The Egyptian Economy

The Egyptian Economy
Current Challenges and Future Prospects

Edited by Hanaa Kheir-El-Din

An Egyptian Center for Economic Studies Publication
The American University in Cairo Press
Cairo New York

First published in 2008 by
The American University in Cairo Press
113 Sharia Kasr el Aini, Cairo, Egypt
420 Fifth Avenue, New York NY 10018
www.aucpress.com

Dar el Kutub No. 20272/07
ISBN 978 977 416 154 4

Dar el Kutub Cataloging-in-Publication Data

Kheir-El-Din, Hanaa
The Egyptian Economy: Current Challenges and Future Prospects / Edited by Hanaa Kheir-El-Din.—Cairo: The American University in Cairo Press, 2008
p. cm.
ISBN 977 416 154 8
1. Economics I. Kheir-El-Din, Hanaa (ed.)
330

1 2 3 4 5 6 7 8 12 11 10 09 08

Designed by Sally Boylan/AUC Press Design Center
Printed in Egypt

About ECES

The Egyptian Center for Economic Studies (ECES) is an independent, non-profit research institute. It was founded in 1992 by leading members of the private sector in Egypt. The mission of the Center is to promote economic development in Egypt by conducting and disseminating applied policy research. The aim is to develop viable policy options for Egypt in light of international experience. Research is conducted in-house by ECES staff and other Egyptian and foreign experts.

ECES publishes and distributes its research in English and Arabic (all research is down-loadable at www.eces.org.eg). The Center's activities are carried out in the spirit of public interest.

For more information, please contact:
The Egyptian Center for Economic Studies
Nile City Towers, North Tower, 8th floor
Corniche El Nil, Cairo 11221, Egypt
Tel.: (20-2) 2461-9037-44 Fax: (20-2) 2461-9045
E-mail: eces@eces.org.eg
URL: www.eces.org.eg

Contents

PART III: Sectoral Issues

Foreword

I would like to thank the Egyptian Center for Economic Studies (ECES) for a topic well chosen. Its importance lies in its assessment of key reforms undertaken in recent years and its discussion of reform prospects in areas such as macroeconomic, institutional, and sectoral reforms. Thus, it contributes to the formulation of long-term development policies. This volume, based on a conference held by ECES in November 2006, also comes at a time when the Egyptian economy is facing several challenges of which five stand out. The first—as elaborated in chapter two of this volume—relates to the challenge of achieving high and sustainable growth rates, which requires investment in the building of new production capacities, and raising productivity. In 2005/2006, the GDP growth rate of the economy reached around 7 percent, an upward trend. Maintaining that momentum, however, requires serious studies like those included in this volume, to establish reliable economic indicators and determine the specific causes of growth.

The second challenge concerns the relation between poverty, economic growth, and income distribution, otherwise known as the social dimension of economic policy. In this respect, one must say that a policy of income distribution will not go far in the face of low output and per capita income. It would be like putting the horse behind the cart. In other words, an effective policy of income distribution must be coupled with continuous efforts to increase growth and output. The one without the other will do the poor no good.

The third challenge is to continue building the structure of our market economy with the aim of reaching a mature social market economy. In the process, Egyptian society has to realize that relative price corrections are warranted to remedy decades of price distortion. Such recognition is important for a smooth transition to a fully fledged market economy.

The fourth challenge concerns the country's rapid population growth. Some progress has already been achieved with respect to tackling this problem, as evidenced by the fall in that growth from close to 3 to less than 2 percent over the past few decades. However, much more needs to be done, as Egypt's population is expected to reach 91 million in the year 2020.

The fifth challenge is the issue of development and democracy. Country experience has shown that achieving real economic development requires the enhancement of democratic processes and the active participation by all segments of society in public decision-making.

Finally, it is important to note that addressing these challenges requires concerted efforts from all agents of society including the government, civil society, and the business community. In other words, we all have to work together to ensure better prospects for the coming generations.

Osman M. Osman
State Minister for Economic Development, Egypt

Acknowledgments

This book comprises research papers presented at the ECES conference "The Egyptian Economy: Current Challenges and Future Prospects." Several people have been instrumental in the completion of this book. I would especially like to thank the ECES Board of Directors for their unwavering support. Thanks are also due to the contributing authors who provided the material that gives this volume its merit. I am also obliged to the following individuals who took part in the conference as discussants, moderators, or active participants: Mounir Abdel-Nour, Sultan Abou-Ali, Tamer Abou-Bakr, Hossam Badrawi, Mona El-Baradei, Adel Beshai, Zine Eddine El-Edrissi. Naglaa El Ehwany, Ibrahim El-Essawi, Samiha Fawzy, Ahmed Galal, Ahmed Ghoneim, Heba Handoussa, Soad Kamel, Safwat El-Nahass, Heba Nassar, Sherif Omar, Amal Refaat, Faika El Refaie, Fouad Sultan, Hisham Tawfik, John Langenbrunner, Mohamed Fathi Sakr, Mohamed Taymour, Mostafa El-Said, Osman M. Osman, and Sherine Al-Shawarby. Thanks are also due to Yasser Selim for editing the research papers, compiling the manuscript, and reading the final proofs; Amr Samir, Niveen El-Zayat, Noha Hamdy, and Sara Al-Nashar for excellent research assistance; and the ECES administration and finance staff for their superb organization of the conference.

Hanaa Kheir-El-Din

Contributors

Tarek Abdelfattah Moursi, *Information and Decision Support Center* and *Cairo University*
Ragui Assaad, *The Population Council*
Omneia Helmy, *The Egyptian Center for Economic Studies* and *Cairo University*
Hanaa Kheir-El-Din, *The Egyptian Center for Economic Studies* and *Cairo University*
Aart Kraay, *The World Bank*
Heba El-Laithy, *Cairo University*
Akiko Maeda, *The World Bank*
Nihal El-Megharbel, *The Egyptian Center for Economic Studies* and *Cairo University*
Mai El Mossallamy, *Information and Decision Support Center*
Sameh El Saharty, *The World Bank*
Tarek Selim, *The American University in Cairo*
Abdallah Shehata Khattab, *The Egyptian Center for Economic Studies* and *Cairo University*
Enas Zakareya, *Information and Decision Support Center*

CHAPTER 1

Overview

Hanaa Kheir-El-Din

The Egyptian economy has undergone several reforms since the early 1990s. However, it was not until mid-2004 that the reform process picked up in speed and intensity. Key initiatives involved rationalizing the tariff structure, stabilizing the exchange rate, and improving the income tax system, which included drastic cuts in income tax rates and a streamlining of tax administration. As a result, the real GDP growth rate increased, inflation fell sharply, and the real interest rate turned positive, in turn during 2005, building economic confidence.

Although such developments reflected positively on the economy, considerable challenges still lie ahead. Output growth, though significantly improved, remains below the level required to absorb labor force growth. Egypt is still lagging in the area of employment creation, with continued concern over rising unemployment. Sectoral policy reforms are also needed to complement efforts aimed at stabilizing the economy and enhancing growth.

This volume comprises research papers that were presented at a conference organized by the Egyptian Center for Economic Studies (ECES) in Cairo on November 21–22, 2006. Its purpose was twofold: to address a wide range of economic challenges centered around the macroeconomy and labor policies in Egypt, as well as to focus on specific sectoral issues related to energy and healthcare. The aim was to evaluate the impact of recent reform policies and highlight priority areas for further reform. The present volume consists of nine papers organized in three parts as elaborated below.

Part I: Macroeconomy

The real GDP growth rate has risen to 5.7 percent in the first half of FY 2005/2006 and again to 6.5 percent in FY 2006/2007. According to the Ministry of State for Economic Development (2007), economic growth is expected to exceed 7 percent in 2007/2008, and to reach 8.5 percent by the end of the sixth five-year plan (2007/2008–2011/2012). Nevertheless, there is growing evidence of increasing income inequality and poverty. The Egyptian economy also experienced significant inflationary pressures due to the pass-through effect of successive devaluations of the pound that culminated in its floatation in January 2003. Inflation increased to 12 percent from May to December 2004, as measured by the consumer price index, while the wholesale price index was 17 percent over the same period. However, inflation declined in early 2005 (EIU 2005; Femise Network 2004).

After severe exchange rate fluctuations, the black-market rate converged toward the bank rate in the second half of 2004. In December 2004, an interbank foreign exchange market was launched and flexibility was restored in setting the exchange rate. Confidence in the convertibility of the Egyptian currency improved, strengthening the pound against the US dollar and other major currencies. The surplus in trade in services helped offset the trade deficit. Proceeds from the export of goods and services grew in 2004 and the current account surplus increased. Official international reserves rose from US$14.8 billion in June 2004 to an excess of US$26 billion in December 2006 (CBE 2007).

This part of the book attempts to address the following questions: how did income distribution and poverty measures evolve with GDP growth achieved over the period 1990/1991–2004/2005? How did monetary policy evolve during the same period and what were the implications for the Egyptian economy? And finally, how did the depreciation of the Egyptian pound affect household welfare?

In Chapter 2, Hanaa Kheir-El-Din and Heba El-Laithy highlight the key features of Egypt's growth over the period 1990/1991–2004/2005. Further, they try to determine whether growth has been associated with improved income distribution leading to a significant reduction in poverty, or whether growth has been combined with deteriorating income distribution, dampening or even reversing the growth effect on poverty. Dividing the period of study into three sub-periods corresponding to the time span that elapsed between successive household income, expenditure, and consumption surveys (HIECS), the analysis proceeds along three levels: the macroeconomic level, which considers the growth experience of Egypt over the past fifteen years; the sectoral level, which addresses the pattern of growth of various sectors of activity, as well as the poverty level in these sectors; and finally the household level, which studies the pattern of distribution and poverty indicators for various expenditure groups.

At the macroeconomic level, the contributions of various sources of GDP growth are explained by decomposing the growth of output per worker into two components: one related to total factor productivity (TFP) growth and the other to the effect of a changing capital–labor ratio. TFP growth contribution increased from a negative value to an increasingly positive one, yet the effect of increasing capital intensity remained predominant. At the *sectoral* level, the composition of GDP remained remarkably stable. Insignificant structural changes in the sectoral pattern of employment and in output per worker within sectors have been observed. At the *household* level, distinctly different patterns were observed in terms of distribution and growth effects on changes in expenditures, driving variations in poverty outcomes over the whole period as well as over successive sub-periods. The first two sub-periods witnessed a reduction in poverty incidence, while the last sub-period (1999/2000–2004/2005) reflected an increased incidence of poverty. Observed divergences between per capita expenditure growth and that of per capita GDP—which have successively shown an average annual real decline versus an average real increase—reflect that GDP growth alone is not sufficient to improve income distribution and to trickle down to the poor, resulting in lower poverty incidence.

Based on these results, and in light of the experience of countries that have succeeded in reducing poverty the fastest, the study concludes that rapid growth has to be combined with effective income redistribution policies. It further highlights specific policies and strategies to promote inclusive growth, simultaneously ensuring high and sustained GDP growth, more equitable distribution, and a rapid reduction in poverty incidence.

In Chapter 3, Tarek Moursi and co-authors examine the structure and stance of monetary policy (MP) and describe their implications for the Egyptian economy, with an emphasis on the period from 1990 through 2005. The study addresses the following questions: should the Central Bank of Egypt (CBE) depend on the interest rate as a policy instrument? Should the CBE advocate an expansionary or a contractionary policy stance? What will be the effect of such a policy on the economy, particularly on output? Should the CBE adopt an inflation-targeting framework? If so, how can it formulate a policy rule?

The analysis is based on a set of policy-oriented models that measure the stance of monetary policy and evaluate the responses of key policy (the interest rate, total and non-borrowed reserves) and non-policy (commodity prices, GDP deflator and real output) variables to policy shocks. The results reveal that the impact of monetary policy shocks on real output and prices has been respectively negligible and ambiguous. Policy shocks have almost no real effect whereas they do impact inflation. This suggests that the effect of monetary policy on the level of real output and on the rate of economic growth in the long run is limited by its capacity to achieve long-run price stability.

The analysis further focuses on the prospects for policymaking by a policy rule instead of the current discretionary monetary decision-making regime. The authors examine whether the current discretionary policymaking process may have led to rule-like based policy decision. Moving to the approach of ***inflation targeting*** that the CBE is currently seeking to adopt as the monetary policy objective, the authors set up a generalized Taylor-type interest rate rule to highlight the recommended CBE nominal interest rate adjustments in response to deviations of inflation from its target and real output from its trend. Focusing on the period from 2001 to mid-2006, the findings indicate that the discretionary monetary regime in Egypt may not be inconsistent with rule-like policy outcomes. The results illustrate a clear trade-off between inflation and interest rate stabilization. Historical and counterfactual simulations indicate that during this period, the CBE has given precedence to reducing the interest rate variance rather than to stabilizing inflation. Simulation scenarios suggest that it is possible to stabilize inflation through policy intervention measures.

In Chapter 4, Aart Kraay investigates the effect of the sharp depreciation of the Egyptian pound that occurred between 2000 and 2005 and particularly in 2003. He focuses his analysis on the impact of these depreciations on household welfare through consumer price variations induced by the changes in the exchange rate. For this purpose, he uses disaggregated monthly consumer price indices to estimate regressions to isolate the extent of the pass-through effect of exchange rate changes on consumer prices. He finds a significant, and very heterogeneous across products, degree of pass-through from the exchange rate to consumer prices. The author then uses household-level data from the last two HIECS for 1999/2000 and 2004/2005 to quantify the welfare effects of these consumer price changes at the household level. The average welfare loss due to the pass-through effect of exchange rate depreciation on consumer price increases was equivalent to 7.4 percent of initial expenditure. Estimated exchange rate pass-through for food items only highlights that this effect disproportionately affected poorer households, confirming the observed higher poverty incidence over the period of study.

Part II: Labor Market Issues

Although Egypt has successfully achieved macroeconomic stability and promising GDP growth prospects, it has been lagging in the area of employment creation, with continued concern over open unemployment and underemployment. This part of the book examines unemployment in Egypt based on a recently released comprehensive survey of labor market conditions compared against the 1998 Egypt Labor Market Survey (ELMS) figures. It further reviews the impact of recent macroeconomic and labor market policies on job creation in Egypt. Finally, it assesses a recently formulated vision of the Government of Egypt (GOE) for a new pension system which aims—according to its announced objectives—at reducing the fiscal burden of the current system while ensuring more equitable benefits to its contributors. Comprising three chapters, this part tries to investigate the following issues: what are the demographic, economic, and institutional factors that shape the process of labor market entry? What is their effect on youth insertion in the labor market and hence on unemployment? How have various macroeconomic and labor policies impacted job creation? And finally, how is the proposed GOE vision of the new pension system expected to impact the government's public deficit as well as contributors and beneficiaries of the system?

In Chapter 5, Ragui Assaad addresses the first two questions using data from the recently released Egypt Labor Market Panel Survey (ELMPS) of 2006. The study shows that there has been a decline in both the relative and absolute size of unemployment in Egypt over the period 1998–2006. It further presents detailed evidence in support of this assertion. The explanation of falling unemployment at a time when it seems so questionable is threefold. *Demographically*, the growth of the working-age population has slowed and the age structure of population has shifted away from the 15–19 age group, which experienced the highest unemployment rates in 1998 to the 20–24 age group. As a result, the composition of the working-age population shifted away from the ages with the highest levels of unemployment, and a drop in unemployment among younger youths was observed. *Economically*, the higher growth rates achieved since 2004 have resulted in employment growth in the private sector for new young male entrants to the labor market. Finally, *institutionally*, the GOE has significantly slowed its hiring, hence reducing the incentive for graduates, especially female graduates, to remain unemployed while queuing for government jobs. This has led to many female graduates withdrawing from the labor market instead of continuing to declare themselves as unemployed. It further explains the observed decline in female participation rates in the 1998–2006 period.

Chapter 6 analyzes the impact of recent macroeconomic and labor market policies on job creation in Egypt. In this chapter, Nihal El-Megharbel shows that reform measures undertaken by the government since mid-2004 to promote investment, boost exports, and reduce the public deficit have not been conducive to employment creation. Furthermore, labor market policies did not succeed in correcting labor market failures due to the short-term nature of these policies. To increase employment, the importance of designing a *national employment strategy* aimed at creating more jobs, especially in sectors with high employment elasticity, is emphasized. This strategy should also attempt to address the mismatch between labor supply and demand. It should further be integrated in Egypt's national development plan. Both macroeconomic and labor market policies should be streamlined and aligned with the objectives of the strategy.

In Chapter 7, Omneia Helmy presents a thorough investigation of the recently outlined vision of the GOE for the new pension system. She gives an *ex ante* assessment of its expected results in light of international experience. She stresses that the gradual implementation of the system would help reduce the short-term burden on the treasury and achieve long-run fiscal sustainability; it would also maintain the redistributive role of the state. Additionally, it would enhance economic efficiency and help develop the capital market. However, Helmy argues that the proposed system would also transfer the burden of risk management from the government to individuals even though the former is better positioned to manage such risks.

To maximize the benefits derived from implementing the proposed system, the study underscores the importance of aligning the maximum monthly contribution with the average economy-wide monthly wage, linking the rate of return on pension funds with the wage growth rate, and putting in place an automatic mechanism to preserve the real value of pensions. As to reducing the risks to individuals, the study stresses the role of the state in establishing appropriate rules and regulations governing the investment of funds in the capital market, in taking measures to reduce the accompanying administrative costs, and finally in ensuring more equitable income distribution.

Part III: Sectoral Issues

After addressing macroeconomic and labor market issues, the volume moves on to discuss sectoral issues of current concern to the Egyptian economy, namely the energy and healthcare sectors. These two sectors were singled out due to their strategic importance as well as insufficient coverage in economic literature in Egypt.

Energy is an essential source of livelihood in modern economies. In Egypt, this sector and related activities constitute around one sixth of the country's GDP, a little less than half of the proceeds from the country's exports of goods and is a strategic resource for future growth. Egypt's oil reserves are quickly depletable with a risk of over-consumption associated with the continued policy of price subsidization; production is aging and net imports of some oil products are already in evidence. On the other hand, natural gas reserves are new and there is a clear trade-off between oil and natural gas as sources of energy. The question is: what should Egypt do with its energy reserves? Should it export its natural gas output and retain oil for domestic consumption, even though such consumption is highly subsidized and puts a strain on the government budget? Or should it mainly export its increasingly scarce oil resources, relying more on relatively abundant natural gas reserves for domestic consumption? A further concern relates to the continued heavy burden of energy subsidies on the fiscal deficit and the likely implications of their removal on various users.

In Chapter 8, Tarek Selim presents an analysis and forecast for Egypt's energy resources until the year 2025. He emphasizes that since Egypt is running the risk of an oil shortage in the near term, its strategic energy policy should shift from oil toward multiple energy sources, including natural gas and alternative energy uses.

The methodology applied is based on optimal resource extraction rates (Hartwick's model) whereby dynamic efficient production schedules, subject to the constraint of sustainable growth rates in consumption, identify future energy requirements. He further proposes detailed strategies for Egypt's energy sector and highlights their expected impact on the economy. They include: the derivation of sustainable production paths for oil and natural gas as strategic energy resources until 2025; the reduction and ultimate removal of energy subsidies by 2017, with oil subsidy removal by 2010; the estimation of required investments for energy self-sufficiency at US$120 billion over ten years for natural gas and 5.25 percent annual investment growth for oil through 2020; and the gradual adoption of alternative energy sources (currently at less than one percent of the country's total energy sources), including solar and nuclear energy to substitute oil with 10 percent alternative energy use by 2015 and 25 percent by 2025. Finally, the chapter outlines a timeline for implementing these strategies.

Chapter 9 is concerned with an important issue related to energy use in Egypt, namely energy subsidies. In this chapter, Abdallah Shehata Khattab investigates the impact of reducing energy (oil products and natural gas) subsidies on energy-intensive industries, applying a partial equilibrium approach. He first selects a sample of sectors and industries that heavily depend on energy products and then measures the impact of subsidy reduction on profitability per ton of production in these industries, holding other factors constant. He further highlights that energy-intensive industries in Egypt benefit most from subsidized energy products, either directly or indirectly. After analyzing the impact of several energy subsidy reductions on production costs and profitability of a sample of leading companies engaged in energy-intensive activities, he concludes that increasing prices of energy products (including both petroleum products and natural gas) and the resulting rise in electricity prices can be absorbed by these companies without having to raise their sale prices proportionately. In other words, energy-intensive industries can adjust to energy subsidy reductions either by choosing not to raise prices—due to their already high profitability ratios—or to increase prices in ways that do not exceed the resulting actual increase in costs.

Now we turn to the other sector considered: healthcare. Egypt has made significant progress in improving the quality of healthcare for its population. However, it is uncertain whether it will be able to achieve the Millennium Development Goals' (MDGs) health target by 2015. The MDGs include ensuring equitable access to health services, improving quality, enhancing health outcomes, securing sustainable financing, improving efficiency, ensuring greater responsiveness, and enhancing citizens' involvement in decision-making. Furthermore, one in five Egyptians (about 13.6 million people) lives in poverty and considerable numbers live just above it. Negative shocks to households, such as disease, are among the key reasons for the high incidence of poverty in Egypt. Disease affects household income by decreasing earnings and raising healthcare expenditure.

Chapter 10 presents an assessment of Egypt's health system, defines the challenges that face it, and proposes strategies for reform. This chapter has been compiled by Sara Al-Nashar, based on a study by Sameh El Saharty and Akiko Maeda and their presentation of the study at the ECES conference. The study indicates that over the past decade, Egypt has achieved an overall improvement in health outcomes, in particular, significant reductions in infant, child, and maternal mortality rates. This improvement is attributable to a combination of factors including: improved access to basic health services, hygiene and safe drinking water, and to improved educational attainment of mothers. However, several deficiencies face the health system in Egypt, particularly the public health system, and raise concerns about its sustainability.

Egypt has a pluralistic health system, consisting of a number of parallel public and private healthcare delivery systems and multiple financing intermediaries. Social health insurance coverage provided through the Health Insurance Organization (HIO) covers about 48 percent of the population, and one-third of the active labor force. Different laws in effect under HIO result in different systems of benefits and co-payments, which complicate the administration of the program. Total spending in the health sector is dominated by direct out-of-pocket payments by households, which account for more than 60 percent of all health expenditure, about 30 percent of expenditures come through the government budget, and 10 percent through social insurance contributions. Between 1996 and 2002, growth in total health spending outpaced economic growth. Private out-of-pocket spending grew faster than public spending, resulting in a higher share of private spending at the end of the period.

The main challenges facing the health system in Egypt include: financing, fragmentation of risk-pooling, inequities in distribution between regions and between rich and poor, and inefficiencies in the public health delivery system. Options and strategies for reform include directing government subsidies toward priority programs and beneficiaries; expanding health insurance coverage; consolidating multiple social insurance programs under a national insurance fund; and enhancing economic incentives to improve the quality and efficiency of government health services.

Concluding Remarks

To conclude, it is important to stress that for reforms to succeed, they must be backed by a strong political commitment as well as realization that any meaningful reform will involve costs for some in the short run, but significant gains for the economy as a whole in the medium and long runs. A communication plan will also be essential to enhance transparency and ensure public support. Reform efforts also need to be continuous to achieve their intended objectives—sporadic reforms, no matter how intense they are, will always fall short of achieving the desired objectives.

References

CBE (Central Bank of Egypt). 2005. *Monthly Statistical Bulletin*, Volume 121–April 2007.

EIU (Economic Intelligence Unit). 2005. *Country Report: Egypt*, UK, May/June.

Femise Network. 2004. *Egypt Country Profile, the Road Ahead for Egypt*. Cairo: December.

Ministry of State for Economic Development. 2007. *The Five-Year Plan for Economic and Social Development (2007/2008–2011/2012) and its First Year Plan (2007/2008)*, Arab Republic of Egypt, April.

PART I

Macroeconomy

CHAPTER 2

An Assessment of Growth, Distribution, and Poverty in Egypt: 1990/91–2004/05

Hanaa Kheir-El-Din and Heba El-Laithy

A prime goal of development efforts is to reduce poverty; to fulfill that goal requires strong, country-specific combinations of growth and distribution policies (Bourguignon 2005). Countries that have combined rapid growth with improved income distribution have reduced poverty the fastest. It has been pointed out that the "quantity and quality of employment of the poor" is a crucial factor in determining how growth would translate into higher income for the poor (Osmani 2003, as quoted in El-Laithy and El Ehwany forthcoming). However, when policies aimed at equity have had a negative effect on growth, the poverty reduction impact has been limited or even negative. Similarly, when growth has been combined with deteriorating income distribution, the poverty reduction impact has also been limited or negative. Thus, investigating the relative importance of growth and inequality factors may be helpful when trying to strike the right balance between equity and pro-growth interventions.

Based on the Egyptian experience since the beginning of the 1990s[1] to date, this chapter tries to explain observed growth in Egypt and to link it to the evolution of poverty over this period. It attempts to identify whether growth has been associated with improved distribution so that they both would lead to a significant reduction in poverty or, conversely, whether growth has been combined with a deterioration in income distribution dampening or even reversing the growth effect on poverty reduction. The period of study has been further divided into three sub-periods corresponding to the time elapsed between the four successive household, income, expenditure, and consumption surveys available for the whole period. The analysis proceeds along three levels of aggregation: the *macroeconomic level* which considers the growth experience of Egypt over the past fifteen years; *the sectoral level* which addresses the pattern of growth of various sectors of activity as well as the poverty levels in these sectors; and finally the *household level*, which studies the pattern of distribution and poverty indicators for various expenditure groups.

The analysis is based on time series and cross-sectional data from Egyptian sources complemented with international sources. The figures for macroeconomic and sectoral GDP and employment were obtained from the Ministry of Economic Development (MOED). Capital stock is derived from the Nehru and Dhareshwar dataset (Nehru and Dhareshwar 1993), and the World Bank database. Distribution and poverty measures are calculated from four successive household income, expenditure, and consumption surveys (HIECS) for the years starting 1990/91 to 2004/05[2] implemented by the Central Agency for Public Mobilization and Statistics (CAPMAS).

The chapter is organized as follows: after this introduction, the next section discusses some key features of the macroeconomic growth experience. This is followed by an investigation of aggregate poverty trends in Egypt and discussion of growth and distribution components of poverty measures. The chapter then moves on to analyze the sectoral patterns of GDP and employment growth and tries to correlate these observed patterns with income distribution and poverty. Finally, it highlights policy requirements of equitable growth and ends with some concluding remarks.

Key Features of Egypt's Growth

GDP Growth (1990/91–2004/05)

During the period considered, the annual rate of real GDP growth averaged 4.2 percent. The growth of GDP was characterized by frequent fluctuations around the average with values ranging between a minimum of -0.503 percent in 1991/92 and a maximum of 6.15 percent in 1997/98, with a standard deviation of 1.71 percent.

After the sharp decline in 1991/92 following the stabilization effort to address the serious internal and external macroeconomic imbalances that Egypt was facing, the reform program managed to reduce these imbalances and to establish conditions for sustainable growth. The growth rate of GDP picked up in 1994/95 to reach a peak exceeding 6 percent in 1997/98 as shown in Figure 2.1. This growth could be attributed to the increase in private investments, largely inventory accumulation rather than gross fixed capital formation and public investments mainly in infrastructure mega projects. However, the Egyptian economy was then confronted with several external shocks. Since 1998/99, the growth rate started to decline due to the combined effect of three external factors: the emerging market crises, the Luxor incident and the sharp decline in oil prices in 1998, and lax economic structural reform efforts. This was followed by the global economic fallout from the September 11 attacks in 2001. The situation was further aggravated by the war on Iraq, the consequent uncertain political conditions in the region, and the sluggish global environment. This slowdown was evident in real sector indicators and in privately conducted business surveys (ERF and FEMISE2 2004, 11–12).

Figure 2.1. Real GDP and Output per Worker Growth Rates (1990/91–2004/05)* (%)

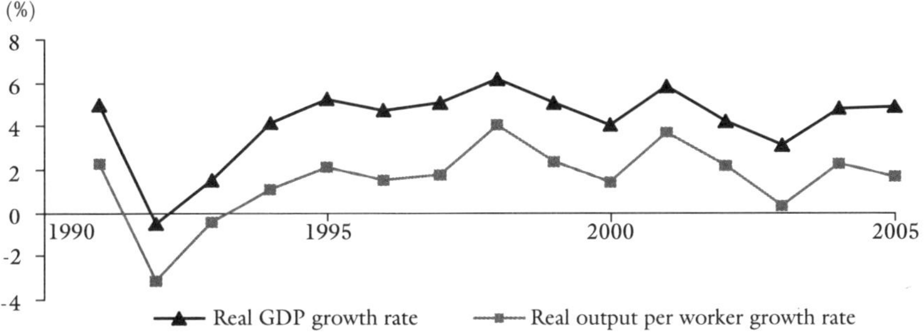

Source: MOED and WDI Database and authors' calculations.
* Years indicated in the figure refer to fiscal years. Thus 2000 refers to fiscal year 1999/2000 starting July 1st 1999 and ending June 30th 2000 and so on.

The slowdown continued in 2001/02, with growth approaching 4.3 percent. Economic activity in 2002/03 remained constrained by a shortage of foreign currency, inactive monetary policy, high real interest rates, and a depressed regional and global environment. In January 2003, the Egyptian pound was floated, resulting in a more than 30 percent depreciation of its value. Real GDP growth rate declined further to around 3 percent, which is far below the Egyptian economy's potential and what is required to reduce the unemployment rate and to provide job opportunities to the new entrants to the labor market. Inflation accelerated. However, growth exceeded 4.7 percent in 2003/04, reached around 5 percent during 2004/05, and was projected to exceed 6 percent by the end of 2005/06 and the beginning of the following year. The recovery has been driven by a rebound in tourism, increased exports of goods and services, a moderate revival in consumption expenditures, and a continuing fiscal expansion associated with a widening budget deficit. Private consumption and investment are expected to further strengthen as personal and corporate tax rates are lowered (UNDP and INP 2005, 86–87).

Sources of Output per Worker Growth: Capital Intensity and Total Factor Productivity

The standard neoclassical growth accounting presumes two potential sources of growth of GDP or aggregate output. The first is explained by the growth of physical inputs used in production. The second is an unobserved residual after accounting for inputs growth. This residual growth (called the Solow residual) represents gains in output due to improvements in the technological efficiency with which physical inputs are utilized, and is defined as total factor productivity (TFP). Such residuals include the effects of factors affecting the motivation of workers; the productivity of capital; levels of education, health, and living standards of members of the society; efficiency in resource allocation; and the acquisition and application of modern technology. It would also contain measurement and unknown statistical errors in output or input data.

Using a linearly homogeneous Cobb-Douglas production function with Hicks-neutral technical progress and two factor inputs, labor and capital (see Appendix 1) and assuming a depreciation rate of 5 percent per year, the share of capital α, or elasticity of output with respect to capital, has been estimated at 0.509.[3] On the basis of these estimates along with observed growth in capital and employment, the relative contributions of these physical inputs to GDP growth could be gauged, then the contribution of TFP to GDP growth could be derived as a residual.

The data show that employment grew over the whole period at an average annual growth rate of 2.63 percent. With few exceptions, annual employment growth during the period 1990/91–2004/05 was remarkably stable, with a relatively small standard deviation of 0.45 percent (see Table A4.4). As a result of the stability of average employment growth, a significant co-variability between output and output per worker, as indicated in Figure 2.1, and between capital and capital-labor ratio growth rates have been observed. Hence, abstracting from output per worker fluctuations, the growth of physical capital would be sufficient to characterize the behavioral structure of real output changes. Furthermore, stability of employment growth accompanied by restrained human capital development and restricted labor skills—arising from an inefficient formal educational system—limit the role of labor participation in the growth process (Kheir-El-Din and Moursi 2007). These observations suggest an alternative way to explain the contributions of various sources of GDP growth by decomposing output per worker into two components: one related to TFP growth and the other related to the effect of changing capital intensity in the economy as shown by the developments in the capital-labor ratio (see Appendix 1). Table 2.1 reflects this decomposition.

Table 2.1. Sources of Output per Worker Growth (average annual increase in %)

	90/91–04/05	*90/91–95/96*	*95/96–99/00*	*99/00–04/05*
Output per worker growth	1.509	0.546	2.349	1.993
From TFP	-0.153	-1.088	0.081	0.782
From increasing k ratio	1.661	1.633	2.267	1.210
Memorandum items in %				
Investment/GDP ratio	21.178	19.824	23.820	20.689
Average annual growth rate of capital per worker	3.325	3.265	4.558	2.410

Source: Authors' estimates based on MOED and WDI database.

Changing Capital Intensity

Figure 2.2 reflects a considerable correlation between output per worker and capital per worker (capital intensity) growth. Not much is known about the structure, vintage, and productivity of capital stock at either the aggregate or sectoral levels in Egypt. Investment flows have been recurrently used to account for the impact of capital changes on output growth (Kheir-El-Din and Moursi 2007).

The most noticeable feature of changes in capital intensity is its continuous decline since 1990/91 until the middle of the 1990s, reflecting the sharp public investment reduction associated with the stabilization effort and unmatched by private investment restrained by low domestic savings. Capital intensity was further boosted by large public investments in mega projects starting 1995/96 and by private investments financed by easily accessible bank credit. By the end of the 1990s, specifically by

1998/99, recessionary pressures undergone by the Egyptian economy and associated with the previously mentioned external shocks and lacking internal structural reforms, capital per worker declined again. Capital intensity was constrained by the reduction in public investments restricted by the widening budget deficit and increasing domestic debt. It was further reduced by contraction in private investment due to declining domestic savings and restrained bank credit, particularly toward the end of the period considered (Dobronogov and Iqbal 2005; and Abdel-Kader 2006). By 2003/04, capital intensity moderately increased, but this rise was not sustained during the following year, due to the recurrent government efforts to relieve unemployment by hiring a few thousand new graduates during the first few years of the 2000s.

Figure 2.2. Output per Worker and Capital per Worker Growth Rates (%)

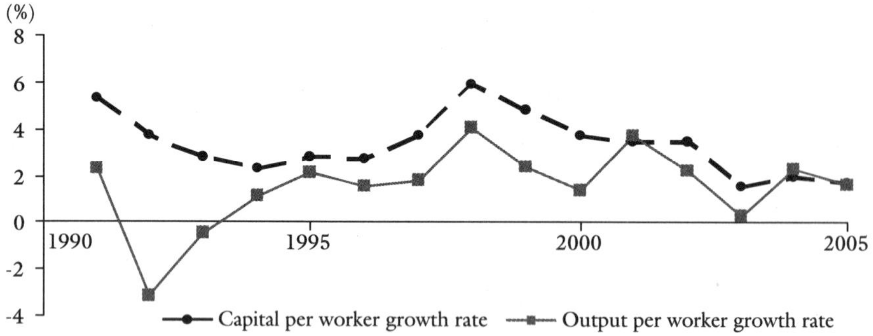

Source: Capital stock was calculated from the Nehru and Dhareshwar dataset and the WDI Database; output per worker was calculated from GDP and employment figures from the MOED and WDI database.

These changes were, to a great extent, associated with growth in output per worker. In Egypt, there has always been a domestic resource gap. The discrepancy between domestic savings and investment has usually been bridged by external financial resources. It is thus plausible to infer that higher levels of investments, through raising the domestic savings rate and bank credit and through encouraging foreign financial capital inflows, would result in an increase in economic growth.

The Role of Technical Progress

Figure 2.3 shows that TFP has been fluctuating during the period 1990/99–2004/05, but has tended to rise moderately toward the end of the period, showing an increased contribution to output per worker annual growth estimated at 0.782 percent by the third sub-period, as indicated from Table 2.1.

During the period 1990/91–2004/05, output per worker increased at a modest annual rate of 1.51 percent. The contribution of TFP growth to output per worker was negative, while capital intensity increases tended to exceed growth in output per worker by around 10 percent.

Dividing the period of study into the three sub-periods, it appeared that these relative contributions to output per worker growth changed considerably. The relative contribution of TFP growth to output per worker growth increased from a negative value, ceding a predominant role to capital intensity to explain changes in output per worker, to an increasingly positive contribution of around 3.4 percent and further almost 40 percent, as derived from Table 2.1.

Figure 2.3. Total Factor Productivity Growth Rate (%)

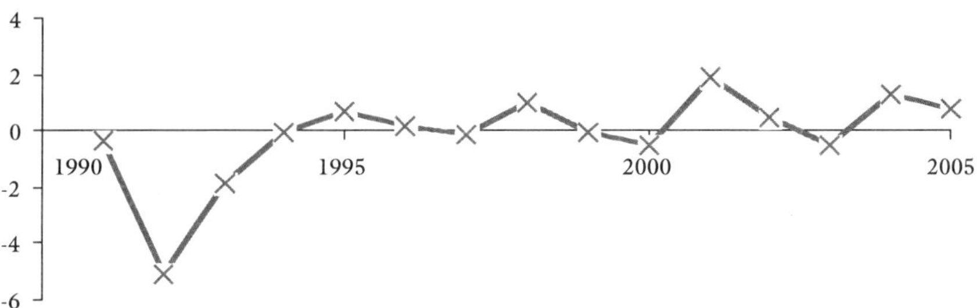

Source: Author's estimates based on MOED data and WDI database.

Thus, over the period considered, TFP growth has played an increasingly relative role in explaining the observed changes in output per worker growth, yet the effect of increasing capital intensity remained predominant. This predominance explains the observed decline of growth rate of output per worker due to a sharp fall in capital intensity associated with the reduction in public investments and the restricted private investments resulting from reduced access to bank credit.

Aggregate Poverty Trends in Egypt

Poverty Measures During the Period 1990/91–2004/05

During the second half of the 1990s poverty in Egypt fell for the first time since the early 1980s. This fall was observed across various poverty measures—incidence, depth, and severity of poverty all declined—based on a household-specific poverty line calculated as the sum of a food poverty line and a non-food poverty line, on the basis of the cost of basic needs (World Bank and Ministry of Planning 2002). This reduction in poverty measures was associated with the rebound of GDP growth in 1994/95, which was sustained till the end of the decade. Starting in 2001/02, Egypt's economic performance slumped in response to the September 11 attacks and the resulting instability in the region. The slowdown in domestic credit reinforced these recessionary pressures. Furthermore, the devaluation following the pound floatation in January 2003 raised the rate of domestic average inflation from 2.4 percent in 2001/02 to 3.2 percent in 2002/03 and further to 8.1 percent in 2003/04,[4] mainly as a result of the pass-through effect of devaluation. Given that poverty in Egypt is fairly shallow, many of those who escaped poverty during the 1990/91–1995/96 sub-period and further during the 1995/96–1999/2000 sub-period may have slipped back into it during the five following years (Table 2.2). In 2004/05, overall poverty in Egypt stood at 19.56 percent using the absolute poverty line. It slightly exceeded the 1995/96 level after a decline in 1999/2000 to 16.7 percent. This means that almost 19.56 percent of the population in Egypt, or approximately 13.6 million people, could not obtain their basic food and non-food needs. The depth of poverty is measured by the poverty gap index, which captures the percentage of shortfall below the poverty line for the whole population. The poverty gap index was 3.9 percent.

Table 2.2. Aggregate Poverty Measures (1990/91–2004/05) (%)

*Indicator**	*1990/91***	*1995/96*	*1999/2000*	*2004/05*
P_0	24.18	19.41	16.74	19.56
P_1	6.54	3.39	2.97	3.90
P_2	2.77	0.91	0.80	1.09

Source: Authors' estimates based on HIECS.

* P_0 is a measure of incidence of poverty; P_1 measures the depth of poverty; and P_2 measures the severity of poverty (Foster, Green, and Thorbecke 1984).

** Based on per capita poverty line, whereas in the subsequent three surveys poverty measures were calculated on the basis of a household-specific poverty line.

As indicated in the table, poverty measures are higher in 2004/05 compared to 1999/2000 and to 1995/96 regardless of poverty measures chosen, although the difference between 2004/05 and 1995/96 might not be significant. Poverty measures from the last three surveys indicate a significant decline in all poverty measures compared to the initial year 1990/91. Dominance analysis was carried out to assess the robustness of these results to the poverty lines applied. Curves for the three poverty measures were plotted using a wide range of values for the poverty line (40 percent to 100 percent of average per capita expenditure for the four survey years. Figure 2.4 illustrates the poverty incidence curves for the HIEC survey years.

In Figure 2.4 the 1990/91 curve intersects with the three other curves for the lower levels of relative poverty lines defined at around 45 percent and 55 percent of the mean annual expenditure per capita. This indicates that the incidence of poverty declined from 1990/91 to 1995/96 and 2004/05 with the lowest poverty lines defined at around 45 percent of the mean per capita expenditure. Incidence of poverty declined further from 1990/91 to 1999/2000 at the lowest end of expenditure distribution for those living at around 55 percent of the mean per capita expenditures. However, poverty incidence in 1990/91 remained lower than in the three subsequent survey years for poverty lines exceeding 45 percent of the mean expenditure in 1995/96 and 2004/05 and 55 percent of the mean expenditure in 1999/2000, suggesting that at poverty lines exceeding these levels, the welfare of poor expenditure groups under these higher poverty lines deteriorated compared to the initial year. Poverty incidence in 1995/96 almost coincided for all poverty lines below 80 percent of per capita expenditure with poverty incidence in 2004/05, but exceeded it for poverty lines above 80 percent of per capita expenditure. Finally, the poverty incidence curve, as well as those for depth and severity of poverty (not shown), in 2004/05 were always above the corresponding curves for 1999/2000, indicating higher poverty, by all measures, in 2004/05 compared with 1999/2000. The decomposition of poverty incidence into growth and redistribution components will explain these observations.

Figure 2.4. Poverty Incidence Curves (1990/91–2004/05)

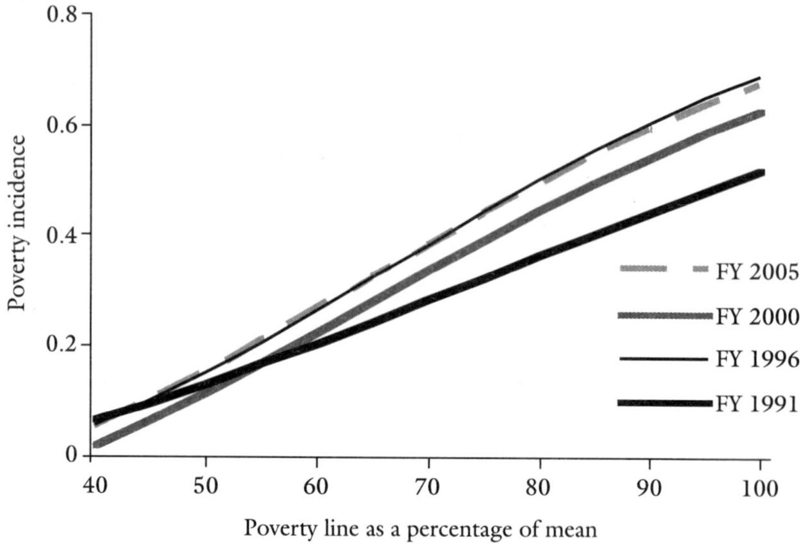

Source: Authors' calculations based on HIECS.

Growth and Redistribution Components of Poverty Measures

Changes in the pattern of income distribution may be assessed by following up the changes in Gini coefficients over the whole period, as well as over successive sub-periods, as reflected in Table 2.3.

Table 2.3. Gini Coefficients from Various HIECS

	1990/91	*1995/96*	*1999/2000*	*2004/05*
Gini coefficients	0.446	0.345	0.362	0.320

Source: Authors' calculations based on HIECS.

Income distribution has generally improved from 1990/91 to 2004/05 as the Gini coefficient declined from 0.45 to 0.32. However, the improvement was not uniform between successive household surveys. Income distribution improved significantly between the first two surveys from 0.45 to 0.35 as agricultural incomes rose sizably as a result of the implementation of the stabilization effort and liberalization of the economy. Liberalization of compulsory delivery prices of the main agricultural crops as well as price liberalization of the major agricultural inputs led to a net increase in agricultural incomes, explaining the observed improvement in income distribution. However, the third survey reflected a slight deterioration in income distribution to 0.36—associated with worsening expenditure distribution in metropolitan governorates, particularly in Upper Egypt (World Bank and Ministry of Planning 2002). Accordingly, the estimated Gini coefficient increased, followed by a decline from 0.36 to 0.32 by 2004/05, reflecting an improvement in expenditure distribution between the most recent HIECS and the previous one of 1999/2000.

Inequality is usually captured by changes in summary indicators of income (expenditure) distribution, such as the Gini index. Yet such change is not necessarily an indicator of change in poverty incidence. This is because what matters is the change in the segment of the Lorenz distribution that lies to the left of the point that indicates the proportion of population in poverty. The index of income distribution may fail to accurately capture a change in this segment if there is a (compensatory) change in the segment of the Lorenz distribution that lies to the right, i.e., that corresponds to higher income brackets. It is quite possible that while distributional changes address equity concerns, there is no absolute gain to the poor. Similarly, pro-rich distributional shifts may come with absolute gains to the poor.

The observed changes in poverty measures can be decomposed into two effects. First there is the effect of a proportional change in all incomes that leaves the distribution of relative incomes unchanged, i.e., a *growth* effect. Second, there is the effect of a change in the distribution of relative incomes, which, by definition, is independent of the mean, i.e., a *distribution* effect. A change in poverty can then be shown to be a function of growth, distribution, and the change in distribution (Datt and Ravallion 1992).

There were various distinctly different patterns over time in terms of distribution and growth effects on changes in expenditures driving the differences in poverty outcomes over the whole period as well as over successive sub-periods (Table 2.4). At the national level and over the whole period covered, the improved distribution effect led to a reduction in poverty incidence by 10.5 percent, while the growth effect was associated with an increase in poverty incidence (P_0), by 5.9 percent, leading to an overall decline in poverty incidence by 4.6 percent. A similar pattern was observed during the first sub-period. However, during the second sub-period, the deterioration in income distribution dampened the favorable growth effect on reducing the poverty incidence, and poverty decreased by only 2.7 percent. Relatively improved growth rates of GDP and slight deterioration in distribution, particularly working against Upper Egypt (World Bank and Ministry of Planning 2002), explain these developments between 1995/96 and 1999/2000. Finally, over the last sub-period (1999/2000–2004/05), an improved distribution effect led to a reduction in poverty incidence (P_0) by 1.8 percent. However, the adverse impact of the slowdown in growth on increasing poverty incidence (4.6 percent) was larger than the effect of improved expenditure distribution (-1.8 percent), leading to an overall increase in poverty incidence by 2.8 percent.

Table 2.4. Growth and Redistribution Effects on Changes in Poverty Incidence P_0, 1990/91–2004/05 (%)

	Change in Incidence of Poverty Due to		
	Growth	*Redistribution*	*Actual Change*
1990/91–2004/05	5.866	-10.486	-4.620
1990/91–1995/96	4.890	-9.660	-4.770
1995/96–1999/2000	-3.631	0.954	-2.677
1999/2000–2004/05	4.607	-1.780	2.827

Source: Authors' calculations based on HIECS.

Elasticities of poverty measures to changes in mean consumption expenditures and to the inequality index shown in Appendix 3 further support these observations.

Growth Incidence Curves

Although the economy's growth rate is usually measured by the rate of growth of per capita real GDP or GNP, changes in income for poverty indicators have to be measured by the change in *personal* or in *disposable* income or expenditure, in terms of which the poverty threshold is defined. Aside from members of households, there are other claimants to GDP or GNP, such as businesses and the government. Shares of different claimants do not necessarily remain unchanged. Thus it is possible, indeed quite normal, for the rate of growth of personal/disposable income (expenditure) to differ from the rate of growth of GDP/GNP. This divergence is an outcome of macroeconomic policies. This point will be taken up further in the next section. Moreover, as mentioned earlier, an improvement in income distribution, as reflected by a decline in the Gini coefficient, is not necessarily associated with a decline in poverty incidence.

A more direct approach to assessing the impact of growth on poverty incidence is to consider growth rates of per capita income or expenditure of the poor. It is common to compare growth of mean incomes across the distribution ranked by income levels, sometimes called "Pen's parade" (following Pen 1971). To assess whether growth is equitable one may calculate, using Pen's parade, the growth rate in the mean income of the poorest percentiles. Table A4.7 in Appendix 4 illustrates the growth of per capita expenditures by deciles over the survey years. Following Ravallion and Chen (2001), the "growth incidence curve" (GIC) shows how the growth rate for a given quantile varies across quantiles ranked by income/expenditure levels.

Figure 2.5 presents the Egyptian growth incidence curve (GIC) for the period 1990/91–2004/05, as well as for the three sub-periods considered. It is worth noting that the real mean per capita expenditure has been declining over the whole period of study, as well as during the first and third sub-periods. It has increased only during the second sub-period 1995/96–1999/2000. GIC for the whole period is decreasing over all quantiles, implying that inequality declined, as higher quantiles are declining more rapidly than lower quantiles. The annualized percentage increase in per capita expenditure is estimated to have exceeded 10 percent for the poorest two percentiles, declined steadily, to reach zero around the 30th percentile and turned negative to reach -2 percent (the average growth of per capita expenditure) around the middle of the eighth decile and continued to decline thereafter. This indicates that over the whole period under consideration, expenditure distribution has markedly improved, with a clear decline in poverty incidence. These developments are also depicted in Table A4.7 of Appendix 4.

Figure 2.5. Growth Incidence Curves for Egypt

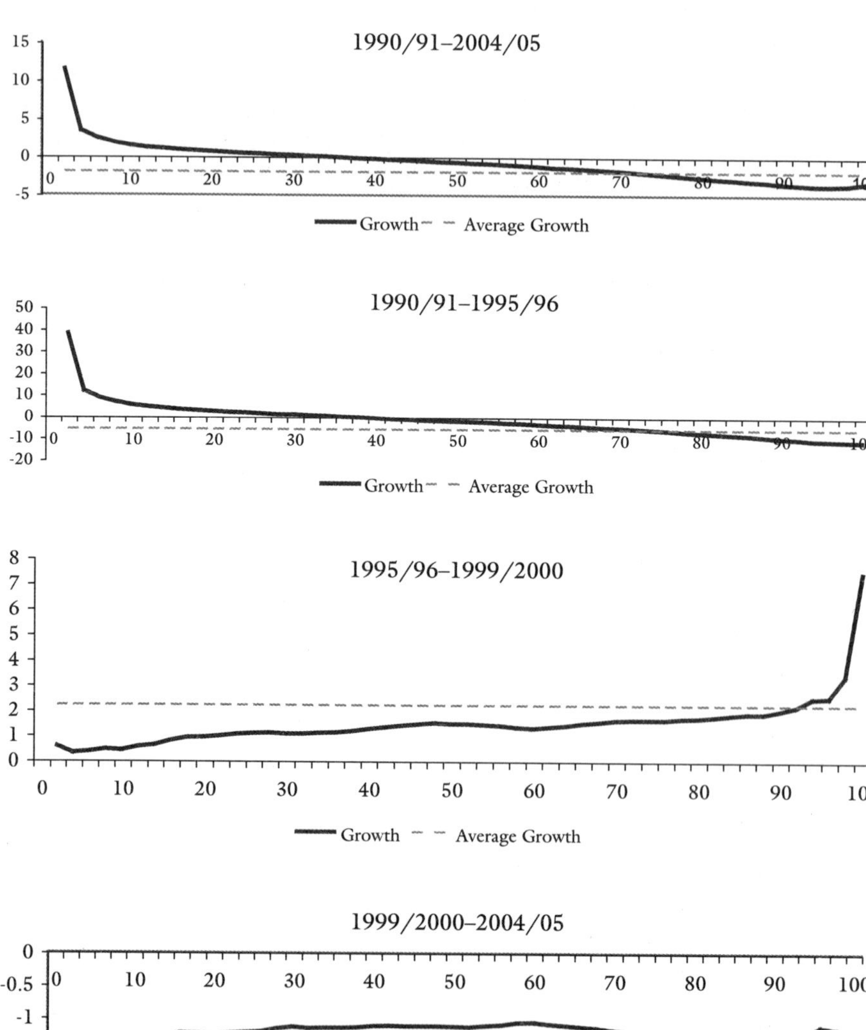

Source: Authors' calculations based on the four successive HIECS from 1990/91 to 2004/05.

However, this pattern has not been uniform over the three sub-periods. The observed improvement in expenditure distribution occurred during the first sub-period (1990/91–1995/96) when a substantial stabilization effort was implemented and price liberalization occurred, particularly in agriculture. This was accompanied by a significant decline in all poverty measures (Table 2.2), and a sharp fall in poverty incidence, as reflected by the decline in GIC over all quantiles, in the corresponding figure. The second sub-period (1995/96–1999/2000) witnessed a reversal of the pattern of expenditure distribution, with a slight increase in poverty measures. The annualized percentage increase in per capita expenditure, estimated to have been below 1 percent for the poorest percentiles, rose steadily to exceed the average growth rates of 2 percent by the 90th percentile and increased drastically for the richest decile. Poverty slightly increased but remained far below its 1990/91 level and expenditure distribution deteriorated by the end of the second sub-period, as per capita expenditure of the poor increased at a much lower rate than the higher expenditure brackets.

The third sub-period reflected a different growth and distribution pattern. Average per capita expenditure declined by around 1.4 percent. However, the decline for the poorest percentiles exceeded 2 percent, remained negative but exceeded the average of 1.4 percent from the middle of the second to around the middle of the ninth decile. It then dropped sharply for the highest percentiles in the tenth decile, indicating a sharp decline in per capita expenditures for the richest. T5hus, by the end of the last sub-period, average per capita expenditure deteriorated in general, but the most affected by this deterioration were the poorest and the richest in the distribution ladder. The intermediate expenditure brackets were relatively less affected by these developments. Table A3.2 in Appendix 3 also confirms these developments. The same results could be obtained by integration on the growth incidence curve (Ravallion and Chen 2001), to estimate the pro-poor index.

Growth of GDP per Capita versus Growth of per Capita Expenditure

As mentioned earlier, the rate of growth of GDP is normally different from that of personal expenditure. This reflects further on the rate of growth of GDP (output) per capita versus that of per capita expenditure. Table 2.5 illustrates the differences between these annual growth rates over the periods considered. Per capita personal expenditure declined annually by around 2.08 percent over the whole period. Yet this decline was not uniform, as the first and third sub-periods witnessed average annual declines of 5.98 percent and 1.43 percent respectively, while during the second sub-period (1995/96–1999/2000), per capita expenditure increased by an annual average rate of 2.18 percent. Per capita real GDP, however, grew over the whole period at an average annual rate of 2.24 percent, showing variations during various sub-periods. The second sub-period reflected a relatively better growth performance exceeding 3 percent annually.

Table 2.5. Average Annual Growth Rates of Real per Capita Expenditures and GDP (1990/91–2004/05) (%)

Real annual growth rate of:	*1990/91–2004/05*	*1990/91–1995/96*	*1995/96–1999/2000*	*1999/2000–2004/05*
Per capita expenditures	-2.08	-5.98	2.18	-1.43
Per capita GDP	2.24	1.40	3.07	2.57

Source: Authors' calculations based on HIECS figures, MOED, and WDI database.

These divergences between per capita expenditure and GDP growth rates result from macroeconomic policies, which affect the relative share of households compared to other claimants to GDP, principally businesses and the government. Such policies include taxes, transfers among claimants to GDP, policies related to wages as well as business practices concerning withheld profits. Further investigation of the reasons behind these divergences is required.

Sectoral Pattern of Growth, Distribution and Poverty

Egypt's Pattern of GDP Growth

Egypt's pattern of growth since the early 1990s can be characterized as follows:

- The Egyptian economy continued to be a service-based economy. Despite fluctuations in their share of GDP, production and social services[5] together exceeded 50 percent of GDP on average during the period considered, while industry and agriculture constituted on average around 33 percent and 16 percent of GDP (Table A4.1 in Appendix 4).
- The sectoral growth rate of value added generated in agriculture was persistently lower than that of industry and services. On average, agricultural value added grew at a modest annual rate of 2.47 percent compared to industry, which grew at 5.9 percent. Industry includes manufacturing and mining, petroleum and petroleum

products, electricity, and construction. The standard deviations of value added for the two sectors were successively 4.15 percent and 5.10 percent. Production and social services, on the other hand, exhibited diverging growth patterns. Production services grew on average at an annual rate of 4.13 percent ranging between -0.45 percent and 8.23 percent with a standard deviation of 2.59 percent, while social services grew at a lower average annual rate of 3.31 percent, within a wider range of -5.53 percent and 8.23 percent and a standard deviation of 4.61 percent (Table A4.2 in Appendix 4).

- Despite diverging growth rates, the sectoral composition of GDP remained remarkably stable, although the share of industry in GDP grew modestly to 36.07 percent by 2004/05 while that of agriculture deteriorated slightly to reach 14.9 percent. Similarly, the share of the two services sub-sectors grew modestly to 32.2 percent for production services whereas it fell to 16.8 percent for social services, as depicted in Figure 2.6 and in Table A4.1 of Appendix 4.

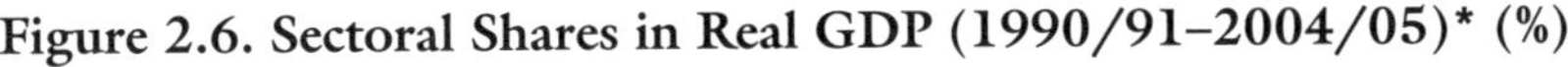

Figure 2.6. Sectoral Shares in Real GDP (1990/91–2004/05)* (%)

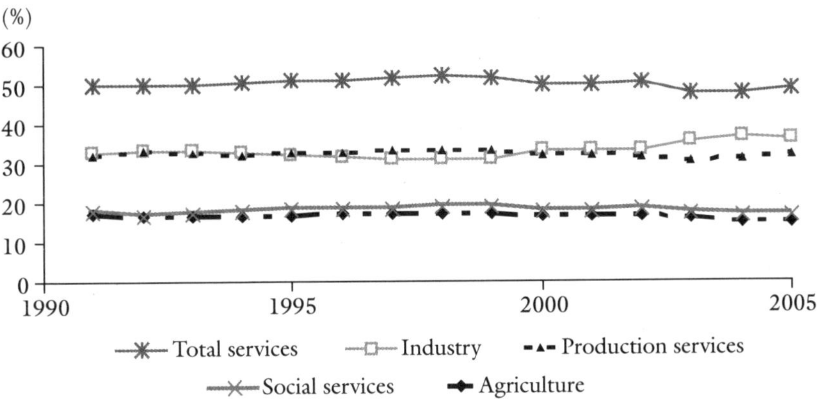

Source: Authors' calculations based on MOED and WDI database.
*GDP is deflated using the WDI database deflator. Base Year = 1991/92.

Changes in employment structure and in sectoral output per worker (as a proxy for labor productivity) can influence both determinants of change in poverty—namely the growth and distribution components. Growth in employment and in output per worker would improve the growth rate in the economy. Moreover, changes in employment structure and in sectoral output per worker would improve income distribution by pushing up the lower relevant segment of the Lorenz distribution. This can only be achieved by increasing employment and enhancing its remuneration, particularly at the lower level of the wage scale in various sectors. This will be discussed sequentially in the following sections.

Shifts of Labor Between Sectors

Economic theory predicts that in a country with a large pool of surplus labor occupied in low-productivity sectors (agriculture and social services in the case of Egypt), rapid growth and industrialization result in relocation of agriculture and other low-productivity labor into the non-agriculture sector, where employment increases rapidly (Lewis 1954). In the process, overall output per worker increases because: (1) labor shifts from less productive sectors to more productive ones, and (2) output per worker within each sector increases because of technology and institutional innovations.

The economy-wide capital-labor ratio should increase as labor moves from less capital-intensive sectors to more capital-intensive ones, and the sectors themselves also become more capital intensive. As labor moves out of agriculture, output per worker there increases and the gap between output per worker in agriculture and the other sectors declines over time. Therefore, as the economy grows, the share of low-productivity sectors in employment declines. This pattern was weakly observed in Egypt as indicated in Figure 2.7. Employment shares show a slightly declining trend in agriculture and social services, and a modest increase in industry and production services.

Figure 2.7. Employment Shares (1990/91–2004/05) (%)

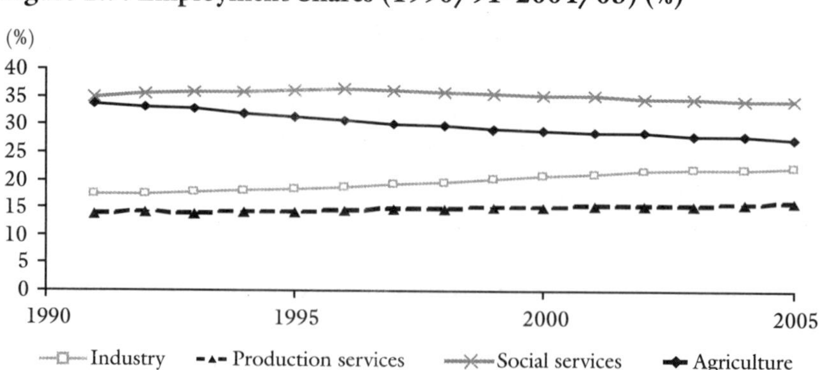

Source: MOED.

In the meantime, output per worker in industry and production services remained high and modestly increased while that in agriculture and social services remained low with a slightly rising trend, as shown in Figure 2.8. Consequently, the ratio of output per worker in industry and production services versus agriculture and social services, dubbed the output per worker gap, remained persistently high although tending to decline over the period of study, as indicated in Tables A4.5, A4.6 in Appendix 4.

Figure 2.8. Sectoral Output per Worker and Output per Worker Gap*

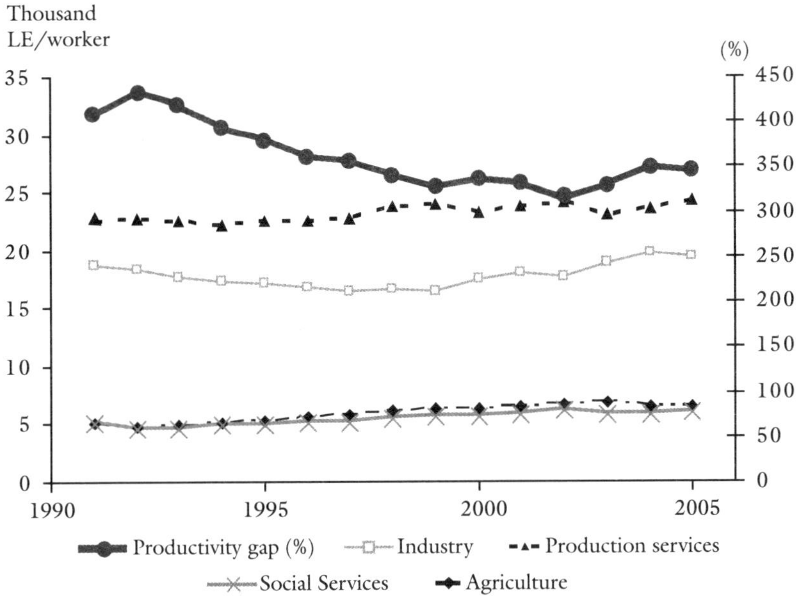

Source: Authors' calculations based on MOED and WDI data.
* The gap is measured as the percentage of output per worker in "industry and production services" to output per worker in "agriculture and social services."

Explaining Sectoral Output per Worker Growth

To further support these findings, overall output per worker growth is decomposition into two sets of components related to labor shifts between sectors and output per worker growth within sectors (Kuijs and Wang 2005; and Appendix 2).

The decomposition results are shown in Table 2.6. They indicate that output per worker growth has been modest over the whole period under consideration, not exceeding 1.535 annually. However, it tended to increase in 1995/96–1999/2000 to 2.38 percent annually from a low 0.566 percent during the first five years of stabilization effort, but declined somewhat to an annual average growth rate of 2.019 percent during the last five years, which were dominated by recessionary pressures. These pressures were only overcome by 2004/05.

With the exception of the first years of the stabilization effort (1990/91–1995/96), where shifts of labor between sectors dominated the low growth of overall output per worker, these labor shifts explained about 30 percent to 36 percent of the increase in overall growth of output per worker, while sectoral increases in output per worker explained the remaining over the last two sub-periods. In general, within sector improvement in output, per worker has been higher in industry than in other sectors. Nevertheless, these improvements have been modest and uneven showing a decline in some sectors of activity during the first sub-period. This indicates that *structural changes in the economy have been lagging, as the sectoral pattern of employment has not significantly evolved over the reform period considered, nor did output per worker within sectors remarkably increase.*

Table 2.6. Sectoral Contributions to Real Output per Worker Growth Rates (1990/91–2004/05) (average annual changes, %)

	90/91–04/05	*90/91–95/96*	*95/96–99/00*	*99/00–04/05*
Overall output per worker growth rate	1.535	0.566	2.382	2.019
(1) From shifts in employment between sectors	0.611	0.473	0.850	0.586
(2) From sectoral output per worker increase	0.923	0.092	1.532	1.434
Agriculture	0.207	0.073	0.518	0.117
Industry	0.420	0.186	0.343	0.763
Production Services	0.171	0.005	0.251	0.307
Social Services	0.125	-0.173	0.420	0.246

Source: Authors' calculations based on MOED and WDI data.

Industry benefited from low prices for energy, electricity, and utilities (including water) and from not being subjected to strictly enforced environmental regulations. Cheap electricity for industry, due to subsidies on natural gas and oil products for power generation, continues to encourage the establishment of energy-intensive and electricity-intensive industries, which did not significantly pay in terms of industrial growth promotion.

Development of the production services sector was not significantly stimulated. It continued to suffer from restrictions, which constrain its performance. A large share of employment continues to be trapped in the low-productivity government sector, with insignificant efforts to upgrade the bureaucracy, which still employs around 72 percent of labor engaged in social services and 24.5 percent of total employment. Similarly, low output per worker agriculture continued to employ more than 27.5 percent of workers in 2004/05. These two low-output per worker sectors together employ more than half the workers in Egypt. Hence the necessity of focusing efforts to enhance output per worker in these two highly labor intensive activities as a prerequisite for a serious growth promotion and poverty reduction strategy.

Poverty and Sector of Employment

Most of the poor rely for their subsistence on the only asset they have: labor. Whether they are able to use this asset to escape poverty largely depends on how successful they are in finding work and how much they are able to earn.

Khan (2005) detected five channels through which employment can reduce poverty: 1) an increase in wage employment; 2) an increase in real wage; 3) an increase in self-employment; 4) an increase in productivity in self-employment; and 5) an increase in the terms of exchange of output of self-employment.[6] Poverty declines if the outcome of these channels is favorable to the poor.

At the national level and according to the 2004/05 HIECS, the poor were over-represented in agriculture, as reflected in Table 2.7. About 43.9 percent of the working poor heads of households were engaged in agricultural activities, compared to 28.9 percent for the entire population, while household heads engaged in industry and both production and social services had a lower share among the poor (a higher share among the non-poor) than their share in the general population. The same pattern was observed over all survey years, reflecting the persistence of poverty in agriculture. This observation is consistent with low output per worker in agricultural activities.

Additionally, regional disaggregation shows that in both urban and rural areas the poor were highly over-represented in agricultural activities in all survey years except in urban areas in 1995/96. They were also over-represented in industrial activities in 1995/96 and in production services in 1990/91 in urban areas, reflecting the poor conditions of those engaged in construction as well as those at the lower wage scale in manufacturing and in production services. Surprisingly, those engaged in social services (which were shown to be mainly employed by the government) represent 21.1 percent of the poor and 25.5 percent in overall employment in 2004/05. Their shares among the poor are also lower than their shares in total employment in both rural and urban areas as well as over all survey years. This indicates that although output per worker in social services, and particularly in government employment, is the lowest among sectors of activity, as reflected in Figure 2.8, the modest but secure and regular government salaries along with the opportunities for moonlighting secure expenditure levels, which reduce the incidence of poverty among those engaged in such employment (see Appendix 4 Table A4.8).

Table 2.7. Percentage Shares of the Poor and Non-poor by Economic Activities of Heads of Households, All Egypt (1990/91–2004/05) (%)

	All Egypt					
	Non-poor	*Poor*	*All*	*Non-poor*	*Poor*	*All*
	1990/91			*1995/96*		
Agriculture	30.44	45.07	34.06	29.72	46.27	33.08
Industry	24.17	18.77	22.83	21.76	19.82	21.36
Production Services	21.14	17.73	20.29	22.36	14.06	20.68
Social Services	24.26	18.43	22.81	26.16	19.85	24.88
Total	100	100	100	100	100	100
	1999/2000			*2004/05*		
Agriculture	27.77	45.83	30.93	25.15	43.88	28.93
Industry	21.88	16.49	20.94	22.66	18.38	21.80
Production Services	23.45	16.36	22.21	25.52	16.66	23.74
Social Services	26.90	21.33	25.92	26.66	21.08	25.54
Total	100	100	100	100	100	100

Source: Authors' calculations based on various HIECS.

The 1999/2000–2004/05 period exhibited employment movements, from social services toward production services in urban areas. Employment for the poor shifted from services to industry in urban areas and from agriculture to industry in rural areas. As output per worker is lower in agriculture than in industry and in social services than in production services, these shifts may well have been the reason for improvements in income distribution observed between 1999/2000 and 2004/05.

The analysis of HIECS data highlights that agriculture is the single most important source of rural employment for the poorest, the landless, and for women. The poorest are mostly employed as agricultural wage-workers. Across income groups, the percentage of wage-workers declines steadily while that of farm self-employment rises. Furthermore, the rural non-poor are likely to be engaged in non-agricultural activities than the poor. Across income groups, the share of total income from non-agricultural sources rises steadily with living standards while agricultural income goes in the opposite direction. Non-farm employment provides more security. HIECS data show that households living on farm income only (or on farm income and transfers) are the poorest and the most affected by fluctuations of agricultural income. The data also show that non-farm self-employment and informal employment in micro enterprises reflect high poverty incidence. These observations highlight the necessity of supporting agricultural development and boosting agricultural output per worker in addition to promoting non-farm self-employment and informal employment in micro enterprises among the poor to ensure inclusiveness of the poor in the growth process.

Economic Policies for Equitable Growth

A last issue is whether there are specific policies and strategies that would simultaneously lead to high and sustained GDP growth, more equitable distribution, and a rapid reduction in poverty, i.e., policies that would secure inclusiveness of the poor as well as pro-growth outcomes. Considering the experiences of countries that have succeeded in significantly reducing poverty along with achieving high and sustained growth, a number of policy choices have to be addressed. Most important are the following:

The Choice of Growth Sectors

Although economic growth is necessary to reduce poverty, the orientation of this process is also important. The selection of which sectors should be given priority in an inclusive growth strategy has to be determined within a poverty reduction growth strategy.

The dual economy models of Lewis (1954) and Fei and Ranis (1965) provided an attempt to understand the role of inter-sectoral linkages, which have been considered essential when formulating a development strategy. Since the 1960s this strategy focused on expanding industrial activities. Most developing countries increased trade barriers to protect the development of domestic manufacturing. Some countries, mostly in Asia, succeeded in developing a competitive industry. However, the strategy did not lead to an internationally competitive industry in Egypt and turned out to be devastating for traditional agricultural production which was heavily taxed to provide cheap inputs to manufacturing and low-cost food to the industrial and urban workforce. This not only affected export revenues but also employment and poverty in both urban and rural areas. Since incomes in agriculture deteriorated, people moved to the city looking for jobs, but the majority ended up in the informal sector or in open unemployment. Hence, poverty increased in both urban and rural areas.

It is now clear that supporting the agricultural sector is necessary to increase its productivity and reduce poverty in the countryside. Reforming the rural environment and increasing net earnings are necessary to increase growth in a sustainable manner in agriculture (Christiansen, Demery, and Kühl 2006).

Results from India showed that agricultural growth is more important than manufacturing growth for poverty reduction (Ravallion and Datt 1996). Even if manufacturing growth matters more for overall growth, agriculture growth is necessary for both employment growth and poverty reduction.

Employment shifts from informal toward modern (formal) sector activities and improving investment and working conditions in micro and small enterprises, in both urban and rural areas, have also been shown to be an important factor in explaining changes in poverty.

The Role of Government

Changes in tax and public expenditure policies are important to achieve immediate poverty alleviation and to support processes that enhance growth and achieve poverty reduction in the longer term.

The efficiency and composition of public expenditures and taxes are critical determinants of growth and poverty reduction. Three types of impact from reallocation of public expenditures and changing the tax structure may be distinguished: 1) when relative prices and factor incomes change, income distribution and poverty will change; 2) the composition of government expenditures affects sectoral productivity and hence labor demand and household incomes; and 3) changes in the supply of public services, such as education and healthcare, impact the households' possibility to acquire human capital (Bigsten and Levin 2001).

Increasing budget deficit pressures in Egypt induce the government to reduce capital expenditures rather than recurrent expenditures particularly the government wage bill and subsidies that have a clear urban bias toward government employment and middle-income households. While protecting urban households from a short- and medium-term income loss, this has a longer-term negative impact on the rural poor as government investments in agriculture and rural infrastructure decline, resulting in a long-term decline in agricultural production. Furthermore, this limits the government's capacity to provide financing, technical support, and training to micro and small enterprises, thus depriving them from an important source of support.

This suggests that an appropriate growth strategy must focus on the special features of poverty in Egypt, which is concentrated in micro and small enterprises and in the agricultural sector. Ensuring the availability of critical inputs for micro and small businesses is thus a priority. Reducing regulatory obstacles to starting, operating, and dissolving small businesses is essential. Increasing poverty-oriented investments in rural areas and supporting agricultural development are all necessary. Also necessary are supporting local governments to plan and implement priority local projects and ensuring the flexibility to involve NGOs, community organizations, and private sector participation in such investments (World Bank and Ministry of Planning 2004).

A reallocation of government expenditures may also improve the supply of health and education services, however, this does not necessarily benefit the poor, as spending on such social services is not well targeted to the poorest households. Thus reallocation of government expenditures is not sufficient. Policies must be based on understanding the factors that govern household decisions concerning healthcare and schooling and on providing the means to ensure better outcomes of subsidized social services for the poor.

Provision of public services in Egypt, as well as in many other countries, is constrained by low levels of public revenues, which could, in principle, be solved by higher levels of taxation. However, increased taxation might constrain private investment and negatively impact future growth and tax revenue collection. Thus, supporting the mobilization of voluntary participation of civil society and the private sector in providing such services on a non-profit basis is warranted. This could be encouraged through various incentive schemes.

Finally, equitable growth strategy should entail measures targeted directly to the poor. Universal subsidies, currently prevailing in Egypt and designed to benefit the whole population, have proven inefficient, distortionary, and fiscally unsustainable, thus constraining long-term growth. Targeting such subsidies is essential; one approach is *self-targeting* which is designed in such a way that only members of the target group find it worthwhile to participate. Another approach is *characteristics* or *indicator targeting*, which relies on making the service or transfer contingent on easily observable characteristics such as sex, age, size of land holding, and/or region of residence.

In sum, the government has to consider two important issues: 1) improved public service delivery is crucial in promoting growth and reducing poverty; 2) tax policies need to be further redesigned in order to satisfy an increasing demand for public services, while providing an enabling environment for private sector and civil society participation and development.

Inclusive Growth and Human Capital

Human capital accumulation has been an important factor in accounting for differences in growth rates and distribution across countries. An extensive literature has developed on the effects of education expansion on growth, yet relatively little is known of its effects on income distribution. The increase in supply of educated workers must be matched by an increase in labor demand, which in turn will depend on economic growth. Egypt's experience has shown a modest contribution of human capital accumulation to growth, as indicated earlier.

Four priority areas of education reform that are especially beneficial for the poor and are likely to increase their potential for future earnings include: 1) combating illiteracy; 2) enhancing access to and reducing costs of education for the poor; 3) improving the quality and relevance of basic and secondary general and technical education; and 4) enhancing access of the poor to higher education (World Bank and Ministry of Planning 2004).

Policy Measures to Reduce Risk and Income Volatility

The World Development Report (World Bank 2000) extends the concept of poverty beyond income and consumption expenditure, education, and health to include risk and vulnerability, as well as voicelessness and powerlessness. Thus emphasis on empowerment and security becomes a crucial component in a poverty reduction strategy. The concept of social capital has been used to describe the ability of individuals to secure benefits as a result of membership in social networks and other social structures. This is particularly important in the areas of microfinance and access to savings facilities.

Rapid and sustainable poverty reduction depends upon the interaction of a wide range of policy measures. The potential for financial development as an instrument of economic management and of poverty reduction will be unfulfilled so long as conventional financial institutions are reluctant to expand their activities beyond their traditional borrowers. Microfinance institutions can play an important role in filling this gap and possibly also help to reduce imperfections in the credit market, improving access to credit for poor households in both urban and rural areas. However, many programs that have been successful in reaching the poor are not financially sustainable and/or are based on individual initiatives that need to be supported, developed, and institutionalized.

Concluding Remarks

The analysis of determinants of economic growth, as measured by growth of output per worker shows that it depends on capital intensity and TFP growth. The accumulation of capital, as reflected by physical investment to GDP ratio, increasing capital to output ratio and average annual growth rate of capital per worker have appeared to be highly correlated with growth. Human capital accumulation due to education showed no significant contribution to growth. Over the whole period of study (1990/91–2004/05), capital intensity growth explained more than the observed growth in output per worker (110.07 percent), reflecting inefficient utilization of investment and a decline in TFP over the whole period. This, in turn, indicates that the efficiency in resource allocation, and the acquisition and application of modern technology have been lagging, and output per worker growth depended primarily on increasing capital intensity. However, following up the relative contributions of capital intensity and TFP growth, it appears that over the three sub-periods considered, the role of TFP growth increased while that of capital intensity declined to reach respectively around 39 percent and 61 percent of output per worker growth during the last sub-period considered.

The evidence reviewed in this study shows that the proportion of Egypt's population living in poverty over the whole period declined. However, the sharpest decline occurred during the first sub-period, when the stabilization and liberalization program started to be implemented. Poverty declined further during the second sub-period in response to the higher growth rate of GDP and output per worker achieved. However, the incidence of poverty tended to rise again toward its incidence level during the first sub-period as a result of the recessionary pressures on the Egyptian economy due to both external and internal factors, mainly lax structural reforms and delayed responses to external shocks. The structural reforms implemented over the last year considered, 2004/05, and the resulting improvement in growth performance has not yet translated into a significant decline in poverty incidence. Over the whole period, poverty remained shallow, reflecting that any increase or decline in output growth may be accompanied by a decline or increase in poverty for those who are close to the poverty line.

The sectoral pattern of growth over the period considered has remained remarkably stable, with marginal shifts of employment from low output per worker sectors (agriculture and social services) to relatively higher output per worker sectors (industry and production services). Furthermore, sectoral output per worker increases remained modest in all sectors, and the gap between relatively high output per worker sectors and low output per worker sectors remained high, although declining. Over the whole period considered, shifts between sectors accounted for around 40 percent of annual output per worker growth, while sectoral output per worker increases accounted for the rest of the modest annual increase of output per worker of 1.5 percent.

In accordance with the low level of output per worker in agriculture, poverty appears to be mostly concentrated in this sector, pointing to the necessity of focusing on supporting growth in agriculture in an attempt to reduce poverty.

The development policy of the government emphasizes the necessity of promoting investment and hence growth as a prerequisite for poverty reduction. The evidence presented highlights that growth alone has not been sufficient to achieve this end. Although GDP growth has been achieved, it was not reflected in improved income distribution, lower poverty, and increased per capita personal expenditure. Hence the need for ensuring that growth reaches households and particularly the poor among them. As mentioned, GDP is shared by agents other than households, such as businesses and the government. The share of each agent is determined, among other factors, by macroeconomic policies, including wage policy, taxation, transfers, and business profit withholding policy.

Empirical evidence shows that countries that have been successful in achieving and sustaining economic growth have also been successful in reducing poverty. However, when growth is associated with improved income distribution, the reduction in poverty is faster, particularly if policies aimed at achieving equity do not negatively impact growth. Policies that enhance equity and ensure inclusiveness should be beneficial to growth. Such policies should aim at building assets for the poor and support demand for these assets; improving provision and targeting of social services; expansion of education; supporting agricultural development and increasing the relative prices of agricultural commodities and the wages of unskilled workers in both urban and rural settings; providing transfers to reduce risk for the poor; and creating an environment conducive to growth. These policies, however, require microeconomic measures aimed at increasing market access for the poor and improving the functioning of such markets; and macroeconomic policies aimed at ensuring stability and improving benefit distribution through progressive taxation and better targeted expenditure allocation. Improving institutions, empowering the poor, and providing good governance are also necessary.

Appendix 1

Aggregate Production Function and Decomposition of Output per Worker

The aggregate production function (APF) may be written as:

$$Y_t = A_t K_t^{\alpha} L_t^{-\alpha} \qquad (1)$$

where Y_t is a linearly homogeneous Coble-Douglas production function with Hicks-neutral technical progress, and two factor inputs: K_t capital stock at constant 1991/92 prices and labor L_t expressed in physical units, the coefficient α, $0 < \alpha < 1$ is the share of capital in income and A_t denotes TFP. The exponents of capital and labor in the APF are set to add up to unity, following the assumption of constant returns to scale.

Dividing by L, taking natural logs and differentiating (1) totally with respect to time, the production function may be expressed in per-worker form as:

$$\dot{y}_t = \alpha\, \dot{k}_t + \dot{a}_t \qquad (2)$$

where the lower case letters, $\dot{y}$ and $\dot{k}$ measure the logarithmic growth rates of output per worker (dy) and of capital per worker (dk); y = ln $\frac{Y}{L}$, k = ln $\frac{K}{L}$.

The variable is an unobserved index of technical progress reflecting the growth in TFP or $\frac{dA}{A}$, a = ln A.

Output per worker growth $\dot{y}$ is thus the sum of two components: the contribution of capital intensity $\alpha\dot{k}$ and the contribution of TFP growth $\dot{a}$.

Appendix 2

Decomposition of Overall Output per Worker Growth Rates Shifts in Employment between Sectors versus Growth in Sectoral Output per Worker

Overall output per worker (y =Y/L) may be defined as:

$$\frac{Y_1 + Y_2 + Y_3 + Y_4}{L_1 + L_2 + L_3 + L_4}$$

where Y_i and L_i (i = 1, ...,4) are sectoral output (value added at constant 1991/92 prices) and sectoral employment, respectively. This definition may be written as:

$$Y = l_1\, y_1 + l_2\, y_2 + l_3\, y_3 + l_4\, y_4 \qquad (3)$$

where, as before, y is overall output per worker, y_i is output per worker in sector i and l_i is the share of sector i in total employment.

By partially differentiating Equation 3 with respect to time and dividing though by y, the growth rate of overall output per worker may be written as:

$$\begin{aligned} g(y) &= g(l_1) \times l_1 \times y_1 + l_1 \times g(y_1) \times y_1 \\ &+ g(l_2) \times l_2 \times y_2 + l_2 \times g(y_2) \times y_2 \\ &+ g(l_3) \times l_3 \times y_3 + l_3 \times g(y_3) \times y_3 \\ &+ g(l_4) \times l_4 \times y_4 + l_4 \times g(y_4) \times y_4 \end{aligned}$$

where g (x) denotes the growth rate of x ($g(x) = \frac{\partial x / \partial t}{x}$). The first column of elements captures the effect of shifts of labor between sectors, while the second column represents the growth in output per worker within each of the four sectors.

Appendix 3

Further Indices of Poverty Incidence

1. Elasticity of Poverty Measures to Mean Consumption and Inequality

How much a given growth rate can reduce poverty levels has changed over time. Elasticity of poverty incidence to changes in the mean consumption expenditure may explain the impact of growth on poverty trends. Table A3.1 shows estimates of the elasticity of poverty measures to growth—i.e., the percentage change in poverty indices, given a percentage change in mean expenditure levels. It appears that poverty in 1999/2000 was more responsive to growth in mean expenditure compared to other survey years, while it was least responsive in 1990/91. This indicates that a given percentage increase in the mean consumption expenditure in 1999/2000 would reduce all poverty measures more than in other survey years, whereas it would reduce them least in 1990/91.

On the other hand, the elasticity of poverty measures to the inequality index (Gini coefficient) was highest in 1999/2000, closely matched by the corresponding elasticities in 1990/91. The elasticities with respect to the Gini index were lower in 1995/96 and in 2004/05. This implies that a given percentage change in Gini indices in the four surveys would change poverty measures in 1990/91 and 1999/2000 relatively more than in 1995/96 and 2004/05, indicating a higher sensitivity of poverty measures to distribution changes in the former two surveys than in the latter two.

Table A3.1. Elasticity of Poverty Measures to Mean Consumption and Inequality

		Consumption Elasticity	*Gini Index Elasticity*
1990/91	P_0	-1.85	3.15
	P_1	-2.79	7.47
	P_2	-3.71	11.75
1995/96	P_0	-3.49	2.77
	P_1	-5.57	6.22
	P_2	-7.68	9.68
1999/2000	P_0	-3.57	3.43
	P_1	-5.74	7.47
	P_2	-7.94	11.54
2004/05	P_0	-3.05	2.83
	P_1	-4.10	5.72
	P_2	1.72	8.22

Source: Authors' calculations based on MOED and WDI data.

2. Pro-poor Index

The pro-poor growth rate (PPG) can be measured by the mean growth rate of expenditure for the poor,[7] defined as those living below the poverty line at the initial date.

Table A3.2 gives PPG measure of the rate of equitable growth for different quintiles. Looking at the whole period (1990/91–2004/05), change in per capita expenditure was slightly pro-poor, growth rate for the poorest quintile was positive (0.6 percent) while it was negative for the other quintiles. For the second quintile, although per capita expenditure declined, it declined less than the higher three quintiles. Growth was highly equitable between 1990/91 and 1995/96, as indicated by the high growth rate in per capita expenditure for the poorest quintile, which rose to 5.74 percent, followed by the 2nd and 3rd quintiles, while the growth rate for the two richest quintiles was negative, indicating a relative decline in their per capita expenditures. During the second sub-period (1995/96–1999/2000) growth fell considerably to 0.58 percent for the poorest quintile, furthermore it was not equitable, as per capita expenditure for the poorest quintile grew at a lower rate than per capita expenditure for the following four quintiles confirming the observed deterioration in expenditure (income) distribution. Finally, the last sub-period, from 1999/2000 to 2004/05, witnessed a decline in per capita expenditures in all quintiles. The highest decline being in the poorest and the richest quintiles, which indicates that the growth experience was not pro-poor, but it was rather in favor of the middle three quintiles which suffered a relatively lower decline than the first and fifth quintiles.

Table A3.2. Growth Rate of per Capita Expenditure for Different Quintiles (PPG) (%)

	20	*40*	*60*	*80*	*100*
1990/91–2004/05	0.60	-0.35	-1.34	-2.75	-2.08
1990/91–1995/96	5.74	2.49	0.25	-2.12	-5.98
1995/96–1999/2000	0.58	0.87	1.08	1.25	2.18
1999/2000–2004/05	-1.42	-1.28	-1.21	-1.22	-1.43

Source: Authors' calculations based on MOED and WDI data.

Appendix 4

Some Additional Tables

Table A4.1. Sectoral Distribution of GDP (Constant Prices) (%)

	Agriculture	*Industry*	*Production Services*	*Social Services*	*Total*
1991	17.37	32.86	32.03	17.74	100.00
1992	16.54	33.34	33.27	16.85	100.00
1993	16.71	33.07	32.89	17.33	100.00
1994	16.87	32.76	32.34	18.03	100.00
1995	16.78	32.30	35.59	18.33	100.00
1996	17.26	31.62	32.61	18.51	100.00
1997	16.95	31.22	33.55	18.28	100.00
1998	17.11	30.86	33.39	18.63	100.00
1999	17.32	30.92	33.11	18.65	100.00
2000	16.74	33.13	32.25	17.88	100.00
2001	16.56	33.33	32.13	17.98	100.00
2002	16.46	33.20	31.85	18.49	100.00
2003	16.34	35.67	30.75	17.24	100.00
2004	15.18	36.87	31.21	16.74	100.00
2005	14.92	36.07	32.21	16.81	100.00

Source: Authors' calculations based on MOED and WDI data.

Table A4.2. Growth Rate of GDP, by Sector of Activity (%)

	Agriculture	*Industry*	*Production Services*	*Social Services*	*Total*
1991	-5.875	20.274	3.147	-3.713	4.984
1992	-5.249	0.946	3.367	-5.527	-0.503
1993	2.533	0.681	0.312	4.390	1.489
1994	5.162	3.150	2.434	8.352	4.152
1995	4.642	3.781	6.037	7.003	5.237
1996	7.678	2.455	4.750	5.728	4.679
1997	3.142	3.670	8.035	3.659	5.000
1998	7.146	4.947	5.630	8.229	6.149
1999	6.261	5.195	4.142	5.117	5.012
2000	0.550	11.470	1.291	-0.297	4.013
2001	4.633	6.412	5.410	6.366	5.783
2002	3.618	3.821	3.290	7.206	4.225
2003	2.309	10.743	-0.446	-3.904	3.083
2004	-2.671	8.331	6.348	1.756	4.790
2005	3.119	2.587	8.226	5.293	4.881
Mean	2.47	5.90	4.13	3.31	4.20
Standard Deviation	4.15	5.10	2.59	4.61	1.71

Source: Authors' calculations based on MOED and WDI data.

Table A4.3. Sectoral Employment Shares (%)

	Agriculture	*Industry*	*Production Services*	*Social Services*	*Total*
1991	33.74	17.31	13.96	34.99	100
1992	33.12	17.38	13.99	35.50	100
1993	32.67	17.73	13.85	35.75	100
1994	32.01	18.14	14.01	35.84	100
1995	31.30	18.46	14.18	36.06	100
1996	30.59	18.79	14.34	36.28	100
1997	30.00	19.13	14.88	35.99	100
1998	29.74	19.59	14.82	35.86	100
1999	29.31	20.21	14.93	35.55	100
2000	28.91	20.75	15.13	35.21	100
2001	28.67	20.97	15.27	35.08	100
2002	28.44	21.79	15.29	34.48	100
2003	28.08	22.00	15.45	34.47	100
2004	27.86	22.10	15.64	34.40	100
2005	27.52	22.39	15.93	34.16	100

Source: MOED.

Table A4.4. Growth Rates of Sectoral and Overall Employment (%)

	Agriculture	*Industry*	*Production Services*	*Social Services*	*Total*
1991	0.94	3.21	3.21	3.82	2.64
1992	0.86	3.15	2.95	4.25	2.74
1993	0.57	3.98	0.94	2.66	1.96
1994	0.94	5.39	4.28	3.29	3.03
1995	0.78	4.89	4.30	3.71	3.07
1996	0.77	4.99	4.22	3.71	3.10
1997	1.15	4.99	7.09	2.35	3.16
1998	1.16	4.49	1.61	1.67	2.05
1999	1.15	5.85	3.34	1.73	2.60
2000	1.19	5.38	4.00	1.60	2.60
2001	1.16	3.09	2.95	1.64	2.00
2002	1.14	5.96	2.13	0.24	1.98
2003	1.50	3.80	3.89	2.76	2.80
2004	1.68	2.93	3.71	2.26	2.47
2005	1.91	4.52	5.10	2.47	3.18
Mean	1.13	4.44	3.58	2.54	2.63
Standard Deviation	0.35	1.03	1.47	1.08	0.45

Source: Authors' calculations based on MOED.

Table A4.5. Output per Worker (Constant Prices) (in thousand LE/worker)

	Agriculture	*Industry*	*Production Services*	*Social Services*	*Total*
1991	5.07	18.69	22.60	4.99	9.8475
1992	4.76	18.29	22.69	4.53	9.5370
1993	4.86	17.71	22.55	4.60	9.4932
1994	5.06	17.33	22.15	4.83	9.5962
1995	5.25	17.15	22.52	4.98	9.7981
1996	5.61	16.74	22.63	5.08	9.9483
1997	5.72	16.52	22.83	5.14	10.1256
1998	6.06	16.60	23.73	5.47	10.5326
1999	6.37	16.49	23.92	5.66	10.7801
2000	6.33	17.45	23.29	5.55	10.9285
2001	6.55	18.01	23.85	5.81	11.3338
2002	6.71	17.65	24.12	6.21	11.5829
2003	6.76	18.83	23.11	5.81	11.6149
2004	6.47	19.82	23.70	5.78	11.8778
2005	6.55	19.45	24.41	5.94	12.0739
Mean	5.87	17.78	23.21	5.36	10.60
Standard Deviation	0.72	1.06	0.70	0.52	0.91

Source: Authors' calculations based on MOED and WDI data.

Table A4.6. Growth Rates of Output per Worker (%)

	Agriculture	*Industry*	*Production Services*	*Social Services*	*Total*
1991	-6.751	16.535	-0.058	-7.252	2.284
1992	-6.061	-2.139	0.409	-9.380	-3.153
1993	1.950	-3.170	-0.619	1.681	-0.459
1994	4.184	-2.130	-1.769	4.897	1.086
1995	3.833	-1.057	1.665	3.174	2.103
1996	6.852	-2.413	0.511	1.947	1.533
1997	1.969	-1.262	0.879	1.275	1.782
1998	5.919	0.435	3.953	6.454	4.019
1999	5.058	-0.617	0.773	3.333	2.350
2000	-0.636	5.783	-2.608	-1.863	1.376
2001	3.433	3.223	2.385	4.653	3.709
2002	2.452	-2.014	1.136	6.953	2.198
2003	0.798	6.692	-4.170	-6.483	0.276
2004	-4.283	5.249	2.544	-0.495	2.264
2005	1.189	-1.849	2.970	2.756	1.650
Mean	1.33	1.42	0.53	0.78	1.53
Standard Deviation	4.16	5.31	2.17	5.00	1.72

Source: Authors' calculations based on MOED and WDI data.

Table A4.7. Percentage Change in per Capita Expenditure by Deciles, 1990/91–2004/05

Population Deciles	*90/91–04/05*	*90/91–95/96*	*95/96–99/00*	*99/00–04/05*
10	2.96	9.92	0.38	-1.60
20	0.82	3.05	0.74	-1.29
30	0.29	1.20	1.03	-1.20
40	-0.15	-0.17	1.12	-1.15
50	-0.63	-1.73	1.40	-1.13
60	-1.11	-3.05	1.36	-1.11
70	-1.68	-4.64	1.45	-1.14
80	-2.43	-6.64	1.62	-1.29
90	-3.23	-8.90	1.84	-1.32
100	-3.63	-11.17	4.40	-1.93
Average Growth	-2.08	5.98	2.18	-1.43

Source: Authors' calculations based on HIECS, CAPMAS.

Table A4.8. Percentage Shares of the Poor and Non-poor by Economic Activities of Heads of Households (1990/91–2004/05)

	Urban			*Rural*			*All Egypt*		
	Percentage Share			*Percentage Share*			*Percentage Share*		
	Non-poor	*Poor*	*All*	*Non-poor*	*Poor*	*All*	*Non-poor*	*Poor*	*All*
					*1990/91**				
Agriculture	7.11	14.09	8.54	56.50	66.72	59.47	30.44	45.07	34.06
Industry	34.07	32.70	33.79	13.11	9.04	11.92	24.17	18.77	22.83
Production Services	29.68	30.05	29.75	11.60	9.13	10.88	21.14	17.73	20.29
Social Services	29.14	23.17	27.92	18.80	15.11	17.73	24.26	18.43	22.81
Total	100	100	100	100	100	100	100	100	100
					1995–96				
Agriculture	5.58	8.34	5.90	46.01	56.23	48.59	29.72	46.27	33.08
Industry	30.91	40.59	32.04	15.57	14.37	15.27	21.76	19.82	21.36
Production Services	34.24	25.22	33.19	14.35	11.13	13.53	22.36	14.06	20.68
Social Services	29.26	25.84	28.87	24.07	18.28	22.61	26.16	19.85	24.88
Total	100	100	100	100	100	100	100	100	100
					1999–2000				
Agriculture	5.93	14.15	6.71	43.32	54.06	45.72	27.77	45.83	30.93
Industry	29.18	26.56	28.93	16.69	13.87	16.06	21.88	16.49	20.94
Production Services	34.24	31.50	33.97	15.77	12.43	15.02	23.45	16.36	22.21
Social Services	30.66	27.79	30.38	24.22	19.65	23.19	26.90	21.33	25.92
Total	100	100	100	100	100	100	100	100	100
					2004–2005				
Agriculture	5.80	15.20	6.74	41.11	50.99	43.78	25.15	43.88	28.93
Industry	29.38	30.55	29.49	17.12	15.37	16.65	22.66	18.38	21.80
Production Services	36.22	31.05	35.71	16.70	13.09	15.73	25.52	16.66	23.74
Social Services	28.60	23.20	28.06	25.06	20.55	23.85	26.66	21.08	25.54
Total	100	100	100	100	100	100	100	100	100

*In the 1990/91 HIEC survey, economic activities are available for heads of households rather than individuals, unlike for the three subsequent surveys. For comparison purposes, figures in this table have been estimated by economic activities of heads of households, which differ from those based on economic activities of individuals available only for the three HIECS for 1995/96, 1999/2000, and 2004/05

Notes

1. The year 1990/91 has been chosen as the initial year of the analysis as it marked a turning point in Egypt's modern economic history with the initiation of the economic reform and structural adjustment program. The program aimed at eliminating macroeconomic imbalances and redressing economic inefficiencies resulting from costly economic policies and institutional deficiencies of the previous decades.
2. The years indicated here and thereafter refer to fiscal years that start July 1st and end June 30th of the next year. The four surveys have been implemented for 1990/91, 1995/96, 1999/2000, and 2004/05.
3. This is smaller than the capital share estimated in Kheir-El-Din and Moursi (forthcoming) for the period 1960–1998, which was found to be 0.606.
4. The domestic average inflation rate is measured here on the basis of the consumer price index (CPI) changes. If measured by the wholesale price index (WPI) it rises from 2.1 percent in 2001/02, to 11.6 percent in 2002/03 and further to 17.8 percent in 2003/04 (CBE various issues).
5. Production services include transportation and communications, Suez Canal, trade, finance, insurance, and restaurants and hotels. Social services include real estate, public utilities, social insurance, and social, governmental, and personal services. The latter activities dominated the social services sub-sector, generating between 85.6 percent and 88 percent of value added in this sub-sector.
6. The analytical framework in this part of the chapter is more fully discussed in Khan (2001).
7. Note that this is not the same as the growth rate in the mean income (or expenditure) of the poor.

References

Abdel-Kader, Khaled. 2006. *Private sector access to credit in Egypt: Evidence from survey data.* Working Paper Series, no. 111. Cairo, Egypt: Egyptian Center for Economic Studies.

Bigsten, A. and J. Levin. 2001. Growth, income distribution and poverty: A review. Paper presented at the WIDER Development Conference on Growth and Poverty, Helsinki 25–26 May.

Bourguignon, F. 2005. *Poverty-growth-inequality triangle: With some reflections on Egypt.* Distinguished Lecture Series, no. 22. Cairo, Egypt: Egyptian Center for Economic Studies.

CAPMAS (Central Agency for Public Mobilization and Statistics). Various issues. *HIECS (Household Income, Expenditure and Consumption Surveys).* Cairo, Egypt: CAPMAS.

CBE (Central Bank of Egypt). Various issues. *Economic Review.* Cairo, Egypt: the Central Bank of Egypt.

Christiansen, L., L. Demery, and J. Kühl. 2006. *The role of agriculture in poverty reduction: An empirical perspective.* Policy Research Working Paper, no. 4013. Washington, D.C.: World Bank.

Datt, G. and M. Ravallion. 1992. Growth and redistribution components of changes in poverty measures: A decomposition with applications to Brazil and India in the 1980s. *Journal of Development Economics* 38: 275–95.

Dobronogov, A. and F. Iqbal. 2005. *Economic growth in Egypt: Constraints and determinants.* Middle East and North Africa Working Paper Series, no. 42. Washington, D.C.: World Bank.

El-Laithy, H. and N. El Ehwany. 2006. Employment-poverty linkages. Towards a pro-poor employment policy framework in Egypt. Unpublished paper submitted to the International Labor Office, Cairo, Egypt.

ERF (Economic Research Forum) and FEMISE (Euro-Mediterranean Forum of Economic Institutes). 2004. *Egypt country profile: The road ahead for Egypt.* Cairo, Egypt: Economic Research Forum for the Arab Countries, Iran, and Turkey.

Fei, J.C.H. and G. Ranis. 1965. Development of the labor surplus economy: Theory and policy. *Canadian Journal of Economics and Political Science* 31 (2): 283–4.

Foster, J., J. Greer, and E. Thornbecke. 1984. A class of decomposable poverty measures. *Econometrica* 52: 761–65.

Khan, A.R. 2001. *Employment policies for poverty reduction.* Issues in Employment and Poverty Discussion Paper, no. 1, Recovery and Reconstruction Department. Geneva: International Labor Organization.

———. 2005. Growth, employment and poverty: An analysis of the vital nexus based on some recent UNDP and ILO/SIDA studies. Paper prepared under the joint ILO-UNDP program on Promoting Employment for Poverty Reduction.

Kheir-El-Din, H. and T. Moursi. 2007. Sources of economic growth and technical progress in Egypt: An aggregate perspective. In *Explaining growth in the Middle East* edited by Jeffrey and Hashem Pesaran. Netherlands: Elsevier.

Kuijs, L. and T. Wang. 2005. *China's pattern of growth: Moving to sustainability and reducing inequality.* Policy Research Working Paper, no. 3767. Washington, D.C.: World Bank.

Lewis, A. 1954. *Economic development with unlimited supply of labor.* The Manchester School of Economics and Social Studies 22: 139–91.

MOED (Ministry of Economic Development). Various issues. Available online at http://www.moed.gov.eg/

Nehru, V. and A. Dhareshwar. 1993. A new database on physical capital stock: Sources, methodology and results. Available online at: http://econ.worldbank.org/WBSITE/EXTERNAL/EXTDEC/EXTRESEARCH0,,contentMDK:20699846~pagePK:64214825~piPK:64214943~theSitePK:469382,00.html

Osmani, S.R. 2003. *Exploring the employment nexus:Topics in employment and poverty.* Report prepared for the Task Force on the joint ILO-UNDP program on Promoting Employment and Poverty.

Pen, J. 1971. *Income distribution.* London: Allen Lane.

Ravallion M. and S. Chen. 2001. *Measuring pro-poor growth.* Policy Research Working Paper, no. 2666. Washington, D.C.: World Bank.

Ravallion, M. and G. Datt. 1996. How important to India's poor is the sectoral composition of economic growth. *World Bank Economic Review* 10: 1–25. Washington, D.C.: World Bank.

UNDP (United Nations Development Programme) and INP (Institute of National Planning, Egypt). 2005. *Egypt human development report. Choosing our future: Towards a new social contract.*

World Bank. 2000. *Attacking poverty.* The World Development Report. Washington, D.C.: World Bank.

———. World Development Indicators, online database. Washington, D.C.: World Bank.

World Bank and Ministry of Planning. 2002. *Poverty reduction in Egypt: Diagnosis and Strategy*, vol. I, report no. 24234–EGT.

World Bank and Ministry of Planning. 2004. *A poverty reduction strategy for Egypt*, report no. 27954–EGT.

CHAPTER 3

The Effect of Some Recent Changes in Egyptian Monetary Policy: Measurement and Evaluation

Tarek Abdelfattah Moursi, Mai El Mossallamy, and Enas Zakareya[1]

Since the beginning of the 1990s through 2005, frequent changes have occurred in the conduct and management of monetary policy in Egypt. The changes have been implemented as part of the reform endeavors by the government and the Central Bank of Egypt (CBE) to stimulate the short-term growth of the real economy. They involved modifications to the operational and intermediate targets of the CBE as well as in the choice of monetary instruments selected to achieve the operating targets. Nevertheless, the principal objectives of monetary policy remained more or less unchanged throughout almost all of that period, focusing essentially on price stability and on the stabilization of the exchange rate. In addition, the CBE principal monetary objectives included several other goals such as increasing the level of output, controlling liquidity growth, raising foreign competitiveness, promoting exports, and establishing confidence in the national currency.

The high inflation rates that came about in the aftermath of the floatation of the Egyptian pound at the end of January 2003 presumably prompted the CBE to espouse price stability and low inflation rates (along with banking system soundness) as the main monetary objective. The importance of realizing price stability as an intervening principal objective of monetary policy was further accentuated by the recent structural reforms, which encompassed the establishment of the Coordinating Council, under the leadership of the Prime Minister, in January 2005 and the Monetary Policy Committee affiliated with the CBE Board of Directors in mid-2005.

Within this setting, the CBE recently restructured the monetary policy framework through the adoption of the overnight interest rate on interbank transactions in lieu of the excess bank reserves as the main operational target. To manage interest rates (including the overnight interbank rate) and implement its monetary policy, the CBE established a new operational framework early in June 2005, known as the corridor system, with a ceiling and a floor for the overnight interest rates on lending from and deposits at the CBE, respectively.

The new system of policy management is based on conventional macroeconomic theorization, which predicts that it would be possible to stabilize prices and control inflationary pressures via monetary tightening.[2] In practice, there are no assurances that the actual results obtained from a monetary contraction would match the theorized facts. In particular instances, an increase in the interest rate could lead to a rise in the price and/or output levels. Such puzzles are likely to jeopardize the effectiveness of the CBE monetary policy and its capacity to check inflation and achieve the price stabilization objective. Consequently, there is a dire need to understand the dynamic behavior of prices and output in response to different monetary policy shocks. Discerning the structure of those responses should also be useful to investigate the prospect of pursuing a monetary policymaking framework based on a formal inflation-targeting approach as proposed recently by the CBE (CBE 2004/2005).

The main object of this chapter is to examine the effect of recent changes in the structure of the monetary policy in Egypt on the monetary system and on the performance of the economy. We begin by measuring the stance of monetary policy in a way that reflects the CBE's operating procedure. The stance is constructed based on an analytical framework that allows the extraction of information about monetary policy from the data on variables of interest. We concentrate on two key policy variables, the bank reserves and the interest rates, which appear to be the main CBE operational policy targets since the end of the 1980s. To maintain the focus on the monetary sector, we avoid imposing any unwarranted restrictions on the relationships between the other macroeconomic variables in the economy. In the process of measuring the stance, we are also able to estimate the size and the direction of the responses to policy shocks of real output, of prices, and of the policy variables themselves. Finally, against the backdrop of the estimated responses, we explore the viability of policymaking by rules rather than by discretion. Furthermore, we argue in favor of implementing constrained discretion, which, it is important to note, turns out to be consistent with the inflation-targeting approach, as a basic framework for monetary policymaking at the CBE.

Our empirical study takes the analytical models introduced by Bernanke and Mihov (1998), Uhlig (2005), and Rotemberg and Woodford (1997 and 1998) as templates to measure the monetary stance; to identify the effects of policy shocks on the economy; and to formulate historical and counterfactual scenarios that assess the implications of different rules on policy decisions, respectively. Our replicas of the analytical models are adapted to consider the realities of the Egyptian economic system and the monetary regime.

The remainder of the chapter proceeds as follows. Section 1 presents a brief historical overview that delineates the main objectives, targets, and instruments of the CBE policy since the beginning of the 1990s. In Section 2, we evaluate the existing measures and direction of monetary policy from the mid-1980s to 2005 using a structural vector autoregression (VAR) that is chosen from a model that nests different possible descriptions of the CBE operating procedures. The selected VAR model is employed for measuring the changes in the stance during the period under investigation. Section 3 considers that model as a point of departure to describe the effect of monetary policy shocks on real output subject to different stylized structural restrictions. Section 4 attempts to identify an underlying monetary policy rule for the CBE and to predict how real output, interest rate, and inflation respond to stochastic disturbances in that rule using a structural VAR model. Section 5 concludes. An Appendix includes additional tables and graphs related to the analysis.

1. Monetary Policy in Egypt 1990–2005: A Narrative

This section presents a brief review of the evolution of the main components of monetary policy in Egypt. The review considers the recent developments in the ultimate objective of the CBE monetary policy, the intermediate and operational targets that were selected to achieve that objective, and the monetary instruments adopted to affect those targets.

During 1990 through 2005, with the exception of 1996/1997, the CBE has continually focused on achieving two principal objectives, namely price stability and exchange rate stability. The monetary policy, however, exhibited overt inconsistencies, particularly during 1992/1993–1996/1997. In 1992/1993, besides price and exchange rate stability, the CBE planned to achieve ostensibly conflicting objectives. While the CBE aimed at controlling the monetary expansion thereby implying a contractionary policy, it also called for a reduction of the interest rate on the Egyptian pound to encourage investment and promote economic growth thereby implying an expansionary stance (CBE 1992/1993). With the onset of the second stage of the economic reform program in the following year 1993/1994, the thrust of the monetary policy shifted to the promotion of growth in the productive sectors as a means of stimulating aggregate productivity (CBE 1993/1994). The CBE primary objective swayed back to the expansionary monetary control/output growth recipe during the 2–year period 1994/1995 to 1995/1996. In 1996/1997, the CBE reverted once more to the objective of economic growth via monetary stabilization.

Alternatively, throughout the period 1990/1991 until 2004/2005, the different proximate targets of monetary policy seemed fairly consistent. The CBE intermediate target entailed the control of the annual growth rate of domestic liquidity measured in terms of the broad money supply, M_2. Similarly, during the entire period under consideration, save 2004/2005, the two operational target components, management of nominal interest rates and the control of banks' excess reserves in local currency at the CBE, remained unchanged. Starting in 2005, the overnight interest rate on interbank transactions was designated as the operational target.

To achieve its targets, the CBE depended mostly on a number of indirect, market-based instruments such as the required reserve ratio, reserve money, and open market operations along with a host of interest rates including the discount rate, Treasury bill rate, 3-month deposit rate, and loan and deposit interest rates. The choice of indirect instead of direct instruments was motivated by the initiation of the monetary policy reform act as part of the country's overall economic reform program. Direct instruments (e.g., quantitative and administrative determination of interest rates using credit and interest rate ceilings) were abolished for the private and the public sectors starting 1992 and 1993, respectively. Consequently, public enterprises were allowed to deal with all banks without prior permission from a lending public bank (Hussein and Nos'hy 2000). The remainder of this section presents a brief overview of the main developments in the use of the monetary instruments since the 1990s.

The CBE relied on the discount rate as a monetary policy instrument during 1990 to 2005. During that period, the discount rate was lowered gradually from 19.8 percent in 1992 to approximately 9 percent by the beginning of 2006 with the hope of promoting investment.[3] To reduce the rigidity in the discount rate, the CBE linked it to the interest rate on Treasury bills. This resulted in a steady decline in the interest rate on Treasury bills, which decreased starting 1992 through 1998. The interest rate on Treasury bills began to recover once again in 2002 only to attain a maximum in the following year.

By January 1991, the CBE had liberalized the *interest rates on loans and on deposits.* Banks were given the freedom to set their loan and deposit interest rates subject to the restriction that the *3-month interest rate on deposits* should not fall below 12 percent per annum. This restriction was cancelled in 1993/1994. Because of the continuous decrease in the discount rate, interest rates on loans (one year or less) also fell during the period 1995 to 1999 before they started to rise again in 2000. The decline in the interest rate on loans led to a reduction in the returns on deposits held in local currency. The local currency deposits, however, were not significantly affected by the fall in the interest rate since the interest rate on the Egyptian pound deposits remained relatively higher than the equivalent rates paid on foreign currencies (El-Asrag 2003).

Open market operations are an important instrument that affects the short-run nominal interest rate through their capacity to absorb and manage excess liquidity in the economy and to sterilize the effect of increases in international reserves. Open market operations in Egypt depend on a number of tools including repurchasing of Treasury bonds, final purchase of Treasury bills and government bonds, foreign exchange swaps, and debt certificates (Abu El Eyoun 2003). The use of open market operations became consistent with the liberalization of the interest rates once the CBE resorted to the market as a means of financing government debt. The primary dealers system, which became effective in July 2004, increased the importance of the open market operations as an instrument of monetary policy.

In 1997/1998, the CBE increased its dependence on an alternative instrument, the *repurchasing operations of Treasury bills (repos)*, to provide liquidity and to stimulate economic growth. The value of these operations increased, reaching LE 209 billion in 1999/2000. The reliance on repos, however, started to decrease in 2000/2001 reaching a minimum in 2002/2003. In 2003/2004, the CBE introduced the *reverse repos of Treasury bills* and permitted *outright sales of Treasury bills* between the CBE and banks through the market mechanism. In August 2005, the CBE notes were introduced instead of the Treasury bills reverse repos as an instrument for the management of the monetary policy.

The *domestic and foreign currency required reserve ratios* represented another key instrument of monetary policy. During the period 1990–2005, the domestic and foreign currency required reserve ratios ranged between approximately 14–15 percent and 10–15 percent, respectively. The changes in the required reserve ratios alone have not been sufficient to determine the variance in the reserves as the formula employed in the calculation of the reserve ratio was subjected to several revisions during 1990–2005.

Apart from the modifications in the structure of the indirect monetary policy instruments, the CBE undertook a number of notable reforms in the *exchange rate* system. At the beginning of the 1990s, Egypt officially implemented a managed float regime, with the exchange rate acting as a nominal anchor for monetary policy. Yet, in reality, the country had adopted a fixed exchange rate regime with the authorities setting the official exchange rate without regard for market forces. This resulted in a highly stable exchange rate for the Egyptian pound against the US dollar and a black market for foreign exchange (El-Asrag 2003). In February 1991, a dual exchange rate regime, which included a primary restricted market and a secondary free market, was introduced to raise foreign competitiveness and to simplify the exchange rate system. The two markets were unified in October 1991. From then until 1998, the Egyptian pound was freely traded in a single exchange market with limited intervention by the authorities to keep the exchange rate against the US dollar within the boundaries of an implicit band (ERF and IM 2004).

The second half of the 1990s was characterized by a tight monetary stance. El-Refaay (2000) detects that tightness based on the observed slowdown in the growth rate of M2 and of reserve money. By 1997, the Egyptian economy had started to feel the crunch of a liquidity crisis owing to internal and external shocks that led to a shortage in both domestic and foreign (i.e., US dollar) currencies. The internal shocks were prompted by a large increase in bank lending, particularly to the private sector. A significant part of the bank credit extended to the private sector in the 1990s was directed to real estate investments. In the absence of matching demand, the relative increase in the supply of housing units made it difficult for the real estate investors to repay their bank loans. The supply-demand mismatch raised the rates of loan default and instigated a liquidity shortage in the banking system. The liquidity crisis was intensified by the large fiscal debt, which was sparked by the government's initiation of several huge projects at the same time including the Toshka Project, al-Salam Canal, North West Gulf of Suez Development Project, and East of Port Said Project (Hussein and Nos'hy 2000). The financing of these projects greatly depended on bank deposits. The strain on bank deposits increased with the accumulation of a large government debt to public and private construction firms. Moreover, external shocks, including the fall in oil, tourism, and Suez Canal revenues and the decrease of workers' remittances from abroad by the end of the 1990s exacerbated the liquidity problem.

The appreciation of the real exchange rate during the 1990s was probably the key factor behind the liquidity shortage. Following the liberalization and unification of the foreign exchange rate in 1991, the nominal exchange rate remained within excessively tight bounds (between LE 3.2–3.4 per dollar). The nominal exchange rate rigidity in conjunction with high real interest rates caused a real appreciation in the value of the Egyptian pound that not only depleted the economy's foreign competitiveness but also triggered significant market speculation. The foreign exchange market instability and the increase in the importation bill—financed through bank loans—created a shortage of US dollars in the economy (Hussein and Nos'hy 2000).

The move to an exchange rate peg during the 1990s was accompanied by accommodating changes in the monetary policy. It was not possible, however, to pursue an active monetary policy with a fixed exchange rate regime. In January 2001, Egypt replaced the de facto Egyptian pound to US dollar peg with an adjustable currency band. Despite those reforms, the Egyptian pound gradually lost about 48 percent of its value against the US dollar over the period 2001–2003 (ERF and IM 2004). On January 29, 2003, the adjustable peg was swapped with a floating exchange rate regime. Under the free float, banks were permitted to determine the buy and sell prices of exchange rates. The CBE was barred from intervention in setting the foreign exchange rate, except to correct for major imbalances and sharp swings (El-Asrag 2003). The move from the managed float system to a flexible exchange rate regime denotes a transformation from an implicit policy rule to a non-committal absence of a monetary policy rule (Bartley 2001 and Mundell 2000). Accordingly, the liberalization of the pound marks the demise of an implicit dual-component monetary rule system with intricate price stability and exchange rate stability rules.

Despite the liberalization of the pound in 2003, the CBE has continued to maintain exchange rate stability as one of its key objectives during the following years, 2004 and 2005. It is difficult to comprehend how the CBE plans to bring about exchange rate stability without frequently resorting to direct controls. We suspect that in the coming months, the CBE might still choose to keep a tight grip on the foreign exchange market. In theory, efficient monetary policymaking, however, tolerates intervention in the foreign exchange market only by means of policy measures. Hitherto, the CBE has a good record on that account. For instance, the fears of dollarization that followed the liberalization of the pound, prompted the CBE to tighten monetary policy through an increase in the rate of interest (CBE 2004/2005).

During the last year, the main objective of the CBE has been to keep inflation low and stable. That objective was cast within the context of a general program to eventually move toward anchoring monetary policy by inflation-targeting once the fundamental machinery needed for its implementation is installed (CBE 2005). Meanwhile, in the transition period, the CBE intends to meet its inflation stabilization objective through the management of the short-term interest rates and control of other factors that affect the inflation rate including shocks to credit and to money supply (CBE 2005). In view of the recent changes in policymaking initiated by the CBE, we anticipate that the upcoming period will see efforts to conduct monetary policy on objective and methodical bases. We believe that good measurement of monetary policy and of the stance during the last 15 years or so should provide a suitable inferential point of departure en route toward the support of those endeavors.

To summarize, the above narrative establishes the importance of price stability as the prime objective of the CBE. We show that since the beginning of the 1990s short-run interest rates and reserves have played a key role as monetary instruments under the control of the CBE for achieving that objective.

2. Measuring Stance and the Impact of Monetary Policy Shocks

This section focuses on measuring the direction of monetary policy to find out whether it has been expansionary or contractionary in the last two decades. Measuring the stance requires the identification of the monetary instruments that can best describe the policy shocks and the selection of a suitable model that can illustrate the behavioral dynamics that explain the structural responses to those shocks. We use the historical information about the CBE operating procedure presented in Section 1 and the Bernanke and Mihov (1998) VAR methodology to measure monetary policy in Egypt and to assess its impact on the economy.

2.1 Theoretical Underpinnings

Contemporary macroeconomic literature draws attention to the drawbacks of intermediate targeting of monetary aggregates. In addition, the monetary aggregates (e.g., M0, M1, or M2) cannot be used to measure neither the stance nor the effects of variations in the central bank operating procedure since they are typically influenced by a variety of non-policy effects (e.g., money demand disturbances) and by changes in policy (Bernanke and Mihov 1998). Consequently, different measures have been proposed for the evaluation of monetary policy.

Strongin (1995) proposes measuring policy by the changes in that portion of nonborrowed reserves that is orthogonal to total reserves.[4] He argues that when the monetary authority is constrained to meet total reserve demand in the short-run, it can effectively tighten policy through reducing the nonborrowed reserves to the extent of forcing the banks to borrow from the discount window. Strongin's approach has several advantages. First, the inclusion of nonborrowed reserves as a policy variable can avoid the price puzzle and other anomalies in the behavior of non-policy variables, e.g., output (Sims 1992, Uhlig 2005, and Bernanke and Mihov 1998). Second, the approach is capable of nesting alternative monetary authority operating procedures because it allows the projection of nonborrowed reserves on total reserves to vary over time (Bernanke and Mihov 1998).[5]

We have seen in Section 1 that interest rates and reserves were regularly utilized as CBE monetary policy instruments during the period 1990–2005. In this section, we provide an analysis of the monetary policymaking process within the context of a VAR framework that includes three policy indicators: total reserves, nonborrowed reserves, and short-term interest rates. Bernanke and Mihov (1998) propose a six-variable semi-structural VAR model that nests a number of quantitative monetary policy approaches within a unified milieu. An important advantage of their approach is that it facilitates the computation of an optimal overall measure of policy stance, which is consistent with the estimated parameters describing the monetary authority's operating procedure and the market for bank reserves. Beside the three policy variables, the VAR model incorporates three main non-policy variables: real GDP, GDP deflator and an index of commodity prices. Like nonborrowed reserves, the exclusion of commodity prices may lead to a price or an output puzzle (Sims (1992), Eichenbaum (1992), Gordon and Leeper (1994), Bernanke and Mihov (1998), and Kim (1999)).

The structure in the VAR model proposed by Bernanke and Mihov (1998) depends on a simple description of the market for bank reserves that is represented in innovation form by the following equations:[6]

$$u_{TR} = -\alpha u_{IR} + v^d \quad (1)$$
$$u_{BR} = \beta u_{IR} + v^b \quad (2)$$
$$u_{NBR} = \phi^d v^d + \phi^b v^b + v^s \quad (3)$$

where u_{TR}, u_{IR}, and u_{NBR} are observable VAR residuals representing the shocks to the banks' total demand for reserves (*TR*), to the interest rate (*IR*), and to the nonborrowed reserves (*NBR*), respectively, and α, β, ϕ^b, and ϕ^d are positive parameters. Equation 1 implies that the innovation in the demand for total reserves depends negatively on the shock in the interest rate (u_{IR}) and on an unobservable VAR residual, v^d, which measures the demand disturbance in the system. Equation 2 shows that the shock to borrowed reserves (*BR*), u_{BR}, depends positively on the innovation in the interest rate and on an unobservable VAR residual, v^b, which represents the disturbance in the portion of reserves that the commercial banks choose to borrow. Finally, Equation 3 describes the behavioral response of the monetary authority to shocks in the demand for total and for borrowed reserves and to policy innovations (v^s). The coefficients ϕ^d and ϕ^b determine the relative importance of the response of the central bank to the different shocks.

Bernanke and Mihov (1998) stipulate that the disturbance term v^s represents the policy shock that needs to be identified. It can be easily shown that the class of solutions for the vector of observable shocks $\boldsymbol{u}=[u_{TR}\, u_{BR}\, u_{NBR}]'$ in the system of equations (1)-(3) is given by $[\alpha(\beta+\alpha)^{-1}\ v^s\ -(\beta+\alpha)^{-1}]'$ such that

$$v^s = -(\phi^d + \phi^b)u_{TR} + (1 + \phi^b)u_{NBR} - (\alpha\phi^d - \beta\phi^b)u_{IR}. \quad (4)$$

With seven unknown variables, α, β, ϕ^d, ϕ^b, v^d, v^b, and v^s, the system is underidentified by one restriction. Bernanke and Mihov also show that the solution of this system nests at least five different models for measuring monetary policy shocks including Bernanke and Blinder (1992) *IR* model, Christiano and Eichenbaum (1992a) *NBR* model, Strongin (1995) *NBR/TR* model, Cosimano and Sheehan (1994) *BR* model, and the Bernanke and Mihov (1998) just identification (*JI*) model. All those models can be determined through imposing a variety of parametric restrictions on the equation coefficients in the solution for $\boldsymbol{u}$.

First, targeting the interest rate so that the monetary authority can fully offset changes in total and in borrowed demand for reserves is equivalent to the parametric restriction ϕ^b=-1 and ϕ^d=1 (Bernanke and Blinder 1992). Second, imposing the constraint ϕ^b=ϕ^d=0 implies that nonborrowed reserve shocks depend only on monetary policy innovations (Christiano and Eichenbaum 1992a). Third, Strongin (1995) assumes that all disturbances in total reserves are attributable to demand shocks (i.e., α=0), which are accommodated by the monetary authority in the short-run through open-market operations and/or the discount window and that the monetary authority does not respond to shocks in commercial bank borrowing (ϕ^b=0). Fourth, targeting borrowed reserves implies the parametric restrictions ϕ^d=1 and $\phi^b=\alpha/\beta$. Since each of those four models imposes two parametric constraints, the resulting solutions are overidentified by one restriction. Finally, Bernanke and Mihov (1998) present an alternative model with the single identifying restriction α=0, thus implying that the shocks in total reserves are exclusively attributable to demand disturbances.

2.2 Data

Equations (1)-(3) and the relevant parametric restrictions were employed to estimate the parameters of a 6–variable semi-structural VAR for each of the five models described above. The VAR estimates are obtained using monthly data for Egypt during the period 1985–2005.

Time series data on real GDP and the GDP deflator were not available at monthly frequency. Following Bernanke and Mihov (1998), the two monthly series were constructed from annual IMF-IFS (2006) data for the period 1981–2005 by state-space methods using the Litterman (1983) temporal disaggregation procedure (Quilis 2004).[7] The consumer price index (CPI) was chosen as a proxy for commodity prices to capture the CBE perceptions about the future behavioral dynamics of inflation. The monthly frequency CPI series as well as the data for total reserves were obtained from the IMF-IFS (2006). The nonborrowed reserves series was computed as the difference between the total reserves less the credit to commercial banks from the CBE, which was also available in the IMF-IFS database. Both the total and the nonborrowed reserves were seasonally adjusted using an autoregression integrated moving average (ARIMA) model of the order ARIMA (3, 1, 0).[8] The total and the nonborrowed reserves series were normalized by a 36–month moving average of total reserves to induce stationarity.

From the mid-1980s to 2005, the CBE used at least four different rates of interest as policy instruments. They include the discount rate, the 3-month deposit rate, the Treasury bills rate and the interbank overnight rate. To maintain a sufficient number of degrees of freedom, it would not be practically feasible to take account of all these interest rates concurrently in a VAR model. We picked the 3-month deposit rate to represent the interest rate component of the CBE operating procedure.[9] Although our choice involves some degree of subjectivity, it is not totally without objective merit.

In Figure 3.1, Panels A and B juxtapose the movements in the 3-month deposit rate with the interbank overnight rate and the Treasury bills rate from 2002–2005 and from 1997–2005, respectively.[10] The shading in the diagrams indicates the periods characterized by co-movement of the 3-month deposit rate and each of the two other rates. It appears that the movements of the Treasury bills and the interbank overnight rates are fairly captured by the variation in the 3-month deposit rate. These eyeball findings are confirmed by Ljung-Box *Q*-statistics estimates (results not reported), which could not reject at the usual levels of significance the correlation between the 3-month deposit rate and each of those rates for different lags and leads. We conclude that, apart from its importance as a key instrument of monetary policy since the mid-1980s, the 3-month deposit rate is a good proxy for other short-term interest rates.

Having the expected correlations with economic growth and M2 provides additional evidence that supports proxying the interest rate disturbances by shocks in the 3-month deposit rate. Panel C in Figure 3.1 contrasts the standardized movement of the 3-month deposit rate with real output growth from 1991–2005. In concurrence with the conventional wisdom, the diagram illustrates that unlike the first half of the 1990s, an inverse relation between the 3-month interest rate and the economic rate of growth generally characterized the period 1997–2005. Alternatively, the expected (negative) correlation between the 3-month deposit rate and M2 prevailed from 1997 to mid-2003 as depicted by the shading in Figure 3.1, Panel D. The anomalous relation between M2 and the 3-month deposit rate, observed since the beginning of mid-2003, emphasizes the limited capacity of the CBE to absorb excess liquidity by means of open market operations without resorting to an increase of the 3-month deposit rate.

Figure 3.1. Relation between the 3MDEP and OVERNIGHT, Tbill, Growth, and M2

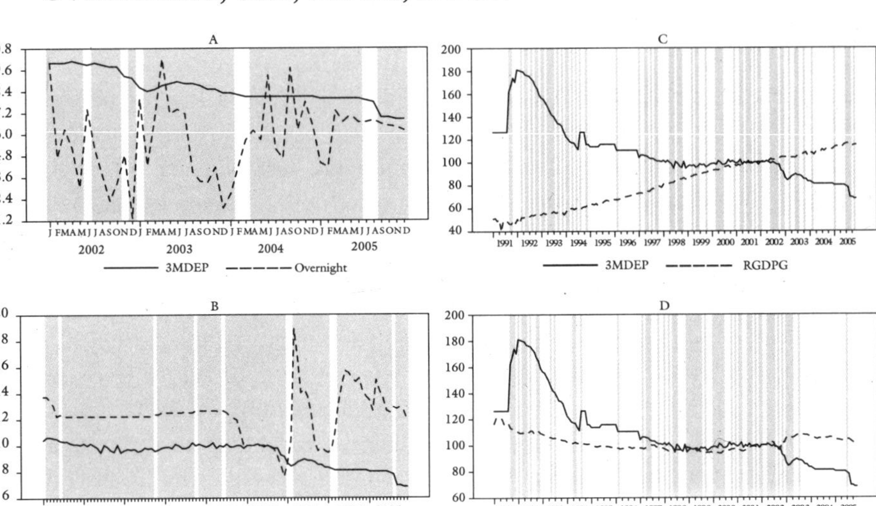

Note: Panel A: The overnight interbank rate (OVERNIGHT) and the 3-month deposit rate (3MDEP) were standardized such that 2002:1=10. The OVERNIGHT series starting 2001:12–2006:7 was obtained from the CBE database (unpublished) and from 2001:2–2001:11 was forecasted using an ARIMA(3,1,0) process (Caporello and Maravall 2004). The shading indicates co-movement of the two series.
Panel B: The Treasury bills rate (Tbill) and the 3MDEP were standardized such that 2002:1=10. Shading indicates co-movement of the two series.
Panel C: RGDPG portrays the growth rate of (detrended) real output. The growth rate and the 3MDEP were standardized such that 2002:1=100. Shading indicates counter-movement of the two series.
Panel D: M2 was normalized by a 36-month moving average of M2 to induce stationarity. Both M2 and 3MDEP were standardized such that 2002:1=100. Shading indicates counter-movement of the two series.

2.3 Estimation of Monetary Stance and Dynamic Responses to Policy Shocks

This sub-section is concerned with the measurement of monetary policy using the Bernanke and Mihov (1998) VAR model. Additionally, it examines the dynamic responses of the key macroeconomic variables to policy shocks. The selected VAR process isolates the monetary shocks in a 6–variable model incorporating 3 policy variables (total bank reserves, nonborrowed reserves, and the 3-month deposit rate) and 3 non-policy variables representing broad macroeconomic conditions and the overall performance of the economy (real GDP, the GDP deflator, and the commodity price index). To identify their model, Bernanke and Mihov (1998) assume there is no feedback from the policy variables to the economy. Hence, the length of the estimation horizon affects the parameter estimates. To identify the influence of the time horizon effect, the VAR parameters were computed for the period 1985:1–2005:12 and for the sub-period 1990:1–2005:12. Estimating the model over different time horizons allows for the possibility of detecting shifts in the regression coefficients. The structural relations implied by equations (1)-(3) were imposed on the coefficient estimates.

Table 3.1 reports the structural VAR parameter estimates and their standard errors obtained from the four overidentified and the just identified models for the complete (1985:1–2005:12) and the sub-sample (1990:1–2005:12) periods.[11] The different VAR specifications were fit with 12 lags in levels of the logs of real GDP, GDP deflator, CPI, and total and nonborrowed reserves and in 3MDEP.[12] The table reports a p-value corresponding to the test of the overidentifying restriction (OIR) and an estimate of the log likelihood function (LLF) for each model. We analyze statistical results portrayed in Table 3.1 to select the preferred model describing the CBE operating procedure and the instruments of policy intervention. We start by analyzing the statistical properties of the parameter estimates for the different models.

The estimate of the coefficient ϕ^d that describes the CBE propensity to accommodate shocks to the total demand for reserves is depicted in Table 3.1 for the NBR/TR and JI models.[13] The values of the estimates of ϕ^d in the whole and the sub-sample periods for both models are very close (between 0.805–0.822), and are highly statistically significant. This implies that the CBE has usually almost fully but not perfectly aimed at offsetting reserve demand shocks during the entire and the sub-sample periods. These findings are naturally inconsistent with the IR and the BR models and the NBR model in which the estimate of ϕ^d is assumed to be restricted either to 1 (i.e., full accommodation) or 0 (no accommodation), respectively. Accordingly, there is a tendency to reject the IR, BR, and NBR models in the selected sample horizons.

The negative parameter estimates for the response to borrowing shocks, ϕ^b, in the whole and the sub-sample periods predicted by the JI model disclose the CBE inclination to offset reserves market disturbances. The estimates, however, are very small in absolute terms and are statistically insignificant. Consequently, since the IR, NBR/TR, and BR models are distinguished primarily by their predictions of ϕ^b, it would not be possible to single out the best one of those models to describe the behavior of the CBE (Bernanke and Mihov 1998).

Table 3.1. Parameter Estimates for Different Models

Standard errors in parentheses

Sample	*Model*	α	β	ϕ^d	ϕ^b	*Test for OIR*	*LLF*
1985:1–2005:12	JI (BM)	0	0.554	0.805	-0.067		2029.596
			(0.498)	(0.033)	(0.088)		
	IR (BB)	0.416	-0.019	**1**	**-1**	0.000	1801.266
		(0.001)	(0.008)				
	NBR (CE)	0.849	0.006	**0**	**0**	0.000	2005.991
		(0.021)	(0.007)				
	NBR/TR (S)	**0**	-0.989	0.805	0	***0.055***	2027.759
			(0.510)	(0.035)			
	BR (CS)	-0.016	0.761	**1**	α/β	0.000	2004.063
		(0.013)	(0.005)				
1990:1–2005:12	JI (BM)	**0**	1.141	0.822	-0.021		1575.583
			(2.545)	(0.040)	(0.066)		
	IR (BB)	0.843	0.083	**1**	**-1**	0.000	1244.835
		(0.000)	(0.000)				
	NBR (CE)	0.758	0.009	**0**	**0**	0.000	1559.144
		(0.011)	(0.009)				
	NBR/TR (S)	**0**	-1.227	0.822	0	***0.352***	1575.150
			(0.904)	(0.039)			
	BR (CS)	0.137	0.251	**1**	α/β	0.000	1500.933
		(0.000)	(0.000)				

Note: IR denotes the BB model assumptions (Bernanke-Blinder 1992), NBR denotes the CE model assumptions (Christiano-Eichenbaum 1992a), NBR/TR denotes the S model assumptions (Strongin 1995), BR denotes the CS model assumptions (Cosimano-Sheehan 1994), and JI denotes the BM model assumptions (Bernanke-Mihov 1998). The imposed parameters for each model are indicated in boldface. The OIR p-values shown in boldface italics are not significant at the 0.05 level implying that the model cannot be rejected at the 5 percent significance level.

Table 3.1 reports the estimates of the slope coefficients, α and β, for all but the JI and the NBR/TR models wherein α is preset by assumption. With the exception of the BR model for the whole sample, the estimates of α have the correct (positive) sign and are statistically significant. The BR model estimate of α for 1985–2005 is negative yet insignificant. The estimated value of α varies considerably between the 0.14–0.85. The small magnitude of α predicted by the BR model for the sub-sample period provides support for the identifying assumption imposed by the JI and NBR/TR models (α=0). The estimates of β are of the correct sign for all the models except the IR and the NBR/TR models for the whole sample and the NBR/TR model for the sub-sample period. Similarly, the estimates of β for the BR model are statistically significant; alternatively, the JI, NBR and NBR/TR models yield insignificant results for the whole and the sub-sample periods. The IR model predicts a significant estimate of β for the whole sample period but the absolute magnitude of the estimated coefficient is relatively very small. This implies that the shocks in the demand for borrowed reserves do depend on the unanticipated disturbances in the borrowing function rather than on the interest rate at which the borrowed reserves are re-lent.

The estimated VAR coefficients are not alone adequate to identify the preferred monetary instruments and operating procedure pursued by the CBE. We, therefore, complement the above analysis by resorting to an evaluation of the performance of the alternative models based on the OIR test results and the LLF estimates.

The OIR for the IR model rejects the BB assumptions with a p=0.000 for the sample as a whole and for the sub-period 1990–2005. Table 3.1 reveals that the NBR model performs poorly according to the p-value criterion. These results suggest that it could have been easier to employ nonborrowed reserves management in comparison with interest rate as an operational target. The BR model that assumes the CBE targets borrowed reserves also fails the OIR test. Unlike the IR and the NBR models that restrict the response of nonborrowed reserves and total reserves demand shocks to 1 and 0, respectively, the NBR/TR treats ϕ^d as a free parameter. The flexibility of the NBR/TR model probably explains its relatively better performance. Table 3.1 shows that the OIR test fails to reject the NBR/TR model for the selected time periods.

In general, the JI and the NBR/TR models yield similar results mainly since they restrict the slope of the demand curve for total reserves to be vertical (α=0).[14] That restriction seems to be readily pinned down by the data at hand. Hence, the JI and the NBR/TR models consistently outperform the others. The LLF estimates reported in Table 3.1 reinforce these findings. However, the overall performance of the JI model surpasses that of the NBR/TR model based on the LLF criterion and on the relatively poorer estimates of β obtained from the latter model.

Despite the relatively superior overall performance of the JI model, it embraces some of the behavioral features of the other models. For instance, the estimated value of ϕ^d (the policy response parameter) for the JI model approaches the theoretical value of 1 as suggested by the IR and the BR models and the estimated coefficient for ϕ^b does not statistically differ from the theoretical value of 0 imposed by the NBR and the NBR/TR models. Thus, the values of the estimated coefficients ϕ^d and ϕ^b for the JI model obviously differ. This confirms that the nonborrowed reserves and the interest rate ought to receive appreciably different weights as indicators of monetary policy with the biggest share of the weight devoted to interest rate smoothing and a minimal share dedicated to the nonborrowed reserves target (see Equation 4).

The variances of the structural shocks to demand for total reserves, to banks borrowings and to policy (v^d, v^b and v^s, respectively) can tell the important role that the policy variable (interest rate) may play as a monetary instrument. Bernanke and Mihov (1998) point out that these variances are not estimated in comparable units and suggest presenting the variance estimates in terms of the share in the interest rate shocks that are attributable to each of the three structural disturbances. Table 3.2 reports the distribution of the variance share estimates for the whole and for the sub-sample periods.

Table 3.2. Contribution of Structural Disturbances to the Variance of the Interest Rate Shocks

	Structural Shock		
	v^d	v^b	v^s
1985–2005	3.889	3.703	92.408
1990–2005	4.076	3.940	91.984

Table 3.2 shows that the policy shocks account for roughly 92 percent of the interest rate variance in 1985–2005 and 1990–2005. This finding provides strong support for the importance of the interest rate as a good policy indicator for the CBE operating procedure. In contrast, borrowing and demand shocks had negligible impact accounting only for about 4

percent of the interest rate variance. During 1985–2005, the CBE apparently had aimed at offsetting the effects of demand and of borrowing shocks on the interest rate. We employed the JI model to measure the monetary policy and to describe the overall operating policy of the CBE. We start by an examination of the dynamic responses of the different variables in the VAR, including the policy measure itself, to policy shocks.

The dynamic effects of a negative policy shock (i.e., tightening) on the variables in the VAR are depicted by means of impulse response functions (IRFs). The IRFs estimated using the JI model for the whole and the sub-sample periods following the interest rate shock are pictured in Figure 3.2 (solid line) over a 48-month response horizon. The shock was normalized to produce a 100 basis-points increase in the 3-month deposit interest rate on impact. The IRFs from a standard non-structural VAR model are also included in the diagram (dashed line) as a benchmark for comparison.

The conventional wisdom says that a monetary policy contraction leads to a rise in the interest rate and a decrease in output, prices and total and nonborrowed reserves (Sims (1972, 1980, 1986, 1992), Eichenbaum (1992), Bernanke and Blinder (1992), Strongin (1995), Christiano and Eichenbaum (1992a, b), and Canova (1995)). The IRFs from the JI model do not show evidence of an output puzzle neither for the whole nor for the sub-sample period as real GDP appears to fall in response to monetary tightening. The standard VAR model implies very weak effects for the shock on real output in each of those periods with some anomalous responses in the first six to twelve months following the shock. In contrast, the JI model IRFs for the GDP deflator and the CPI indicate an obvious price puzzle that prevails throughout the whole sample period with both prices rising in response to the shock (Figure 3.2A). It would also be difficult to rebuff the price puzzle during the sub-sample period despite the fall in prices (especially the CPI) that occurs one year after the shock. The standard VAR IRFs portray the correct responses for prices with just a trace of a price puzzle that is detected with the whole sample data. Like output, the price responses, particularly those implied by the non-structural VAR, remain relatively small owing to sticky price responses, model misspecification and/or measurement errors.

Figure 3.2. Responses of Policy and Non-policy Variables to a Contractionary Shock for the JI (-) and Non-structural (--) VAR Models

A. 1985–2005

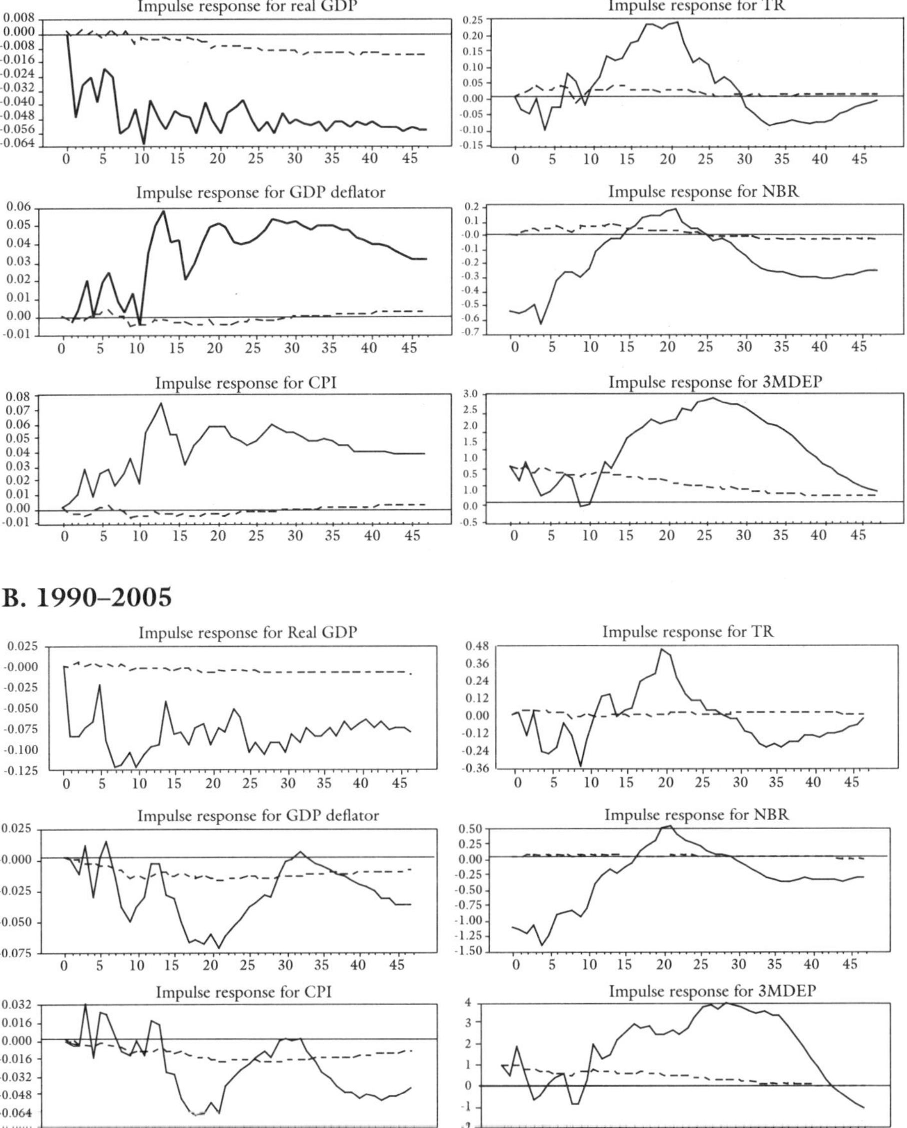

Figure 3.2 demonstrates that the dynamic responses of the total and of the nonborrowed reserves described by the non-structural VAR IRFs are inconsistent with the prior expectations. The IRFs for the JI model, however, depict the correct responses for these variables except from the 15th to the 30th month following the shock. Moreover, the diagram illustrates that the impact of the shock on the non-policy variables (real output and prices) is much smaller than its effect on the policy variables. Such a difference might exist because of misspecification errors. It may also arise owing to the presence of propagation mechanisms that affect the reserves market relatively more than the rest of the economy.

The dynamic responses of the variables to the shock cannot alone provide information on the effects of changes in the implicit policy rule on the economy and on monetary stance.[15] To estimate the effect of variation in that rule, we computed a simple indicator of monetary policy stance that articulates the anticipated (endogenous) and unanticipated (exogenous) components of policy. In practice, the indicator can provide a qualitative description of the overall behavior of the CBE and a measure of the general monetary conditions in the economy that allows for the detection of different episodes of monetary tightness or ease.[16] Equation 4 specifies the index of monetary stance (Bernanke and Mihov 1998). We employ the parameter estimates obtained using the JI VAR model in the construction of the index.

Figure 3.3 sketches the overall index of the monetary stance (top panel) and its exogenous (middle panel) and endogenous (bottom panel) components graphed for the period 1985–2005. The peaks and troughs in the index identify episodes of monetary easing and tightening, respectively. The top two panels in Figure 3.3 show that most of the period 1987–1996 was characterized by a tight stance, especially during the fourth quarter of 1991 through 1993. The following period, 1996–2004, witnessed an easier stance.

Despite a decline in the 3MDEP, the stance index indicates an unexpected monetary tightening in 2005. We are not exactly sure what caused the tightening. One possibility is that the impact of the rise in the overnight interbank interest rates in that year on shocks in the market for total and nonborrowed reserves has beset the effect induced by the fall in the 3-month deposit rate.

To summarize, the estimated stance index faithfully traces the episodes of monetary easing and tightening from the mid-1980s through 2005. The JI model, from which the stance was derived, however, is not capable of emulating the a priori theoretical responses of important variables, particularly real output, to policy innovations. We have found that the impact of monetary policy shocks on the size and on the direction of change in real GDP and in prices was either negligible or ambiguous. The anomalous responses of total and of nonborrowed reserves to policy shocks (Figure 3.2) could possibly lead to such a puzzling outcome.

Figure 3.3. Total Measure and Exogenous and Endogenous Components of Monetary Stance 1985–2005

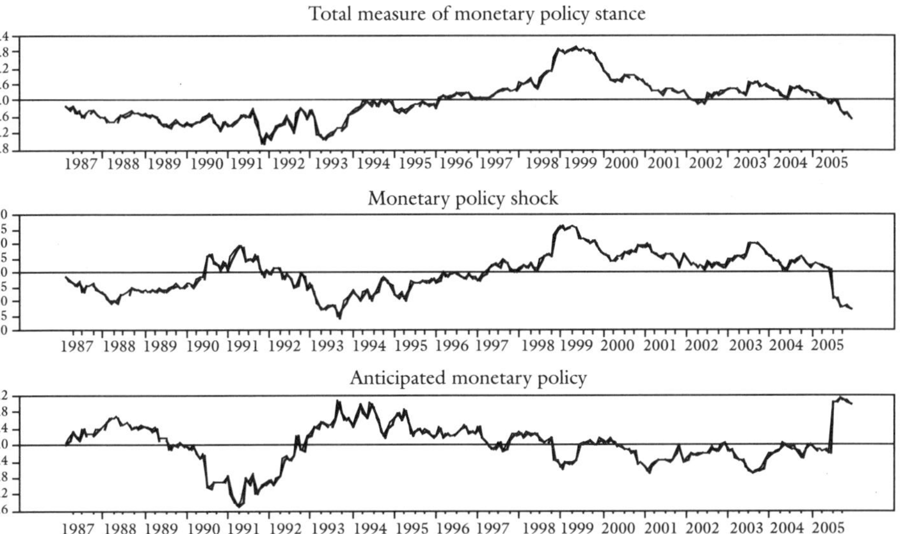

Note: The overall stance is rescaled to have 0 mean and the same variance of 3MDEP. The unanticipated and anticipated components are rescaled to have the same variance of the unanticipated and anticipated components of 3MDEP, respectively. The latter components of 3MDEP are decomposed using the Hodrick-Prescott (HP) filter.

3. The Effect of Monetary Policy on Output

This section considers the effect of policy shocks on real output responses after imposing restrictions on the IRFs of nonborrowed reserves and of prices to ensure the consistency of their dynamic behavior with the prior expectations. We use the *pure-sign-restrictions* methodology proposed by Uhlig (2005). The restrictions are set up such that a negative monetary policy shock does not lead to decreases in the interest rate or to increases in the prices or nonborrowed reserves for a certain period following the shock. Meanwhile, no restrictions are imposed on the response of real output, which is *agnostically* identified by the model output (Uhlig 2005). It becomes, therefore, critical to select a time horizon (K) for the sign-restrictions to hold following the shock.

At the outset, we obtained a set of benchmark IRFs from our non-structural 6-variable VAR model using the standard Cholesky decomposition. The monthly data from 1981–2005 described in sub-section 2.2 were employed in the estimation.[17] The VAR was estimated with 12 lags in levels of the logs of real GDP, the GDP deflator, the CPI, and total and nonborrowed reserves and in level of 3MDEP.[18] This ordering of the variables allows monetary policy shocks to be identified in the VAR with the innovations in the 3MDEP ordered sixth (Figure A1, I). We fit the same model identifying a monetary policy shock with 3MDEP innovations reordered fourth before the nonborrowed and the total reserves as proposed by Uhlig (2005) (Figure A1, II).

The IRFs and the corresponding error bands are sketched in Figures A2, II for a 5-year period following the shock. The diagrams reveal that the endogenous behavior of the response functions to the policy shock seems qualitatively insensitive to the choice of ordering of the variables in the VAR. The response of the policy variable to its own shocks is not exactly consistent with the prior predictions. The negative monetary shock brings about an initial immediate increase in the 3MDEP by about 25 basis points, after which the interest rate starts declining very gradually. The waning effect of the shock dissipates after about 60 months. Figures A2, II also show that the initial response of total reserves to a policy shock is unexpectedly positive for the first four years following the shock. The dynamic response of nonborrowed reserves is generally more realistic although it takes roughly two years to be consistent with the prior expectations. It is likely that the puzzling (positive) price response due to the negative monetary shock can lead to a fall in the real interest rate, which may in turn tempt the CBE to unduly accumulate rather than de-accumulate reserves.

A one-standard-deviation contractionary shock reduces real output nearly all through the response horizon. We detect a bit of an output puzzle in the third month after the shock with 3MDEP ordered last à la Bernanke and Mihov. The identification of the policy shock implied by that ordering might not always be appropriate. However, when the policy shock is ordered fourth, the output puzzle becomes even more distinct (Figure A1, I). Figure A1 panels I and II disclose that despite the relatively tight standard error bands for real output during the first two years following the shock, they seem to straddle the no-response line at 0. In addition, during the remainder of the response horizon, the error bands are too wide. We, therefore, conclude that the effect of a policy shock on the size and sign of the response of real output is ambiguous.

Figures A2 I and II demonstrate other antinomies. We observe a persistent price puzzle that could not be mitigated by reordering the policy variable shock in the VAR. The price puzzle is not the only problem that taints the response functions for the GDP deflator and the CPI. The price movements in the commodity market are normally larger and more flexible in comparison with the aggregate price changes. Figures A2 I and II indicate comparable amplitude for the responses of the GDP deflator and the CPI to the policy shock especially during the first six months of the response horizon. In the next six months, the amplitude of the IRF of the GDP deflator exceeds that of the corresponding IRF of the CPI. This unexpected relation between the IRFs of the GDP deflator and the CPI may be due to deliberate doctoring of the CPI data in order to dodge social unrest by dampening price perturbations and pinning down the official inflation rate.

We resort to the pure-sign-restrictions approach (Uhlig 2005) to rectify the theoretically unreasonable responses of reserves and prices to monetary shocks. The 6-variable VAR described above is employed in the estimation of the responses of the variables to the policy shock, which is ordered fourth in the model. The estimation begins by defining a parameterized impulse vector that imposes non-positive sign-restrictions on the IRFs of the prices (the CPI and the GDP deflator) and nonborrowed reserves and non-negative sign-restrictions on the IRF of 3MDEP. We specify the parameterized restrictions to identify a one-standard-deviation in size contractionary policy shock.

The choice of the time horizon (K) in which the sign restrictions are forced to hold is somewhat arbitrary. To check the sensitivity of the predicted responses to the choice of K, we compare the results estimated using four different values for K=2, 5, 11, and 23 corresponding to time horizons of 1 quarter, 6 months, 1 year and 2 years, respectively, following the initial shock. Figure 3.4 portrays the impulse responses of the variables in the VAR for K=5 after restricting the responses of prices, nonborrowed reserves and 3MDEP as described above.

Figure 3.4. Impulse Responses with Pure-Sign Approach for *K*=5

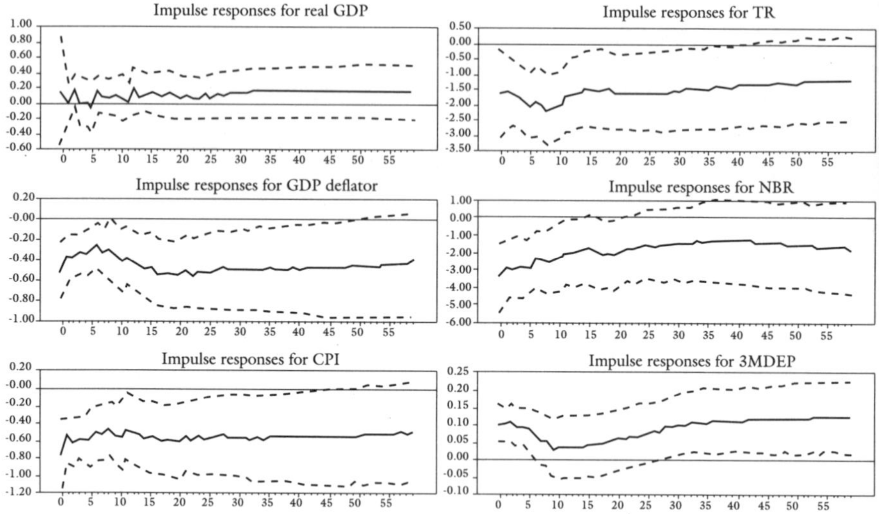

Impulse responses for real GDP

Impulse responses for TR

Impulse responses for GDP deflator

Impulse responses for NBR

Impulse responses for CPI

Impulse responses for 3MDEP

Note: The contractionary monetary shock is chosen equal one standard deviation in size. The solid (—) and the dashed (--) lines represent the IRFs and the ±0.2 standard error bands. The estimates are simulated with 200 draws and 200 sub-draws using an adjusted version of the Uhlig2 RATS program (Estima 2004 and Doan 2004).

The agnostically identified IRF for real output (Figure 3.4) differs significantly from the one based on the Cholesky identification (Figure A1). The agnostic response of real output for *K*=5 seems insensitive to the contractionary shock. Figure A2 confirms the real output invariance for various values of *K*. For each of the four selected values of *K*, the ±0.2 standard error bands appear to flank the IRF of real output around the no response line at 0. Figure A3 sketches the boundaries for the range of IRFs for real output that satisfy the sign-restrictions while varying the restriction horizon. As *K* is increased, the boundary range for the real output response becomes tighter as the upper boundary is displaced downward and the lower boundary is shifted upward. Hence, a longer restriction horizon tends to distribute the responses of real output closer to the no response line with IRFs drawing nearer to 0.

To summarize, our findings decisively show that monetary policy shocks in Egypt virtually have no real effect. Consequently, we conclude that in the long run, money is neutral to the extent that monetary policy shocks would only have an effect on the rate of inflation. The tighter IRF bands observed for the longer restriction horizons corroborate that deduction since they imply that interest rate shocks are associated with relatively stronger real variation of output in shorter runs.

4. Monetary Policymaking by a Rule

Driven by the country's need for a more flexible monetary regime that is conducive to growth, the monetary policy in Egypt recently underwent a sea change. The CBE publicly announced its intention to pursue inflation targeting as the principle objective within a framework that focuses on price stability as the main policy target (CBE 2005). The analytical approach employed so far, which has been concerned primarily with measurement of the monetary policy and stance, cannot be easily extended to deal with the intricate complexities that arise in the process of setting up the stage for the adoption of an inflation-targeting approach. This section considers some of the basic issues related to the evaluation of the prospective potency of inflation targeting as a mechanism for price stabilization. The analysis is conducted in the context of exploring the possibility for the implementation of monetary policy by a rule.

To our knowledge, historically the CBE has been dependent on policymaking by discretion rather than by a policy rule. Two empirical issues deserve special attention once we start seeking a substitute for the prevailing discretionary regime. The first questions whether the CBE should depend exclusively on specific rule(s) in policymaking or simply make use of policy rule(s) to guide the discretionary decisions. More importantly, the second issue considers whether the existing discretionary framework has ever resulted in *rule-like* policy outcomes and arrangements. If so, then it would become potentially easier to instate a monetary regime that allows making policy and taking decisions in conjunction with explicit rules. We tackle both issues in the following sub-sections 4.1 and 4.2.

4.1 Rules versus Discretion: A Cursory Overview

The question of implementing monetary policy by a rule vis-à-vis discretion is at least as old as Friedman's (1960) x-percent rule that dates back to the early 1960s. Nevertheless, that question is usually bound to stir up a lively debate, traversing disputes concerning whether monetary policy should be implemented by strict rules or by pure discretion to explore the overall framework for monetary policymaking.[19] In this study, we focus only on the pragmatic aspects of that debate. In addition, we promote the idea of deriving policy rules to guide the decision-makers in Egypt toward improving their discretionary judgment. Such an approach represents a compromise between strict rules and pure discretion. We reckon that approach would be more realistic not only because of its theoretical advantages (discussed hereafter) but also owing to its potential scope for reconciling the CBE's long historical experience in discretionary policymaking with the current demands for the implementation of inflation targeting.

The strict rules approach has several advantages. Ironclad policy rules are characterized by simplicity, transparency, predictability, consistency, and credibility. They increase the likelihood of insulating monetary policymaking from the effect of exogenous political pressure and rule out problems of time inconsistency.[20] On the down side, they are rigid, too mechanical, and completely lack the necessary flexibility to accommodate unanticipated shocks that affect the relationship between the rates of growth of money, output, and prices or to anticipate appropriate responses due to exogenous shifts in the monetary sphere. Moreover, the rules approach is generally prone to inconsistencies in situations where there might be conflicting targets (e.g., stabilizing the exchange rate and keeping a low and stable level of inflation). At the other extreme, advocates of pure discretionary authority hail its flexibility in confronting and accommodating unforeseen developments in the economy and in the monetary sphere without the oversimplification underlying the rules-based approach. Unfettered discretion, however, is exposed to serious deficiencies. The list of drawbacks includes low credibility, susceptibility to political intervention, and unwarranted confidence in the ability of the policymakers' decisions to guide economic policy. So, while the pure discretionary monetary policy has its obvious limitations, unbreakable policy rules have not been implemented in practice because of the real instability that they may create (Bernanke (2003a), Meyer (2002), Gramlich (1998), and Buchanan (1983).

Bernanke and Mishkin (1997) propose a more sensible approach—dubbed constrained discretion—that finds a middle ground between pure discretion and strict rules. Under constrained discretion, the policymakers are strongly committed to keeping low and stable levels of inflation but at the same time they are endowed with sufficient flexibility to respond to unanticipated adverse shocks to the economy and to the money markets. In addition, constrained discretion requires the monetary authority to stabilize the variance in the use of resources subject to imperfections in the information on economic conditions and on the impact of policy (Bernanke 2003a).

Constrained discretion is closely related to the inflation-targeting approach and, thus, to the idea of employing a policy rule for monetary decision-making. On one hand, the operational aspects of monetary policy involved in inflation-targeting are similar to those of constrained discretion;[21] and both approaches attempt to limit the variance in output and employment subject to keeping low and stable rates of inflation.[22] On the other hand, inflation targeting emphasizes the importance of transparency and of timely communication of policy decisions and measures to the public. These prerequisites of inflation targeting should be able to improve the overall performance and management of monetary policy to the extent of achieving greater consistency in decision-making and enhanced central bank accountability, which are themselves preconditions for the constrained discretion framework.[23]

To summarize, omniscient discretion does not exist. The preceding discussion espouses constrained discretion as a basis for the design of monetary policy. The constrained discretion framework draws on policy rules. However, the rules act only as a means for supplying the policymakers with general roadmaps and quantitative guidance that can inform their discretionary decisions without precluding their prerogative to adjust to structural changes and real world conditions in order to reach stabilizing policy actions. In that respect, the policy rules are not a substitute for the decision-makers' judgment but rather an input in the judgmental process (Feldstein 1999). In the following sub-section, we present an empirical model for Egypt that can be used to make the constrained discretion framework operational.

4.2 Estimating a Policy Rule for Egypt

Does it make sense to estimate a policy rule, knowing that decision makers at the CBE have been implementing policy by discretion? To answer the question just posed, we must first understand the objective of having a policy rule. The quest for a policy rule is typically motivated by either one of the following two objectives. A rule can be employed, normatively, to design policy and to prescribe stabilizing responses conditional on incoming data and information. Alternatively, it could be derived to describe the way the decision makers have conducted the monetary policy during a specified period (Bernanke 2003a and Gramlich 1998). The second objective is sufficiently broad to permit the description of policymaking processes even for discretionary regimes. Good discretionary policy requires systematic decisions. And we should be able to represent those decisions by a rule-like construct (i.e., an implicit rule) that can explain the monetary policymaking choices. The following analysis aims at unveiling the implicit historical CBE policy rule and evaluating its policy relevance. The evaluation is conducted by means of a set of counterfactual simulation scenarios that study the economic and policy relevance and implications of the estimated rule in comparison with alternative hypothetical rules.

We assume that the contemporary monetary policymaking is driven by the CBE ambition to formally implement inflation targeting. Taylor (1993) proposes a systematic perspective for modeling inflation targeting by a rule.[24] Interestingly the Taylor rule turns out to be consistent with the prerequisites of the constrained discretion framework. Moreover, it permits the description of the monetary policy by a feedback rule that gives great discretionary authority to the decision makers to pursue the selected policy and to respond readily to deviations between the actual and the target levels of policy and non-policy variables.

Sections 2 and 3 underscore the central role of the interest rate as a policy instrument. Hence, we presume that it would be more realistic to estimate a quantitative Taylor rule for the nominal interest rate. Because there is no formal policy rule, we try to keep things simple by specifying a small model with only three variables: real output, CPI inflation, and overnight interbank rate (the policy variable) and by focusing on the recent period February 2001 through July 2006.[25] The (nominal) interest rate rule was estimated using the optimization-based econometric framework proposed by Rotemberg and Woodford (1997a, 1998, and 1999).

Rotemberg and Woodford introduce a generalization of the basic Taylor rule in which the monetary authority determines the nominal interest rate not only depending on the history of output and inflation but also as a function of the interest rate itself. The policy rule was derived from a structural econometric model based on a choice theoretic approach and assumes an intertemporal optimizing behavior for producers and consumers of goods and services. The optimization framework is articulated within a rational expectations model. The model, therefore, embodies many more dynamics than the simple Taylor rule. A detailed discussion of the methodology developed by Rotemberg and Woodford is beyond the scope of this chapter. To simplify the interpretation of our results, however, we sketch a general outline of the empirical steps that were needed to estimate the CBE policy rule following the Rotemberg and Woodford (1997a, 1997b, and 1998) guidelines.[26]

Initially, a trivariate just identified unrestricted structural VAR model with real output, inflation rate, and the overnight interbank rate was fit to estimate the implied empirical policy rule and to determine the response of the economy to stochastic disturbances in it. In the second step, a theoretical model was proposed as an explication of the unrestricted VAR results. The theoretical model has been designed to account for the stylized responses of real output and inflation to policy shocks assuming that output and prices may not change immediately owing to the shocks because of decision lags. We calibrated the theoretical model using selected values for a set of parameters that describe the behavior of agents in the economy. Table A1 gives a brief description of these parameters and reports the values that were chosen for the calibration according to subjective beliefs about the realities of the Egyptian economy. The values of two of those parameters were freely determined by an optimization algorithm that minimizes a penalty function defined as the sum of squared differences between the theoretical and empirical impulse responses for output, inflation, and interest rate in the first four months following a policy shock. The three discrepancies were given equal weights in the objective function as suggested by Rotemberg and Woodford (1997a).[27] Finally, the results from the quantitative theoretical model and the empirical VAR were used to identify the historical shock series for the structural equations. The shock processes together with the values selected for the calibration parameters (Table A1) were in turn employed to simulate different historical paths and examine alternative counterfactual scenarios that explicate the consequences of hypothetical monetary policy rules on the economy.

The parameters of the empirical VAR model, including the overnight interbank interest rate (R), CPI inflation rate (π), and detrended real GDP (y), were estimated using monthly data for the period 2001:2–2006:7. A short estimation time horizon (5.5 years) has been selected to minimize the probability of major structural shifts in the policy regime. Table A2 displays the parameter estimates of the unrestricted VAR.

The coefficient estimates of the feedback policy rule are reported in the column labeled R_t. The overall responsiveness of the overnight interbank rate to inflation and output shocks can be captured by means of long-run multipliers. The multipliers measure the variation in the overnight rate because of a permanent change in the levels of output and inflation. The long-run multipliers were computed using the policy rule parameter estimates and the long-run values for inflation (π^*) and the overnight interbank rate (r^*). The long-run estimates of π^* and r^* are 5.0 percent and 9.2 percent respectively, thus implying a long-run-average real overnight interbank rate of 4.2 percent. The long-run multipliers are given by

$$r - r^* = 0.93(\pi - \pi^*) + 11.17y. \qquad (5)$$

Our findings show that the long-run inflation rate is relatively high. If the CBE were to set the inflation target equal to the long-run value of 5 percent, then the nominal interest rate would have to range between 9 percent and 10 percent in order to keep the real interest rate at a reasonable level that would preclude a fall in bank reserves and the adverse consequences of dollarization. Continuing to maintain interest rates at those high levels might preserve reserves but the excessive rates of interest would inevitably end up leading the economy to low long-run levels of growth.

Equation 5 shows that either a level of output that is higher than the trend or an inflation rate that exceeds the target would raise the overnight interbank rate. The output multiplier indicates that the nominal interest rate is extremely sensitive to the output gap. This sensitivity reflects the underlying rigidities in the economy as it takes a large increase in the interest rate to return output back to the trend when output rises above the natural level. In addition, the inflation multiplier is just a little bit less than 1. Hence, a fall in the inflation rate implies a relatively smaller amount of decrease in the nominal interest rate leading to a marginal increase in the short-run real interest rate and consequently to a negative effect on growth.

The estimated coefficients of the policy rule (Table A2) imply a considerable degree of interest rate smoothing since the parameter estimates for the lagged endogenous variable are all positive and sum to 0.79. The estimates also show that an increase in the inflation rate does not have a significant effect on the overnight interbank rate until the next month.

The IRFs derived from the estimated VAR (Figure A4) depict the response of each variable in the model to a one-standard-deviation monetary policy shock that raises the overnight interbank rate just over 0.2 percent. The behavioral dynamics of the overnight interbank rate and inflation generally satisfy the prior expectations. The policy shock immediately raises the overnight rate. However, the overnight rate falls noticeably during the first month following the shock and gradually gets back to normal after one year. The inflation rate declines with the monetary tightening. The sharpest fall in inflation occurs one month following the shock, at the same time when the interest rate decreases sharply. There appears a tad of a price puzzle after three months following the shock as inflation begins to rebound to the no response level of 0. The effects of the shock on interest rate and on inflation dissipate completely after twelve and four months respectively, following the initial impulse. Though the output level returns to the no response level almost at the same time as inflation does, its estimated response is not always consistent with the prior expectations. Output first declines owing to the negative shock. The fall in output is reversed after one month following the shock and this unanticipated response persists during the next two months. Consequently, in contrast with the earlier findings (see Sections 2 and 3) we discover that during the period 2001–2006, although the price puzzle is no longer significant, an apparent output puzzle occurs in response to the policy shock.

The anomalous responses of real output and to a lesser extent inflation may be attributed to the complex structural dynamics that cause reversals in their behavior once the interest rate starts to return to its normal level. Because the interest rate falls slowly, the economic agents may no longer be surprised by the shock and hence are able to adjust their expectations accordingly. Moreover, since, by that time, the inflation rate has already started to return back (increase) to its steady-state value, the real interest rate falls, thereby bringing about reversals in the responses of output and prices. Because producers normally have better access to information in comparison with consumers, the output reversal takes place almost seven weeks ahead of the price reversal.

The impulse responses of the empirical VAR are employed (given the values selected for the calibration parameters displayed in Table A1) to tailor the structure of the theoretical model so that it is consistent with the dynamic characteristics of the data used in the estimation. The theoretical IRFs of output, inflation, and interest rate are plotted in Figure A4 as solid lines. The diagram shows that none of the theoretical IRFs can perfectly match the predicted point estimates of the empirical VAR responses either in terms of magnitude or in terms of the persistence of the effect of the shock on each variable.

The responses implied by the theoretical model are considerably larger than those obtained from the actual VAR. Both models indicate that the interest rate gradually returns to normal one year following the shock. The theoretical and empirical IRFs of the policy variable, however, connote different dynamics. The actual IRF of the interest rate exhibits a sharp decline during the first month following the shock. According to the theoretical model, it takes twice that time for the interest rate to fall significantly. The theoretical response of inflation also reaches a minimum two months following the shock. Unlike the empirical VAR, the theoretical model demonstrates an unequivocal price puzzle that persists for roughly two months, albeit that inflation falls during the first three months following the shock. Finally, despite the marked difference between the real output dynamics of the theoretical and empirical VARs, the two models demonstrate an output puzzle that takes place concurrently in different periods following the shock (Figure A4).

The poor tracking of the theoretical responses points to a specification error that probably arises due to the poor precision of the empirical VAR estimates. It also highlights the deficient specification of the theoretical model that ignores the effect of the coefficients of the estimated policy rule on the nature of the theoretical responses of output and inflation to the policy shock (Rotemberg and Woodford 1998). The importance of the differences between the theoretical and the empirical IRFs should not be exaggerated. Even with those discrepancies, the theoretical model may still be able to capture the behavioral dynamics of the data underlying the empirical VAR. One way to predict the correspondence between the theoretical and the empirical models is through comparing the second moments for the data with those from the structural model. The nine panels in Figure A5 plot the cross-correlation functions of the three series for the theoretical (solid line) and the empirical (dashed line) VAR models. The chart shows that with the exception of output, the theoretical model accounts for the second moments of the data to similar degree as the unrestricted actual VAR. In particular, the diagram illustrates that the theoretical model efficiently captures the same degree of persistence of inflation implied by the empirical model. It also reproduces the interest rate smoothing as does the empirical VAR.

The fitness of the structural model can be tested differently through examining its capacity to simulate the variations in real output, inflation, and the overnight interbank rate in the presence of Rotemberg-Woodford type historical shocks. We conduct those simulations in the following sub-section and make use of them to understand the effects of alternative counterfactual monetary policy rules on the performance of the economy.

4.3 Policy Rule Simulations under Alternative Scenarios

In this sub-section, we study the interest rate feedback effects for the estimated historical policy rule as well as for alternative hypothetical rules. Figure 3.5 graphs the actual data (dashed line) along with two model simulations. The first (HSIM3) depicts a simulated policy rule with Rotemberg-Woodford type series of historical policy and non-policy (real) shocks (solid line). The dash-dot line (-.) represents an alternative policy rule that is simulated with the historical series of real shocks only (HSIM2).[28]

Figure 3.5 discloses that the HSIM3 graphs trace the actual inflation and overnight interbank rate series accurately, particularly since the second quarter in 2003. The HSIM3 simulation of inflation, however, seems to follow the actual series more precisely in comparison with the overnight rate. Conversely, the HSIM3 fails to convincingly track real output except from mid-2005 until the end of the simulation horizon when a marginal improvement in tracking is discernable. That improvement possibly proceeds from the enhanced management of the financial markets starting

2003 and from the implementation of a more focused monetary policy that culminated with the selection of the overnight interbank rate as the key operational target in 2005.

Figure 3.5 illustrates the critical effect of monetary policy shocks on the performance of the economy. The diagram portrays considerable differences between the HSIM3 and the HSIM2 simulated paths for each of the three series. The deviation is relatively more pronounced for real output but it is also noticeable for the interest rate prior to 2004. These findings indicate that during the simulation horizon, stochastic disturbances to monetary policy had a significant influence on output and on the interest rate. In contrast, random shocks to monetary policy had much less important consequences on the rate of inflation.

Figure 3.5. Actual and Simulated Paths with and without a Monetary Shock

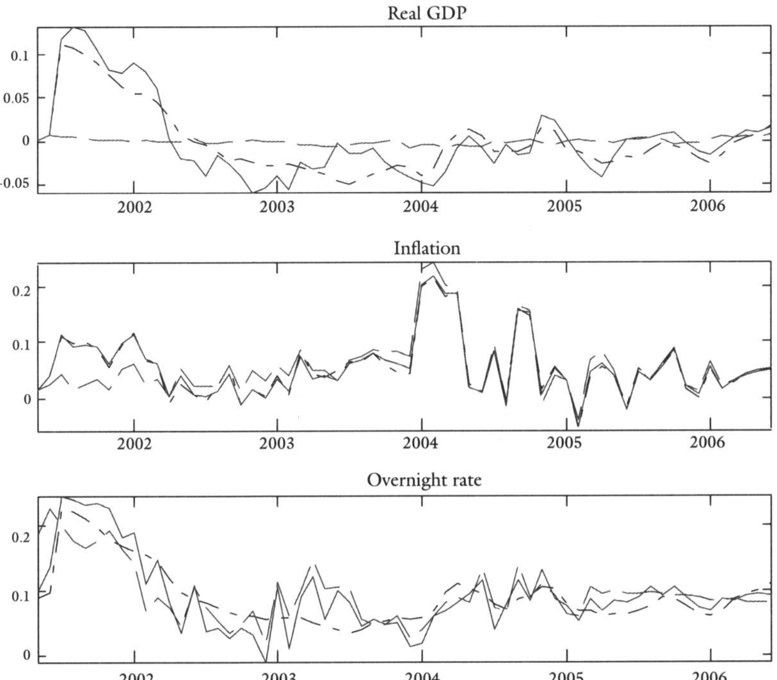

Note: The dashed line (--) represents the actual data and the solid (—) and dash-dot (-.) lines represent the HSIM3 and the HSIM2 simulations, respectively. The Taylor rule coefficients obtained from the estimated feedback policy rule for inflation (θ_π) and real output (θ_y) are 0.082 and 1.163, correspondingly.

Table 3.3 provides further evidence on the important role that monetary policy has to play in terms of its contribution to the variances in real output, inflation and interest rate. The table reports the variances for each of these variables under the HSIM3 and the HSIM2 historical simulations employing the estimated feedback rule with and without the stochastic disturbance term. In addition, the table depicts analogous variance estimates for various counterfactual Taylor-style (1993) feedback monetary policy rules with different arbitrary values for θ_π and θy.[29]

We immediately notice that all the HSIM3 variances are greater than the corresponding HSIM2 variances owing to the effect of monetary policy shocks. With very few exceptions, the predicted variances are larger than one would normally expect. For example, HSIM3 predicts that a monetary policy shock accounts for approximately 32 percent and 15 percent of the variance in inflation and in interest rate respectively, and for almost 2.5 percent of the variance in the deviation of real GDP from the trend. These large moments imply that unexpected stochastic variation in the CBE monetary policy has been significantly more important than the systematic component, which leaves the CBE excessively vulnerable to unanticipated shocks and economic instability. Such vulnerability is likely to interfere with the capacity of the CBE to design sound monetary policy and calls for swift implementation of more resilient reforms that could enforce the CBE objectives and reduce its exposure to the perils of economic disturbances. We believe that a major step in the right direction involves a shift in the orientation of the monetary policy toward the implementation of constrained discretion. This obviously should entail the introduction of some organizational prerequisites capable of bringing about essential institutional adjustments that could lead to enhanced transparency, independence, and credibility of the CBE monetary policy, more reliable data and finer forecasts.

Table 3.3 examines the effects on the economy of a variety of counterfactual monetary regimes represented by simple Taylor-type rules in comparison with the estimated historical policy rule. The modeling options for the feedback rule are distinguished by the values given to the parameters θ_π and θ_y. A specific policy rule implies higher inflation or output stabilization the bigger the values of the response parameters θ_π or θ_y, respectively. The variation among the predicted variances manifests the significant differences in the policy impact of the different monetary rules. For instance, consider the output from two counterfactual policy scenarios: (i) an output stabilization regime that is parametrically determined by the values θ_π=1 and θ_y=5 and (ii) an inflation stabilization policy represented by θ_π=10 and θ_y=0 (Table 3.3). The relatively larger response to deviations of output from its trend (θ_y=5) reduces dramatically the variance in output fluctuations from 51.3 percent to 1.2 percent. The major decrease in output volatility is associated with an equally sharp contraction of the variance in the interest rate. Meanwhile, the output stabilization scenario is accompanied by a large rise in the volatility of inflation from 9.5 percent to 28.2 percent owing to the 90 percent increase in θ_π.

Table 3.3. Predicted Stationary Variances of Real Output, Inflation, and Interest Rate under Alternative Monetary Rules

	Var (R)	*Var (y)*	*Var (π)*	*Var (π-Eπ)*	*Var{E (y-y^s)}*	*Loss from Variability*
				HSIM3		
Historical policy with shock	15.423	2.443	31.754	19.147	40.461	46.551
Historical policy without shock	8.006	1.288	31.466	19.133	39.306	45.989
θ_π=1.5, θ_y=0.5	75.131	57.066	21.128	16.114	14.508	29.004
θ_π=1, θ_y=5	30.109	1.219	28.213	17.793	33.531	41.011
θ_π=10, θ_y=0	949.435	51.327	9.494	9.233	0.732	12.232
θ_π=1.5, θ_y=1	61.432	24.417	19.548	16.396	10.738	26.619
				HSIM2		
Historical policy with shock	12.936	1.351	30.024	19.134	35.413	43.635
Historical policy without shock	5.520	0.196	29.735	19.120	34.258	43.073
θ_π=1.5, θ_y=0.5	65.877	42.788	20.362	16.002	12.709	27.786
θ_π=1.0, θ_y=5	26.651	0.860	26.747	17.786	28.937	38.467
θ_π=10, θ_y=0	937.262	41.585	9.373	9.177	0.539	12.049
θ_π=1.5, θ_y=1	54.899	17.991	19.370	16.340	10.329	26.330

Note: The variance estimates for inflation and interest rate are calculated in annualized percentage points; they are computed for real output as a percentage deviation from its potential level.

How do the variances predicted under the historical simulation compare with those that come from the counterfactual experiments? The historical policy rule implies that the current CBE monetary policy has devoted substantial attention to the stabilization of output and interest rates with less consideration given to the reduction of the variance in inflation. This seems in stark contradiction with the CBE's announced objective to keep low and stable levels of inflation. Actually, the results displayed in Table 3.3 disclose a clear tradeoff between the costs of the deviation of inflation from its expected (target) value (Var(π-Eπ)) and the interest rate variance: higher costs of deviation are associated with large interest rate variance. In general, the historical monetary policy rule implies that the CBE has attached relatively lower cost—in comparison with the counterfactual scenarios—to inflation stabilization thus sacrificing price stability in order to dampen monetary volatility and gain credibility from interest rate stability. By such deviation between the announced policy (price stability) and the realized objective (interest rate stability) the CBE takes the risk of being held accountable for time inconsistency transgression.

To summarize, the results show that the monetary policy can play a critical role in adjusting the dynamic behavior of output and inflation just by focusing on achieving price stability. Despite the constructive measures that have been taken recently by the CBE to reform the monetary sector, more effort is required to fine-tune the performance of monetary policy. More synchronization between the monetary objectives and the actual policy realization seems badly needed to evade the problem of time inconsistency. If the CBE were to focus, by whatever means, on targeting inflation (as we think it should), it should overtly take the necessary steps required to achieve that objective without worrying too much about meeting other targets such as the reduction of variance in interest rate. After all, this is what transparency and credibility are all about.

5. Concluding Remarks

Our results reveal that during the recent period, the impact of monetary policy shocks on real output and on prices was negligible and ambiguous, respectively. Hence, we conclude that policy shocks have an impact only on the rate of inflation with almost no real effect. We take this as evidence supporting the long-run neutrality of money. Naturally, this does not mean that the monetary policy is not important. What it means, however, is that the effect of monetary policy on the level of real output and on the rate of economic growth in the long run is limited by its capacity to achieve long-run price stability.

The study sheds light on the prospects for monetary decision-making by a policy rule as a substitute for the current discretionary decision-making regime. Egypt has a long history of monetary policy-making by discretion rather than by rules. The disadvantages of such a system are well known. Discretionary policy in Egypt has usually had limited success—at least since the 1990s—in achieving a myriad of occasionally conflicting economic and monetary objectives including inflation and output stabilization, motivating real GDP growth, interest rate smoothing, exchange rate stability, and restraining liquidity expansion.

In line with the mainstream literature, we advocate implementation of the constrained discretion framework that finds a middle ground between the pure discretion and the strict rules approaches. It also permits the decision makers to remain committed to some target via a policy rule but at the same time allows sufficient flexibility to respond to unanticipated adverse shocks to the economy and to disturbances in the money markets. The literature shows that constrained discretion is closely related to the inflation-targeting framework, which involves the idea of employing a policy rule.

Picking up on the theme of inflation targeting, we estimated a variant of the Taylor-type interest rate feedback rule à la Rotemberg and Woodford (1998) as part of a system for real output, inflation, and overnight interbank rate determination. The estimation model zoomed in on the recent period from 2001 to mid-2006. Our findings disclose that the discretionary monetary regime in Egypt may not be inconsistent with rule-like policy outcomes. The results illustrate a noticeable tradeoff between inflation and interest rate stabilization. Moreover, historical simulations point to a problem of time inconsistency. During the period under consideration, the CBE has given precedence to the reduction of the interest rate variance rather than to the stabilization of inflation. Counterfactual policy-oriented scenarios suggest that it might be possible to improve the capacity of the CBE in stabilizing inflation through abiding by policy intervention measures that can appropriately influence the responses of the (nominal) interest rate to deviations of inflation from its target value and of real output from its trend.

Appendix 1

I. Tables

Table A1. Values Selected for Calibration Parameters

Parameter	*Description*	*Value***
α	Determines the average length of time during which individual prices remain in effect. Chosen value assumes prices do not change within 3 quarters	0.660
β	Discount factor	0.217
θ	Constant elasticity of substitution (assumed > 1)	10.000
η	Elasticity of output with respect to hours worked	0.700
ω	Elasticity of marginal disutility of producing output with respect to an increase in output: $\varepsilon_y - \sigma + ((1-\eta-/\eta)$	**0.977**
FE	Frisch elasticity of labor supply with respect to the real wage: $1/\eta(\varepsilon_{wy} - \sigma)$	**2.605**
ε_{wy}	Elasticity of average real wage with respect to variation in output (assuming variations in output that are not associated with shifts in preferences or technology)	**0.571**
σ	Free parameter*	***0.023***
γ	Free parameter*	***0.845***
κ	$(1-\alpha)(1-\alpha\beta)\ (\omega+\sigma)/\alpha(1+\omega\theta)$	**0.041**
Ψ	$(1-\gamma)/\alpha\gamma$	**0.278**

Note: *The free parameters (σ and γ) are computed by minimizing a criterion function whose value equals the sum of squared differences between the theoretical and empirical impulse responses for output, inflation and interest rate in the first 4 months following a policy shock, with equal weights given to the three discrepancies that make up that sum.

**Boldface italics font indicates the optimal values for the free parameters from the optimization model and boldface font indicates the parameter values that are computed residually given the other parameter values.

Table A2. Unrestricted Trivariate VAR Estimates: 2001:1–2006:7

Standard errors in parentheses

Independent Variables[*]	R_t	π_{t+1}	y_{t+1}
π_{t+1} (ϕ_3)			0.004
			(0.008)
R_t (μ_0)		-0.002	-0.010
		(0.249)	(0.014)
R_{t-1} (μ_1)	0.407	-0.533	-0.002
	(0.128)	(0.252)	(0.015)
R_{t-2} (μ_2)	0.256	0.030	0.018
	(0.136)	(0.253)	(0.014)
R_{t-3} (μ_3)	0.127	0.311	-0.005
	(0.130)	(0.236)	(0.013)
π_t (ϕ_0)	0.082	0.442	-0.005
	(0.077)	(0.139)	(0.009)
π_{t-1} (ϕ_1)	-0.059	-0.019	-0.018
	(0.083)	(0.150)	(0.008)
π_{t-2} (ϕ_2)	0.172	0.036	0.014
	(0.077)	(0.144)	(0.008)
y_t (θ_0)	1.163	-6.271	0.692
	(1.479)	(2.674)	(0.156)
y_{t-1} (θ_1)	-0.127	5.334	0.073
	(1.682)	(3.024)	(0.173)
y_{t-2} (θ_2)	1.305	-1.075	0.070
	(1.489)	(2.696)	(0.150)
Constant	-0.055	0.051	0.047
	(0.035)	(0.064)	(0.043)
R^2	0.687	0.395	0.621
Durbin-Watson statistic	1.840	1.968	1.893

Note: [*]Coefficient symbol in parentheses.

II. Graphs

Figure A1. Impulse Responses to a Contractionary Monetary Policy Shock Using Lower Triangular Cholesky Decomposition

I. Variable Identifying Policy Shock Ordered Sixth

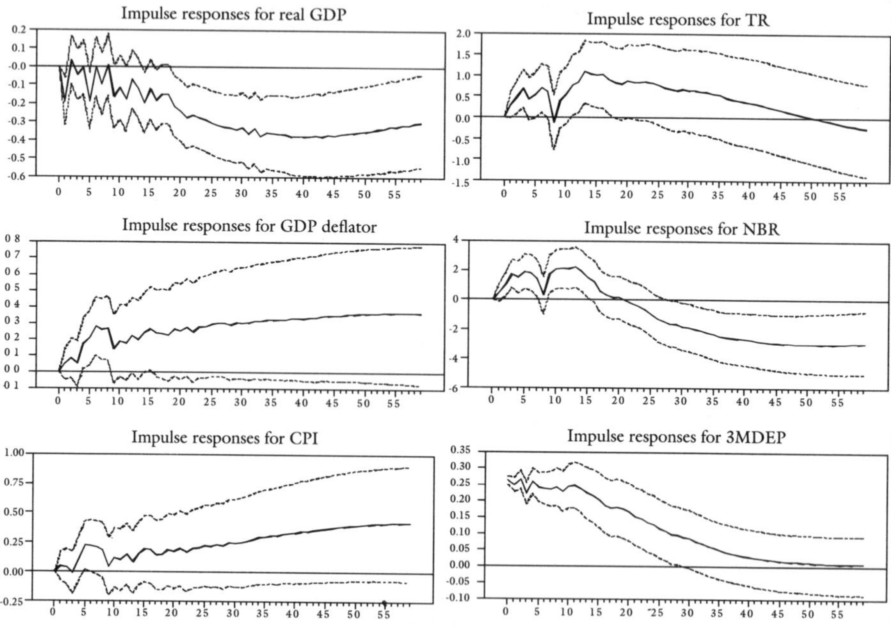

II. Variable Identifying Policy Shock Ordered Fourth

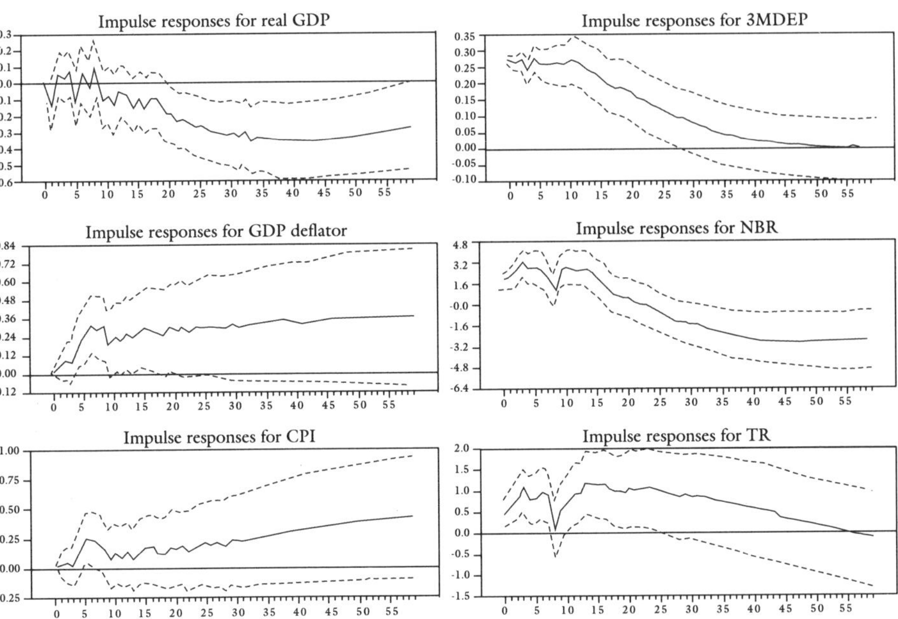

Note: The diagram depicts the IRFs (the middle solid (—) line) for a contractionary monetary shock identified with a one standard deviation rise in the 3MDEP rate. The dashed (--) error bands correspond to the 0.16 and 0.84 fractiles of the response distribution generated from 50,000 draws using Estima's (2004) *monteva2* procedure based on Sims and Zha (1999). Except for the difference in the sample estimation horizon, the IRFs computed in Figure A1, I are analogous to those portrayed in Figure 3.2A with the 3MDEP ordered sixth (rather than fourth) after TR and NBR à la Bernanke and Mihov. The IRFs and error bands portrayed in Figure A1, II and Figure A1, I are similar save for the ordering of the variables.

Figure A2. Impulse Responses Ranges with Pure-Sign Approach for Real GDP

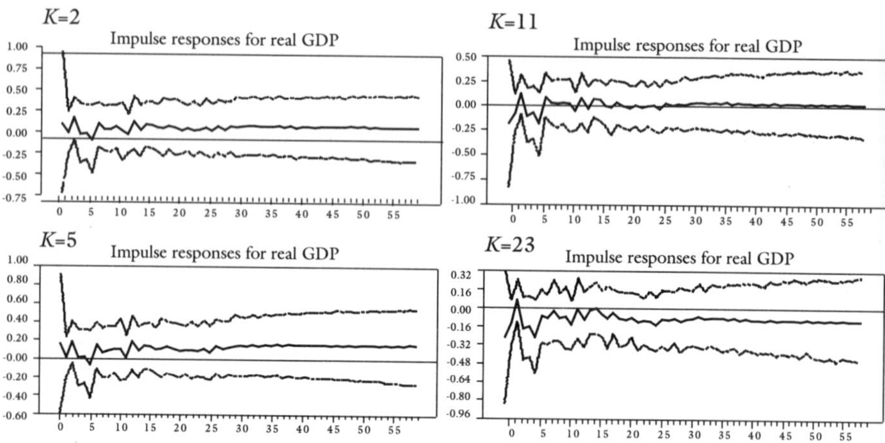

Note: The negative monetary shock is set equal one standard deviation in size. The solid lines (—) represent the IRFs; the dashed lines (--) indicate the ±0.2 standard error bands. The estimates are simulated with 200 draws and 200 sub-draws using an adjusted version of the Uhlig2 RATS program (Estima 2004 and Doan 2004).

Figure A3. Impulse Responses Ranges for Real GDP with Pure-Sign Approach

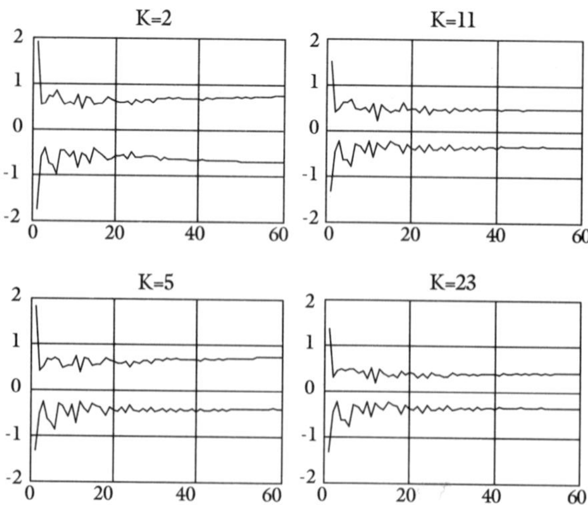

Note: The range of IRFs is defined for a negative monetary shock chosen equal one standard deviation in size when imposing the sign-restrictions for *K*=2, 5, 11, and 23. The estimates are simulated with 50,000 uniform draws using an adjusted version of the Uhlig1 RATS program (Estima 2004 and Doan 2004).

Figure A4. Actual and Theoretical Responses to a Monetary Policy Shock

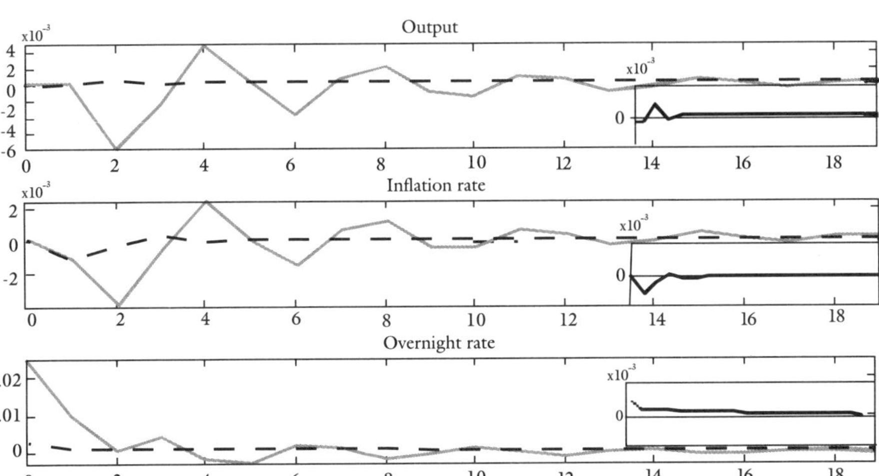

Note: The dashed (--) and the solid (—) lines indicate the actual point estimates and the theoretical responses of the IRFs, respectively. The inserts portraying the actual IRFs are incorporated to facilitate exposition.

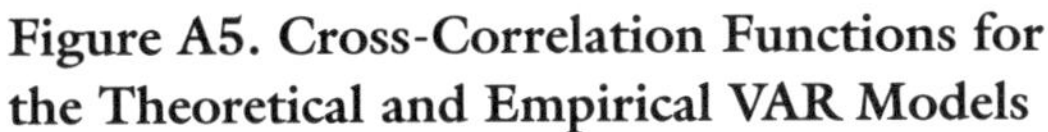

Figure A5. Cross-Correlation Functions for the Theoretical and Empirical VAR Models

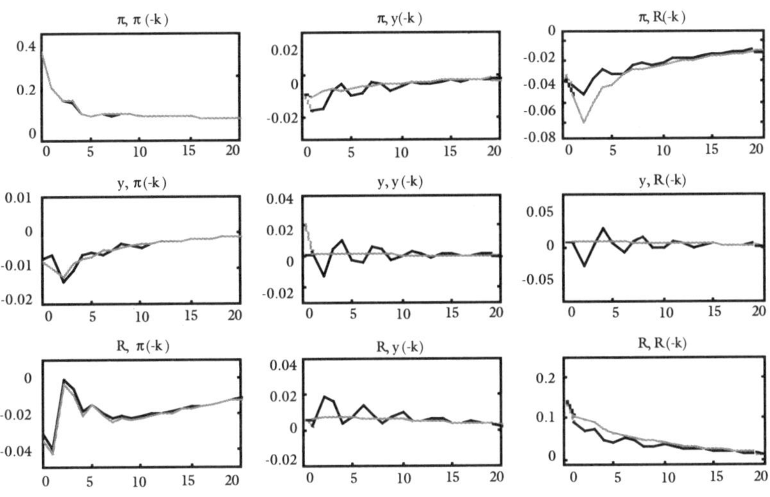

Note: The dashed line (--) represents the cross-correlation function for the unrestricted VAR characterizing the actual data and the solid line (—) represents the theoretical cross-correlation function.

Notes

1. Tarek Abdelfattah Moursi is at the Department of Economics, Faculty of Economics and Political Science, Cairo University and is an economic consultant at the Information and Decision Support Center (IDSC); Mai El Mossallamy and Enas Zakareya are economists at the IDSC. This study was conducted as a joint project between the IDSC and the Egyptian Center for Economic Studies (ECES). We would like to thank Hanaa Kheir-El-Din, director of the ECES, for suggesting the topic, for valuable comments, for partial financial support, and for continuous encouragement. We are extremely indebted to the IDSC and to its director, Magued Osman, who offered an exquisite and unmatched atmosphere for carrying out our research. We are also grateful to Sultan Abou-Ali, professor of economics at Zagazig University, for his comments on an earlier draft of this chapter. Our genuine gratitude extends to Wafik Younan (IDSC) for outstanding management support, Ahmed El Tawanssy (IDSC) for his generous endeavors to provide us with unpublished Central Bank of Egypt data, and Keity George (IDSC) for her superb efficiency in providing electronic and analogue library support. Ahmed Abdel Tawab spent valuable IDSC time to write up the Matlab code required for minimizing the difference between the theoretical and the estimated impulse response functions used in the policy rule analysis. We are extremely indebted to him; definitely, without his efforts, Section 4 would not have come into being. We are grateful to Heidy Aly, Enas Ali, and Dina Rofael, all at the IDSC, for research assistance. An unabridged version of this chapter can be obtained from the IDSC upon request.
2. Standard macroeconomic theory a priori suggests that a contractionary (expansionary) monetary shock raises (decreases) the interest rate, reduces (increases) the level of prices and lowers (raises) real output.
3. The discount rate is typically considered a poor operational monetary policy instrument because it is usually subjected to strong administrative control. Thus, shocks in the discount rate do not always account for variation in the monetary stance (Bernanke and Mihov 1998).
4. Nonborrowed reserves are defined as the difference between the total bank reserves with the monetary authority less bank borrowed reserves at the reserve discount window.
5. For instance, a policy targeting nonborrowed reserves presumes that they do not respond to changes in total reserves (Christiano and Eichenbaum 1992a) while an interest rate targeting strategy assumes that nonborrowed reserves respond one to one to shocks in total reserves (Bernanke and Blinder 1992).
6. Equation 2 is slightly different from the one presented by Bernanke and Mihov (1998) to comply with the structure of the estimated VAR model for Egypt.
7. Bernanke and Mihov (1998) employ the Chow and Lin (1971) temporal disaggregation procedure. We took advantage, however, of Litterman's (1983) method for distributing the low frequency real GDP and GDP deflator series. Besides the trend, seven high frequency indicator variables (oil price [UK Brent], real exports and imports, real Suez Canal dues, real M1, real quasi-money, and real exchange rate with respect to the US CPI) were utilized in the disaggregation of the real GDP series. The series real exports and imports, real Suez Canal dues, real M1, and real quasi-money were deflated using the wholesale price index (WPI) (IMF-IFS 2006). The annual GDP deflator was distributed using two high frequency (monthly) interpolator variables: CPI and WPI.
8. We employed the Tramo and Seats method (Caporello and Maravall 2004) for the seasonal adjustment. Alternatively, the series were seasonally adjusted with the Ratio-to-Moving-Average (RTMA) method (Wichern and Reitsch 2001). Both seasonal adjustment methods rendered qualitatively similar VAR estimates.

9. The monthly data for the 3-month deposit rate were obtained from the CBE (2006) database and the IMF-IFS (2006).
10. The Treasury bills and the interbank overnight rate policy instruments were introduced in different periods. The selected time horizon for analyzing the movement in those instruments differs accordingly.
11. The BFGS algorithm was employed in the estimation of the structural VAR models.
12. The lag length for all the models was determined using a 6-variable unrestricted VAR. The non-policy variables in the VAR were ordered prior to the policy variables as follows: real GDP, GDP deflator, CPI, total reserves, nonborrowed reserves and 3-month deposit rate. The SBC criterion was used to choose the VAR lag length for the whole sample and the sub-sample periods.
13. The estimate for ϕ^d was determined freely only in the case of those two models.
14. In particular, the NBR/TR and the JI models yield identical estimates for ϕ^d for the whole and the sub-sample periods.
15. The monetary policy in Egypt has been carried out by discretion rather than by a policy rule. In Section 4, we argue that the existing discretionary framework has often resulted in rule-like policy outcomes.
16. A formal analysis of the effect of shocks in the policy rule requires setting up a more elaborate structural model with stronger prior restrictions. This is done in Section 4.
17. Uhlig (1994 and 2005) suggests fitting the VAR without a constant or a time trend to improve the robustness of the results at the expense of slight misspecification. We follow suit.
18. The choice of lag length is based on the SBC criterion.
19. A strict policy by rules regime implies that policymakers commit to setting policy instruments according to available data and forecasts via the specification of a simple publicly announced formula without the possibility of any discretionary modification regardless of the policy outcomes. Alternatively, under pure discretion the policymakers commit in advance only to actions based on their best value judgment and the information set that is available to them.
20. Time inconsistency problems arise when policymakers pursue a different policy than the one to which they have been committed.
21. Both approaches share the operational aspects pertaining to the assessment of the structure of the economy and the identification of the policy instruments.
22. In extreme inflation-targeting situations, the monetary authority is constrained to achieve a specified inflation target.
23. In particular, there are three main prerequisites for inflation targeting. The first requirement for a country to implement inflation targeting is to guarantee the autonomy/independence of its central bank to manage monetary policy. This provides the central bank with flexible discretionary power that allows it to choose the most appropriate monetary policy instruments to achieve the inflation target and to enhance the credibility of the policy. The second prerequisite is linked to the idea of central bank transparency. It requires the provision of a communications strategy between the central bank and both the financial markets and the public (Bernanke 2003b). Accordingly, the central bank should provide public timely information about its objectives, strategies, and decisions through publishing inflation reports and minutes of its decision-making meetings. The third prerequisite stipulates that the central bank should rely on powerful models to predict inflation (Allen 2003). Besides, inflation targeting demands the availability of an accurate and reliable consumer price index that can measure inflation correctly.
24. The Taylor (1993) rule specifies how the nominal interest rate should be adjusted in response to deviations of real output from its potential level (trend) and inflation from its target rate. Thus, the Taylor rule considers both the policy and non-policy

choices. Taylor rules are not the only type. Besides price-level stability Taylor-style rules, the monetary authority may adopt different rules such as a base money growth rule, M2 rule, or a nominal income growth rule (McCallum 2002).

25. We utilized the temporally disaggregated monthly frequency data for real GDP and the CPI inflation series described earlier to estimate the policy rule. The monthly overnight interbank rate was provided by the CBE (unpublished).
26. The adjusted Matlab code from Rotemberg and Woodford (1997b) is used with the *solds* and *reds m-files* for solving dynamic systems (http://www.columbia.edu/~mw2230/Tools) to estimate the theoretical policy rule and to conduct the related historical simulation experiments.
27. The choice of free parameters in this study differs from the original selection suggested by Rotemberg and Woodford (1997a and 1998). Our choices have been largely influenced by the convergence properties of the optimization model solution. The Matlab code, employing *cmaes.m* Version 2.40 (CMAES 2006) used for the minimization was prepared by Ahmed Abd El Tawab.
28. In other words, we assume that the historical sequence of monetary policy shocks is equal to zero.
29. We consider the simple Taylor feedback rule specification $r_t = \theta_\pi \pi_t + \theta_y y_t$.

References

Abu El Eyoun, M. 2003. *Monetary policy in Egypt: A vision for the future* (in Arabic). Working Paper Series, no. 78. The Egyptian Center for Economic Studies (ECES).

Allen, William. 2003. Inflation-targeting–an overview. Lecture to the Egyptian Banking Institute.

Bartley, Robert L. 2001. Dervish Lira, Peso Mariachi. *Wall Street Journal*, March 5.

Bernanke, B.S. 2003a. Constrained discretion and monetary policy. Remarks before the Money Marketeers of New York University, New York.

———. 2003b. A perspective on inflation-targeting. Remarks at the Annual Washington Policy Conference of the National Association of Business Economists, Washington, D.C.

Bernanke, B.S. and A.S. Blinder. 1992. The federal funds rate and the channels of monetary transmission. *American Economic Review* 82 (4): 901–921.

Bernanke, B.S. and Frederic Mishkin. 1997. Inflation-targeting: A new framework for monetary policy? *Journal of Economic Perspectives* 11 (Spring): 97–116.

Bernanke, B.S. and I. Mihov. 1998. Measuring monetary policy. *Quarterly Journal of Economics* 113 (3): 869–902.

Buchanan, James M. 1983. Monetary research, monetary rules and monetary regimes. *Cato Journal* 3 (Spring), (1): 143–146

Canova, Fabio. 1995. VAR: Specification, estimation, testing and forecasting, in Pesaran, H. and M. Wickens, eds., *Handbook of Applied Econometrics*, 31–65, London: Basil Blackwell.

Caporello, G. and A. Maravall. 2004. Tramo and Seats Program (TSW). Banco de España, Spain.

Central Bank of Egypt (CBE). 1990/1991 to 2004/2005. *Annual report* (in Arabic). CBE, Cairo, Egypt.

———. 2005. Monetary policy statement. CBE, Cairo, Egypt, *http://www.cbe.org.eg*.

———. 2006. The discount rate and interest rates on deposits and loans in Egyptian pounds. CBE, Cairo, Egypt, http://www.cbe.org.eg/timeSeries.htm,

———. Unpublished. Monthly interbank rates on Egyptian pound.

Chow, G. and A.L. Lin. 1971. Best linear unbiased distribution and extrapolation of economic time series by related series. *Review of Economic and Statistics* 53 (4): 37–375.

Christiano, Lawrence and Martin Eichenbaum. 1992a. Liquidity effects and the monetary transmission mechanism. *American Economic Review* 82 (2): 346–353.

———. 1992b. Identification and the liquidity effect of a monetary policy shock. In Cukierman, A., Hercowitz, Z., Leiderman, L. (eds.), *Political economy, growth and business cycles.* Cambridge, MA: MIT Press.

CMAES. 2006. http://www.bionik.tu-berlin.de/user/niko/cmaes060523.m.

Cosimano, Thomas and Richard Sheehan. 1994. The federal reserve operating procedure, 1984–1990: An empirical analysis. *Journal of Macroeconomics* 16 (summer): 573–88.

Doan, Tom. 2004. New developments in VAR modeling. Prepared for RATS User's Group Meeting Trinity College.

Economic Research Forum (ERF) and Institut de la Mediterranée (IM). 2004. *Egypt country profile, the road ahead for Egypt.* A report by ERF, ERF Egypt.

Eichenbaum, Martin. 1992. Comments on 'interpreting the macroeconomic time series facts: The effects of monetary policy' by Christopher Sims. *European Economic Review* 36 (5): 1001–1011.

El-Asrag, H. 2003. The performance of monetary policy in Egypt during the period (1997–2003) (in Arabic). Paper presented at the 24th Egyptian economists' conference. Cairo, Egypt.

El Mossallamy, Mai. 2004. Analyzing the behavior of inflation in Egypt: A modern approach (in Arabic). Unpublished MA Thesis, Department of Economics, Faculty of Economics and Political Science, Cairo University.

El-Refaay, F. 2000. The issue of liquidity in Egypt: Reasons and solutions (in Arabic). Working Paper Series, no. 41.The Egyptian Center for Economic Studies (ECES).

Estima. 2004. RATS User's Guide Version 6. Estima, Evanston, IL, USA.

Feldstein Martin. 1999. Comment on interest rate rules in an estimated sticky price model. In John B. Taylor (eds.), *Monetary policy rules*, National Bureau of Economic Research. University of Chicago Press.

Friedman, Milton. 1960. *A program for monetary stability.* New York: Fordham University Press.

Gordon, D.B. and E.M. Leeper. 1994. The dynamic impacts of monetary policy: An exercise in tentative identification. *Journal of Political Economy*, 102 (6): 1228–1247.

Gramlich, Edward M. 1998. Monetary rules. Remarks at the Samuelson Lecture before the 24th Annual Conference of the Eastern Economic Association, New York, New York.

Hussein, K. and A. Nos'hy. 2000. What caused the liquidity crisis in Egypt? International Center for Economic Growth (ICEG), http://www.iceg.org/NE/projects/financial/liquidity.pdf.

IMF-IFS. 2006. International Financial Statistics, CD-ROM. International Monetary Fund, June.

Information and Decision Support Center (IDSC). 2005. Index for the performance of the financial economy. IDSC, Cairo, Egypt.

Kim, S. 1999. Does monetary policy matter in the G-7 countries? Using common identifying assumptions about monetary policy across countries. *Journal of International Economics* 48 (2): 387–412.

King, R.G. and M.W. Watson. 1996. Money, prices, interest rates and the business cycle. *Review of Economics and Statistics* 78 (1): 35–53.

Litterman, R.B. 1983. A random walk, Markov model for the distribution of time series. *Journal of Business and Economic Statistics* 1 (2): 169–173.

Lucas, Robert E. 1976. *Econometric policy evaluation: A critique.* Carnegie Rochester Conference Series on Public Policy 1: 19–46.

McCallum, Bennett T. 2002. The *Wall Street Journal* position on exchange rates. http://www.somc.rochester.edu/Apr02/McCallum.pdf.

Meyer, Laurence H. 2002. Rules and discretion. Remarks at the Owen Graduate School of Management, Vanderbilt University, Nashville, Tennessee.

Mundell, Robert. 2000. Currency areas, exchange rate systems, and international monetary reform. Paper given at Universidad del CEMA, Buenos Aires, Argentina.

Quilis, Enrique M. 2004. A Matlab library of temporal disaggregation methods: Summary. Instituto Nacional de Estadstica, Paseo de la Castellana, 183, 28046 - Madrid (Spain).

Rotemberg, J. J. and M. Woodford. 1997a. An optimization-based econometric framework for the evaluation of monetary policy. In *NBER Macroeconomics annual*, ed. Ben Bernanke and Julio J. Rotemberg, 297–346. Cambridge, MA: MIT Press.

———. 1997b. Notes on the programs for Rotemberg and Woodford an optimization-based econometric framework for the evaluation of monetary policy. *NBER Macroeconomics Annual.*

———. 1998. *An optimization-based econometric framework for the evaluation of monetary policy: Expanded version.* NBER Technical Working Paper Series, no. 223, Cambridge, Mass.: National Bureau of Economic Research.

———. 1999. Interest rate rules in an estimated sticky price model. In John B. Taylor (eds.) *Monetary policy rules.* National Bureau of Economic Research.

Sims, Christopher A. 1972. Money, income and causality. *American Economic Review* 62(4): 540–552.

———. 1980. Macroeconomics and reality. *Econometrica* 48: 1–48.

———. 1986. Are forecasting models usable for policy analysis. *Minneapolis Federal Reserve Bank Quarterly Review* 10(1): 2–16.

———. 1992. Interpreting the macroeconomic time series facts: The effects of monetary policy. *European Economic Review* 36: 975–1011.

Sims and Zha. 1999. Error bands for impulse responses. *Econometrica* 67(5): 1113–1155.

Strongin, Steven. 1995. The identification of monetary policy disturbances: Explaining the liquidity puzzle. *Journal of Monetary Economics* 35 (3): 463–497.

Taylor, John. 1993. Discretion versus policy rules in practice. *Carnegie-Rochester Conference Series on Public Policy* 39: 195–214.

———. 1999. *Monetary policy rules.* Chicago: University of Chicago Press for the National Bureau of Economic Research.

Uhlig, Harald. 1994. What macroeconomists should know about unit roots: A Bayesian perspective. *Econometric Theory* 10: 645–671.

———. 2005. What are the effects of monetary policy on output? Results from an agnostic identification procedure. *Journal of Monetary Economics* 52: 381–419.

Wichern, Hanke, J.D. and A. Reitsch, A. 2001. *Business forecasting*, 7th edition, 155–157. New York: Prentice Hall.

CHAPTER 4

The Welfare Effects of a Large Depreciation: The Case of Egypt 2000–2005

Aart Kraay[1]

Between 2000 and 2005 Egypt experienced a large nominal depreciation of the Egyptian pound, much of it concentrated around a sharp decline in early 2003. The objective of this paper is to assess the welfare implications of the large changes in consumer prices that accompanied this movement in the exchange rate. To address this issue I first isolate the component of observed price changes during this period that are due to the depreciation. I do this by estimating disaggregated exchange rate pass-through regressions, using monthly consumer price index (CPI) data over the period July 2000 through June 2005, for eight regions in Egypt, disaggregated into 20 different goods and services.[2] The fitted values from these regressions provide estimates of the effect of the depreciation on 160 different price indices. Disaggregation of exchange rate pass-through to this level is important, as there is considerable heterogeneity across commodities in the response of domestic consumer prices to the exchange rate. In particular, I find that on average, exchange rate pass-through was greater for food items than for non-food items, and varied considerably even within food items. Regional variation in pass-through is also present, but is not as large as across consumption items.

I then bring the estimated price changes due to the depreciation for each of these 160 different price indices to the household survey for Egypt, to investigate their welfare effects. I empirically construct estimates of the compensating variation associated with these price changes for each household. In particular, I estimate how much higher (or lower) each household's total expenditure would have to be in order to attain the pre-depreciation level of utility at post-depreciation prices.[3] This compensating variation consists of two parts. The first is the change in the cost of households' initial consumption bundles as a result of depreciation-induced price changes. The second captures changes in household behavior in response to these price changes. A modest methodological contribution of this paper is to show how these substitution effects can be estimated easily given the (pseudo-) panel dimension of the data that I have for Egypt. I find that most of the compensating variation is captured by the direct effect, which averages 7.4 percent of initial expenditure, and is statistically significantly (although quantitatively modestly) higher in poorer households. I find that there is a great deal of heterogeneity across households in the estimated size of the welfare effect of the depreciation. Most of this heterogeneity is due to differences in consumption patterns across households. A policy implication of this heterogeneity is that it would be difficult to accurately target any kind of subsidy program to offset the effects of the depreciation.

Three major qualifications regarding these results should be kept in mind. First, a significant limitation of this paper is that I am only able to study the welfare effects of depreciation-induced changes in consumer prices. The depreciation is likely to have had heterogeneous effects on the incomes of different households as well. With imperfect labor mobility, for example, it is plausible that households employed in exporting sectors would have seen increases in earnings, while households employed in import-competing industries would have seen declines in earnings, as a result of the depreciation. Unfortunately, however, the Egyptian household survey data that I use provide only very limited information on the economic sector of employment, and so I cannot investigate these kinds of effects, and their distributional consequences in any detail.[4]

A second limitation is the fairly coarse level of aggregation at which I am able to estimate the exchange rate-induced component of price changes. As discussed further below, by working at this coarse level of aggregation, I am likely to be underestimating the scope that households have for adjusting their expenditure patterns in response to price changes. This in turn means that I am likely to be overestimating the adverse welfare effect of the depreciation, which could be substantially smaller than what is reported here.

Third, I stress that I am looking at the welfare effects of depreciation-induced changes in consumer prices over a fairly short period with a fairly large depreciation, and this time horizon drives the finding of significant welfare losses. However, looking at exchange rate changes over other horizons would naturally lead to different conclusions. For example, the depreciation in the trade-weighted nominal exchange rate between 2000 and 2005 was preceded by an even larger trade-weighted nominal *appreciation* in the previous five years between 1995 and 2000. In fact, for the entire period between 1995 and 2005, the trade-weighted nominal exchange rate *appreciated* by about 20 percent. If the pattern of exchange rate pass-through to disaggregated consumer prices was similar during this earlier period, then one can interpret the welfare losses sustained between 2000 and 2005 as just a partial reversal of the welfare gains experienced during the appreciation between 1995 and 2000.

1. The Depreciation and Consumer Price Changes

Figure 4.1[5] shows the evolution of the nominal exchange rate and consumer price index in Egypt between 1995 and 2005. The pound was pegged to the US dollar between 1995 and 1999, followed by a moderate depreciation during 2000 and 2001. In 2002 the pound was again pegged to the US dollar, but during 2003 it depreciated sharply by 31 percent against the dollar, and by 41 percent in trade-weighted terms.[6] The consumer price index increased by 6.2 percent during 2003 and by another 10.8 percent during 2004. As shown in Table 4.1, the trade-weighted exchange rate depreciated cumulatively by 26.2 percent between 2000 and 2005, and the exchange rate *vis-à-vis* the dollar depreciated by 52.2, while consumer prices rose by 27.6.

The key question I address in this section is the effect of the large depreciation during 2003 on disaggregated consumer prices. Table 4.2 reports the cumulative growth rate between July 2000 and June 2005 of the disaggregated components of the consumer price index that I have for Egypt.[7] A quick glance at this table reveals that price changes have varied considerably across expenditure items and to a lesser extent across regions. Most striking is the behavior of food prices, which increased faster than the overall consumer price index. Taking a simple average across regions, overall consumer prices increased by 28 percent, but food prices increased by 38 percent, implying a 10 percent increase in the relative prices of food. In the remainder of this section, I investigate in detail the contribution of the depreciation of the Egyptian pound to these absolute and relative price changes.

1.1 Empirical Framework

As shown in Table 4.2, I have monthly data on the consumer price index disaggregated into 31 goods and services, for eight regions in Egypt. Because of difficulties in mapping the expenditure items in the CPI to the household survey, I will work with a somewhat more aggregated set of 20 of these expenditure items that correspond to expenditure categories in the household survey. I model the consumer price of item i in region r in month t as follows:

$$P_{irt} = \left(P^{N}_{irt}\right)^{\alpha_{ir}} \cdot \left(P^{T}_{irt}\right)^{1-\alpha_{ir}} \qquad (1)$$

where P^N denotes the price of the non-traded component and P^T denotes the price of the traded component of that item. To simplify notation, we can think of the non-traded component as capturing both purely non-traded goods within this item, as well as non-traded distribution costs associated with the traded goods. Accordingly we can think of P^T as the price of imported goods "on the dock" in Egypt. Concretely, one of our disaggregated items is fruit. P^T would therefore be the price of imported fruit "on the dock," while P^N is a price index of non-traded fruit as well as the distribution costs associated with both kinds of fruit.

Following the large empirical literature on exchange rate pass-through, I model the logarithm of this import price as a linear function of the log exchange rate and a measure of foreign marginal costs of production:[8]

$$\ln P^{T}_{irt} = \beta_{0ir} + \beta_{1ir}(L) \cdot \ln E_t + \beta_{2ir}(L) \cdot \ln C_t + u_{irt} \qquad (2)$$

where E is the exchange rate, C is a proxy for foreign marginal costs, and u is an error term that I assume is independent of the exchange rate. I do not have any direct measure of foreign marginal costs of production disaggregated by product. I therefore simply introduce an aggregate foreign cost variable, which is a trade-weighted average of the monthly producer price index in Egypt's five largest trading partners for which this data exist.[9] Note that I allow the extent of foreign cost pressures on export prices to vary by product and region. $\beta_1(L)$ and $\beta_2(L)$ are polynomials in the lag operator, so that I allow current and lagged values of the exchange rate and foreign costs to affect import prices in order to capture slow adjustment.

Taking log differences of (1) and using (2) gives the growth rate of the consumer price as a function of the growth rate of the exchange rate:

$$\Delta \ln P_{irt} = \alpha_{ir} \cdot \Delta \ln P^{N}_{irt} + (1-\alpha_{ir}) \cdot \left(\beta_{0ir} + \beta_{1ir}(L) \cdot \Delta \ln E_{t} + \beta_{2ir}(L) \cdot \Delta \ln C_{t} + \Delta u_{irt}\right) \quad (3)$$

The effect of current and lagged changes in the exchange rate on consumer prices is given by $(1-\alpha_{ir}) \cdot \beta_{1ir}(L)$, and this is the key parameter of interest for this section. It is important to note that the sensitivity of consumer prices to the exchange rate is likely to be substantially smaller than the sensitivity of border prices to the exchange rate. This is because consumer prices contain a substantial non-traded component, both in the form of non-traded items themselves, as well as distribution costs. I do not have direct information on the size of these distribution margins in the case of Egypt, although in principle these can be extracted from input-output tables for Egypt. In industrial countries, these distribution margins are typically quite substantial, averaging 30–50 percent of the prices paid by consumers (Campa and Goldberg 2006).

Unfortunately, however, I cannot simply estimate Equation 3 econometrically since I do not directly observe the price of the non-traded component of each good, P^{N}. I also cannot ignore this term and treat it as part of the error term in a regression since movements in the non-traded component of goods prices might be spuriously correlated with movements in the exchange rate. In particular, during much of the period of interest there were across-the-board increases in nominal prices in Egypt together with a depreciation in the exchange rate, and at least part of these price increases were likely driven by purely domestic factors.

To address this problem I assume that the growth rate of the non-traded component of the price of each item in each region consists of a common component and an idiosyncratic component that is orthogonal to movements in the exchange rate:

$$\Delta \ln P^{N}_{irt} = \Delta \ln P^{N}_{rt} + v_{irt} \quad (4)$$

I assume further that I can approximate the common component of non-traded goods prices with a simple average of a few items in the consumer price index that appear to be primarily non-traded on *a priori* grounds. These are domestic services, and restaurant and hotel services.[10] These two assumptions (of a common component in non-traded goods prices, approximated by these two particular prices) are clearly strong ones and open to debate. However, it is not clear what good alternatives might be available. Although the results that follow are based on this assumption, I have tried three alternatives, and found that the estimates of pass-through are not very different. One possibility is to try to model explicitly purely domestic sources of inflation, for example by including measures of growth in the money supply in the regression. I experimented with this but found it difficult to obtain reasonable estimates of the effect of money growth on disaggregated consumer prices. Another possibility is to simply allow for a time trend in the regression for each good, to capture the upward trend in domestic prices during the period. A third possibility is to simply ignore the domestically induced changes in non-traded goods prices and drop them from the regressions.

In any case, denoting the growth rate of the simple average of these items in each region as $\Delta \ln \hat{P}^{N}_{rt}$, I obtain the following empirical specification:

$$\Delta \ln P_{irt} = \gamma_{0ir} + \gamma_{1ir}(L) \cdot \Delta \ln E_t + \gamma_{2ir}(L) \cdot \Delta \ln C_t + \gamma_{3ir} \cdot \Delta \ln \hat{P}^{N}_{rt} + e_{irt} \qquad (5)$$

where $\gamma_{0ir} = (1-\alpha_{ir}) \cdot \beta_{0ir}$ is the intercept; $\gamma_{1ir}(L) = (1-\alpha_{ir}) \cdot \beta_{1ir}(L)$ captures the effect of the exchange rate on consumer prices; $\gamma_{2ir}(L) = (1-\alpha_{ir}) \cdot \beta_{2ir}(L)$ captures the effect of foreign costs on consumer prices; $\gamma_{3ir} = \alpha_{ir}$ captures the contribution of changes in non-traded goods prices; and $e_{irt} = \alpha_{ir} \cdot \Delta v_{irt} + (1-\alpha_{ir}) \cdot \Delta u_{irt}$ is the error term. Since this composite error term is by assumption uncorrelated with the right-hand-side variables, I can estimate Equation 5 by ordinary least squares. In practice, I measure all growth rates as monthly observations on quarterly log differences, and I allow for 3-, 6-, and 9-month lags of these growth rates in the estimation. Since I have monthly data from July 2000 through July 2005 this gives me 60 monthly data points on which to estimate this specification for each item and region.

1.2 Results

I first calculate the long-run pass-through coefficient as the sum of the coefficients on the current and lagged exchange rate variables, i.e., $\hat{\gamma}_{1ir}(1)$, for each of the 160 product-region combinations for which I have data. Figure 4.2 provides a visual summary of the pass-through estimates, and Table 4.3 reports some summary statistics. In the top panel of the graph I report pass-through estimates for some aggregate categories, and in the bottom panel I report estimates for disaggregated food items. I organize the pass-through estimates by product, and use box-plots to show the distribution across the eight regions of our estimates of pass-through for each product. In Figure 4.3 I generate the same box-plots by product category, but now reporting the t-statistics associated with the test of the hypothesis that the long-run pass-through coefficient is zero. There are several striking features of these two figures and table:

- *Estimates of the long-run impact of the exchange rate on consumer prices are quite substantial for many products.* The median long-run estimated pass-through effect was 19 percent, indicating that 19 percent of the movement in the trade-weighted exchange rate was reflected in consumer prices. Many of the estimated pass-through coefficients are much higher, with the 75th percentile equal to 47 percent pass-through.
- *Estimates of pass-through vary substantially across products.* The most notable difference is between food and non-food items, with much higher estimates of pass-through for food items. In particular, pooling all regions, the median estimate of pass-through for food items is 0.43, while for non-food items it is only 0.07 (see the second column of Table 4.3). In the top panel of Figure 4.2, the pass-through estimates for an aggregate price index for food, beverages, and tobacco are clearly much higher than for other non-food categories shown. This is true also for many individual food products as shown in the bottom panel of Figure 4.2.
- *Estimates of pass-through are in most cases very statistically significant.* This can be seen in Figure 4.3, which reports the distribution of t-statistics associated with the null hypothesis that the long-run estimated pass-through effect is zero. For almost all food items, and for some non-food items, these t-statistics are quite large, indicating highly significant estimates. For several non-food items, however, estimated pass-through effects are not significantly different from zero, and in some cases are even negative (peculiarly, for entertainment, the estimates are significantly negative). As these negative pass-through estimates are difficult to interpret, I will set them to zero in the subsequent analysis of welfare effects.

Unfortunately, there are few studies of exchange rate pass-through to disaggregated consumer prices in developing countries to which we can compare these results. Campa and Goldberg (2006) study a sample of 21 OECD countries and document that the median (across countries) pass-through of the exchange rate to the consumer price index is 17 percent, which is quite similar to the median (across goods) pass-through estimates reported here for Egypt. Choudri and Hakura (2001) estimate exchange rate pass-through to the aggregate CPI in a sample of 71 developed and developing countries. They find an average long-run pass-through of 35 percent in a group of moderate-inflation countries including Egypt, and 24 percent for Egypt itself, which is slightly higher than the median (across commodities) estimate reported above. Frankel, Parsley, and Wei (2005) report a substantially higher estimate of pass-through of 42 percent for a set of eight very specific branded commodities, pooling data from a sample of 76 developed and developing countries. However, several of the commodities they consider are food, alcohol, and tobacco products, and in the case of Egypt I find substantially higher pass-through for such commodities.

The estimated change in consumer prices due to the depreciation can be obtained by multiplying the pass-through estimates by the observed change in the exchange rate. Between 2000 and 2005, the trade-weighted exchange rate that I use depreciated by 26.2 percent (see last column of Table 4.1). I therefore multiply the estimates of pass-through reported in Figure 4.2 by 26.2 percent to obtain the estimated change in consumer prices due to the depreciation. To take a specific example, the estimate of pass-through for meat and poultry in Cairo is 0.43, implying that the depreciation increased the price of this product category in Cairo by 11 percent. The actual change in the price of meat and poultry in Cairo was 43 percent, so that roughly one-quarter of the observed increase in the price of this item in Cairo was due to the depreciation.

More systematically, I calculate the ratio of the exchange-rate induced change in each price to the actual observed price change for each of the 20 goods in eight regions in Egypt, and summarize these ratios using box-plots in Figure 4.4, while the last column of Table 4.3 reports summary statistics. For the median consumption item, 19 percent of the observed growth in nominal prices can be attributed to the depreciation, with an interquartile range from 6 percent to 34 percent. Since the estimated pass-through coefficients are substantially bigger for food than for non-food items, our estimates of the exchange rate-induced price changes are also much bigger for food items, where the median is 31 percent, as opposed to 10 percent for non-food items.

These higher rates of pass-through for food items give a first indication of the distributional consequences of the depreciation. Since poorer households devote a greater share of expenditure to food items, the price changes associated with the depreciation would have had a larger effect on them. In the next Section, I document in more detail the welfare effects of these price changes.

2. Estimating the Welfare Impact of Exchange Rate Induced Price Changes

The next step is to take the estimates of the changes in prices induced by movements in the exchange rate and calculate their welfare effects.

2.1 Empirical Framework

I use the compensating variation as a standard measure of welfare effects of price changes. In particular, let e(u,p) denote the expenditure function, i.e.,

$$e(p,u^*) \equiv \min p'x \quad s.t.\ u(x) > u^* \qquad (6)$$

where p is an nx1 vector of prices, x is an nx1 vector of quantities demanded, u(x) is a well-behaved utility function, and u* is a reference level of utility. Let p_0 denote the reference prices prevailing in 2000, the time of the initial household survey, and let $\Delta p \equiv p_1 - p_0$ denote the vector of price changes that were caused by the depreciation between 2000 and 2005, that I have isolated empirically in the previous section. The compensating variation measures the change in expenditure that would be required in order for households to achieve their pre-depreciation utility u* at the post-depreciation set of prices, p_1:

$$cv = e(p_1,u^*) - e(p_0,u^*) \qquad (7)$$

I will empirically approximate the compensating variation using a second-order Taylor expansion of the expenditure function around the initial period prices:[11]

$$cv \approx \Delta p' \frac{\partial e(p,u^*)}{\partial p} + \frac{1}{2} \Delta p' \frac{\partial^2 e(p,u^*)}{\partial p \partial p'} \Delta p \qquad (8)$$

where the matrices of first and second derivatives of the expenditure function are evaluated at p_0. Using Shephard's Lemma and the fact that compensated and ordinary demands are equal at the initial optimal allocation, I can write this approximation to the compensating variation as a share of initial expenditure e_0 as:

$$\frac{cv}{e_0} \approx \frac{\Delta p' x_0}{e_0} + \frac{1}{2 \cdot e_0} \Delta p' \frac{\partial h(p,u^*)}{\partial p'} \Delta p \qquad (9)$$

where h(p,u*) is the Hicksian or compensated demand function.

The interpretation of this expression is straightforward. The first term captures direct effect of price changes, which is just the change in the cost of purchasing the initial consumption bundle, x_0, expressed as a share of initial total expenditure, e_0. In particular I can write the direct effect of the price changes in proportional terms as:

$$\frac{\Delta p' x_0}{e_0} = \sum_i w_i \cdot \frac{\Delta p_i}{p_i} \tag{10}$$

where $w_i = \frac{p_{i0} \cdot x_{i0}}{e_0}$ is the share of good i in initial total spending and $\frac{\Delta p_i}{p_i}$ is the proportional change in the price of good i. Thus, the direct effect of the price changes, as a share of initial expenditure, is just a weighted average of the growth rate of the prices of each good, with weights equal to the initial expenditure shares.

Considering only this direct effect would overstate the welfare effect of the price changes because it does not take into account how households change their spending patterns in response to price changes. If households can substitute away from goods that become relatively more expensive, then the direct effect of the price changes will exaggerate the welfare effects since it assumes no such substitution is possible. Estimating these substitution effects is therefore important, although substantially more involved. One direct approach is to econometrically estimate a demand system over the various consumption goods, using data from the household survey, and retrieve from this an estimate of the matrix of price derivatives of the compensated demand function $\frac{\partial h}{\partial p'}$. Doing so, however, requires data on goods prices at the household level. In the case of the Egyptian household survey, I have some information on unit values for individual consumption items. However, at the more aggregated level at which the exchange rate pass-through estimates are calculated, these unit values become very difficult to interpret.[12]

In this paper I take a different and computationally much simpler approach that exploits the fact that I have two household surveys for Egypt, for 2000 and 2005. The basic idea is to use information on observed changes in expenditure shares over this period to back our estimates of the substitution effects. The key simplification of this approach is that it obviates the need to estimate an entire demand system, but instead requires only estimates of the expenditure elasticities for each consumption item. As long as prices faced by individual households are orthogonal to total expenditure, these elasticities can be estimated by simple regressions of expenditure shares on total expenditure alone.

To implement this idea, I first need to relate observed changes over time in quantities demanded to the substitution effects of interest. Taking a first-order approximation to changes in the observed ordinary demand function I have:

$$\Delta x(p,e) \approx \frac{\partial x(p,e)}{\partial p'} \Delta p^* + \frac{\partial x(p,e)}{\partial e} \Delta e \qquad (11)$$

where x(p,e) is the ordinary demand function; Δx(p,e) are the changes in quantities demanded between 2000 and 2005; and Δp^* is the vector of overall price changes between 2000 and 2005. Note that Δp^* refers to overall price changes during this period, while Δp above refers only to the depreciation-induced component of price changes. Next I can use the Slutsky equation, which expresses the observable elasticities of the ordinary demand function in terms of the unobservable elasticities of the compensated demand function, i.e.,

$$\frac{\partial x(p,e)}{\partial p'} = \frac{\partial h(p,u)}{\partial p'} - \frac{\partial x(p,e)}{\partial e} x(p,e)' \qquad (12)$$

Substituting Equation 12 into Equation 11 and rearranging results in:

$$\frac{\partial h(p,u)}{\partial p'} \Delta p^* \approx \Delta x(p,e) - \frac{\partial x(p,e)}{\partial e} \Delta x(p,e)'p \qquad (13)$$

Suppose momentarily that we were interested in evaluating the welfare effects of the full set of price changes between 2000 and 2005, i.e., Δp^*, as opposed to simply those price changes induced by the depreciation, i.e., Δp. Then I could simply pre-multiply Equation 13 by $\Delta p^{*\prime}$ and I would have the substitution component of the compensating variation on the left-hand-side, expressed in terms of observables on the right-hand side. In particular, on the right-hand side of Equation 13 I have observed changes in quantities demanded, Δx, and the derivatives of demand with respect to total expenditure, $\frac{\partial x}{\partial e}$, that can readily be estimated from available data on expenditure shares and total expenditure at the household level.

Unfortunately, however, things are more complicated in this case since I want to obtain an estimate of substitution effects in response to depreciation-induced price changes, $\Delta p'\frac{\partial h(p,u)}{\partial p'}\Delta p$, not substitution effects in response to overall price changes, $\Delta p^{*\prime}\frac{\partial h(p,u)}{\partial p'}\Delta p^{*}$. In order to make progress, I make one further, and non-trivial, assumption, that the Slutsky matrix $\frac{\partial h}{\partial p'}$ is diagonal, i.e., that all compensated cross-price elasticities are zero. In this case, Equation 13 simplifies to:

$$\left(\frac{\partial h_i}{\partial p_i}\cdot\frac{p_i}{h_i}\right)\cdot\frac{\Delta p_i{}^{*}}{p_i}\approx\frac{\Delta x_i}{x_i}-\left(\frac{\partial x_i}{\partial e}\cdot\frac{x_i}{e}\right)\cdot\sum_j w_j\cdot\frac{\Delta x_j}{x_j} \qquad (14)$$

Given estimates of the expenditure elasticities $\left(\frac{\partial x_i}{\partial e}\cdot\frac{x_i}{e}\right)$ I can solve (14) for the compensated own-price elasticities $\left(\frac{\partial h_i}{\partial p_i}\cdot\frac{p_i}{h_i}\right)$. Finally, I can substitute these into Equation 9 to obtain the following estimate of the substitution effect:

$$\frac{1}{2\cdot e_0}\Delta p'\frac{\partial h(p,u^{*})}{\partial p'}\Delta p\approx\frac{1}{2}\cdot\sum_i w_i\cdot\left(\frac{\partial h_i}{\partial p_i}\cdot\frac{p_i}{h_i}\right)\cdot\left(\frac{\Delta p_i}{p_i}\right)^2 \qquad (15)$$

Clearly the assumption of a diagonal Slutsky matrix is a restrictive and unappealing one. However, as I discuss later, we shall see that estimated substitution effects for the full set of price changes Δp^{*}, which do not require this restriction, are quite similar in magnitude to the estimated substitution effects associated with the exchange-rate induced changes in consumer prices. This gives some comfort that this assumption is not too misleading. Moreover, it is worth remembering that this restriction does not imply that the cross-price elasticities of ordinary demands are zero. Rather, it restricts the effect of changes in the price of good i on the quantity demanded of good j to operate through the income effect of the change in the price of good j (i.e., the price change multiplied by the initial spending share), multiplied by the income elasticity of good j.

2.2 Results

I begin by reporting estimates of the direct effects of price changes, which I summarize in Figure 4.5, graphing the estimated compensating variation on the vertical axis against log total household expenditure on the horizontal axis. In particular, these direct effects are calculated for each household as the sum across all expenditure items of initial spending shares times the percentage change in the price of each item due to the depreciation, setting negative pass-through estimates to zero. We shall see shortly that our estimates of the substitution effect are generally quite small, and so it makes sense to focus on the direct effects first. Several observations can be made based on this figure:

- *The estimated compensating variation is non-trivial for the vast majority of households.* The income loss associated with the direct effect of exchange rate-induced price changes for the median household is 7.4 percent of initial expenditure. The 5th and 95th percentiles of the distribution of compensating variations at the household level are 4.9 and 9.9 percent of initial expenditure, respectively.
- *The estimated compensating variation is significantly higher for poorer households, although the magnitude of the effect is modest.* A simple regression of the compensating variation on log total expenditure gives a slope coefficient of -0.01. Since the log-difference in total expenditure between households at the 95th and 5th percentile of the expenditure distribution is about 2, this implies that the estimated real income loss due to the depreciation is about two percentage points of initial expenditure higher at the 5th percentile of the income distribution than at the 95th percentile. Controlling for household characteristics (log age and sex of household head and log household size) and regional effects raises the slope coefficient to -0.016, implying a 3.2 percentage point difference in the income effect of the depreciation between rich and poor households. This adverse distributional effect of the depreciation is consistent with our finding that pass-through for food items was higher than for non-food items, coupled with the observation that the share of food in total expenditure is higher for poorer households.

- ***There is enormous heterogeneity across households in the size of the estimated compensating variation.*** A simple regression of the compensating variation on log total expenditure delivers an R-squared of only 17 percent. Including household characteristics and regional dummies raises this to 38 percent, leaving the majority of the cross-household variation in the estimated compensating variation unexplained. In the case of Indonesia, Friedman and Levinsohn (2002) find even greater heterogeneity, with similar regressions explaining only 11 (26) percent of the variation across rural (urban) households in the estimated compensating variation.

Figure 4.6 disaggregates the direct effect of the price changes by rural and urban households. To construct this figure I order households from poorest to richest within rural and urban areas. I then construct a rolling average over 100 households of the estimated compensating variation, and plot it against the percentile rank of the middle household of each group in the entire combined rural and urban expenditure distribution. Over most of the income distribution (and particularly from the 20th percentile on up) the rural compensating variation is slightly higher than for urban households. This figure also shows that the relationship between the compensating variation and income levels is fairly flat over most of the range of the expenditure distribution, and tails off sharply for the richest 10 percent or so of (mostly urban) households. It is also worth noting that the estimates of the compensating variation for rural households is likely to be overstated relative to urban households. This is because rural household's net consumption of food items is likely to be smaller than their gross consumption when compared with urban households, and the depreciation in the exchange rate disproportionately increased food prices.

Table 4.4 reports the mean and standard deviation of the compensating variation by region and by quintile of the expenditure distribution. Regionally, the estimated compensating variation ranges from a low of 6.7 percent in the border region to a high of 8.4 percent in rural Lower Egypt. Within each region the estimated compensating variation declines as we move to successively higher quintiles of the expenditure distribution.

I next investigate further why there is so much heterogeneity across households in the estimated direct effect of depreciation-induced price changes, with the help of a simple decomposition exercise. Adding household subscripts h in Equation 10, I can decompose the direct component of the compensating variation for each household as follows:

$$\frac{\Delta p_h{}' x_{0h}}{e_{0h}} = \sum_i w_{ih} \cdot \frac{\Delta p_{ih}}{p_{ih}}$$
$$= \sum_i \overline{w}_i \cdot \overline{\frac{\Delta p_i}{p_i}} + \sum_i \overline{w}_i \cdot \left(\frac{\Delta p_{ih}}{p_{ih}} - \overline{\frac{\Delta p_i}{p_i}} \right) \tag{16}$$
$$+ \sum_i \left(w_{ih} - \overline{w}_i \right) \overline{\frac{\Delta p_i}{p_i}} + \sum_i \left(w_{ih} - \overline{w}_i \right) \left(\frac{\Delta p_{ih}}{p_{ih}} - \overline{\frac{\Delta p_i}{p_i}} \right)$$

where $\overline{w}_i$ is the average across all households of the share of item i in total consumption, and $\overline{\frac{\Delta p_i}{p_i}}$ is the average across all households (effectively, across all regions since I don't have within-region price variation) of depreciation-induced price changes. The first term in this decomposition is the compensating variation for a hypothetical household facing average price changes and having average expenditure shares. The value of this is 7.5 percent which is (almost) the mean effect, and is the same across households. The remaining terms vary across households and isolate the different sources of cross-household variation in the estimated compensating variation. The first of these captures cross-household variation due to cross-household differences in price changes (since it holds the expenditure shares fixed for all households). The second captures differences due to cross-household differences in expenditure shares, keeping price changes constant, and the third term captures purely household- and price-specific variation. The standard deviations across households of these three components are 0.6 percent, 1.5 percent, and 0.3 percent. This suggests that cross-household differences in expenditure shares are the most important source of cross-household differences in the welfare effects of the depreciation, while price differences (across regions, in our case) are less important, but still non-trivial.

I next examine the poverty impacts of these price changes. To do this, I begin with the 2000 distribution of expenditure across households in Egypt. I then subtract from each household the direct estimate of the compensating variation to arrive at a counterfactual distribution of expenditure which reflects the losses due to the subsequent depreciation. I then calculate the change in the headcount measure of poverty between these two distributions, for Egypt as a whole, and by regions. The results are summarized in Table 4.5. The first column provides the benchmark estimates of the headcount for 2000, by region. The figures report the percent of households falling below the household-specific poverty lines calculated by El-Laithy, Lokshin, and Banerji (2003). The second column uses the same poverty lines, but replaces the actual distribution of expenditure with the counterfactual distribution reflecting the welfare losses due to the depreciation, and the third column reports the difference between the two. For Egypt as a whole, the estimated welfare effects of the depreciation can be interpreted as raising the headcount measure of poverty by 5 percentage points. The effects are lower in the major metropolitan centers of Egypt, with poverty increasing by 2 percent from a low base. Rural areas of Egypt saw the largest absolute increase in the headcount of 6.4 and 6.7 percent in lower and upper Egypt respectively, but from a much higher base. Not surprisingly, the ranking of poverty impacts across regions is quite similar to that of welfare effects across regions in Table 4.4. The final column of Table 4.5 shows the actual headcounts by region in 2005 for reference. It is interesting to note that the estimated poverty impacts of exchange-rate-induced changes in consumer prices are substantial when compared with the overall change in poverty between 2000 and 2005.

I finally consider the role of substitution effects in response to the price changes induced by the depreciation. In order to implement Equations 14 and 15 I need information on changes over time on spending on each of the 20 expenditure items. Although I have access to the 2000 and 2005 household surveys, unfortunately these are not true panels but repeated cross-sections. I therefore employ cohort techniques to estimate the changes in spending shares, and from this the substitution effects. In particular, for the 2000 and 2005 household surveys I construct cohorts based on four education categories, five age categories, and seven regional categories, for a total of 140 cohorts. For each cohort I calculate the average spending shares across the 20 expenditure items in the 2000 and 2005 surveys. Using the household-level variation within each cohort in the 2000 survey, I also estimate cohort-specific income elasticities for each expenditure share. Finally, I combine these ingredients with our estimates of the depreciation-induced price changes, to estimate the substitution effect.

The results of this exercise are summarized in Figure 4.7, which plots the estimated direct and substitution components of the compensating variation against log total expenditure at the cohort level. The estimates of the direct effect at the cohort level is quite similar to what I estimated at the household level, except that unsurprisingly there is less variation given that I now have data only for 140 cohorts that by construction are more homogeneous in their spending shares than the underlying data. The more interesting point is the comparison of the relative magnitudes of the direct and substitution effects, with the latter much smaller (in absolute value) than the former. The mean (across cohorts) substitution effect is just -0.2 percent of initial expenditure, as compared with a mean (across cohort) direct effect of 6.6 percent of initial expenditure. This suggests that substitution effects are small, and the bulk of the welfare effect of the price changes is picked up by the direct effects that we have already discussed.

Clearly this estimate of the substitution effects is just an approximation, and one might ask whether it is reasonable to find such small substitution effects. Two factors suggest that these small estimates may not be too far from the truth. The first is simply the fairly coarse level of aggregation at which data limitations force us to carry out the analysis. Concretely, the scope households have for substituting between, say, food and rent, is much smaller than it is for substituting between higher or lower quality in the purchase of a particular food item. While such substitution undoubtedly occurs, it is not something that we are going to be able to pick up at this level of aggregation. We also note that Friedman and Levinsohn (2002), who use more finely disaggregated set of 155 food items and 64 non-food items, find much larger substitution effects that offset on average between one-third and one-half of the direct effects. However, these authors also argue that their estimates are probably an extreme upper bound on the magnitude of the substitution effects.

One might nevertheless worry that assuming zero cross-elasticities of substitution is driving the results. Recall that this assumption was necessitated by the fact that the quantity changes we observe in the panel are responses to the full set of price changes observed between 2000 and 2005, and not just the depreciation-induced price changes. I can however calculate the income and substitution effects associated with the full set of observed price changes over this period, and then the calculation of the latter will not require any assumptions about cross-elasticities of substitution (recall Equation 13 and the discussion immediately below). I have done this, and for the full set of price changes, I find that the substitution effects are still very small relative to the direct effects. While these two calculations are not strictly comparable because they refer to different sets of price changes, they do suggest that the scope for substitution is lower at coarser levels of disaggregation.

3. Conclusion

This paper has empirically investigated the welfare effects of the large depreciation in Egypt between 2000 and 2005 operating through exchange-rate induced changes in consumer prices. I find a significant, and very heterogeneous across products, degree of pass-through from the exchange rate to consumer prices. On average, the welfare cost of these price changes was 7.4 percent of households' initial expenditure. Since estimated pass-through for food items was significantly greater than for non-food items, the effects of the depreciation disproportionately affected poor households.

One should however keep in mind three major caveats about these results. The first is that I have looked only at the effects of the exchange rate working through consumer prices. The depreciation is also likely to have had heterogeneous impacts on the earnings of households employed in different sectors, and these effects are not captured for lack of (a) detailed information in the household survey of the sector of employment of households, and (b) evidence on the effects of exchange rate changes on wages across sectors in Egypt.

A second caveat is that data limitations have also forced me to work at a fairly high level of aggregation. At this coarse level of aggregation, estimated substitution effects in response to price changes are small, and so I am likely to be overestimating the effects on household welfare. Consider for example the study of the Indonesian depreciation of 1997 by Friedman and Levinsohn (2002). They worked with a much more highly disaggregated set of expenditure items, and found that substitution effects were roughly half the size of the direct effects. If similar substitution behavior occurred for households in Egypt in response to the (much smaller) set of price changes, but was missed at the coarse level of aggregation at which I have worked, then the adverse welfare effects of the depreciation will be considerably overstated and could be much smaller.

Finally, as noted in the introduction, I have studied the welfare effects of depreciation-induced changes in consumer prices over a fairly short period with a fairly large depreciation, and this time horizon drives the finding of significant welfare losses. It is important to note that the depreciation in the trade-weighted nominal exchange rate between 2000 and 2005 was preceded by an even larger trade-weighted nominal *appreciation* in the previous five years between 1995 and 2000, and that over the entire period between 1995 and 2005, the trade-weighted nominal exchange rate *appreciated* by about 20 percent. If the pattern of exchange rate pass-through to disaggregated consumer prices was similar during this earlier period, then one can interpret the welfare losses sustained between 2000 and 2005 as just a partial reversal of the welfare gains experienced during the appreciation between 1995 and 2000.

Appendix

Table 4.1. Exchange Rates and Consumer Prices, 2000–2005 (Annual Change, December over December)

	2000	*2001*	*2002*	*2003*	*2004*	*2005*	*Cumulative*
Trade Weighted Nominal Exchange Rate	-3.0%	-7.4%	0.1%	41.3%	4.4%	-9.2%	26.2%
Nominal Exchange Rate	8.1%	16.6%	3.3%	31.2%	1.0%	-7.9%	52.2%
Consumer Price Index	2.2%	2.4%	2.9%	6.2%	10.8%	3.1%	27.6%

Table 4.2. Disaggregated Price Change (Cumulative Growth Rate, July 2000–June 2005)

Log change in price index, 2005:6 over 2000:7

					Lower Egypt	Upper Egypt	Lower Egypt	Upper Egypt
	Cairo	*Alex*	*Canal*	*Border*	*Urban*	*Urban*	*Rural*	*Rural*
All Items	0.26	0.29	0.30	0.28	0.23	0.29	0.28	0.28
Food Beverage & Tobacco	0.38	0.39	0.41	0.37	0.41	0.39	0.36	0.34
Bread & Cereals	0.21	0.21	0.21	0.26	0.30	0.22	0.35	0.44
Meat & Poultry	0.43	0.42	0.43	0.40	0.44	0.43	0.34	0.30
Fish	0.50	0.47	0.53	0.54	0.45	0.47	0.42	0.42
Milk & Cheese	0.38	0.41	0.40	0.41	0.45	0.44	0.49	0.46
Oil & Fats	0.43	0.40	0.42	0.40	0.45	0.42	0.39	0.36
Fruits	0.61	0.59	0.62	0.47	0.59	0.54	0.36	0.36
Vegetables	0.25	0.40	0.59	0.31	0.47	0.43	0.56	0.28
Pulses	0.34	0.33	0.42	0.32	0.35	0.37	0.31	0.34
Sugar & Sweets	0.38	0.37	0.17	0.44	0.40	0.41	0.32	0.34
Other Foodstuff	0.31	0.28	0.28	0.29	0.27	0.29	0.21	0.21
Beverages	0.23	0.24	0.35	0.23	0.25	0.26	0.23	0.23
Tobacco	0.31	0.31	0.42	0.30	0.31	0.30	0.28	0.28
Clothing & Footwear	0.22	0.24	0.23	0.21	0.27	0.27	0.24	0.27
Clothing	0.22	0.24	0.22	0.18	0.28	0.27	0.22	0.25
Fabrics	0.33	0.28	0.28	0.33	0.32	0.36	0.41	0.45
Footwear	0.21	0.25	0.29	0.31	0.25	0.26	0.21	0.22
Clothing Manufacture	0.06	0.21	0.23	0.18	0.18	0.16	0.08	0.13
Rent, Power & Fuel	0.10	0.13	0.11	0.10	0.10	0.08	0.13	0.13
Rent & Water	0.11	0.15	0.13	0.11	0.11	0.12	0.13	0.14
Energy & Fuel	0.06	0.09	0.08	0.10	0.10	0.04	0.16	0.11
Furniture & Equipment	0.26	0.25	0.28	0.21	0.22	0.25	0.21	0.21
Furniture	0.21	0.19	0.19	0.17	0.18	0.18	0.18	0.17
Maintenance Products	0.28	0.29	0.28	0.25	0.25	0.26	0.23	0.24
Domestic Services	0.29	0.26	0.73	0.22	0.23	0.26	0.19	0.19
Medical Care	0.12	0.19	0.21	0.22	0.18	0.11	0.18	0.16
Medical Products	0.16	0.16	0.16	0.17	0.16	-0.01	0.16	0.16
Physician & Hospitals	0.08	0.22	0.26	0.27	0.19	0.20	0.20	0.16
Transport & Communications	0.30	0.29	0.34	0.33	0.37	0.48	0.30	0.29
Private Transportation	0.21	0.21	0.25	0.26	0.24	0.13	0.25	0.24
Purchased Transportation	0.17	0.14	0.23	0.24	0.24	0.41	0.24	0.24
Communications	0.55	0.60	0.63	0.62	0.67	0.43	0.64	0.62
Recreation & Education	0.14	0.17	0.14	0.19	0.15	0.10	0.11	0.16
Equipment	0.13	0.12	0.10	0.11	0.12	0.12	0.11	0.12
Entertainment & Cult. Serv	0.14	0.20	0.15	0.23	0.16	0.16	0.12	0.21
Education	0.15	0.06	0.15	0.19	0.14	0.17	0.10	0.10
Miscellaneous	0.19	0.18	0.20	0.21	0.21	0.21	0.17	0.17
Personal Care	0.15	0.14	0.18	0.18	0.19	0.18	0.14	0.14
Restaurants & Hotels	0.26	0.26	0.28	0.27	0.26	0.27	0.25	0.25
Mean	0.25	0.26	0.30	0.27	0.28	0.27	0.26	0.25
SD	0.13	0.12	0.16	0.12	0.13	0.13	0.13	0.11

Table 4.3. Summary Statistics on Pass-Through Estimates and Price Changes

	Actual Price Change 2000:7 - 2005:6	*Estimated Pass-Through Coefficient*	*Estimated Share of Price Change Due to Devaluation*
Overall			
25th Percentile	0.21	0.05	0.06
50th Percentile	0.28	0.19	0.19
75th Percentile	0.40	0.47	0.34
Food			
25th Percentile	0.28	0.30	0.20
50th Percentile	0.37	0.43	0.31
75th Percentile	0.43	0.63	0.46
Non-food			
25th Percentile	0.15	-0.03	-0.03
50th Percentile	0.21	0.07	0.10
75th Percentile	0.26	0.15	0.18

Table 4.4. Estimated Compensating Variation, by Region and Quintile of Expenditure Distribution

			Mean by Quintile of Expenditure Distribution				
	Mean	*Std.Dev.*	*Lowest*	*Second*	*Third*	*Fourth*	*Highest*
All Egypt	0.074	0.015	0.081	0.077	0.075	0.073	0.065
Metropolitan	0.072	0.016	0.083	0.077	0.073	0.069	0.055
Cairo	0.071	0.018	0.084	0.077	0.073	0.068	0.052
Alexandria	0.070	0.015	0.080	0.075	0.072	0.068	0.057
Canal	0.077	0.014	0.086	0.081	0.079	0.075	0.066
Border	0.067	0.013	0.072	0.068	0.068	0.066	0.062
Lower Egypt Urban	0.072	0.013	0.077	0.074	0.073	0.071	0.064
Upper Egypt Urban	0.072	0.015	0.079	0.075	0.074	0.071	0.061
Lower Egypt Rural	0.084	0.013	0.088	0.085	0.085	0.083	0.080
Upper Egypt Rural	0.070	0.010	0.073	0.071	0.070	0.069	0.066

Table 4.5. Poverty Impacts of Depreciation-Induced Price Changes

	Headcount Measure of Poverty (Percent of Households)			
	2000 Actual	*Counterfactual With Devaluation Only*	*Difference*	*2005 Actual*
All Egypt	16.7	21.8	5.0	19.6
Metropolitan	5.1	7.1	2.0	5.7
Cairo	5.0	6.9	1.9	4.6
Alexandria	6.2	8.3	2.1	8.0
Canal	3.4	5.7	2.2	5.7
Border	9.9	12.5	2.6	14.5
Urban Lower Egypt	6.5	9.4	3.0	9.2
Urban Upper Egypt	19.3	24.0	4.7	18.6
Rural Lower Egypt	11.8	18.2	6.4	16.8
Rural Upper Egypt	34.2	40.8	6.7	39.1

Figure 4.1. Exchange Rates and Consumer Prices, 1995–2005

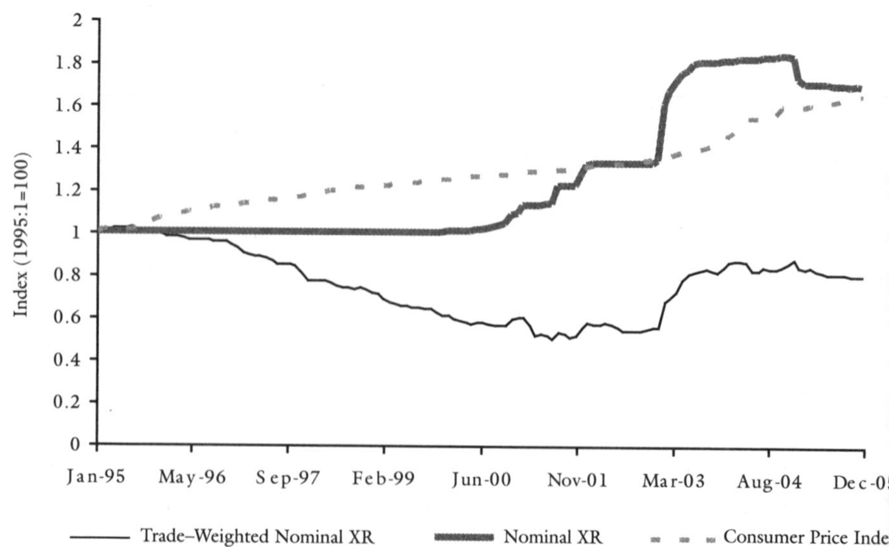

Figure 4.2. Distribution of Estimated Long-Run Exchange Rate Pass-Through to Consumer Prices

Aggregate Items

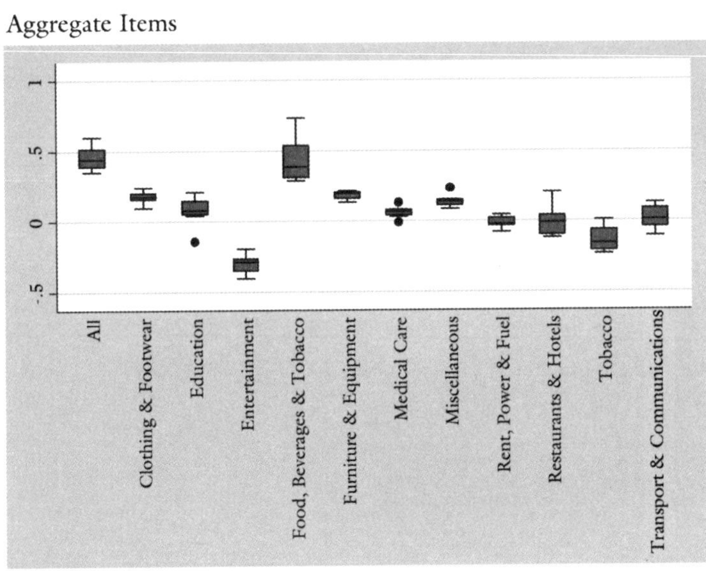

Disaggregated Food Items

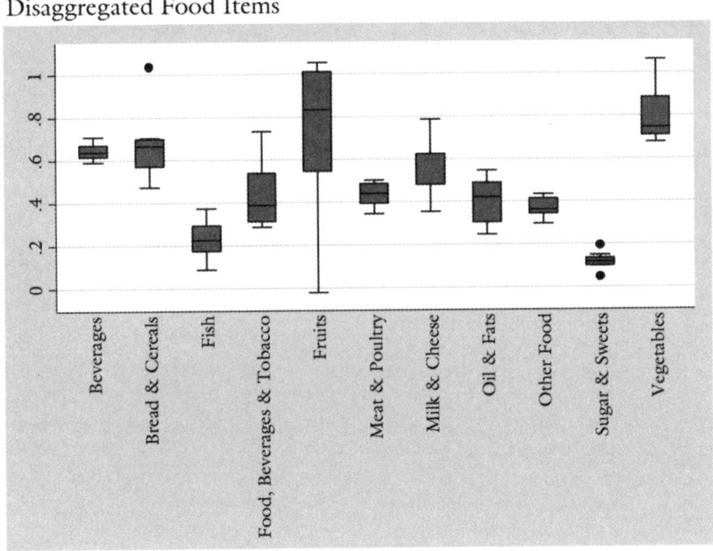

Figure 4.3. Distribution of Significance of Estimated Long-Run Exchange Rate Pass-Through to Consumer Prices

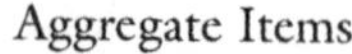
Aggregate Items

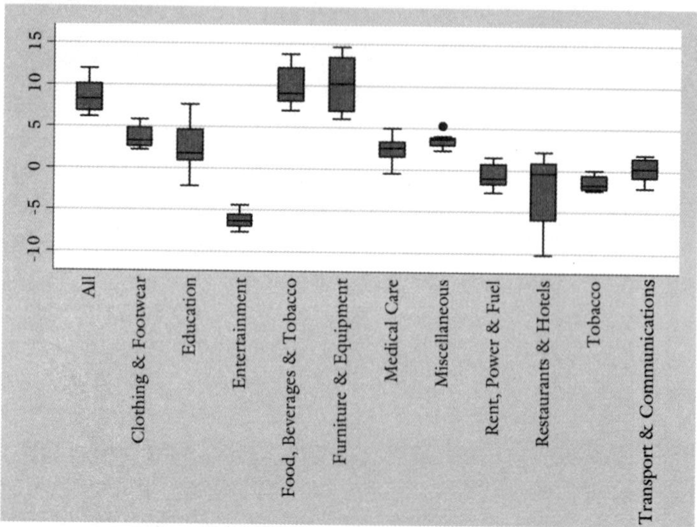

Disaggregated Food Items

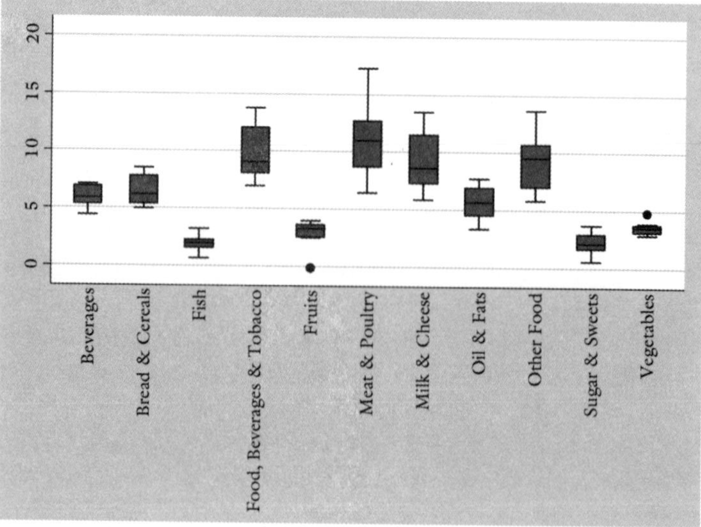

Figure 4.4 Distribution of Share of Observed Price Changes 2000–2005 Due to the Exchange Rate Depreciation

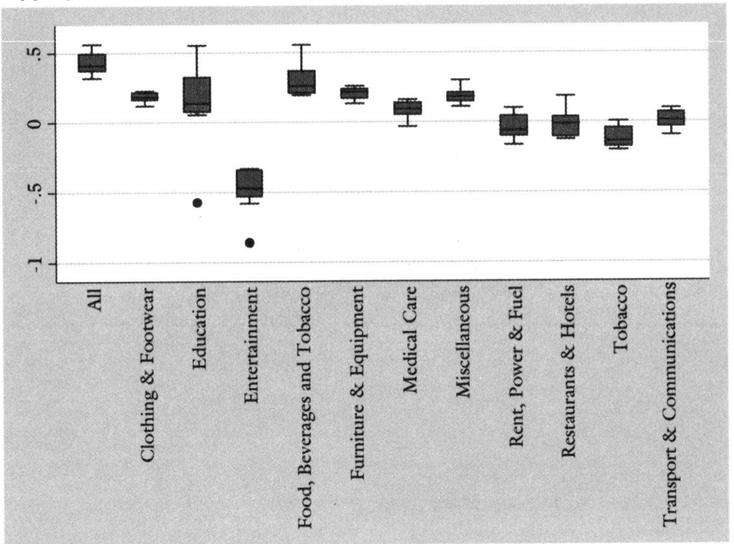

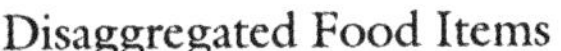

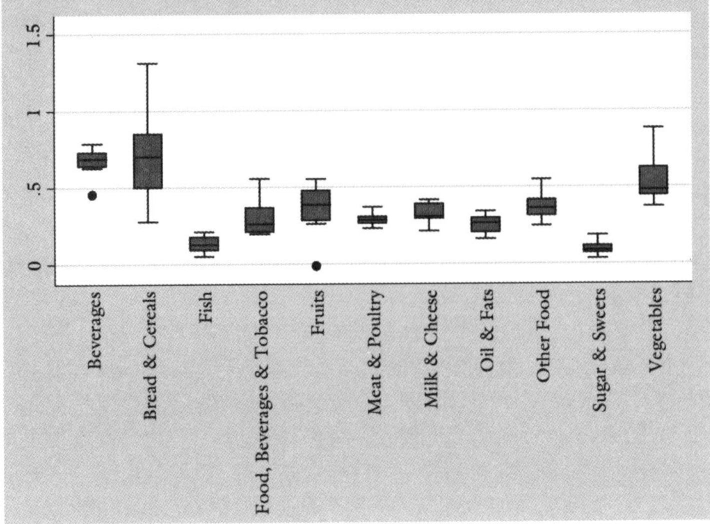

Figure 4.5. Direct Effects of Price Changes on Welfare
(Compensating Variation Calculated as Percent Change in Total Expenditure Required to Purchase Initial Consumption Basket)

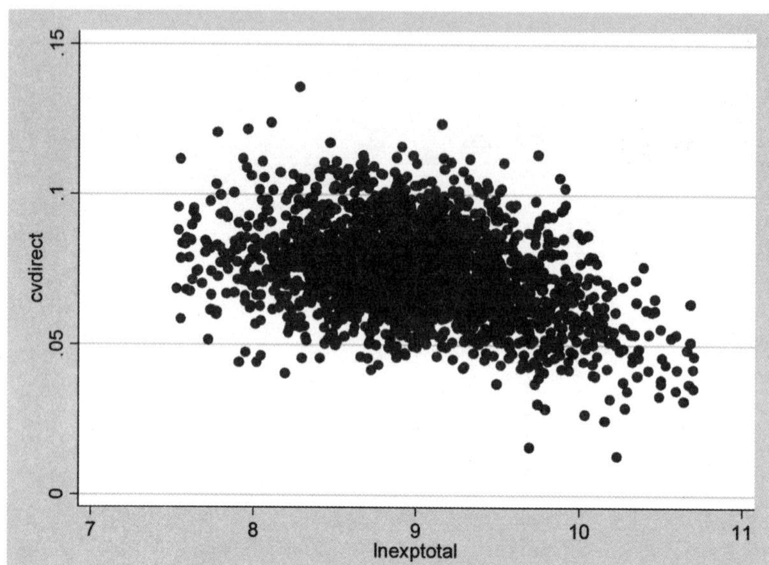

Figure 4.6. Direct Effects of Price Changes on Welfare
(Compensating Variation Calculated as Percent Change in Total Expenditure Required to Purchase Initial Consumption Basket, Rolling Average of 100 Households Ranked by Total Expenditure)

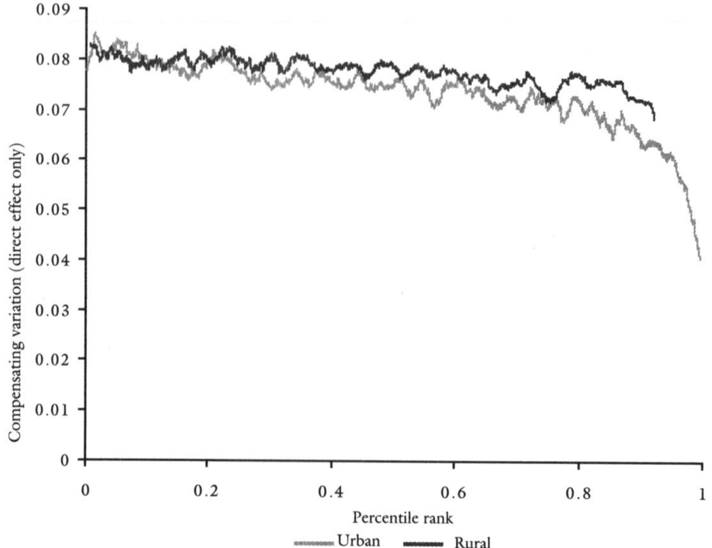

Figure 4.7. Direct and Substitution Effects of Price Changes on Welfare at the Cohort Level

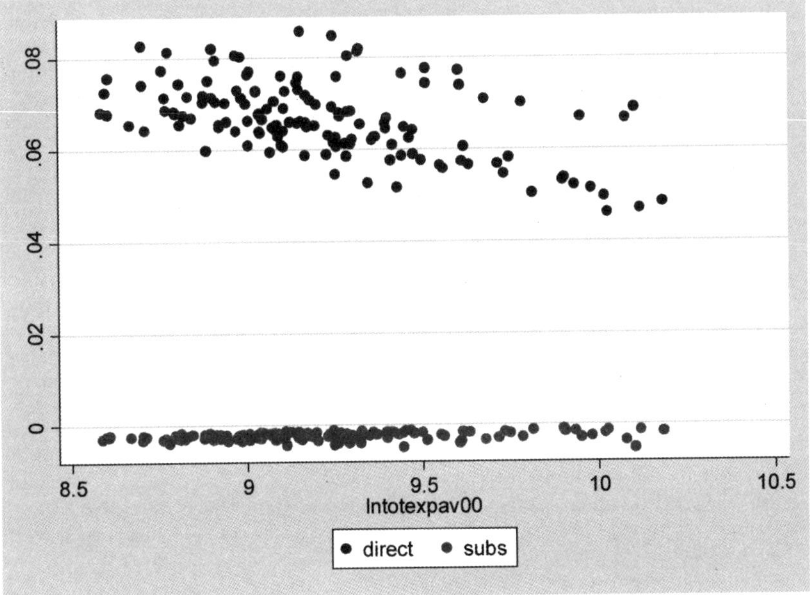

Notes

1. 1818 H Street N.W, Washington, DC, 20433, akraay@worldbank.org, http://econ.worldbank.org/staff/akraay. This chapter was prepared as background for the 2007 Egypt Poverty Assessment. I would like to thank without implication Sherine Al-Shawarby, Heba El-Laithy, Faika El-Refaie, Francisco Ferreira, Jed Friedman, Michael Lokshin, Martin Ravallion, Luis Serven, and conference participants at the Egyptian Center for Economic Studies for helpful discussions. The views expressed here are the author's and do not reflect those of the World Bank, its executive directors, or the countries they represent.
2. The regions dictated by the disaggregation available in the CPI data are Cairo, Alexandria, Canal, border, Upper and Lower urban, and Upper and Lower rural. The commodity disaggregation is dictated by overlap between expenditure categories in the household survey and the CPI data.
3. See Friedman and Levinsohn (2002) for a similar exercise investigating the welfare effects of relative price changes following the depreciation in Indonesia during the East Asian crisis of 1997. The main difference with this paper is that they do not estimate exchange rate pass-through to consumer prices but, reasonably enough in the case of the enormous depreciation of the rupiah, assume that all of observed price changes were due to the depreciation. Ferreira et al. (2004) study the distributional consequences of a large depreciation in Brazil, using a sectorally-disaggregated macro model to quantify the effects of the depreciation on wages and prices, and then linking this to a household survey.
4. See Chen and Ravallion (2004) for an effort to look at the effects of relative price changes on household consumptions and incomes, in the case of China, and Ferreira et al. (2004) for the case of Brazil.
5. All tables and figures cited in text are listed at the end of this chapter.
6. The trade-weighted exchange rate index used here is constructed using data from Egypt's 25 largest trading partners in 2000. I use fixed weights based on these countries' shares in Egypt's imports in 2000. During this period there were some exchange controls in place and the parallel exchange rate *vis-à-vis* the US dollar diverged significantly from the official rate (in levels). This raises the question of whether it is more appropriate to use the parallel market rate. For the analysis that follows, what matters is the exchange rate at which importers actually transact. If they have access to foreign currency at official (parallel) rates then the official (parallel) rates are appropriate. Absent information on this, and absent data on parallel rates *vis-à-vis* all trading partners, I use the trade-weighted official rates. However, in unreported results I obtain very similar estimates of pass-through using the parallel market rate *vis-à-vis* the US dollar. This is because although the two series diverge somewhat in levels, in differences they track each other quite closely over the period I consider.
7. We would like to thank the staff of CAPMAS for kindly assembling this dataset.
8. See for example Campa and Goldberg (2005) for a justification of this particular specification. Burstein, Eichenbaum, and Rebelo (2005) document the importance of non-traded components of traded goods prices and their role in real exchange rate fluctuations.
9. These are the United States, Germany, Italy, Great Britain, and Japan. Saudi Arabia and France are among Egypt's top five sources of imports in 2000 but do not report monthly producer price indices.
10. Other clearly largely non-traded items are rent and education. However, prices of these items are tightly controlled in Egypt and movements in them are unlikely to properly reflect movements in overall non-traded goods prices.

11. This approach is also taken by Friedman and Levinsohn (2002). An alternative is Vartia (1983), who shows how to get the exact comparison of utility in time 0 and time 1, by numerically integrating demand functions. The disadvantage of this approach is that it relies on parametric estimates of the entire demand system that are difficult to implement empirically.
12. Friedman and Levinsohn (2002) implement an approach originally due to Deaton (1988, 1990) who shows how to estimate demand systems when only unit value data are available.

References

Burstein, Ariel, Martin Eichenbaum, and Sergio Rebelo. 2005. Large devaluations and the real exchange rate. *Journal of Political Economy* 113(4): 742–784.

Campa, Jose Manuel and Linda S. Goldberg. 2005. Exchange rate pass-through into import prices. *Review of Economics and Statistics* 87(4): 679–690.

———. 2006. Distribution margins, imported inputs, and the sensitivity of the CPI to exchange rates. Manuscript, Federal Reserve Bank of New York (http://www.newyorkfed.org/research/economists/goldberg/).

Chen, Shaohua and Martin Ravallion. 2004. Welfare impacts of China's accession to the World Trade Organization. *World Bank Economic Review* 18(1): 29–57.

Choudri, Ehsan and Dalia Hakura. 2001. *Exchange rate pass-through to domestic prices: Does the inflationary environment matter?* IMF Working Paper No. 01/194.

Deaton, Angus. 1988. Quality, quantity and spatial variation of price. *American Economic Review* 78(3): 418–431.

———. 1990. Price elasticities from survey data: Extensions and Indonesian results. *Journal of Econometrics* 44(3): 281–309.

El-Laithy, Heba, Michael Lokshin, and Arup Banerji. 2003. *Poverty and economic growth in Egypt.* World Bank Policy Research Department Working Paper No. 3068.

Frankel, Jeffrey, David Parsley, and Shang-Jin Wei. 2005. *Slow pass-through around the world: A new import for developing countries?* NBER Working Paper No. 11199.

Ferreira, Franciso, Phillippe Leite, Luiz Pereira da Silva, and Paolo Picchetti. 2004. Can the distributional impacts of macroeconomic shocks be predicted? A comparison of the performance of macro-micro models with historical data for Brazil. World Bank Policy Research Department Working Paper No. 3303. Washington, D.C.: World Bank.

Friedman, Jed and James Levinsohn. 2002. The distributional impacts of Indonesia's financial crisis on household welfare: A "rapid-response" methodology". *World Bank Economic Review* 16(3): 397–423.

Vartia, Yrjo. 1983. Efficient methods of measuring welfare change and compensated income in terms of ordinary demand functions. *Econometrica* 51(1): 79–98.

PART II

Labor Market Issues

CHAPTER 5

Unemployment and Youth Insertion in the Labor Market in Egypt

Ragui Assaad

It is well-established by now that the unemployment problem in Egypt is essentially one relating to the labor market insertion of a growing and increasingly educated youth population. The vast majority of the unemployed are under the age of 30, educated at least up to the intermediate level, and have never worked before. An analysis of the dynamics of unemployment in Egypt must, therefore, focus on the process of labor market entry and examine the demographic, economic, and institutional factors that shape this process.

Using data from the recently released Egypt Labor Market Panel Survey (ELMPS) of 2006, the study shows that there has been a decline in both the relative and absolute size of unemployment in Egypt in the period from 1998 to 2006. This result is puzzling to many and understandably has been met with a degree of skepticism, if not outright rejection. It thus requires some detailed scrutiny and, if confirmed, some explication. This chapter presents detailed evidence in support of a declining rate and level of unemployment in Egypt, as well as supporting evidence on the process of labor market entry for youth. It also presents what is regarded as a credible explanation for these trends on the basis of demographic, institutional, and economic arguments.

With regard to unemployment indicators, the study relies essentially on international recommendations to define unemployment and economic activity, but presents estimates based on some variations in definitions that are still consistent with international recommendations. The main variations have to do with the operationalization of the active search requirement in determining who is unemployed and the use of the market or extended definition of economic activity in determining who is employed. The picture of declining unemployment is essentially robust to these changes in definitions, although the levels and rates themselves clearly change according to the definition used.

After examining the evidence of unemployment rate, the number of unemployed, and the pattern of unemployment by sex, urban/rural location, age, and education, the study examines the reasons for unemployment in an attempt to determine whether unemployment is voluntary or involuntary. It then moves to a detailed examination of the process of labor market insertion, including an analysis of how the duration of unemployment has changed over time and how the duration from school to work has changed. It finds that for young men, labor market insertion is occurring faster in 2006 than it was in 1998. The period of transition from school to work is shorter in 2006 than in 1998, and the unemployment durations are shorter as well. For young women, the reduction of unemployment appears to be at least partly due to greater withdrawal from the ranks of the unemployed into economic inactivity rather than to more rapid entry into employment. This contrast along gender lines is quite important and requires careful analysis and interpretation. In either case, however, the change in the labor market insertion process for both males and females is consistent with falling unemployment rates.

To gain further understanding of the process of labor market insertion and how it is changing over time, the study moves to an examination of the trend in the number and composition of new entrants over time and of the labor market prospects that they face. This is made possible by an innovation in the ELMPS 06 that allows us to identify not only the timing of entry into the labor market, but also the detailed characteristics of the first job (that lasted more than six months) for everyone in the survey that has ever worked before, irrespective of their current labor market status. Because this information is available for people who entered at different times, it allows us to characterize the labor market facing new entrants from as far back as 1975 to the latest full year covered by the survey, 2005.

In terms of explicating the trend of falling unemployment at a time when it seems so counterintuitive to so many, this study offers the following explanation. Unemployment in Egypt is essentially driven by three essential factors: (i) the growth and age composition of the working-age population, (ii) the institutional distortion introduced by government hiring policies that induce queuing for government jobs among educated workers, and (iii) the rate of economic growth that drives the growth of employment in the private sector. In terms of all three of these factors, the situation in 2006 has objectively improved over what it was in 1998. Demographically, the growth of the working-age population has slowed and the age structure of the youth population has shifted away from the 15–19 age group, which experienced the highest unemployment rates in 1998, to the 20–24 age group. This resulted in a compositional shift away from the ages with the highest levels of unemployment and a drop in unemployment among younger youths. Institutionally, the government has significantly slowed its hiring, reducing the incentive of graduates, especially female graduates, to remain unemployed while queuing for government jobs. The removal of this incentive to queue actually resulted in many female graduates, whose reservation wage was above the private sector wage but below the government's overall compensation package, to simply withdraw from the labor market rather than continue to declare themselves to be unemployed. This essentially explains the observed drop in participation rates among technical secondary and post-secondary graduates in the 1998–2006 period. Finally, economically, the pickup in growth rates in the 2003–2006 period has resulted in an acceleration of employment growth in the private sector, leading to earlier transitions into employment, at least for young new male entrants.

The remainder of this chapter will present a brief description of the data used in this analysis, examine the trend in youth unemployment, the characteristics of the unemployed and the search strategies they utilize, and finally, examine the evidence supporting the argument laid out above regarding the factors behind the decline in youth unemployment.

1. The Egypt Labor Market Panel Survey of 2006 (ELMPS 06)[2]

The Egypt Labor Market Panel Survey (ELMPS 06) is a follow-up survey to the Egypt Labor Market Survey of 1998 (ELMS 98), which was carried out in November-December 1998 by the Economic Research Forum (ERF) in cooperation with the Egyptian Central Agency for Public Mobilization and Statistics (CAPMAS)—the main statistical agency of the Egyptian government. ELMS 98 was carried out on a nationally representative sample of 4816 households[3] and was designed to be comparable to the special round of the Egyptian Labor Force Sample Survey carried out in October 1988 (LFSS 88). The ELMPS 06 is the second round of what is intended to be a periodic longitudinal survey that tracks the labor market and demographic characteristics of the households and individuals interviewed in 1998, any new households that might have formed as a result of splits from the original households, as well as a refresher sample of households to ensure that the data continue to be nationally representative. The fieldwork for ELMPS 06 was carried out from January to March 06.

1.1 Sample

The final sample of 8,349 households is made up of 3,684 households from the original ELMS 98 survey, 2,167 new households that emerged from these households as a result of splits, and a refresher sample of 2,498 households. Of the 23,997 individuals interviewed in 1998, 17,357 (72 percent) were successfully re-interviewed in 2006, forming a panel that can be used for longitudinal analysis. The 2006 sample contains an additional 19,743 "new" individuals. Of these, 2,663 individuals joined the original 1998 households, 4880 joined the split households, and 12,200 were part of the refresher sample of households.

The original sample of the ELMS 1998 was selected from 200 primary sampling units (PSUs) across Egypt. Urban PSUs were over-sampled and constituted 140 of the total and rural PSUs made up the remainder. The 1998 sample was a two-stage stratified random sample selected from a master sample prepared by CAPMAS. The PSUs included in the master sample were selected according to the probability proportional to size (PPS) method. The refresher sample of 2,500 households was selected from an additional 100 PSUs randomly selected from a new master sample prepared by CAPMAS, of which 46 were urban PSUs and 54 were rural PSUs.

The attrition that occurred in the original 1998 sample was mostly random in nature since it resulted from the loss of records containing identifying information for the 1998 households at CAPMAS. Of the 1,115 households that could not be re-interviewed, 615 are due to loss of records and the remainder is made up of expected losses due to total relocation of the household, death of all household members, or refusal to participate in the survey.[4]

1.2 Questionnaire

The questionnaire for the ELMPS 06 is closely based on that used in the ELMS 98 to ensure comparability of the data over time, but adds to the earlier questionnaire several critical modules that would permit a more in-depth study of marriage dynamics in Egypt. The questionnaire is composed of three major sections: (i) a household questionnaire administered to the head of household or the head's spouse that contains information on basic demographic characteristics of household members, movement of household members in and out of the household since 1998, ownership of durable goods and assets, and housing conditions; (ii) an individual questionnaire administered to the individual him or herself containing information on parental background, detailed education histories, activity status, job search and unemployment, detailed employment characteristics, migration histories, job histories, time use, earnings, fertility, a module on costs of marriage, and a module on women's work; (iii) a household enterprise and income module that elicits information on all agricultural and non-agricultural enterprises operated by the household as well as all income sources, including remittances and transfers.

For the purpose of this study, one of the main innovations of the ELMPS 06 questionnaire is the collection of data on the detailed characteristics of the first job. Combined with information on the timing of labor market entry, this information can provide an excellent description of the labor market conditions facing new entrants over time. Although the previous two surveys included job histories as well, the histories contained information on the current job and the two jobs (or labor market statuses) previous to it, which may or may not include the first job. Since the information on first job is now collected for all those who ever worked before, including those who have currently retired or withdrawn from the workforce, it does not suffer from the problem of selective exit from the sample, except due to reasons of death or migration abroad. It is, however, subject to the same recall problems that all retrospective questions suffer from.

In an addition to the unemployment module of the survey, several questions on the use of fixed and mobile phones, the internet, and personal computers in job search were added.

2. The Evolution of Unemployment in the Egyptian Economy

Unemployment is clearly a major concern in Egypt and it is therefore essential to ensure that at least the trend in unemployment, if not the level itself, is measured accurately. According to six different estimates based on various definitions of unemployment and of economic activity, unemployment has declined across the board in the 1998–2006 period, after having risen significantly in the 1988–1998 period. Although the decline is fairly broad, cutting across urban and rural areas and across regions, rural areas appear to have experienced a sharper decline in unemployment than urban areas, and most surprisingly the decline is greatest in rural Upper Egypt. The study will examine these various estimates after a brief discussion of the definitions used to obtain them.

2.1 Definitional Issues

This study uses three definitions of unemployment—standard, broad, and narrow—with the main difference between them being the way in which the search requirement is operationalized. I also use two definitions of economic activity—the market and extended definitions—which differ in whether production and process of primary goods for own consumption is treated as economic activity or not. The combination of these two sets of definitions leads in all to six estimates of the number of unemployed and the unemployment rate. The market definition of economic activity is not available in the LFSS 1988, so any comparisons with 1988 involve the extended definition only.

All three definitions of unemployment we use require that the individual to have not worked a single hour or to have been attached to a job during the week prior to the interview, to have desired work, and to have been available to start work within two weeks of getting a job offer. The differences among them lie in the way the active search requirement is operationalized. The *standard* definition requires that the individual have engaged in some search activity, but, in keeping with previous Egyptian practice, some of this search activity need not be limited to a three-month reference period prior to the interview. Specifically, if the individual had signed up to the centralized graduate employment queue or registered in a public employment office, they are considered to be searching even if such an application or registration was prior to the three-month reference period. Other methods of searching must have occurred within the three-month reference period for the individual to be considered searching for work. The *narrow* definition requires that the individual engage in active search by a method other than registering in a public employment office during the three months prior to the interview. The *broad* definition drops the search requirement altogether and thus includes the discouraged unemployed among the ranks of the unemployed. All that is needed for someone to count as unemployed under the broad definition is to be not working, desiring to work, and to be available for work within two weeks of getting an offer. Hence, among the three definitions the broad one provides an upper bound, the narrow definition a lower bound, and the standard definition falls somewhere in between.

Under the *market* definition of economic activity, only work for the purpose of producing goods and services for market exchange counts as work, so that subsistence workers can be considered unemployed if the rest of the definition of unemployment applies to them. Under the *extended* definition, any work for the purpose of producing or processing primary goods for own household consumption—i.e., subsistence work—also counts as economic activity. As such, a person engaged in such subsistence economic activity would not count as unemployed even though they may be desiring, available, and searching for market work. Thus, the use of the extended definition of economic activity reduces the estimate of the number of unemployed compared to the market definition. More importantly, it reduces the estimate of the unemployment rate even more because it significantly increases the estimate of the labor force, which is in the denominator of the unemployment rate.

2.2 Estimates of Aggregate Unemployment

As shown in Figures 5.1a and 5.1b, the rate of unemployment and the number of unemployed have declined or remained the same between 1998 and 2006, according to all six estimates used. Within the market definition of economic activity, the standard definition of unemployment shows that the rate of unemployment has fallen from 11.7 percent in 1998 to 8.3 percent in 2006, a 30 percent relative decline. The absolute number of unemployed has decreased from 2.0 million to 1.9 million in the same period. The other estimates using the market LF definition show similar declines.

The estimates based on the extended definition of economic activity can be compared to 1988 and can therefore give us a trend across a longer period. The main pattern here is that unemployment rates in 2006 have essentially gone back to close to what they were in 1988, although the number of unemployed has clearly increased significantly compared to 1988. The magnitudes of relative decline in the unemployment rates between 1998 and 2006 using the extended definition are slightly lower than those found using the market definition and the number of unemployed shows stability rather than decline with this definition.

As mentioned above, the difference between the broad and standard definitions is made up of the discouraged unemployed who did not engage in any search activity, although they report desiring to work and being available for it. By the market definition of economic activity, the number of discouraged unemployed has gone from 381 thousand in 1998 to 296 thousand in 2006, a 22 percent relative decline. The numbers are slightly lower based on the extended definition, but the trend is the same. By this definition, there are slightly more discouraged unemployed in 2006 than there were in 1988 (259,000 vs. 246,000).

The difference between the standard and narrow definitions is made up of people who have done no other search activity except register in a public employment office or with the centralized graduate employment scheme. This is a fairly good indicator of those who are exclusively searching for a public sector job. The number of "government-only" searchers by the market labor force definition has also declined from 1998 to 2006 from 141,000 to 125,000, a rate of decline of 11 percent.

Figure 5.1a. Unemployment Rate According to Various Definitions of Unemployment and Labor Force, 1988, 1998, 2006

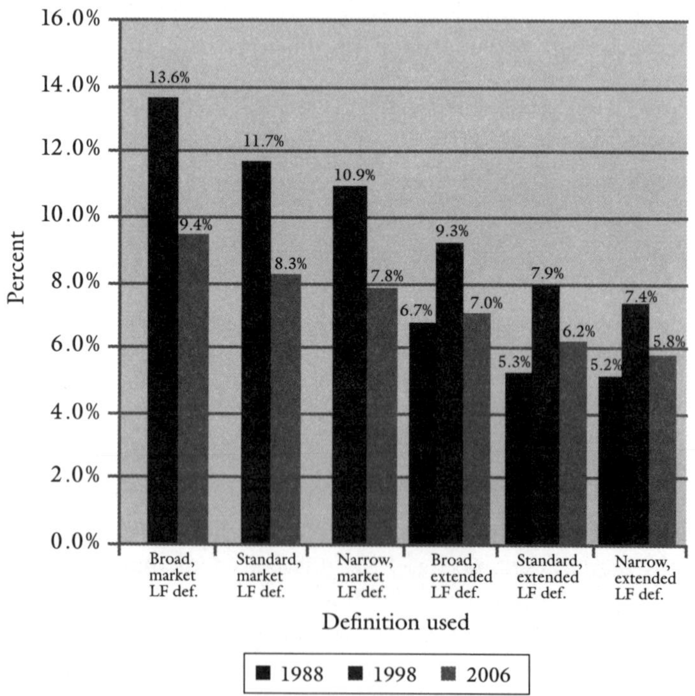

Figure 5.1b. Number of Unemployed According to Various Definitions of Unemployment and Labor Force, 1988, 1998, 2006

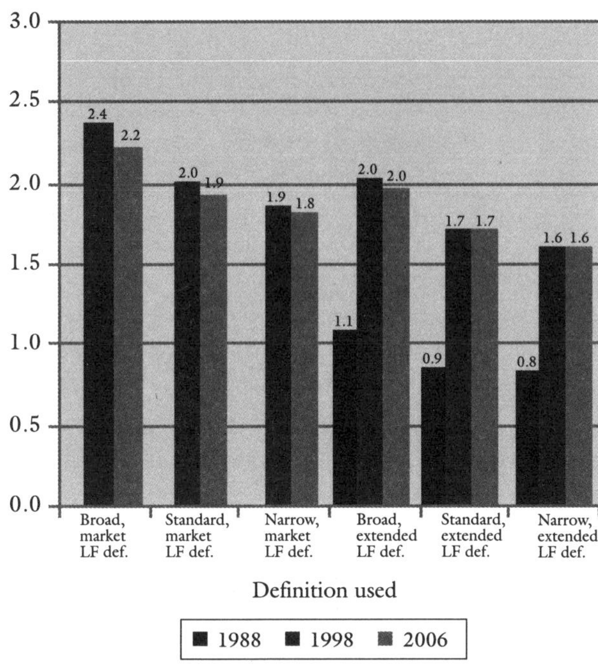

2.3 The Pattern of Unemployment by Sex, Urban/Rural Location, and Region

The detailed results on the pattern of unemployment by sex and urban/ rural location according to all six definitions of unemployment used and for the discouraged unemployed and the "government-only" searchers are shown in Tables A1 and A2 in the Appendix. The following discussion will focus on the results for the standard definition of unemployment using the market and extended definitions of the labor force, and will refer to the estimates obtained from the other definitions only if they add to the analysis.

As shown in Figure 5.2a, men started with significantly lower unemployment rates than women, but their rates declined at about the same relative rates, going from 7.0 percent to 4.7 percent as compared to women's, which went from 27.6 percent to 18.6 percent, maintaining a female to male ratio of unemployment of about 4:1. The decline in unemployment was proportionally greater in rural areas, which went from 12.2 percent to 7.0 percent, than in urban areas, which went from 11.0 percent to 10.0 percent. Both men and women in rural areas experienced a near halving of their unemployment rates.

As shown in Figure 5.2a, the highest rates of unemployment in 1998 were recorded for rural females (33.3 percent). Their rates were about 50 percent higher than those for urban females and nearly five times as high as those of urban males if the standard definition is used. By 2006, the rural female unemployment rate had dropped significantly from 33.3 percent to 17.4 percent, and is now lower than that of urban females, which is 20.0 percent. This sharp decline in rural female unemployment rates requires further analysis because it is unlikely that labor markets for educated rural women, who are the ones most likely to report unemployment, have improved this much.

While we will get back to this issue later, suffice it to say that the sharpest drop in the number of rural female unemployed was among the "government-only" searchers, i.e., women who did nothing but register in a government employment office. Their absolute numbers decline from 86,000 in 1998, or 14 percent of rural female unemployed, to 59,500 in 2006, or 10 percent of rural female unemployed. This is a clear indication that many educated rural women who were queuing for government jobs in 1998 have given up hope of getting such jobs and are now simply not seeking work at all. They are not even among the discouraged unemployed, because the number of the latter has declined. Many of them have left the labor force altogether as indicated by falling participation rates among educated women.

The sex and urban/rural patterns of unemployment are quite similar if we use the extended definition of economic activity, but now we are in a position to compare with 1988. As shown in Figure 5.2b, the downward trend between 1998 and 2006 holds for all subgroups using the extended definition, but, in this case, the reduction for women is relatively less than for men because the extended female labor force did not grow at the same pace as the market female labor force.

The observed broad-based decline in unemployment rates in the 1998–2006 period comes after a period of fairly widespread increases in unemployment in the previous decade. According to the estimates based on the extended definition, which are the only ones available for 1988, standard unemployment is still higher in 2006 (6.2 percent) than it was in 1988 (5.3 percent) (see Figure 5.2b). This result holds for both males and females and for urban and rural areas. It is only for urban females that unemployment, according to the extended definition of economic activity, is actually lower in 2006 than it was in 1988.

Figure 5.2a. Unemployment Rate by Gender and Urban/Rural Location, Ages 15–64

Standard Unemployment Definition and Market Labor Force Definition

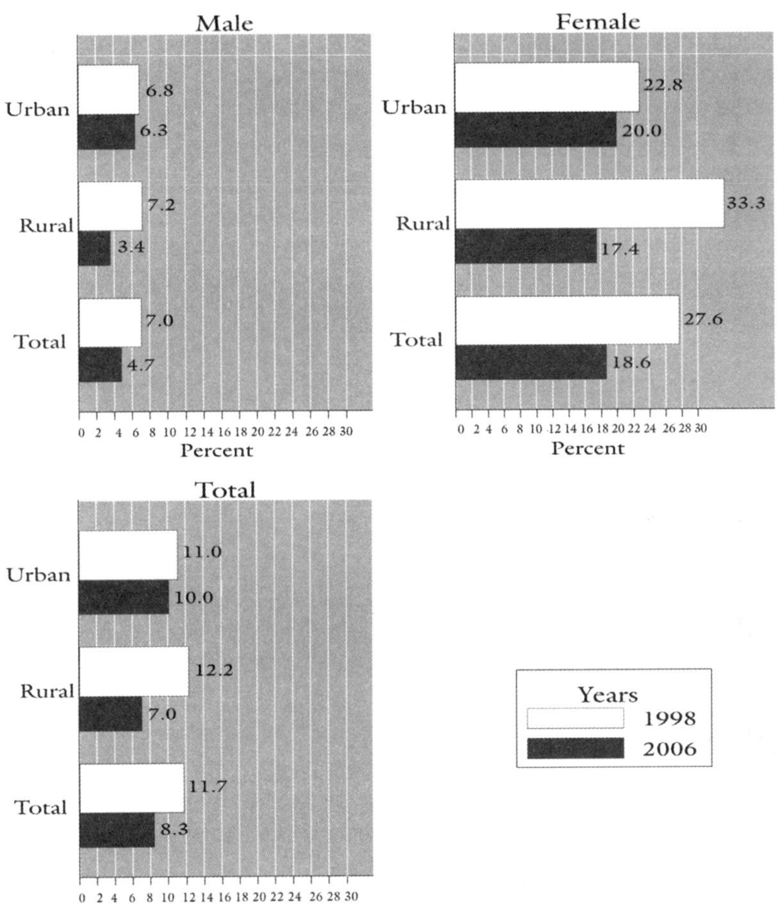

Figure 5.2b. Unemployment Rate by Gender and Urban/Rural Location, Ages 15–64

Standard Unemployment Definition and Extended Labor Force Definition

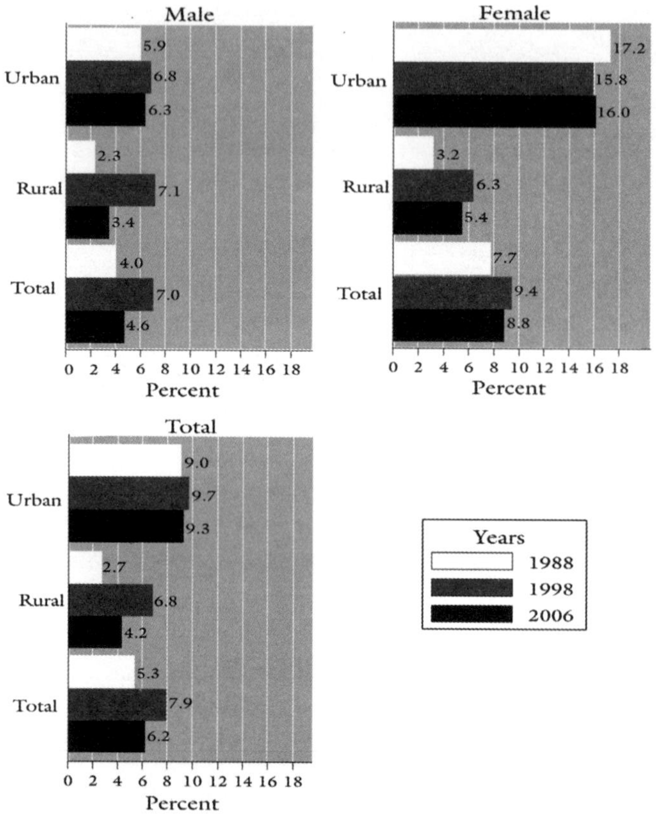

The regional pattern of unemployment is shown in Figures 5.3a and 5.3b according to the standard definition of unemployment and the market and extended definitions of economic activity, respectively. Again, the study will focus the discussion on the standard definition using the market definition of economic activity, but the observed patterns are generally consistent across definitions. Greater Cairo is the only region that saw no decline in unemployment in the 1998–2006 period, although it started out at fairly low levels compared to the national average. In fact, the unemployment rate in Greater Cairo increased for males from 5.4 percent to 6.9 percent, leading to an increase in the overall unemployment rate. The decline was fairly even in relative terms in all the other urban regions, which include Alexandria and the Suez Canal Cities, as well as urban Upper and Lower Egypt. The greatest decline in unemployment was in the two rural regions, where it declined by 39 percent in rural Lower Egypt and 45 percent in rural Upper Egypt.[5]

Lower Egypt, with both its urban and rural sub-regions, was the region with the highest unemployment rates in 1998. Urban Lower Egypt continues to be the highest unemployment region in 2006, but unemployment rates in rural Lower Egypt are now below those of all urban regions except for that of urban Upper Egypt. Female unemployment rates in Lower Egypt remain particularly high at 31 percent in urban areas and 26.5 percent in rural areas of the region. These persistently high unemployment rates among women in Lower Egypt reveal an increasing desire to seek work among an increasingly educated young female population, but with suitable work opportunities for these young women being still fairly limited.

Figure 5.3a. Unemployment Rate by Region and Sex, Ages 15–64

Standard Unemployment Definition and Market Labor Force Definition

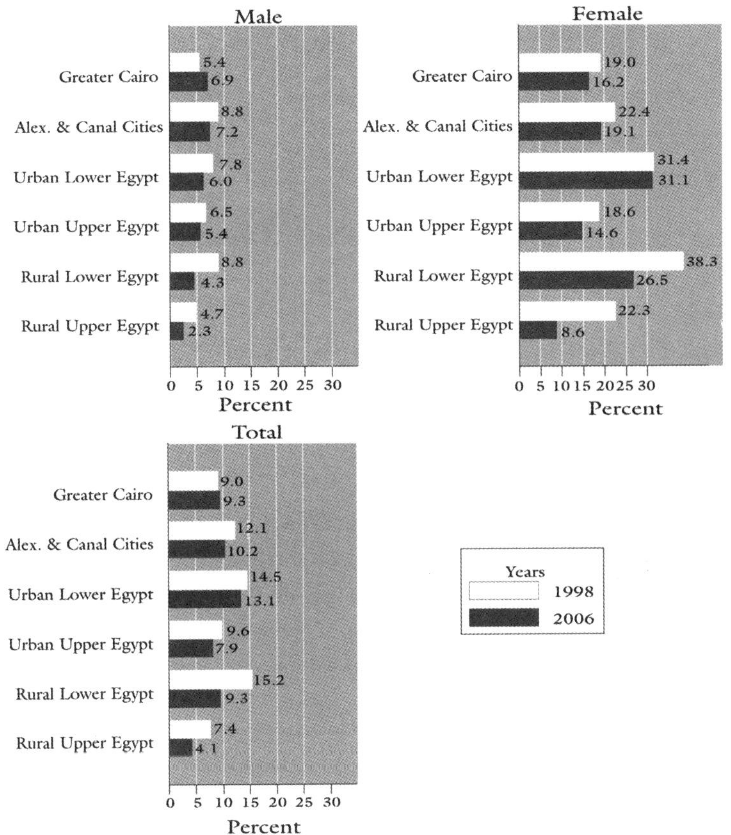

Figure 5.3b. Unemployment Rate by Region and Sex, Ages 15–64
Standard Unemployment Definition and Extended Labor Force Definition

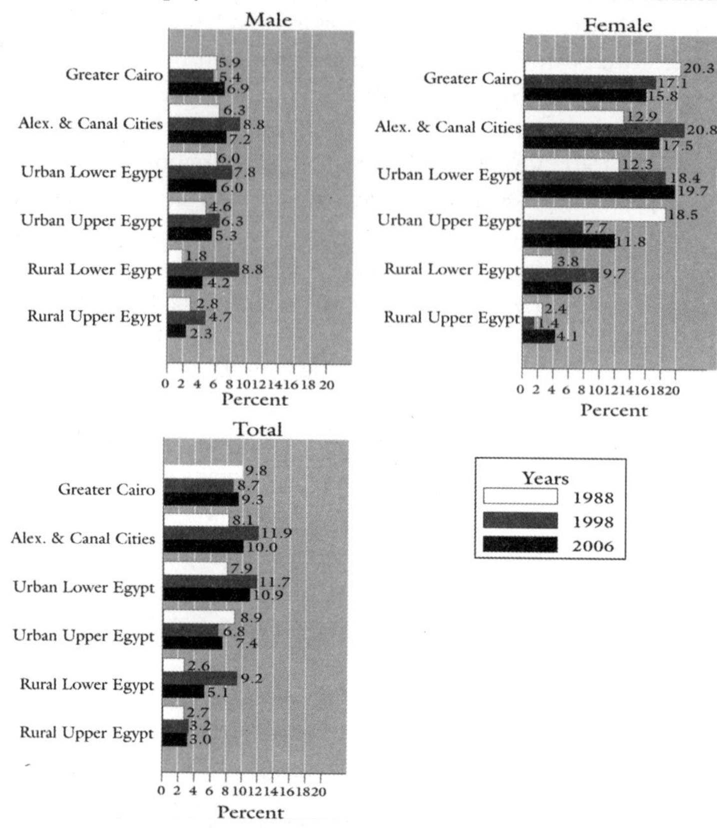

2.4 The Age Pattern of Unemployment

It is well established that unemployment in Egypt is essentially a labor market insertion phenomenon, meaning that it essentially affects youth. As the youth bulge ages, we would expect unemployment rates to decline unless the age pattern of unemployment changes and rates increase at older ages as the bulge moves into these ages. This has fortunately not been the case in Egypt over the 1998–2006 period, at least for males. As shown in Figure 5.4, the highest unemployment rates are reached during the age interval 18–23, the age of completion of secondary school and university degrees and, therefore, first labor market entry. Peak unemployment is at a slightly older age for females than for males. Moreover, urban females are the only group for which unemployment seems to be shifting to older ages as the youth bulge ages. For other groups the age profile is either stable or shifting downward.

In urban areas unemployment rates for very young male youths (15–18) have declined as their share of the population declined. In rural areas, all young males have experienced a sharp decline in unemployment. Comparison with 1988, using the extended definition of economic activity, shows that male youth unemployment is just slightly higher in 2006 than in 1988.

For females, the lower left-hand corner of Figure 5.4 shows that unemployment rates using the market definition of economic activity have declined for urban females under the age of 27, with the more significant declines experienced by those 15–19 years old. There is evidence of an increase in female unemployment rates in urban areas for women between the ages of 27 and 35, an indication that unemployment is shifting to older ages among urban females. In rural areas, the decline in female unemployment is larger and extends all the way to age 35. The picture for women using the extended definition of unemployment is not much different (lower right quadrant of Figure 5.4). While unemployment rates in 2006 are lower for 15–19 year-old women than in 1988, they are higher than in 1988 for women 25–34. Thus it appears that the aging of the youth bulge is negatively affecting young adult women in this age range.

To understand how the age pattern of unemployment translates into changing overall unemployment rates, we need to analyze it in light of the changing age structure of the population. Figures 5.5a and 5.5b show the age distribution of the population from 1988 to 2006 in urban and rural areas. What is immediately apparent from these figures is that a child bulge observed in 1988, and centered around age 4, has turned into an adolescent bulge in 1998 centered around age 14, and into a youth bulge in 2006 centered around age 22. A new child bulge is emerging in 2006, which is the result of the large number of potential young mothers, a clear manifestation of the so-called population momentum phenomenon. The urban and rural age structures are fairly similar, except for more pronounced child and adolescent bulges in 1988 and 1998, respectively, in rural areas where fertility rates are higher.

Combining the age structure information with the age pattern of unemployment, we can see that the drop in the proportion of young working-age adults (15–19) between 1998 and 2006 was also accompanied by a fall in their unemployment rates in both urban and rural areas. This portends the beginnings of a period of reduced pressure on the labor market brought about by the ageing of the youth bulge. This trend is further reinforced by a drop in unemployment rates among older youths (20–24) in rural areas that is happening despite the rapid demographic growth of that group.

2.5 The Educational Pattern of Unemployment

In contrast to the relative stability of the age pattern of unemployment from 1998 to 2006, the pattern of unemployment by education has exhibited some important changes during this period. As shown in the left-hand side of Figure 5.6, unemployment rates in 1998 were low at low levels of education, increased sharply for technical secondary graduates and then fell off again for post-secondary institute and university graduates.[6] In 2006, unemployment rates remain low for people with lower levels of education, increase for technical secondary graduates, but increase even more for post-secondary and university graduates, in most cases. In fact, university graduates are the only educational group to have experienced an increase in unemployment between 1998 and 2006. All other groups have seen a decline in unemployment; in many cases quite large declines. Rural-based technical secondary graduates had the highest unemployment rates in 1998 and experienced some of the most significant declines (from 16 percent to 6 percent for males and from 63 percent to 41 percent for females). Nevertheless, unemployment rates among female graduates with technical secondary degrees remain extremely high. As we will show below, much of the drop in unemployment may be due to exit from the labor force due to discouragement rather than to an increase in employment rates.

An examination of the right-hand side of Figure 5.6, which shows the educational pattern of unemployment using the extended labor force definition, allows us to compare to the situation in 1988. The pattern in 1988 was roughly similar to 1998, with unemployment being highest for technical secondary graduates.[7] Unemployment rates at different education levels in 2006 are either similar to or below their levels in 1988, except for university graduates where they are noticeably higher.

To understand the impact of the educational pattern of unemployment on overall unemployment, one must consider it in conjunction with the changing distribution of the population by educational attainment, which is shown in Figures 5.7a and 5.7b. The most important development in the educational arena is the sharp rise in the proportion of technical high school graduates in the working-age population, mostly at the expense of the proportion of illiterates and literates without a diploma. Technical secondary graduates now make up over 30 percent of the male working-age population, in both urban and rural areas, up from about 20 percent in 1998. They also make up over a quarter of the female working-age population up from about 15 percent in 1998. The proportion of university graduates has also increased, but from a much smaller base and mostly in urban areas.

Figure 5.4. Male Unemployment Rates by Age, and Urban/Rural Location

Standard Unemployment Definition and Market Labor Force Definition

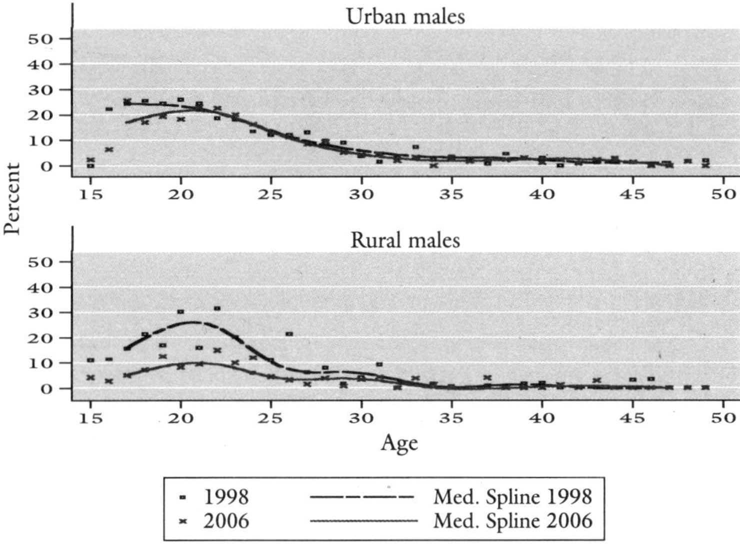

Female Unemployment Rates by Age, and Urban/Rural Location

Standard Unemployment Definition and Market Labor Force Definition

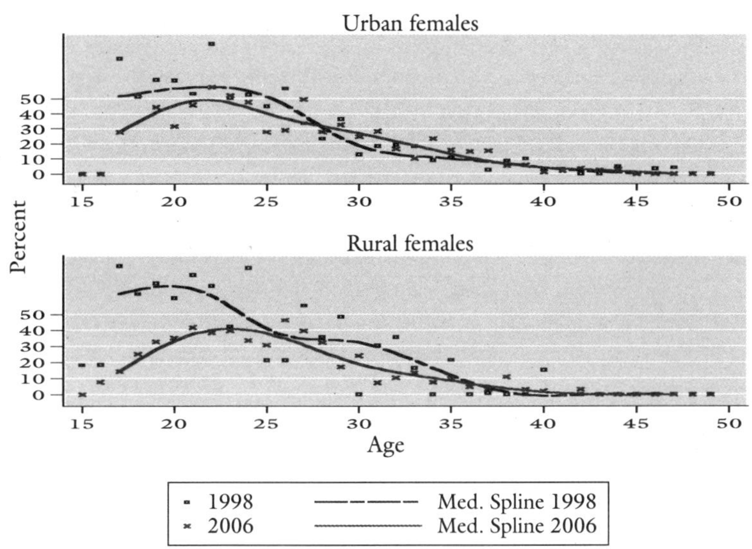

Figure 5.4. *(continued)*

Male Unemployment Rates by Age, and Urban/Rural Location

Standard Unemployment Definition and Extended Labor Force Definition

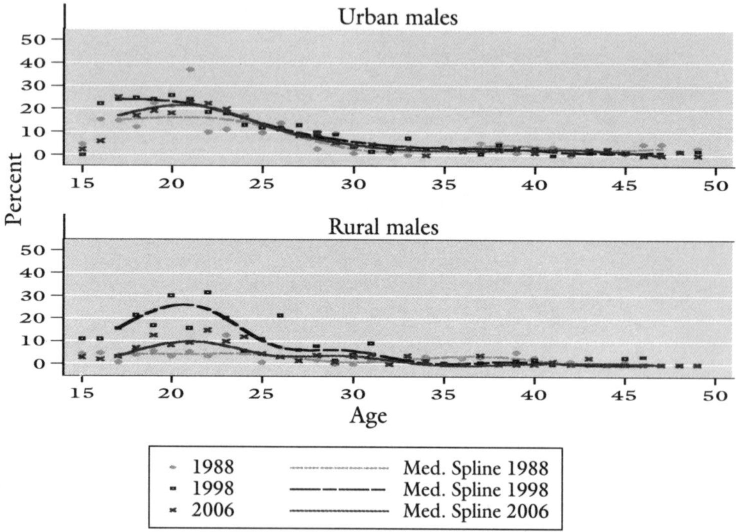

Female Unemployment Rates by Age, and Urban/Rural Location

Standard Unemployment Definition and Extended Labor Force Definition

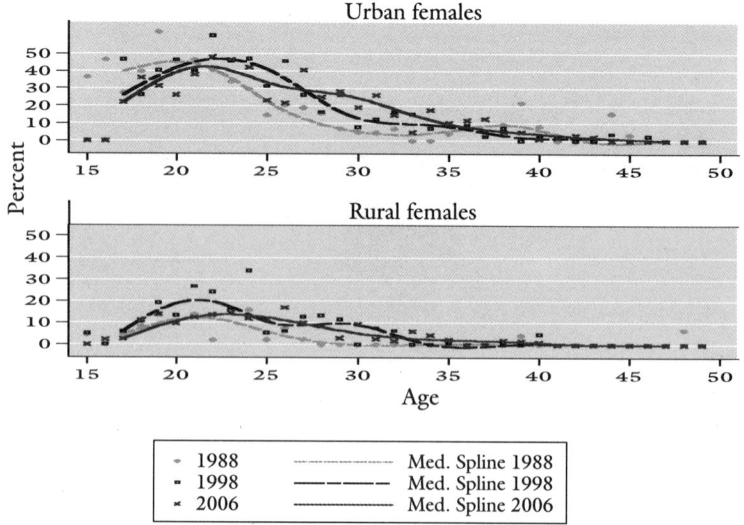

Figure 5.5a. Age Distribution of the Urban Population

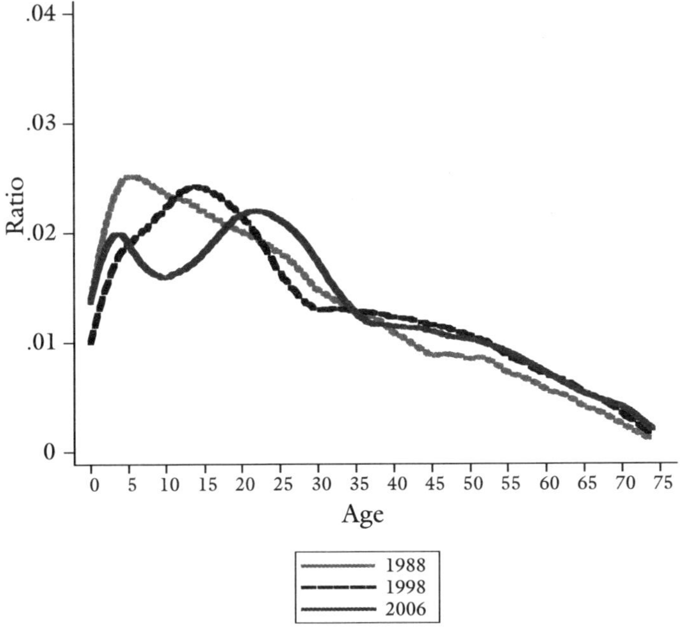

Figure 5.5b. Age Distribution of the Rural Population

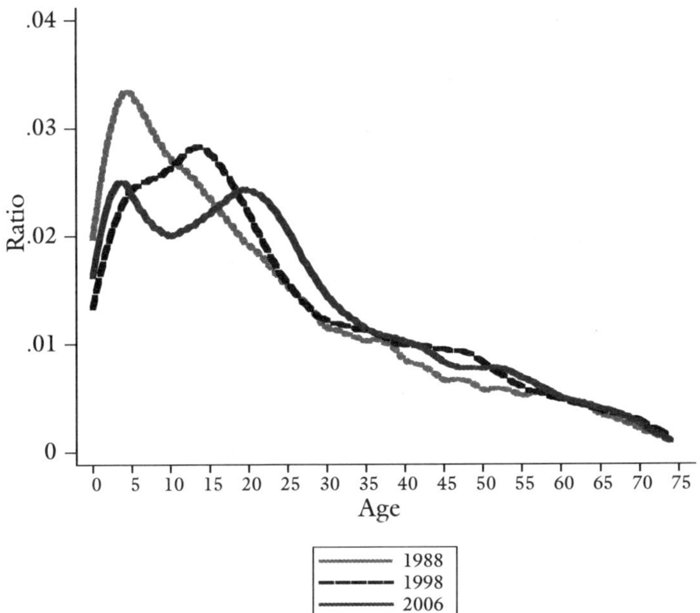

Given the significant jump in unemployment as educational attainment moves from a middle school certificate to a technical secondary certificate, we would have expected overall unemployment to increase due to this compositional effect had there been no change in the educational pattern of unemployment over time. In actual fact, the unemployment rates of technical secondary graduates have dropped sufficiently, so that the overall rate of unemployment declined despite the rapid expansion in the number of graduates. This is particularly true of rural technical graduates, whose unemployment rates have declined significantly despite the rapid growth in their numbers. This decline alone accounts for most of the large declines we noted earlier in the rural unemployment rate. The increase in unemployment among university graduates has countered the trend of falling unemployment among secondary school graduates, but since they are fewer in number, it had a smaller overall impact. The smaller decline in unemployment in urban areas is partly due to a lesser decline in unemployment among urban technical graduates than among their rural counterparts and the larger proportion of university graduates in the urban working-age population.

2.6 Recapping the Explanations for the Decline in Unemployment in the 1998–2006 Period

There are three potential explanations for the decline in unemployment in the 1998–2006 period in Egypt, which can be roughly categorized as demographic, institutional, and economic. On the demographic side, the slower growth of the 15–19 age group, a group with traditionally high unemployment rates, has resulted in both a drop in their unemployment rates as well as a compositional shift in favor of lower unemployment. This group constituted 20.9 percent of the working-age population in 1998, but only 17.4 percent in 2006. This shift can be clearly seen in Figures 5.5a and 5.5b and the accompanying drop in their unemployment rates can be seen in Figure 5.6. Unemployment did not shift to older ages as the youth bulge shifted, because unemployed young people, after a given period of searching, eventually adjust their expectations to the realities of the labor market and accept the jobs that are on offer to them. As a labor market insertion phenomenon, unemployment in Egypt is essentially the result of educated young people searching for jobs that meet certain minimum initial expectations. That is why unemployment rates are highest closest to the age of entry, which is 18 for most new entrants now. As the search process lengthens, they not only gather more information about the labor market that they face, but they also adjust their expectations downward, eventually

Figure 5.6. Male Unemployment Rates by Educational Attainment and Urban/Rural Location, Age 15–64

Standard Unemployment Definition and Market Labor Force Definition

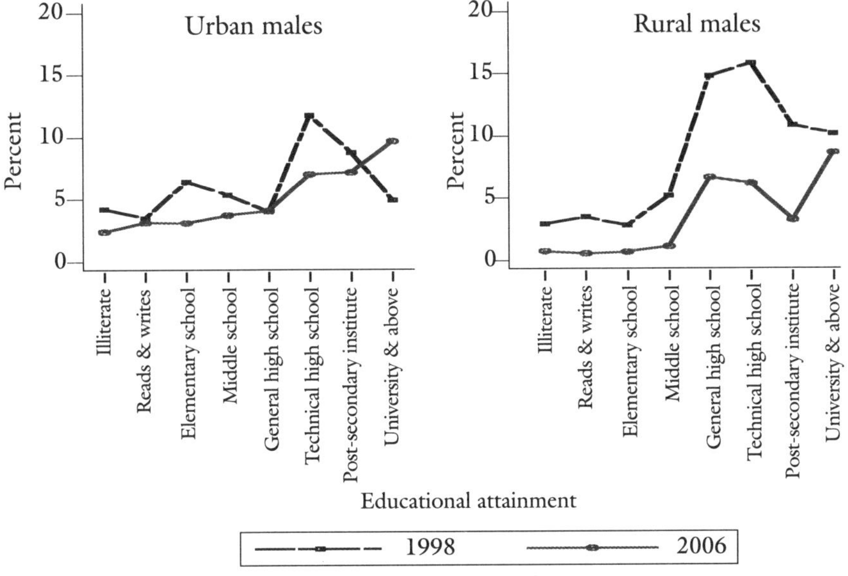

Female Unemployment Rates by Educational Attainment and Urban/Rural Location, Age 15–64

Standard Unemployment Definition and Market Labor Force Definition

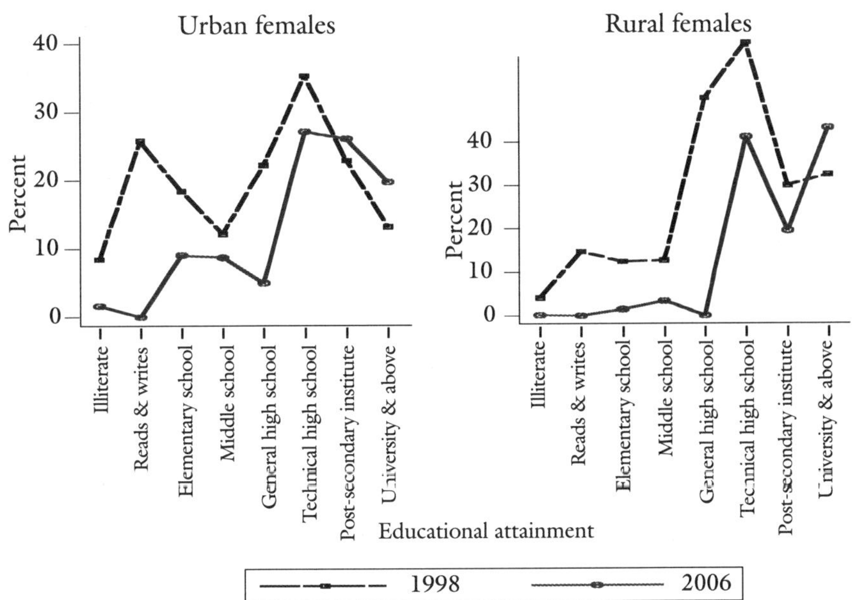

Figure 5.6. *(continued)*

Male Unemployment Rates by Educational Attainment and Urban/Rural Location, Age 15–64

Standard Unemployment Definition and Extended Labor Force Definition

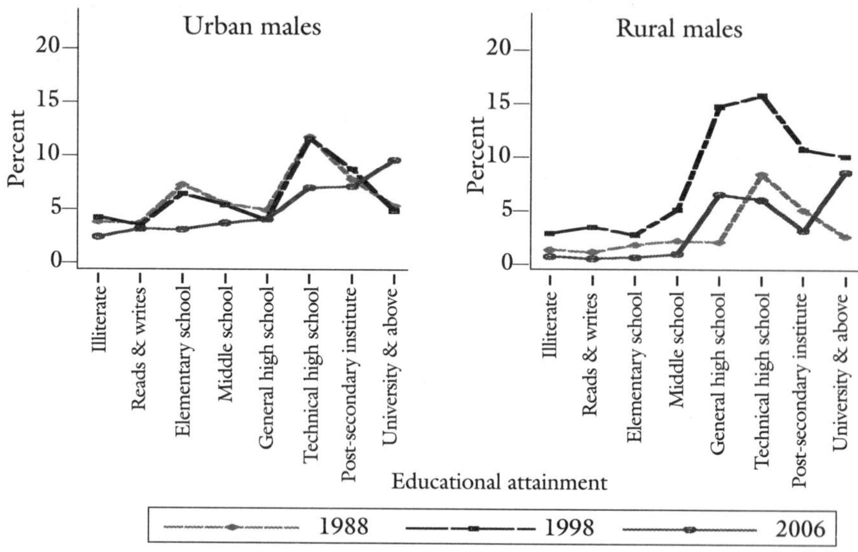

Female Unemployment Rates by Educational Attainment and Urban/Rural Location, Age 15–64

Standard Unemployment Definition and Extended Labor Force Definition

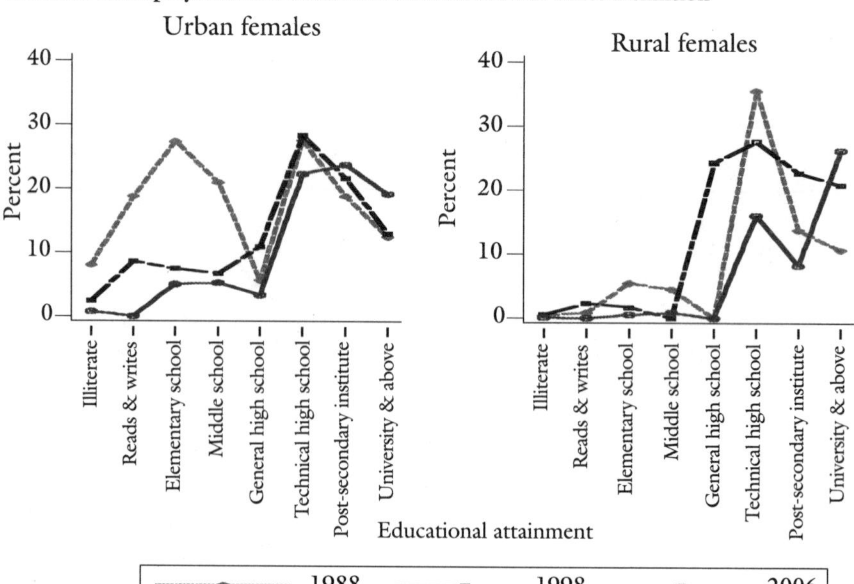

Figure 5.7a. Distribution of the Male Population by Educational Attainment and Urban/Rural Location, Ages 15–64, 1988–2006

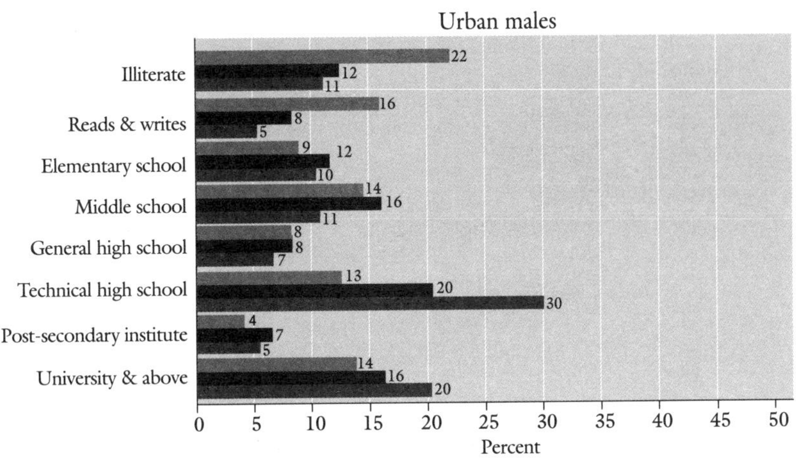

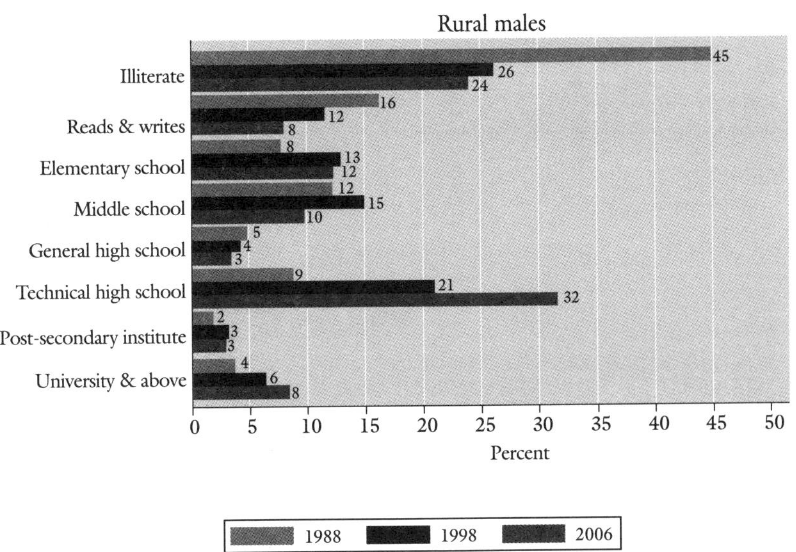

Figure 5.7b. Distribution of the Female Population by Educational Attainment and Urban/Rural Location, Ages 15–64, 1988–2006

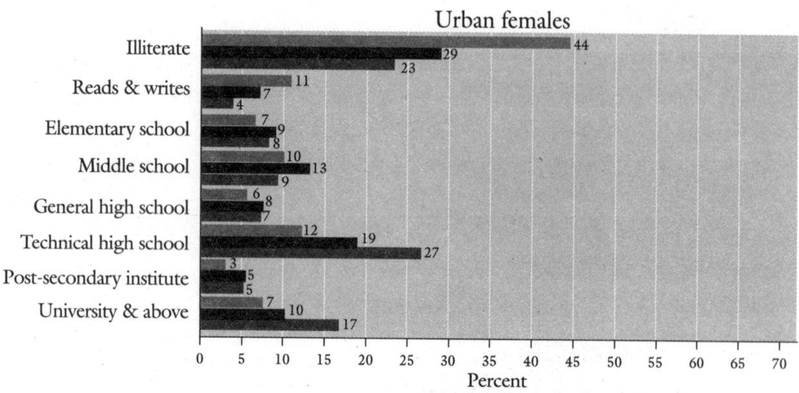

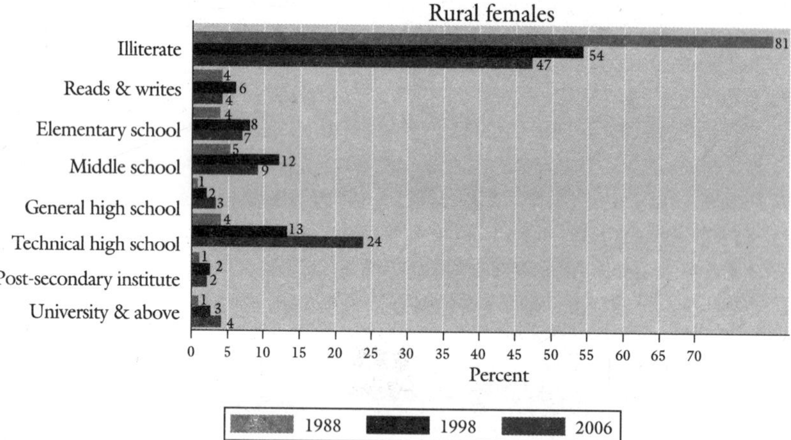

accepting some sort of employment, even if such employment would have been deemed unacceptable to them at first.

On the institutional side, the dramatic slowdown in government hiring in the 1998–2006 period has finally sent a clear message that it is no longer worthwhile to queue for government jobs. In many cases the lack of an incentive to queue may mean a more rapid entry into private sector work, and as we will see below, this could well be the case for males. In others, the lack of queuing may result in simply not declaring oneself to be seeking employment and therefore be captured among those who are outside the labor force. This may well be what is happening among educated young women whose reservation wages (or opportunity cost of time) lies above the prevailing private sector wage rates, and the total value of the government compensation package. Faced with wages in the private sector that are much lower than those obtained by their male counterparts, these women may prefer to leave the workforce rather than accept these low-paid private sector jobs. In the past, because there was a positive probability of getting government employment, they would declare themselves as seeking employment and therefore were counted among the unemployed. Now that the probability of government employment is drastically lower, there is little incentive to continue seeking such jobs.

Evidence for this proposition can be inferred by looking at the pattern of female employment in government by educational level over time and comparing it to the pattern of female labor force participation by education level. These two patterns are shown in Figures 5.8 and 5.9. It is clear from Figure 5.8 that employment rates in the government have fallen significantly for educated women between 1988 and 2006. For instance, the proportion of working-age technical high school graduates employed in government declined from 30 percent in 1988 to 23 percent in 1998 to 15 percent in 2006. The proportion of other graduates working in government also declined but at a somewhat slower pace. Figure 5.9 shows that these declines are directly reflected in the participation rates of educated women. The participation rate of working-age technical high school graduates, according to the extended definition of the labor force, was 80 percent in 1988, of which 22 percent was unemployment and 30 percent was government employment. It fell to 68 percent in 2006, of which 9 percent was unemployment, and 15 percent government. Thus, falling government employment rates for that group was accompanied by increasing employment outside government (from 28 percent to 44 percent) and increasing non-participation (from 20 percent to 32 percent), but not by increasing unemployment.

The third reason for the fall in unemployment is the increase in the pace of private sector employment growth from 1998 to 2006. As shown in Figure 5.10, the growth rate of private wage employment was 5.3 percent per annum as compared to 4.6 percent per annum for total employment and 3.5 percent per annum for the market labor force as a whole. Private non-wage work has also grown rapidly, especially in rural areas. Overall it grew at 7.4 percent per annum, and in rural areas it grew at 8.7 percent per annum.

The rapid growth of non-wage work in rural areas is probably the main reason for the much larger drop in unemployment there.[8] Non-wage work constituted 45 percent of total employment in rural areas in 2006, up from 35 percent in 1998. Among males, its share grew from 33 percent of total employment to 39 percent.

A closer examination of non-wage employment in rural areas reveals that it is mostly concentrated in agriculture, with trade occupying a distant second place. The proportion of non-wage employment in agriculture increased from 61 percent in 1998 to 69 percent in 2006 and that of trade dropped from 23 percent to 16 percent in the same period. Among males, the proportion engaged in transport and construction has increased significantly. The share of males in transport has grown from 3.1 percent to 4.6 percent of total non-wage employment in rural areas from 1998 to 2006. The share in construction has increased from 1.7 percent to 3.4 percent in the same period. Despite the growth of these sectors for males, the rural non-wage economy remains dominated by agriculture and what happens in this sector determines the health of the rural economy.

Figure 5.8. Ratio of Employment of the Female Working Age Population in Government by Educational Attainment, Urban/Rural Location, Ages 15–64

Extended Labor Force Definition, 1988–2006

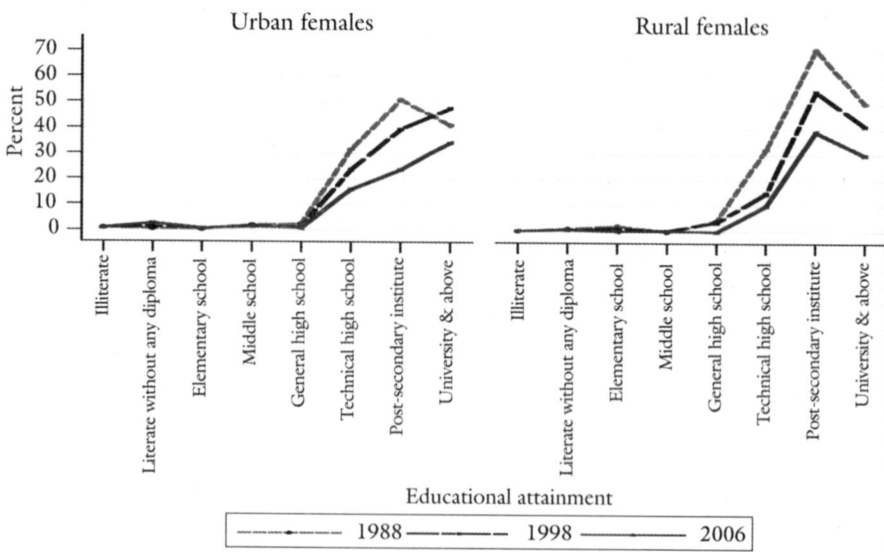

Figure 5.9. Female Labor Force Participation Rates by Educational Attainment, Urban/Rural Location, Ages 15–64

Extended Labor Force Definition, Search is Required, 1988–2006

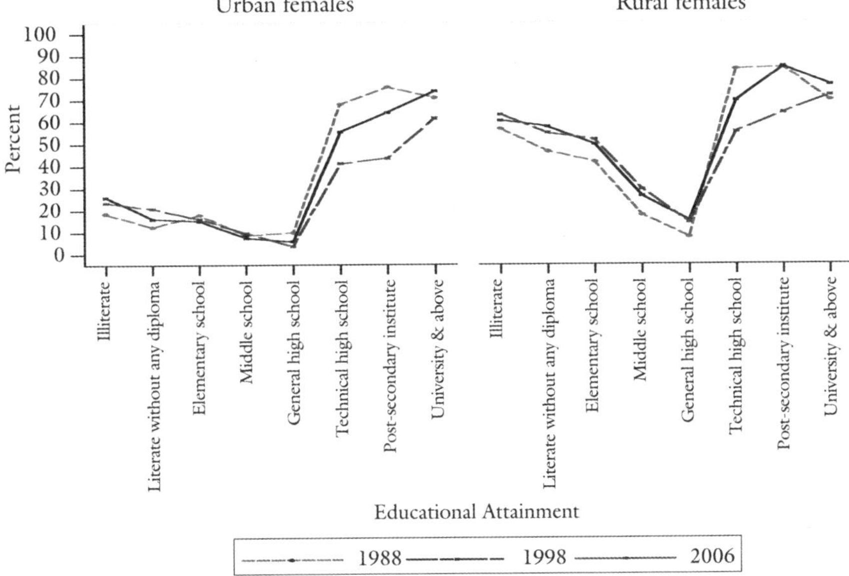

Figure 5.10. Employment Growth Rates by Sector and Urban/Rural Location, 1998–2006

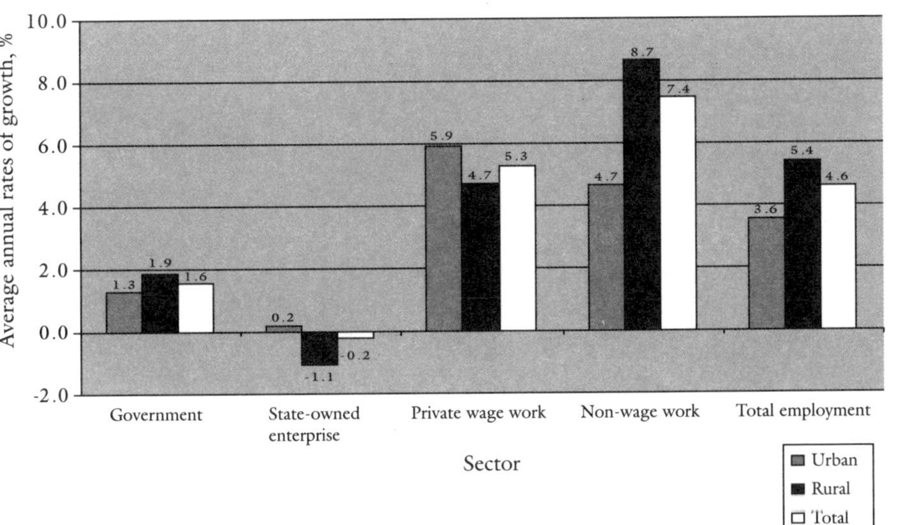

3. Changes in the Reported Reasons for Unemployment

Unemployment is often classified as voluntary and involuntary depending on the reason the individual provides for being unemployed. All three surveys inquired about the reason for being unemployed, with one of the reasons listed being inability to find any job opportunities whatsoever, which could be interpreted as involuntary unemployment. Other reasons referred to inability to find a job that is appropriate along various dimensions, which could be interpreted as involuntary. These dimensions include qualifications, pay, workplace, location, as well as an "other" category. We should be aware, however, that there is still a degree of individual choice among people responding that they are totally unable to find any job. Most of the unemployed in Egypt are educated, because most uneducated people simply cannot afford to remain unemployed and thus either find or create jobs for themselves—jobs that most educated people, with their higher expectations, would find unacceptable. The openly unemployed are therefore all people who are unwilling to take any job and are able to invest some time searching for a job with minimum attributes.

As shown in Table A3a in the Appendix, the proportion of the unemployed (according to the standard unemployment definition and market labor force definition) claiming to be unable to find any jobs has declined from 62 percent in 1998 to 53 percent in 2006, suggesting that unemployment is becoming more voluntary. This decline is observed among both males and females, but is sharper among males. It is also apparent in both urban and rural areas, but is more pronounced in rural areas. The proportion of "involuntary unemployed" was larger among males than among females in 1998 but that order has now been reversed. It was also much higher in rural than in urban areas and is now only slightly higher.

Among those responding that unemployment was for lack of an appropriate job, 52 percent said in 2006 that they could not find jobs that matched their qualification, which is unchanged from the proportion in 1998 (see Appendix Table A3b). Twenty-one percent said that there were no jobs at an acceptable level of pay, up from 12 percent in 1998. Eighteen percent said that the job was not at an appropriate workplace, down from 22 percent in 1998. It is noteworthy that the proportion of women who gave that reason in 2006 (22 percent) was much higher than that of males (13 percent). This confirms that social appropriateness of the workplace is a much more important factor for women than for men. Not finding a job at a suitable location was also a reason more frequently mentioned by women than by men.

These results on reason of unemployment confirm that a great deal of unemployment in Egypt results from a mismatch between the expectations of graduates in terms of the kind of job they should be getting and what the labor market has to offer them.

We repeated the analysis of reported reason for unemployment for the discouraged unemployed. The results show that the rate of involuntariness actually increased among the discouraged from 59 percent in 1998 to 65 percent in 2006. Thus, those who stopped searching truly feel that their chance of finding any job is limited. The vast majority of the discouraged (68 percent) are women who have probably stopped searching because they believe that the only job they are likely to get is a government job.

4. The Labor Market Insertion Process

Since unemployment in Egypt is essentially a problem of labor market insertion of first-time entrants in the labor market, it is important to understand how the process of insertion has changed over the study period. We begin by establishing that unemployment in Egypt is, in fact, a new entrants' phenomenon then move to an examination of the duration of unemployment and how it varies across groups and over time, go on to a brief examination of the school-to-work transition process and then end with an analysis of the changing labor market environment facing new entrants over time.

4.1 The Proportion of New Entrants among the Unemployed

As shown in Figure 5.11a, the proportion of new entrants among the unemployed has continued to climb, confirming that unemployment in Egypt is essentially a problem of youth insertion in the labor market. The proportion of new entrants increased from 74 percent in 1998 to 82 percent in 2006. It is slightly higher in rural areas than in urban areas, but much higher among women than among men. The increase is across the board, but most pronounced for urban males, followed by urban females. As a result, the urban/rural differences in the proportion of new entrants have narrowed over the study period. Figure 5.11b shows the same information using the extended definition of the labor force, thus allowing us to compare to 1988. It confirms that the proportion of new entrants has continued to rise steadily since 1988. It went from 57 percent in 1988 to 80 percent in 2006 according to this definition. Most of the increase from 1988 to 1998 in the proportion of new entrants was in rural areas, unlike the situation in 1998 to 2006. It therefore appears that the proportion of new entrants among the unemployed increases more when the improvement in the unemployment situation is more limited.

Figure 5.11a. Proportion of New Entrants Among the Unemployed by Gender and Urban/Rural Location, 1998–2006

Standard Unemployment Definition and Market Labor Force Definition

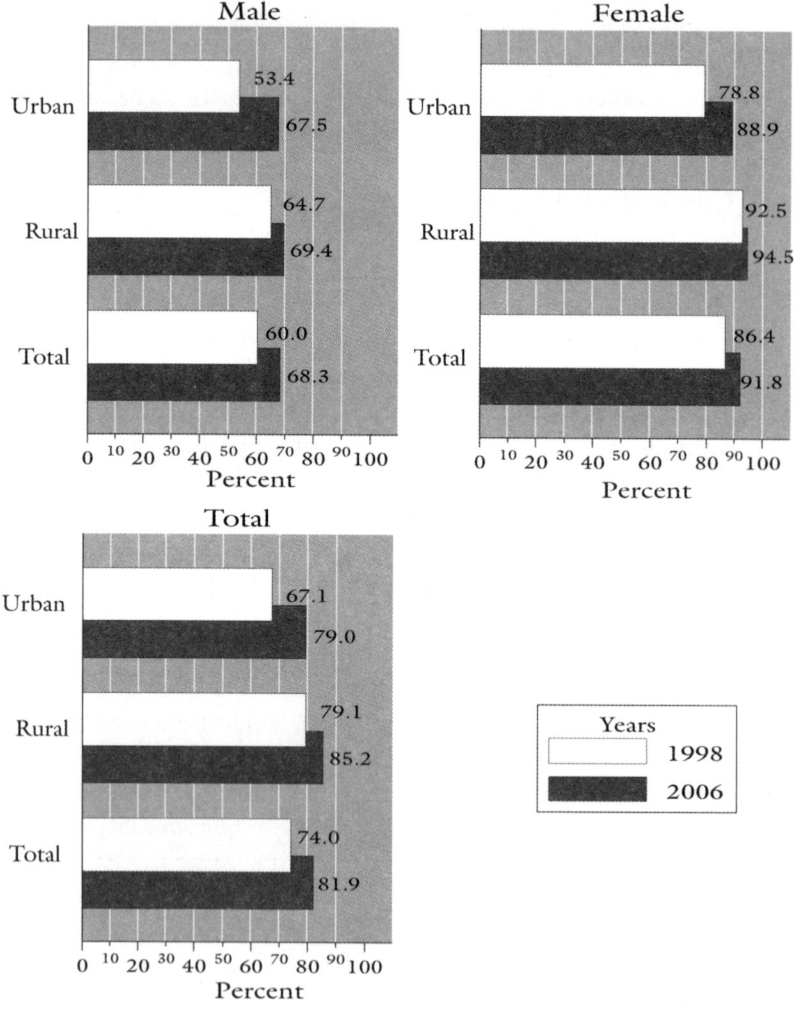

Figure 5.11b. Proportion of New Entrants Among the Unemployed by Gender and Urban/Rural Location, 1988–2006

Standard Unemployment Definition and Extended Labor Force Definition

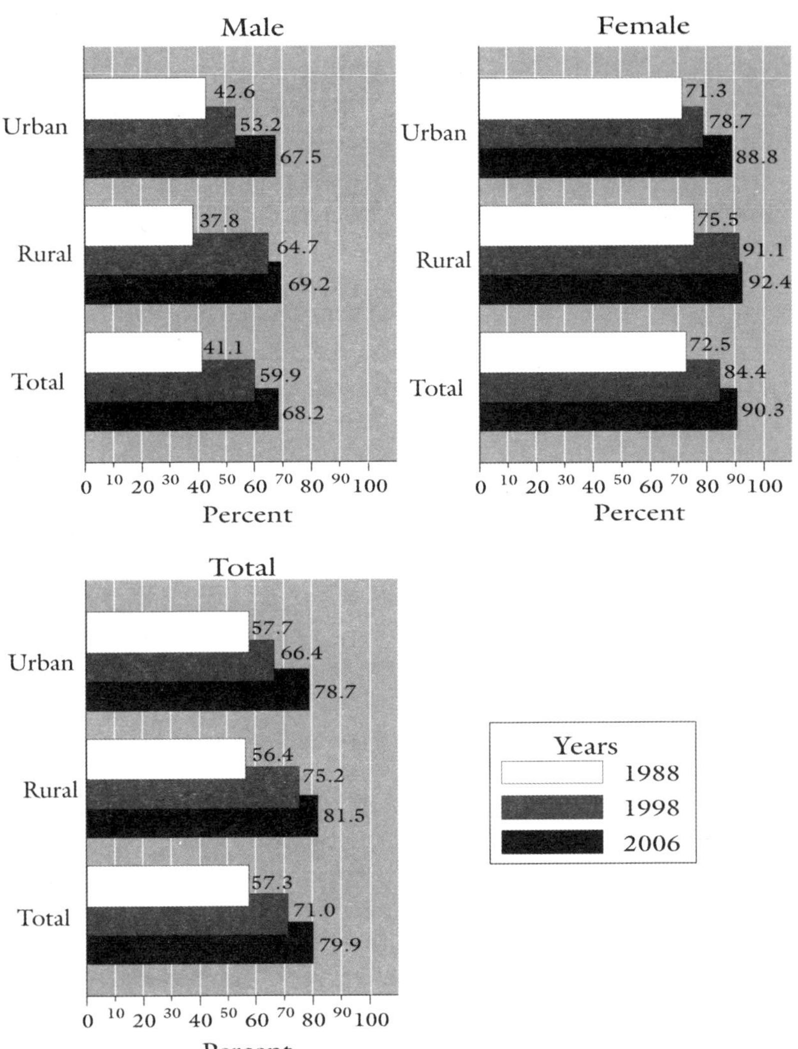

4.2 The Duration of Unemployment

We examine in this section changes in the median and 75th percentile of duration of unemployment by sex and urban/rural location from 1998 to 2006. We do so for the three definitions of unemployment laid out above but for only the market definition of the labor force. This sort of analysis must be interpreted with some caution because it does not take into account the fact that all the durations we are actually observing are censored. In other words, we only observed unemployment durations for those who are currently unemployed, but not for those who were unemployed and later became employed. We also don't take into account the change in the proportion of those who did not experience any unemployment over time. It is quite possible for durations as measured in this way to increase with improving labor market conditions if the short-duration workers get jobs first, leaving behind the truly hard to employ. A fuller analysis that takes into account the censoring problem is beyond the scope of this study.

As shown in Table A4 in the Appendix, it appears that the median duration of unemployment (using the standard, market definition) has stayed the same at 24 months from 1998 to 2006. However, this masks some compositional changes, because the median duration has increased for both males and females. For males, it went up from 12 to 18 months and for females it increased from 24 to 36 months. The 75th percentile duration has not changed, however, for both males and females, and stands at 36 and 72 months respectively. There appears to be no systematic differences in duration of unemployment between urban and rural areas, although unemployment durations for females in rural areas appear to have lengthened significantly.

Women who only used government search mechanisms have the longest median duration in 2006 at 84 months, up from 48 months in 1998. This group is made up for the most part of women who are primarily seeking government employment and are willing to queue for such employment for extended periods of time. The dramatically shorter durations for men in this category in 2006 indicates that this category now includes primarily men who have just started searching and have not yet had a chance to use other search mechanisms. Those in the long-term queue for government jobs among men have presumably already given up and accepted work in the private sector.

While the pattern of change across time is somewhat inconclusive because of the censoring problem discussed above, we can still glean useful information about the gender and urban/rural pattern of unemployment duration.

4.3 The Duration of the Transition from School to Work

Because we have information on the time the individual left or finished school and the time they started work, we can study the transition from school to work independently of the unemployment status of the individual. Since we have durations in this case for those who already started work as well as those who did not, we can correct for censoring by using survival analysis and Kaplan-Meir failure charts. The main limitation here is that duration is measured in discrete increments of one year rather than weeks, so that we are unable to obtain a very fine-grained picture of transition from school to work. As shown in Figure 5.12, these charts provide the cumulative probability of having obtained a first job by year since the individual left school.

Figure 5.12 shows that young male new entrants are entering their first job earlier in 2006 than in 1998, but that young females are entering at the same rate as before. In 1998, 50 percent of male school leavers had found their first job within two years of leaving school, down from three years in 1998. Seventy-five percent found jobs in 2006 within five years of leaving school, whereas in 1998 it would have taken nearly eight years for that proportion to find jobs. The female rates of transition from school to work are much lower and don't exceed 25 percent even after 15 years. There is no perceptible improvement in the transition time from 1998 to 2006 for women.

Figure 5.12. Failure of Duration to Obtain First Job, by Gender, Ages 15–29, 1998 and 2006

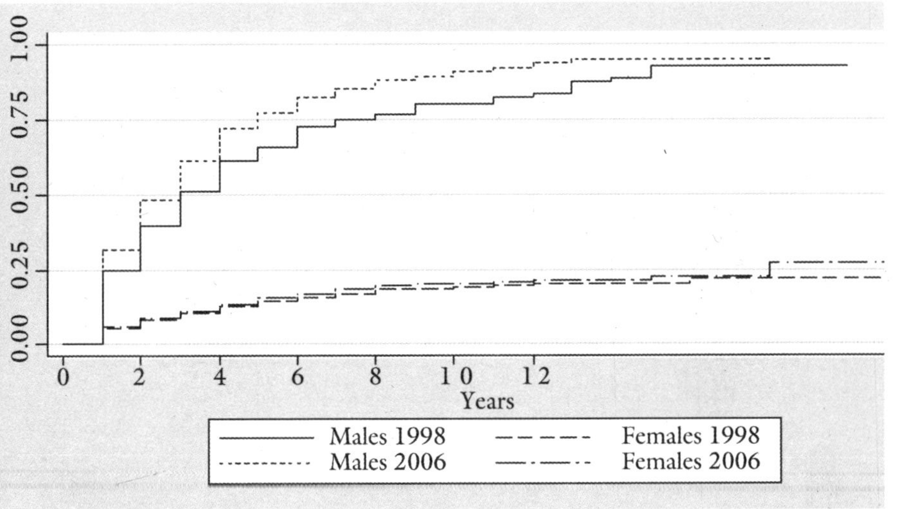

4.4 The Evolution and Changing Composition of New Entrants

The ELMPS 06 data allow us to study the pattern of labor market entry across time by exploiting a question to all individuals, irrespective of their current employment status, about whether or not they had worked before (for a minimum duration of at least six months), and, if so, when they had started work and what were the characteristics of their first job. Aside from problems associated with recall, the main problem associated with these data has to do with the possibility of selection out of the sample due to death or migration abroad. Since those who entered since 1975 are less likely to have died, we limit our period of analysis to the 1975–2005 period. Because of potential problems with recall, no particular significance should be given to year-on-year fluctuations, but only to general trends. Accordingly, we present a four-year moving average to abstract away from these annual fluctuations.

As shown in Figure 5.13, the number of new entrants has climbed steadily from about 400 thousand per year in the mid 1970s to about 900 thousand in the first half of this decade. It should be kept in mind that this is the gross number of new entrants and not the net increment to employment, which was about 680 thousand per year in the 1998–2006 period. As shown in the figure, the proportion of females among new entrants increased from about 23 percent in the mid-1970s to 30 percent the early1980s, a time when the government workforce was expanding rapidly. It then stagnated at this level until 1990, only to decline back to 23 percent by 1996. This period is characterized by slower growth government hiring and de-feminization in non-governmental wage work (See Assaad 2006a). The period since 1996 saw a rapid rise in the proportion of women among new entrants, so that by 2005 it had reached nearly 35 percent. This is in line with other data that show a rapid increase in female employment in the private sector, especially in textiles and garments and food processing manufacturing, and in white-collar service jobs.

Figure 5.13. Evolution of the Number of New Entrants and their Distribution by Sex, 1975–2005

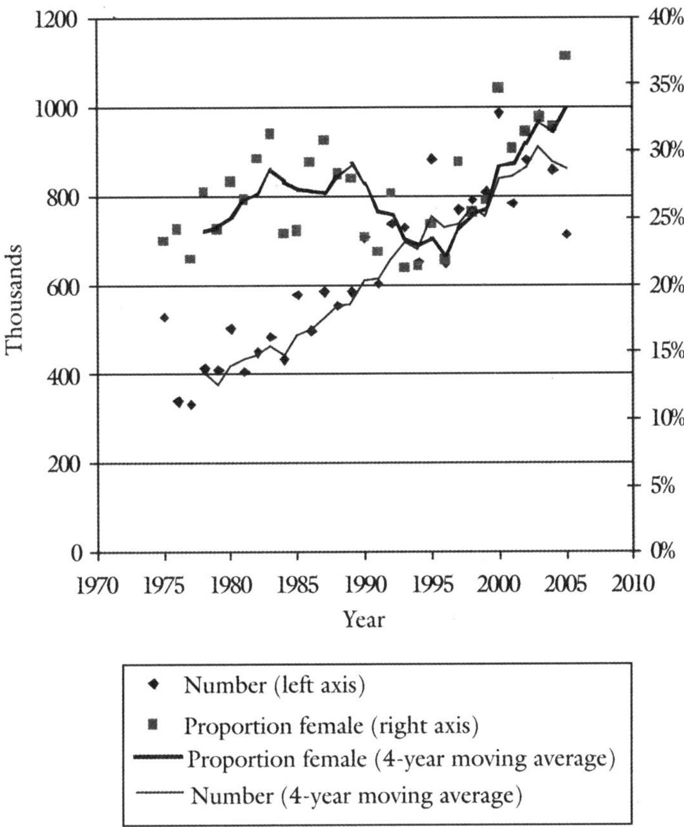

The educational composition of new entrants has also changed significantly over time as reflected in Figure 5.14. The proportion of those without any educational credentials dropped from close to 45 percent in the mid-1970s to about 15 percent in 2005. This secular decline was matched by a dramatic increase in the share of new entrants with secondary educational credentials, which went from nearly 20 percent in 1975 to over 40 percent in 2005. The vast majority of these secondary degree holders are technical secondary graduates since nearly all of general secondary graduates continue onto post-secondary degrees. The share of those with only elementary or preparatory education (classified here as basic education) increased somewhat in the 1980s but then declined again in the 1990s and 2000s.

Figure 5.14. Distribution of New Entrants by Educational Attainment, 1975–2005

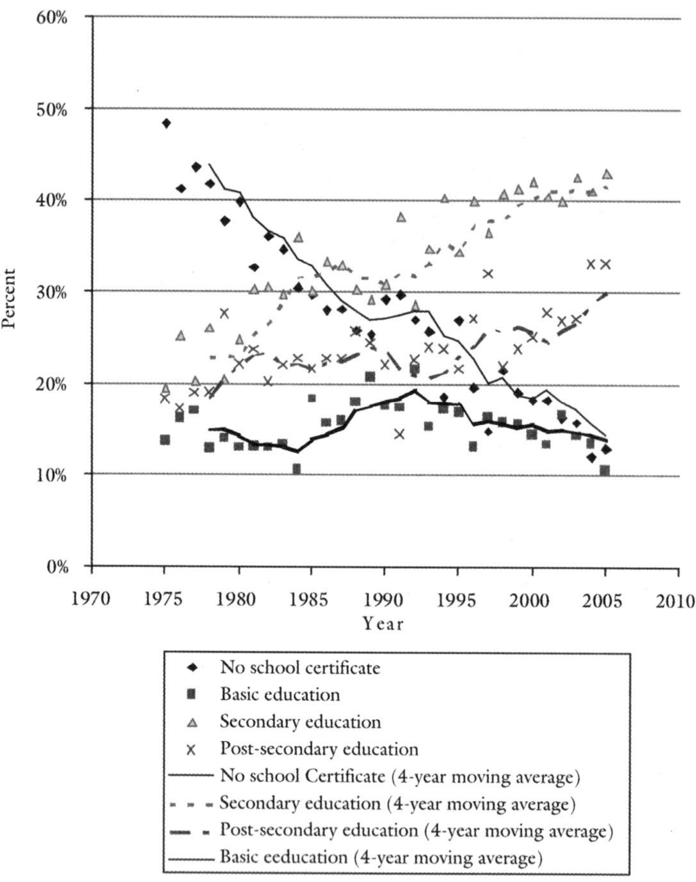

The share of post-secondary graduates, most of whom are university graduates, was more or less stable at a little less than 25 percent from the late 1970s to the mid 1990s, but then started to increase significantly after that. This dramatic change in trend corresponds to a shift in policy a few years earlier when the number of admissions to university was increased significantly after a period of relative stability (see Assaad 2006b). This rapid increase in the number of new entrants with university degrees in the 1998–2005 period could well be responsible for the fact that unemployment rates among this group have increased during this period. This contrasts to the relative stability in the share of secondary school graduates during the same period, a group that has seen its unemployment rates decline.

What sort of jobs are these new entrants getting? We classify jobs along a rough job quality scale, starting with the most secure to the least secure, although there are clearly other dimensions to job quality beside the level of security. At the top we have public sector jobs, which include jobs in the government and the state-owned enterprises, followed by formal jobs in the private sector. These are regular jobs covered by legal contract and/or social insurance coverage. These are followed by informal, but regular, jobs in the private sector. These are jobs where the individual has regular employment but does not benefit from either a legal contract or social insurance. Irregular wage employment comes next. These are made up of intermittent and seasonal wage employment in the private sector, which is almost always without social protection. Finally, we end up with non-wage employment, which technically includes employers, self-employed and those working for their family enterprise at no wage. In actual fact, non-wage employment for a new entrant is almost entirely as unpaid family workers, with a small fraction as self-employed.

It can clearly be debated whether irregular wage employment in the private sector is more or less secure than non-wage work. Non-wage work is probably a rather heterogeneous category that includes highly lucrative stable jobs as well as very marginal work. We therefore don't take a particular position about the ordering of these two categories at the moment.

The distribution of new entrants by the type of first job they obtain is shown in Figure 5.15. As indicated, the share of the public sector in first jobs has dropped steadily from about a third in 1975 to nearly 15 percent by 2005, with the steepest drop occurring in the early 1990s. The share of private formal employment was fairly low and stagnant through the 1980s, began increasing in the 1990s, stagnated in the early 2000s, and picked up again since 2003. Overall, the share of the private formal sector rose from about 5 percent in the mid 1970s to about 10 percent in the mid 2000s. The type of employment that has truly taken over from the public sector in the distribution of first jobs in the past three decades is private, informal, but regular wage employment. Its share increased dramatically in the 1980s from around 15 percent to 25 percent. Its increase slowed a bit in the late 1980s and early 1990s but resumed in the mid 1990s, only to slow down again in the late 1990s and early 2000s. Nonetheless, it now constitutes over 30 percent of all first jobs. A comparison of the rates of growth of formal and informal regular employment among first time entrants since 1990 reveals that formal employment has grown more rapidly at 4.4 percent per annum compared to informal regular employment, which has grown at 3.3 percent per annum, although formal employment is clearly growing from a much lower base.[9]

Figure 5.15. Distribution of New Entrants by Type of First Job (%), 1975–2005

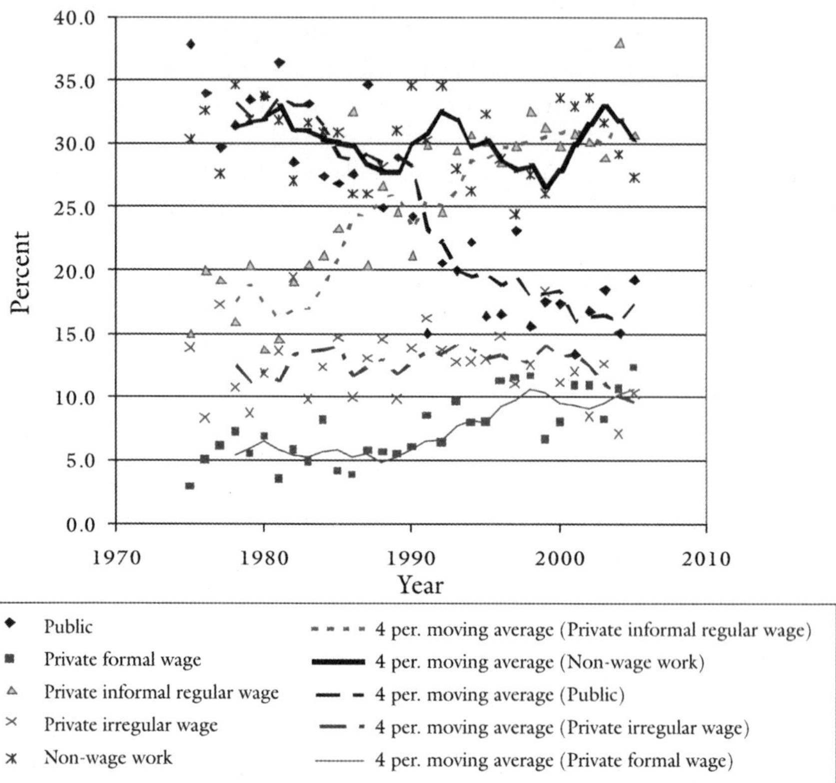

Irregular wage work, a type of work closely associated with construction and agriculture, and also highly associated with poverty, provided somewhere between 10 and 15 percent of first jobs throughout the period. It appears, however, that this type of employment, which is also associated with lower levels of education, is starting to decline in recent years.

Non-wage employment continues to be a very important source of jobs for new entrants. It has essentially provided around a third of all first jobs since 1975, with periodic fluctuations around that level. The period of very rapid increase in the share of informal regular employment in the 1980s saw a decline in non-wage employment. This happened again in the mid to late 1990s. Starting at about 2000, non-wage employment started to increase again. We should note that nearly half of non-wage jobs in 2006 are in agriculture, so that an increase in non-wage employment is probably a mark of employment growth in this sector.

5. Conclusion

In light of the review of trends and patterns of unemployment since 1998, this study concluded that there was indeed a widespread decline in unemployment over that period that affected men and women equally, but that was more marked in rural than in urban areas. This declining trend is robust to various changes in the definition of employment and of economic activity and affects both the rate of unemployment as well as the absolute number of unemployed. The only groups to have been left out of this declining unemployment trend are urban women between the ages of 28 and 34 and university graduates. The increase in unemployment for university graduates could well be due to the rapid acceleration in the number of new university graduates entering the labor market since 2000.

In explicating this declining unemployment trend, the study put forth three sets of explanations. A set related to demographic shifts, focused primarily on the relative size of the 15–19 age group, a set related to the slowdown of government hiring and its impact on job search and queuing behavior especially among educated females, and a set related to employment growth in the private sector, and the growth of non-wage employment in rural areas. Although the slowdown in government hiring has reduced the incentive to queue for government jobs, and therefore lower unemployment, this effect is obtained mostly through reduced labor force participation among educated women—the ones eligible for government employment—rather than through increased employment. These are the women whose reservation wage (or opportunity cost of time) is higher than the very low wages the private sector is currently offering young female new entrants with secondary and post-secondary qualifications, leading them to stay out of the labor market altogether. On the employment front, much of the expansion is in non-wage jobs on family farms and in family enterprises. It is not yet clear what sort of incomes this type of activity is able to generate. It can be clearly seen from the labor market entry data that public employment plays an increasingly limited role in the absorption of new entrants. Private sector formal employment is growing, but from a very low base. The increasingly educated new entrants are mostly finding work in informal, but regular, jobs in the private sector, as well as in non-wage employment. Irregular wage employment, which is associated with high vulnerability to poverty, appears to be declining. The main question that remains then is the quality of the jobs that are being created in the informal regular segment of the labor market and in the non-wage segment, and whether earnings from these jobs allow people to support a decent standard of living.

Appendix

Table A1. Number of Unemployed and Unemployment Rate by Sex and Urban/Rural Location, Ages 15–64

Market Labor Force Definition, Using Different Search Criteria, 1998–2006

	Urban				*Rural*				*All Egypt*			
	1998		*2006*		*1998*		*2006*		*1998*		*2006*	
Broad Definition:	'000s	%	'000s	%	'000s	%	'000s	%	'000s	%	'000s	%
Male	485.20	8.2%	519.30	6.9%	641.40	8.5%	378.50	3.8%	1,126.7	8.4%	897.9	5.2%
Female	562.00	25.7%	653.90	22.8%	699.30	36.9%	680.30	19.9%	1,261.3	30.9%	1,334.2	21.2%
Total	1,047.20	12.9%	1,173.20	11.3%	1,340.70	14.2%	1,058.80	8.0%	2,387.9	13.6%	2,232.1	9.4%
Standard Definition:												
Male	396.90	6.8%	469.40	6.3%	533.50	7.1%	337.90	3.4%	930.4	7.0%	807.3	4.7%
Female	478.40	22.8%	552.80	20.0%	598.20	33.3%	575.60	17.4%	1,076.6	27.6%	1,128.4	18.6%
Total	875.30	11.0%	1,022.20	10.0%	1,131.80	12.2%	913.50	7.0%	2,007.0	11.7%	1,935.7	8.3%
Narrow Definition:												
Male	383.20	6.6%	454.80	6.1%	522.50	7.0%	323.80	3.3%	905.7	6.8%	778.6	4.5%
Female	448.80	21.7%	516.40	18.9%	511.90	29.9%	516.20	15.9%	960.7	25.4%	1,032.5	17.3%
Total	832.00	10.5%	971.10	9.6%	1,034.40	11.3%	840.00	6.4%	1,866.4	10.9%	1,811.1	7.8%
Government Search Only:												
Male	13.60		14.70		11.10		14.10		24.7		28.7	
Female	29.60		36.40		86.30		59.50		115.9		95.9	
Total	43.30		51.10		97.40		73.60		140.6		124.6	
Discouraged Unemployed:												
Male	88.40		49.90		107.90		40.60		196.3		90.5	
Female	83.50		101.10		101.10		104.70		184.6		205.8	
Total	171.90		151.00		209.00		145.30		380.9		296.3	
Employment												
Male	5434.2		6974.4		6928.3		9469.4		12362.5		16443.8	
Female	1621.2		2216.5		1197.7		2732.5		2818.9		4948.9	
Total	7055.4		9190.8		8126		12201.9		15181.3		21392.7	

Table A2. Unemployment by Gender and Urban/Rural Location, Ages 15–64

Extended Labor Force Definition, Using Different Search Criteria, 1988–2006

	Urban						*Rural*						*All Egypt*					
	1988		*1998*		*2006*		*1988*		*1998*		*2006*		*1988*		*1998*		*2006*	
	'000s	%	'000s	%	'000s	%	'000s	%	'000s	%	'000s	%	'000s	%	'000s	%	'000s	%
Broad Definition:																		
Male	356.5	7.3%	483.8	8.2%	519.3	6.9%	179.9	3.2%	638.7	8.4%	376.1	3.8%	536.4	5.1%	1,122.5	8.3%	895.5	5.1%
Female	388.5	20.0%	501.6	18.0%	617.5	18.4%	176.9	4.5%	420.0	7.3%	456.9	6.4%	565.4	9.6%	921.7	10.7%	1,074.4	10.2%
Total	745.0	10.9%	985.4	11.3%	1,136.9	10.5%	356.9	3.7%	1,058.7	7.9%	833.1	4.9%	1,101.9	6.7%	2,044.1	9.3%	1,969.9	7.0%
Standard Definition:																		
Male	282.4	5.9%	395.4	6.8%	469.4	6.3%	126.7	2.3%	533.5	7.1%	335.5	3.4%	409.1	3.9%	928.9	7.0%	804.9	4.6%
Female	321.5	17.2%	430.9	15.8%	523.1	16.0%	125.4	3.2%	361.0	6.3%	382.5	5.4%	446.9	7.7%	791.9	9.4%	905.6	8.8%
Total	604.0	9.0%	826.3	9.7%	992.5	9.3%	252.1	2.7%	894.6	6.8%	718.0	4.2%	856.0	5.3%	1,720.9	7.9%	1,710.6	6.2%
Narrow Definition:																		
Male	282.4	5.9%	381.8	6.6%	454.8	6.1%	126.7	2.3%	522.5	7.0%	321.4	3.3%	409.1	3.9%	904.2	6.8%	776.2	4.5%
Female	308.0	16.6%	406.2	15.1%	487.8	15.1%	116.5	3.0%	299.1	5.3%	343.0	4.9%	424.5	7.4%	705.3	8.4%	830.9	8.1%
Total	590.5	8.9%	787.9	9.3%	942.6	8.8%	243.2	2.6%	821.6	6.3%	664.4	3.9%	833.6	5.2%	1,609.5	7.4%	1,607.1	5.8%
Government Search Only:																		
Male	0.0		13.6		14.7		0.0		11.1		14.1		0.0		24.7		28.7	
Female	13.5		24.7		35.3		8.9		61.9		39.5		22.4		86.7		74.8	
Total	13.5		38.4		49.9		8.9		73.0		53.6		22.4		111.4		103.5	
Discouraged Unemployed:																		
Male	74.1		88.4		49.9		53.2		105.2		40.6		127.3		193.6		90.5	
Female	67.0		70.7		94.4		51.5		59.0		74.4		118.5		129.7		168.8	
Total	141.1		159.1		144.3		104.8		164.2		115.0		245.8		323.3		259.4	
Employed:																		
Male	4,525.3		5,435.7		6,979.0		5,422.7		6,937.8		9,556.7		9,948.0		12,373.5		16,535.7	
Female	1,551.8		2,288.6		2,740.3		3,793.4		5,372.5		6,698.4		5,345.2		7,661.1		9,438.7	
Total	6,077.1		7,724.2		9,719.3		9,216.1		12,310.3		16,255.1		15,293.2		20,034.6		25,974.5	

Table A3a. Reasons of Unemployment By Gender, Urban/Rural Location, Ages 15–64

Standard Definition of Unemployment. Market Labor Force Definition, 1998–2006

	Urban				*Rural*				*All Egypt*			
	1998		*2006*		*1998*		*2006*		*1998*		*2006*	
	'000s	%	'000s	%	'000s	%	'000s	%	'000s	%	'000s	%
Absolutely no Job Opportunity												
Male	238.73	60.3%	240.92	51.3%	368.52	69.8%	174.00	51.5%	607.25	65.7%	414.92	51.4%
Female	228.82	48.2%	288.21	52.1%	395.33	66.1%	322.12	56.0%	624.15	58.2%	610.33	54.1%
Total	467.55	53.7%	529.13	51.8%	763.85	67.8%	496.11	54.3%	1231.40	61.7%	1025.25	53.0%
No Appropriate Job Opportunity												
Male	157.02	39.7%	228.50	48.7%	159.54	30.2%	163.91	48.5%	316.56	34.3%	392.40	48.6%
Female	246.26	51.8%	264.55	47.9%	202.89	33.9%	253.51	44.0%	449.15	41.8%	518.06	45.9%
Total	403.27	46.3%	493.05	48.2%	362.43	32.2%	417.42	45.7%	765.70	38.3%	910.47	47.0%
All Unemployed												
Male	395.74	100.0%	469.42	100.0%	528.06	100.0%	337.90	100.0%	923.80	100.0%	807.33	100.0%
Female	475.08	100.0%	552.76	100.0%	598.22	100.0%	575.63	100.0%	1,073.30	100.0%	1,128.39	100.0%
Total	870.82	100.0%	1,022.19	100.0%	1,126.28	100.0%	913.53	100.0%	1,997.10	100.0%	1,935.72	100.0%

Table A3b. Reason for Unemployment Among those Unable to Find Appropriate Job Opportunities By Gender, Urban/Rural Location, Ages 15–64

Standard Definition of Unemployment. Market Labor Force Definition, 1998–2006

	Urban				*Rural*				*All Egypt*			
	1998		*2006*		*1998*		*2006*		*1998*		*2006*	
	'000s	%	'000s	%	'000s	%	'000s	%	'000s	%	'000s	%
No Work Corresponding to Qualifications												
Male	62.21	39.6%	103.78	45.4%	81.72	51.2%	89.25	54.4%	143.93	45.5%	193.03	49.2%
Female	126.45	51.3%	148.42	56.1%	120.44	59.4%	127.01	50.1%	246.89	55.0%	275.43	53.2%
Total	188.67	46.8%	252.20	51.2%	202.16	55.8%	216.25	51.8%	390.83	51.0%	468.45	51.5%
No Work at Acceptable Pay												
Male	24.75	15.8%	58.55	25.6%	29.78	18.7%	48.32	29.5%	54.53	17.2%	106.87	27.2%
Female	14.98	6.1%	31.74	12.0%	19.40	9.6%	55.66	22.0%	34.38	7.7%	87.41	16.9%
Total	39.72	9.9%	90.29	18.3%	49.18	13.6%	103.98	24.9%	88.90	11.6%	194.27	21.3%
No Work at Suitable Organization												
Male	39.36	25.1%	35.40	15.5%	29.09	18.2%	14.63	8.9%	68.45	21.6%	50.03	12.7%
Female	66.02	26.8%	64.56	24.4%	35.23	17.4%	47.47	18.7%	101.26	22.5%	112.03	21.6%
Total	105.38	26.1%	99.97	20.3%	64.32	17.7%	62.09	14.9%	169.70	22.2%	162.06	17.8%
No Work at Suitable Location												
Male	11.11	7.1%	8.26	3.6%	6.71	4.2%	7.72	4.7%	17.82	5.6%	15.98	4.1%
Female	27.79	11.3%	15.96	6.0%	11.15	5.5%	17.72	7.0%	38.95	8.7%	33.68	6.5%
Total	38.91	9.6%	24.22	4.9%	17.86	4.9%	25.44	6.1%	56.77	7.4%	49.65	5.5%
No Work Available for Other Reasons												
Male	19.58	12.5%	22.52	9.9%	12.24	7.7%	3.99	2.4%	31.82	10.1%	26.51	6.8%
Female	11.01	4.5%	3.87	1.5%	16.66	8.2%	5.66	2.2%	27.67	6.2%	9.52	1.8%
Total	30.60	7.6%	26.38	5.4%	28.90	8.0%	9.65	2.3%	59.50	7.8%	36.03	4.0%
All those with no Appropriate Job Opportunity												
Male	157.02	100.0%	228.50	100.0%	159.54	100.0%	163.91	100.0%	316.56	100.0%	392.40	100.0%
Female	246.26	100.0%	264.55	100.0%	202.89	100.0%	253.51	100.0%	449.15	100.0%	518.06	100.0%
Total	403.27	100.0%	493.05	100.0%	362.43	100.0%	417.42	100.0%	765.70	100.0%	910.47	100.0%

Table A4. Unemployment Duration (in Months); Median and Third Quartile by Gender and Urban/Rural Location, Ages 15–64

Market Labor Force Definition, Using Different Search Criteria, 1998–2006

	Urban				*Rural*				*All Egypt*			
	1998		*2006*		*1998*		*2006*		*1998*		*2006*	
	q50	q75	q50	q75	q50	q75	q50	q75	q50	q75	q50	q75
Broad Definition:												
Male	12.0	25.0	18.0	36.0	12.0	36.0	12.0	36.0	12.0	36.0	15.0	36.0
Female	24.0	72.0	36.0	60.0	24.0	60.0	48.0	84.0	24.0	60.0	36.0	72.0
Total	24.0	48.0	24.0	48.0	24.0	48.0	36.0	60.0	24.0	48.0	24.0	60.0
Standard Definition:												
Male	12.0	24.0	24.0	36.0	12.0	40.0	15.0	36.0	12.0	36.0	18.0	36.0
Female	24.0	84.0	36.0	72.0	24.0	60.0	48.0	84.0	24.0	72.0	48.0	84.0
Total	24.0	60.0	24.0	60.0	24.0	48.0	36.0	66.0	24.0	60.0	36.0	60.0
Narrow Definition:												
Male	12.0	24.0	24.0	36.0	12.0	36.0	18.0	36.0	12.0	36.0	18.0	36.0
Female	24.0	84.0	36.0	66.0	24.0	60.0	48.0	84.0	24.0	60.0	42.0	72.0
Total	24.0	48.0	24.0	60.0	24.0	48.0	36.0	60.0	24.0	48.0	36.0	60.0
Government Search Only:												
Male	48.0	60.0	8.0	24.0	168.0	168.0	6.0	12.0	60.0	168.0	6.0	12.0
Female	84.0	84.0	60.0	108.0	48.0	96.0	84.0	120.0	48.0	96.0	72.0	108.0
Total	60.0	84.0	24.2	78.0	48.0	108.0	60.0	96.0	48.0	96.0	48.0	96.0

Notes

1. The author gratefully acknowledges the excellent research assistance provided by Niveen El-Zayat in the preparation of this chapter.
2. The Labor Force Sample Survey (LFSS) 1988 and ELMS 1998 are described in some detail in Assaad (2002).
3. The five border governorates of Matruh, New Valley, Red Sea, North and South Sinai were excluded from the original sample due to their remoteness and limited populations.
4. For more details, see Barsoum (2006).
5. It should be noted that by the extended measures the decline in both standard and broad unemployment was greater in rural Lower Egypt than in rural Upper Egypt.
6. The results for general high school graduates should be interpreted with caution since very few such graduates actually join the labor force. Most simply go on to higher education.
7. Unemployment rates in 1988 were also unrealistically high for lower educated urban females, probably due to some measurement problem.
8. Although there is some question about the rate of growth of female non-wage work in rural areas because of measurement problems, the rate of growth of rural male non-wage work, which does not suffer from these problems, was a healthy 6.1 percent per annum.
9. If the comparison is started in 1975 instead of 1990, the rates would be 6.1 percent per annum for formal employment vs. 5.6 percent per annum for informal regular employment.

References

Assaad, Ragui. 2002. The transformation of the Egyptian labor market: 1988–1998. In *The Egyptian labor market in an era of reform.* Ragui Assaad (ed.), 3–64. Cairo: American University in Cairo Press.

———. 2006a. Why did economic liberalization lead to feminization of the labor force in Morocco and de-feminization in Egypt? In *Gender impact of trade liberalization in the MENA region.* Tunis: Center for Arab Women Training and Research.

———. 2006b. Institutions, household decisions and economic growth in Egypt. In *Explaining growth in the Middle East.* Hashem Pesaran and Jeffrey Nugent (eds.). Amsterdam: North Holland Elsevier.

Barsoum, G. 2006. Egypt labor market panel survey 2006: Final Report. Cairo: The Population Council.

CHAPTER 6

The Impact of Recent Macro and Labor Market Policies on Job Creation in Egypt

Nihal El-Megharbel[1]

There is growing consensus that job creation poses a major challenge for the Egyptian economy. Some 750,000 new jobs need to be created annually to absorb new entrants to the labor market and reduce the annual unemployment rate currently estimated at 11 percent (CAPMAS 2006b). The labor market suffers from a demand-supply mismatch as well as a discrepancy between the outcome of the education system and skill requirements of businesses. Meanwhile, the government remains a major source of non-agricultural employment, as the private sector has fallen short of creating enough jobs to absorb the growing labor force. In addition, the informal sector continues to be the main refuge for low-productivity and low-income employment.

These trends started in the 1970s, became more intense during the 1980s, and have been worsening since the 1990s. Two main factors could be responsible. Firstly, with the government adoption of the employment guarantee scheme in the 1960s, job creation policies were overlooked and employment targets were never incorporated in macroeconomic policies. Moreover, the national employment scheme adopted in 2001 was not part of the national development plan. Secondly, the government tended to deal with job creation through piecemeal, scattered measures and then only in emergencies. In other words, there was no comprehensive strategy for employment.

In light of poor government management of employment and job creation, the question is: what macroeconomic and labor market policies should be adopted to increase employment? To answer this question, the chapter reviews recent macroeconomic and labor market policies, highlights their shortcomings, and suggests some broad measures that could help improve their impact on employment. The chapter comprises four main sections. Following the introduction, section one presents a brief analysis of the Egyptian labor market. Sections 2 and 3 examine successively the impact and limitations of recent macroeconomic and labor market policies on job creation. They also offer a set of proposals to improve the impact of these policies on employment. Section 4 concludes.

1. Main Characteristics of the Labor Market in Egypt

This section summarizes the main characteristics of the Egyptian labor market in order to identify key problems affecting employment creation. The following overview includes basic information on population, labor force, employment, unemployment, and the informal sector.

1.1 Demographic Perspectives

Egypt's population reached 71,348 million in December 2005, 51.2 percent of which are males. During the period 1995–2005, the population increased by almost 20 percent, despite efforts to reduce the annual population growth rate from 2.1 percent in the late 1990s to 1.93 percent in 2005 (IDSC 2007). The share of the age group between 15 and 64 years to total population increased from 57 percent in 1995 to 62 percent in 2005 (World Bank 2007).

1.2 Characteristics of the Labor Force

Egypt's labor force increased from 17 million in 1995 to 22 million in 2005, at an average annual growth rate of 2.8 percent. In addition, the participation of the population in economic activities measured by the ratio of the labor force to the working-age population between 15 and 64 years increased from 29 to 31 percent during the same period (World Bank 2007 and CAPMAS 2006b). The higher growth of the labor force compared to population growth, and the increase in the participation rate of the working-age population were translated into a rise of unemployment, especially that the necessary measures to create enough jobs were inadequate.

1.3 Employment and Unemployment

Employment among the 15–64 age group amounted to 19.3 million in 2005. The sectoral distribution of employment indicates that almost one third of the employed are working in agriculture and fisheries characterized by low value added and productivity. The manufacturing sector, characterized by its forward and backward linkages, employs only 11.5 percent of total workers. The trade and maintenance, and construction sectors were able to absorb only 11.1 and 8.5 percent of employment, respectively. Employment distribution by sector of ownership demonstrates that almost 25.8 percent work in the government and 4.5 percent in the public sector, while the private sector employs 69.7 percent (CAPMAS 2006b).

Unemployment increased from 10.3 percent in 2004 to 11.2 percent in 2005; 7.1 percent for males and 25.1 percent for females. Almost 92 percent of the unemployed were young people in the 15–29 age group. The majority of the unemployed were new entrants to the labor market, who were seeking a job for the first time. Unemployment was distributed evenly between both urban and rural areas. It was mainly concentrated among secondary school graduates (62 percent) and university graduates (27 percent) (CAPMAS 2006b).

1.4 The Informal Labor Market

The Egyptian economy is characterized by a large and growing informal sector that has been a major source of job creation for some time. However, the jobs created in this sector are not *decent* enough in terms of wage, sustainability and work conditions. Moreover, a lot of jobs in the formal sector lack security and stability due to the absence of social security coverage and work contracts, as employers refuse to enter into binding work contracts and complain about the high cost of the social security system.

Population census data[2] indicate that informal employment reached 2.4 million, 2.9 million, and 4.8 million workers in 1976, 1986, and 1996 respectively (El Ehwany and El Laithy 2006), as measured by the number of workers out of establishments and those working in establishments with less than five workers, exclusive of agriculture. Informal employment can also be measured using Labor Force Sample Survey (LFSS) data, in which case it will be defined as the number of private sector workers employed outside establishments (including agriculture). Under this definition, informal employment reached 8.3 million in 2004, and rose to 9 million in 2005,[3] representing 47 percent of total employment. Approximately 20 percent of informal employment was among females, representing 48 percent of total female employment (CAPMAS 2006b).

1.5 Labor Market Imbalances

It is obvious that the labor market in Egypt suffers from major distortions, namely the supply and demand mismatch in terms of job quantity, and the mismatch between skills required by employers and those offered by workers. These distortions are mainly the outcome of prolonged policies that failed to promote economic growth and increase employment.

The employment guarantee program implemented from the 1960s through the 1980s resulted in overstaffed government and public sectors, which became unable to bear the burden of the increasing wage bill. The Open Door policy adopted in the 1970s failed to create enough jobs despite the increase in growth rates, due to inadequate investment policies. Furthermore, the decline in oil prices and increasing dependence on foreign borrowing during the 1980s slowed down economic growth and employment creation. Additionally, the economic reform and structural adjustment program (ERSAP) adopted in the early 1990s resulted in a slowdown of economic growth and reduction in employment.

Despite efforts exerted by the government to boost economic growth and promote job creation, the early years of the new millennium witnessed a sharp recession that negatively impacted job creation. The Egyptian economy was hit by several external shocks that affected its performance, including the East Asian financial crisis during the late 1990s, the decline in oil prices, as well as internal shocks such as the Luxor terrorist attacks against tourists in 1997. These shocks were also topped off by the negative consequences of the September 11 attacks in 2001 and the American occupation of Iraq in 2003.

It is also worth noting that the government failed to adopt adequate labor market policies to overcome the shortcomings of macroeconomic policies and to face the consequences of the different internal and external shocks. The following two sections analyze recent macroeconomic and labor market policies and their impact on job creation.

2. Assessment of the Impact of Macroeconomic Policies on Job Creation in Egypt

The following subsections evaluate the impact of recent investment, trade, and other macroeconomic policies on job creation. They provide policy recommendations in light of international experience.

2.1 Investment Policies

Increasing employment requires higher investment levels and allocating more investments to labor-intensive activities. Despite the slight increase in investment from 19.04 percent in 2004/2005 to 19.92 percent in 2005/2006, it is still below the level needed to create more jobs in the economy. For an incremental capital-output ratio of four, the investment rate must reach 28 percent to achieve a growth rate of 7 percent (Sakr 2003). Considering that the average employment elasticity for the whole economy was 0.3 in 2004/05, a growth rate of 7 percent would increase employment by 2.1 percent.

In addition, investments are mainly allocated to those sectors with low employment intensity of growth. The distribution of investment by economic activity (Figure 6.1) shows that the sectors with low employment elasticities such as transport, communication and the Suez Canal (0.20), mining (0.16), and social services (0.18) receive the largest shares of investments amounting to 19.9, 17.9, and 15.1 percent respectively, in 2004/05. While the activities with the highest employment elasticities that can create more jobs such as manufacturing (0.61), trade, finance and insurance (0.55) and construction (0.51) receive lower shares of investment, amounting to 13.2, 12.3, and 2 percent respectively, during the same year (MOP 2006). At the same time, the average cost per job in the economy increased from LE 60,000 in the 1980s to LE 100,000 in 2004, reflecting poorly on direct employment creation (IMC 2005; Fawzy 2002).

Figure 6.1. Distribution of Investments and Employment Elasticities by Sector in 2005

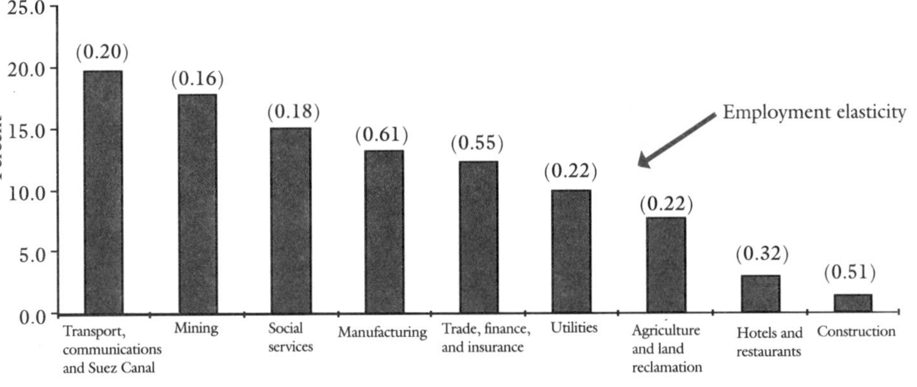

Source: www.mop.gov.eg.

During the last few years, the government made several attempts to increase FDI inflows and succeeded in raising it from US$ 3.9 billion in 2004/05 to US$ 6.1 billion in 2005/06. FDI in non-petroleum sectors increased from US$ 1.4 billion to US$ 4.3 billion,[4] during the same period (CBE 2006). In addition, FDI is expected to increase to US$ 8 billion in 2006/07.

However, recent surveys by the World Bank (2006) and the World Economic Forum (Global Competitiveness Report 2006–07) ranked Egypt in a lower position in terms of business environment and competitiveness (World Bank 2006; WEF 2006). Both reports stressed the importance of improving the business environment by removing all bureaucratic impediments to investment, including dealing with local governments, and dispute settlement. It is worth noting that country experience has shown that improving the investment environment, in terms of starting a business, securing property rights, improving contract enforcement, and dispute settlement procedures, encourages foreign and domestic investment and induces employment (Lopez-Garcia 2006).

Boosting investment also entails increasing domestic savings, stimulating the capital market, reforming the banking sector, and accelerating the privatization process. Besides increasing the investment level, its pattern should also be altered toward increasing employability. Services and labor-intensive manufacturing industries should be encouraged since they have strong forward and backward linkages with other sectors. It is worth noting that establishing industrial clusters has positive effects on job creation, especially for labor-intensive industries such as textiles, furniture, and automotives. Production clusters for means of transportation in the Netherlands, information technology in Ireland and the automotive industry in Austria increased employment opportunities in these countries (Harasty 2004).

2.2 Trade Policy

During the last few years, the government undertook rigorous reforms to accelerate trade liberalization and increase exports through reforming the tariff structure, eliminating non-tariff barriers (NTBs) and adopting a more flexible foreign exchange regime. International experience has shown that the European and East Asian countries that succeeded in increasing employment were among the countries most open to trade. The share of exports to GDP in these countries ranged from 40 to 77 percent. Some of these countries, such as Denmark, devalued their currencies against the currencies of their major trade partners, to boost exports as a means of increasing employment. During the 1990s, Malaysia adopted a dual strategy for import-substitution and export promotion, which resulted in a rapid and sustained decline in unemployment. Labor-intensive, export-oriented industries absorbed the majority of unskilled labor and by the late 1980s Malaysia was a net importer of labor (Harasty 2004).

To increase exports, the Egyptian government implemented two rounds of tariff reduction. In 2004, tariffs were cut to 9.1 percent on average, and the number of ad valorem tariff bands was reduced. In addition, service fees and import surcharges were removed (Ghanem 2006). In February 2007, customs tariffs were reduced on 1,114 articles, including raw materials, and intermediate and consumer goods. The new modifications reduced the average tariffs by almost 25 percent. Moreover, Egypt concluded a number of trade agreements with its main trading partners, namely the EU, the US, and Arab countries. It was expected that the dynamic effects of these agreements would stimulate growth, trade, competition, investment, and employment.

Despite trade liberalization efforts, which resulted in increased non-oil exports, Egypt's export structure remains heavily dominated by resource-based and low-tech exports, which account for nearly 90 percent of manufactured exports.[5] The dominance of resource-based and low-tech exports and the slow pace of diversifying Egypt's export structure into medium- and high-tech activities signal a risk of a gradual decline of its international market share, as the share of low-tech exports in the world market is retreating rapidly.

Figure 6.2. The Share of Egyptian, Turkish and Chinese Manufactured Trade in European and MENA Markets, 1995–2004 (%)

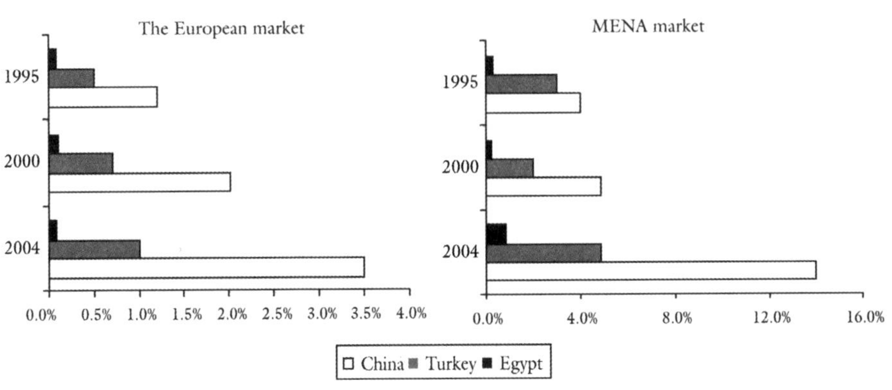

Source: Noureldin, Albaladejo, and El-Megharbel 2006.

In addition, Egypt is losing its share in both the European and MENA markets to competitors such as China and Turkey, especially in labor-intensive textiles and clothing industries.[6] Figure 6.2 shows that Egypt's share of manufactured trade in the European market remained almost stagnant during the period 1995–2004, standing at less than one percent; while the shares of Turkey and China doubled then tripled during the same period. Although Egypt enjoyed a higher share in manufactured trade in MENA market compared to the European market, that share remains low despite the slight increase in 2000 and 2004.

The impact of Egypt's trade agreements on employment is so far negligible. The Egypt-EU Partnership Agreement was restricted to Egyptian tariff dismantling and to the reduction of barriers to EU imports of agricultural products. The Agreement did not address the issue of employment directly; it was only through the funds that Mediterranean Development Aid (MEDA) projects received that employment was targeted. These projects include mainly the Social Fund for Development (SFD) and the Industrial Modernization Program (IMP). In addition, the European Neighborhood Policy (ENP)[7] aims to support the neighbors' priorities regarding political, security, economic, and cultural cooperation. Obviously, employment is not directly targeted (Kamel Rizk and El-Megharbel 2006).

The Ministry of Trade and Industry estimated that 150,000 workers in the textile sector would lose their jobs due to the elimination of the Agreement on Textiles and Clothing (ATC). In a counter move, the government signed the Qualifying Industrial Zones (QIZ) protocol in December 2005. An analysis of the impact of the QIZ protocol revealed that few firms benefited from the agreement. Survey results[8] showed that the majority of firms that export under the QIZ protocol were already exporting to the US and to other markets as well. However, these firms were able to increase their exports to the US under the QIZ protocol, contributing to higher employment (Refaat 2006; Ministry of Trade and Industry 2006).

Despite these short-term gains, it should be noted that these agreements are relatively new and their full impact cannot be assessed accurately. Moreover, to increase their expected benefits, with respect to exports and job creation, a major improvement is required in the performance and competitiveness of the Egyptian manufacturing industries. Moving from low technology to medium and high technology and to higher value-added exports, as well as competing on quality rather than on prices, are important prerequisites for export promotion and creation of *decent* jobs.

The benefits of trade agreements cannot be fully realized unless Egyptian firms become more competitive in international markets. A more comprehensive export promotion strategy that coordinates the different trade agreements is required. These agreements should be used as a catalyst to upgrade and modernize Egyptian manufacturing industries to meet international market standards and gain a foothold in the global production and supply chains. In addition, agreements could be negotiated with the Arab oil-rich countries concerning labor mobility and working conditions as part of the Greater Arab Free Trade Agreement (GAFTA) (Handoussa and El-Oraby 2004).

2.3 Monetary and Fiscal Policies

Promoting economic growth and investment and ultimately increasing employment requires that monetary and fiscal policies be aligned with these objectives. Monetary policy influences job creation through inflation, foreign exchange and bank credit, while fiscal policy affects employment through public spending, taxes and transfers.

2.3.1 Monetary Policy

The attempts of monetary policy to stabilize the foreign exchange market and curb inflation[9] during the past two years had a positive impact on economic growth and investment. However, the lack of bank finance remains a major shortcoming. Credit extended to the private sector has been declining over the past few years, despite the increase in banks' liquidity. This could be explained by the increase in non-performing loans (NPLs), lack of information about the creditworthiness of borrowers, and banks' preference of low-risk investments (Abdel-Kader 2006).

Lack of finance has been repeatedly cited by private sector firms as the main constraint facing business in Egypt. Firms, especially SMEs, claim that tight credit terms, especially collateral requirements and high interest rates are the main impediments they face in acquiring bank credit. However, banks are still the main source of finance for these firms due to the lack of other sources of finance such as the capital market (Abdel-Kader 2006).

International experience has shown that the availability of banking credit has a positive impact on job creation. In a survey carried out by the Canadian Federation of Independent Business (CFIB) in October 1998, one out of four firms surveyed said they were willing to hire more staff if the terms and conditions of banking credit are improved (CFIB 1999). A recent World Bank study showed that easy access to finance for European and Central

Asian firms contributed the most to employment creation in the private sector. The study also noted that high real interest rate or cost of credit negatively affected employment in these countries (Lopez-Garcia 2006).

In light of international experience, a more developed financial market will have positive effects on employment creation in the private sector. Lowering interest rate, easing credit policies, and speeding up the privatization of banks will encourage the establishment of new firms and the expansion of existing ones, ultimately raising employment.

2.3.2 Fiscal Policy

The new income tax law enacted in July 2005 reduced the tax burden by 50 percent, eliminated tax exemptions and benefits, and simplified the tax structure and administration. These reforms aimed at increasing disposable income, widening the tax base, and enhancing economic growth. In addition, the government adopted a two-year plan to streamline and modernize the tax administration and increase the efficiency of collection. Unlike previous reports, the recent 2006–2007 Global Competitiveness Survey indicated that tax regulations and tax rates are not considered the most problematic factors for doing business in Egypt (WEF, several issues).

These results are consistent with empirical evidence showing that increased taxes in European countries contributed to the decline of employment (Dhont and Heylen 2004). In addition, the previously cited World Bank study noted that lowering taxes and applying a simple and transparent tax system would encourage the establishment of new firms and raise employment in European and Asian countries (Lopez-Garcia 2006).

Despite the expected positive impact of recent tax reforms on investment, employment, and growth, the large fiscal deficit and public debt that the Egyptian economy witnessed recently represent major constraints for growth and investment. The net outcome of these contradicting effects could not be predicted. Consequently, more efforts are needed to reduce public debt and to control the fiscal deficit in order to promote economic growth, increase investment, and create more jobs (Refaat 2007).

To sum up, the reform measures that the government undertook in the last two years to promote investment, boost exports, curb inflation, and improve public finances, fell short of increasing employment. More rigorous and continuous reforms are required to improve the business environment, encourage labor-intensive investment, promote medium- and high-tech exports, create a more developed financial market, and reduce public debt and government deficit. In addition to the role of macroeconomic policies in stimulating employment, it is also important to examine the impact of labor market policies on job creation. This will be discussed in the next section.

3. Assessment of Labor Market Policies in Egypt

Labor market policies are defined as government interventions used to correct for failures in the labor market. There are three sets of labor market policies: active, passive, and institutional policies. Despite the extensive use of these policies in most developed countries, empirical evidence has shown that they do not succeed in developing countries, due to the lack of administrative capacity and scarcity of the monitoring and evaluation tools considered crucial for their implementation. The following sub-sections evaluate the impact of both active and institutional labor market policies[10] on the Egyptian labor market.

3.1 Active Labor Market Policies (ALMPs)

Active labor market policies (ALMPs) might affect the demand side by creating additional jobs directly through public works programs. They might also be supply-side interventions by training the unemployed to meet the requirements of the labor market. In some cases, they are used to correct for failures in the education system. Further, they can provide a link between both sides of the labor market through employment offices and labor market information. During the 1990s several countries, including Egypt, used different active labor market programs to overcome labor market malfunctions.

3.1.1 Public Works Programs

The public works program (PWP) implemented through the SFD aimed mainly to improve infrastructure in rural and deprived urban areas as well as to create jobs. However, these projects, which included roads, water supply, and sewage, were capital intensive and the share of workers' wages did not exceed 30 percent of total cost on average. During the period 1994–2000, PWP created more than 6,000 permanent jobs and more than 100,000 temporary jobs. Yet, the extension of these jobs beyond the duration of the project is questioned (De Gobbi and Nesporova 2005).

The National Program for Integrated Rural Development, known as the Shorouk program, is another example of a PWP. This program aimed at providing job opportunities in rural areas in order to close the socio-economic gap between rural and urban areas. The investment required for this program was estimated at LE 267 billion during the period 1994–2017. The program provided more than 4,000 villages and rural communities with potable water, wastewater treatment, electricity, and health and education services. In addition, it created 59,000 permanent jobs and 123,000 temporary ones during the period 1994–2000. This confirms doubts about the continuity of the jobs created by public works programs (Abdel Fatah 2004).

PWPs implemented in Hungary present a good example of the impact of these programs on job creation. In 1996, Hungary established the National Council for Public Works, including representatives of different ministries to assess projects and allocate funds for those selected. Moreover, regional public works councils were established to supervise the implementation of the different projects. In 2000, 52 programs were approved hiring around 5,000 workers, with a total cost of HUF 2 billion. The most important advantage of these programs was the on-the-job training supported by the labor market fund to improve the employability chances of workers after the completion of the projects (Harasty 2004).

It should be noted that in order to improve the employability effect of PWPs, projects must be carefully designed to ensure labor-intensity. In addition, on-the-job training must be provided to upgrade workers skills according to market requirements to increase their opportunities to land decent jobs after the completion of these projects.

3.1.2 Micro and Small Enterprise (MSEs) Development Programs

These include the Mubarak Solidarity Program launched in 1996, which extends loans to small projects. This program allocated LE 65.3 million at an interest rate of 3 to 4 percent to 2.6 million beneficiaries. The Small Enterprise Development Organization (SEDO) affiliated to the SFD is another example of these projects. During the period 1994–2000, SEDO created around 465,000 permanent jobs and almost 59,000 temporary jobs. The Productive Family Program, Bank Nasser, businessmen associations, and credit guarantee programs also provide financial support to MSEs, to promote job creation.

These programs are not very effective in terms of employment creation and their impact does not go beyond the loan duration. Further, the impact of these programs on job creation is limited due to the lack of follow-up and evaluation mechanisms. The death rate of these firms is very high due to limited expertise, lack of demand, and constrained borrowing procedures (De Gobbi and Nesporova 2005). In 2005, the government launched "The National Strategy for Microfinance" with the main objective of providing financial services to the poor and MSEs. The strategy also aims to establish a microfinance industry and integrate it in the development of the financial sector. However, the impact of this strategy on MSEs development and employment creation has yet to be assessed.

In what follows, the study will present some success stories for MSEs development. In 2000, the International Labor Organization (ILO) and a number of non-governmental organizations (NGOs) collaborated on a project to provide business development training to four ethnic groups in Vietnam. The program was successful as 80 percent of the trainees received loans to start a business. More than 67 percent of these loans were invested in non-farm projects. The effectiveness of these programs depended on the loans extended to trainees to establish businesses and on closely monitoring and evaluating the development of these projects (Christensen and Lamotte 2001).

The Philippine Exporters Confederation provided training programs for new entrepreneurs and sub-contracted them to produce some products that were exported through well-established exporters. These programs increased employment, especially for females (Philexport Pioneers 2003). The Japan Small Business Corporation supports MSEs by enhancing the capacity of policy makers, local government representatives, and NGOs working in the field of MSEs development (Harasty 2004).

The main lessons learned from these experiences are related to the problems that MSEs encounter in Egypt. These firms lack expertise and could benefit a great deal from capacity building programs and from establishing close links with exporters and large firms, to overcome weak demand and the need for marketing plans. Moreover, a large number of NGOs are providing technical and financial support to MSEs, therefore raising the capacity of these NGOs could reflect positively on MSEs.

3.1.3 Availability of Labor Market Information

The Ministry of Manpower and Migration (MoMM) gathers information through its network of local employment offices regarding job vacancies and announces them in its monthly bulletin. Most of these vacancies are blue-collar jobs with low salaries. In addition, these offices lack the skills required for proper screening of jobseekers. Consequently, the placement rate reached through the monthly bulletin is usually very modest. Table 6.1 shows that government employment offices provided only 16 percent of the main and secondary jobs, while 33 percent of these jobs were made available through direct contacts and applying directly for jobs, and 26 percent by friends and relatives (CAPMAS 2006a).

Table 6.1. Distribution of Channels of Getting Jobs

Getting main and secondary jobs	*Share of total (%)*
Contacted firms, applied for a job vacancy	33
Friends or relatives	26
Governmental recruitment office	16
Competition	12
Private recruitment office	5
Other	5
Newspapers and other ads.	3
Total	100

Source: CAPMAS (2006a).

The Canadian International Development Agency (CIDA) and the United States Department of Labor (USDOL) initiated a project to upgrade public employment services in Egypt. The project developed 27 employment offices, one per governorate. In addition, more than 60 offices were developed by MoMM with the assistance of CIDA. The new offices focus mainly on employment services and are not concerned with other activities such as labor inspection and labor relations (Kamel 2006).

The Australian Job Network, established in 1998, provides an example of best practices in the field of employment offices and labor market information. The job network included around 200 government and private institutions, with the main objective of securing long-term jobs for the unemployed. The network provides training for job seekers in job search skills and assists them in writing and updating resumes, preparing applications, and preparing for interviews. In three months, the network secured jobs or provided training for 73 percent of job seekers. Korea also provides a good example in providing labor market information and job placement services through its Employment Stabilization Program (Harasty 2004).

Employment offices play an important role in providing information and advice for job seekers. Upgrading employment offices and raising their technical capacities will help bridge the gap between labor market demand and the supply of skills.

3.1.4 Human Resource Development Policies

The 2006 Egypt Labor Market Panel Survey (ELMPS) revealed that 15.5 million workers, representing 69 percent of total employment (around 22.5 million workers) acquired their skills through technical education and vocational training (TEVT). Table 6.2 shows the distribution of the skills acquired by these employees through different channels. Public sector firms were the least interested in acquiring skills. Government and formal private sector employees gained skills mainly through regular vocational education. Informal private workers received on-the-job training through the craftsmen with whom they work and through family members (CAPMAS 2006a).

Table 6.2. Distribution of the Skills Acquired by Employees in Different Employment Sectors

	Channels of Skill Acquirement					
Employment Sector	*Regular Vocational Education*	*Regular Vocational Training*	*Through Contractors*	*Through Craftsmen*	*Other*	*Total*
Government	67	36	2	4	4	26
Public Sector	8	14	1	3	2	5
Formal Private Sector	17	22	4	18	10	14
Informal Private Sector	7	15	14	51	71	41
Unidentified	1	13	79	25	13	14
Total Shares	100	100	100	100	100	100
Total Number	5,185,995	718,674	533,209	3,161,194	5,942,442	15,541,514

Source: CAPMAS (2006a).

In general, private sector firms do not provide their employees with adequate training, with the exception of very limited on-the-job training for basic production skills. Only a small number of large local firms and transnational corporations (TNCs) allocate some resources for training and use modern training methods. This could be explained by lack of awareness of the benefits of training, and the fear of poaching trained workers by other firms. In addition, the government does not provide any incentives to encourage firms to engage in training programs, such as sharing the costs of training, or providing tax holidays for firms involved in such activities.

A major problem facing TEVT is the large number of informal workers who do not receive proper training, except on-the-job training, which is usually incomplete and outdated, and limited training courses offered by some NGOs. In addition, despite the large amounts of funds available to TEVT, it still suffers from fragmentation of efforts and the large number of various bodies involved.[11]

These market failures could be addressed through incentive schemes for in-house training, disseminating best training practices, and awareness campaigns of the benefits of training in improving efficiency and cutting costs, especially overseas training. There is an increasing trend to involve private sector firms in the design and delivery of training, but these efforts are still limited and require more involvement of businesses. Despite the initiatives undertaken, the impact remains limited due to lack of coordination among different stakeholders active in this field (ETF 2005). Spain, Malaysia, and the Philippines are good examples of countries that adopted skills development and vocational training programs that succeeded in increasing employment (Harasty 2004).

To conclude, ALMPs have not been effective in creating jobs. This could be explained by the fact that these programs are dispersed and lack coordination among them. Moreover, ALMPs should be considered as short-term solutions to overcome labor market failures. Consequently, the impact of these policies on job creation should not be overstated. These policies must also be aligned with macroeconomic policies in a global framework of a national employment strategy that aims at increasing employment.

3.2 Institutional Policies of the Labor Market

Institutional policies include labor market regulations and wage policies. This section analyzes the impact of the labor law and minimum wage policy on job creation in Egypt.

3.2.1 Labor Market Regulations

Theoretical analysis has shown that the effect of labor market regulations on employment and unemployment is ambiguous. Consequently, researchers turned to focus on empirical investigation to reach a conclusion. The majority of these studies suggested that labor market regulations have two conflicting effects: they reduce unemployment while at the same time represent a major barrier for employment. In addition, empirical evidence has shown that the high labor cost associated with stringent labor market regulations affect employment negatively, especially female and youth employment (OECD 2004).

The Labor Law enacted in 2003[12] accorded employers more flexibility, especially in relation to termination of contracts for well-established economic reasons. However, the impact of this law on job creation is so far uncertain. It is evident that public sector jobs are still more attractive because of the high level of protection they provide in relation to termination of workers' contracts, social insurance, and other benefits such as the comfortable working hours that allow workers to moonlight to raise their income. In addition, informal employment reached 47 percent of total employment according to the 2005 LFSS. These facts reflect the limited impact of labor regulations on creating jobs in general and *decent* jobs in particular.

The social security system in Egypt provides wide coverage as it includes government, public, and private sector workers, informal employment, employees working abroad, and some vulnerable groups.[13] In 2004/2005, employees covered by the social security system were estimated at 93 percent. However, the social security system is criticized for its high contribution rates, which discourage both employees and employers from paying their contributions and reporting actual wages. In addition, the maximum wage according to which the social security contributions are calculated is very low. Another significant disadvantage of the system is the lack of financial sustainability (Helmy 2006a).

Empirical evidence has also shown that labor market regulations support protected workers and raise their bargaining power. Recently, a number of public and private sector firms witnessed strikes by workers protesting against late payment and complaining of delayed promotion, among other things. The government met some of the workers' demands and promised to consider their employment situation in the near future.

Broadly, labor market regulation should strike a balance between increased labor market flexibility and relatively high social protection for workers. The Danish model of labor market regulation presents a good practice in this respect. Labor market regulations in Denmark provide a mix of flexible labor market, generous welfare system for the unemployed, and active labor market programs that help the unemployed to join the labor market, especially for the young unskilled unemployed. However, it should be noted that this system is expensive, as the Danish government allocated 5 percent of its GDP to both active and passive labor market programs (OECD 2004). Labor market regulations in Egypt might need to be revised to include more incentives for employers to increase employment, especially for females and young graduates. More importantly, these regulations should also be integrated into a national employment strategy.

3.2.2 Minimum Wage Policy

The impact of minimum wage policy on employment is controversial. Several studies claimed that minimum wage affects employment positively, while others showed they have negative effects on employment. Empirical evidence suggests that minimum wage is close to the average wage in developing countries, suggesting that minimum wage regulations are not enforced. Consequently, raising the minimum wage would harm young, unskilled, and female workers. In addition, labor regulations are poorly enforced in these countries, hence a large proportion of workers are engaged in the informal sector, earning less than the minimum wage. When unemployment is relatively high, both workers and employers will not have any incentive to comply with minimum wage regulations (Neumark and Wascher 2004).

The actual average monthly minimum wage in the public sector enterprises amounted to LE 168, while it is only LE 154 in the private sector. Usually, private sector firms ignore the minimum wage and the social insurance requirements determined by the Labor Law. In addition, the non-wage benefits offered by public sector jobs make them more attractive than private sector jobs. In general, wages have declined significantly in real terms over the past few decades (Helmy 2006b).

In order to raise minimum wages and at the same time avoid the negative effects on vulnerable groups, it might be useful to reduce the social insurance contributions of both employer and employee, especially for females and young people. In addition, labor market regulations in general and those related to minimum wage in particular should be enforced to ensure compliance by private sector firms.

4. Conclusion

Job creation is among the most important challenges facing the Egyptian economy. Despite increased economic growth, unemployment is still high and the capacity of the economy to generate enough jobs especially in the private sector remains limited. In addition, the labor market suffers from a mismatch between demand and supply of adequate skills. The poor performance of the labor market can be explained by a number of factors including macroeconomic and labor market policies. The government undertook several reform measures to boost economic growth, increase investments, and raise the competitiveness of the Egyptian economy. However, the Egyptian economy is still suffering from major shortcomings, such as an unfavorable business environment, poor export performance, severe fiscal imbalance, and low levels of investment. In addition, labor market policies have so far been unable to address the mismatch between demand and supply or to resolve other market failures. The impact of active labor market policies and regulations has been limited, reflecting poor policy design and lack of coordination between macroeconomic and labor market policies and regulations. Moreover, it should be noted that macroeconomic and labor market policies were not adequately coordinated to serve the objective of increasing job creation.

In order to increase employment, a national employment strategy should be designed with the objective of creating more jobs, especially in those sectors with the highest employment elasticity. The strategy should also attempt to address the mismatch between labor supply and demand. More importantly, it should be made an integral part of Egypt's national development plan.[14] Finally, both macroeconomic and labor market policies should be revised in light of the shortcomings highlighted, taking into consideration the lessons drawn from best practices and international experiences.

Notes

1. This study was presented in the first annual ECES conference on the Egyptian economy entitled "The Egyptian Economy: Current Challenges and Future Prospects," November 21–22, 2006, and in the workshop on *"Employment Policies in Arab Mediterranean Countries: How Are They Reacting to Trade Liberalization and Social Change?"* as part of the 8th Mediterranean Research Meeting, held in Florence March 21–25, 2007. The author would like to thank Professors Hanaa Kheir-El-Din, Naglaa El Ehwany, and Ragui Assaad for their help and support during the preparation of the study. Thanks also go to Professor Soad Kamel and Ummuhan Bardak for their valuable comments.
2. Egypt carries out a population census every ten years. The preliminary results of the 2006 census were released recently, while the cross tabulation data that could be used to estimate the size of informal employment have not been disclosed yet.
3. It is worth noting that the size of informal employment using the census and LFSS is not comparable. LFSS data do not provide cross tabulation of employment by sector, economic activities, or "outside or inside of establishment" criteria.
4. Of which US$ 3.3 billion in greenfield projects and expansion of existing ones and US$ 906 million as privatization proceeds.
5. Out of Egypt's most important 20 groups of exports (those with the highest average export value during the period 1990–2004), eight product groups are primary exports. These include crude oil and natural gas, cotton, rice, aluminum, unprocessed vegetables and fruits, as well as stone, sand and gravel. The other 12 export groups are concentrated in the resource-based and low-tech export categories. A few exceptions are in the medium-tech export category, such as further-processed iron and steel; sanitary, heating, and lighting equipment; plastics, packaging material, automotive components, and some household appliances (Noureldin, Albaladejo, and El-Megharbel 2006).
6. It should be noted, however, that Egypt was able to increase its exports of textiles and clothing to the US mainly due to the QIZ protocol (Pigato and Ghoneim 2006).
7. ENP was adopted by the EU and its Mediterranean partners, Russia, Ukraine, Byelorussia, Moldavia, Azerbaijan, and Georgia.
8. Namely two surveys: the Egyptian Center for Economic Studies Survey (49 firms) and the Ministry of Trade and Industry/Industrial Modernization Center Survey (257 firms).
9. However, these positive effects could very well be reversed by the recent increase in inflation during late 2006 and early 2007.
10. Passive labor market policies are income support policies that include early retirement schemes, workers shareholders associations, social protection programs, and unemployment benefits. They will not be discussed since they are generally used to protect the unemployed and laid-off workers without increasing their employability.
11. The funds allocated to TEVT include the Training Finance Fund (TFF) established under the Labor Law. According to the law, a one percent levy on net profits of firms employing 10 or more workers will be allocated to this fund. The levy is expected to yield between LE 300 million and LE 400 million a year. Another fund was provided through the EU Technical, Vocational and Educational Training Reform Program with a total amount of 33 million from the EU and an equal amount from the Egyptian government. Moreover, the World Bank offered a $15 million loan for the Skills Development Project (SDP), which started in 2004 and is expected to continue for four years. Other TEVT projects include the National Skills Standards Project (NSSP), the Productivity and Vocational Training Department (PVTD), and the training programs provided by the Ministry of Reconstruction and Housing, the Ministry of Social Solidarity, and the Ministry of Military Production. There is also

the Mubarak-Kohl Initiative (MKI), the human resource development program under the Industrial Modernization Centre (IMC), and the Industrial Training Center.

12. This law relates to private sector workers and employees while civil service workers are governed by Law 47 of 1978.
13. Those who receive Sadat pension.
14. It should be noted that Egypt is part of the ILO Youth Employment Network (YEN) and MoMM is currently working on designing a national plan of action for youth employment.

References

Abdel Fatah, Mahmoud Mansour. 2004. Employment flexibility in Egypt. Employment Strategy. Department, ILO, March, unpublished.

Abdel-Kader, Khaled. 2006. *Private sector access to credit in Egypt: Evidence from survey data.* ECES Working Paper Series, no. 111. Egypt: the Egyptian Center for Economic Studies.

CAPMAS (Central Agency for Public Mobilization and Statistics). 2006a. Egypt Labor Market Panel Survey (ELMPS), Unpublished.

———. 2006b. Labor Force Sample Survey, August.

CBE (Central Bank of Egypt). 2006. *Monthly Statistical Bulletin*, October.

CFIB (Canadian Federation of Independent Business). 1999. Small business outlook for 1999: Results of CFIB survey on business expectations. www.cfib.ca

Christensen, Jens Dyring, and David Lamotte. 2001. Ethnic Minorities – Emerging Entrepreneurs in Rural Viet Nam: A Study of the Impact of Business Training on Ethnic Minorities. SEED Working Paper No. 13 InFocus Programme on Boosting Employment through Small Enterprise Development Job Creation and Enterprise Department, ILO, Geneva.

De Gobbi, Maria Sabrina, and Alena Nesporova. 2005. *Towards a new balance between labor market flexibility and employment security for Egypt.* Employment Strategy Papers, no. 10. Geneva: ILO, Employment Policies Unit.

Dhont. Tine and Freddy Heylen. 2005. Fiscal policy, employment and growth: Why is the EURO area lagging behind? Paper presented at the European Economic Association Conference, Amsterdam, August.

El Ehwany, Naglaa and Heba El Laithy. 2006. Employment–poverty linkages.Towards a pro-poor employment policy framework in Egypt, unpublished paper submitted to the International Labour Office. Cairo, Egypt.

European Training Foundation (ETF). 2005. Country overview on labor market policies in Egypt. Working document.

Fawzy, Samiha. 2002. *Investment policies and unemployment in Egypt* (in Arabic). ECES Working Paper Series, no. 68. Cairo: the Egyptian Center for Economic Studies.

Ghanem, Amina. 2006. An assessment of policies and reforms since July 2004. In the Egyptian Competitiveness Report: 2005–2006.

Handoussa, Heba and Nivine El Oraby. 2004. *Civil service wages and reform: The case of Egypt.* ECES Working Paper Series, no. 98. Egypt: the Egyptian Center for Economic Studies.

Harasty, Claire. 2004. *Successful employment and labor market policies in Europe and Asia and the Pacific.* ILO, Employment Strategy Papers Series, no. 4.

Helmy, Omneia. 2006a. *The new pension system in Egypt.* ECES Working Paper Series, no. 116. Egypt: the Egyptian Center for Economic Studies.

———. 2006b. *Towards developing the minimum wage policy in Egypt.* ECES Policy Viewpoint Series, no. 18. Egypt: the Egyptian Center for Economic Studies.

IDSC (Information and Decision Support Center). 2007. Accessed at: www.IDSC.gov.eg.

IMC (Industrial Modernization Center). 2005. Egypt's industrial development strategy. Industry: The engine of growth (unpublished).

Kamel, Maggie. 2006. *Situation analysis of youth employment in Egypt.* Report prepared by the Centre for Project Evaluation and Macroeconomic Analysis (PEMA). Ministry of International Cooperation, October.

Kamel Rizk, Soad and Nihal El-Megharbel. 2006. The impact of the EUROMED Partnership Agreement on employment in eight southern Mediterranean countries: The case of Egypt. Unpublished report, June.

Lopez-Garcia. Paloma 2006. *Business environment and labor market outcomes in Europe and Central Asia countries.* World Bank Research Working Paper, no. 3885.

MOP (Ministry of Planning). 2006. Accessed at: www.mop.gov.eg, October 2006.

Neumark, David, and William Wascher. 2004. Minimum wages, labor market institutions, and youth employment: A cross-national analysis. *Industrial and Labor Relations Review.*

Noureldin, Diaa, Manuel Albaladejo, and Nihal El-Megharbel. 2006. Industrial competitiveness: Engine of growth? In the *Egyptian Competitiveness Report*: 2005–2006. Egyptian National Competitveness Council (ENCC). Cairo, May.

OECD. 2004. Employment protection and regulation and labor market performance. In *OECD Employment Outlook*, July.

Pigato, Miria and Ahmed Ghoneim. 2006. *Egypt after the end of the multi-fiber agreement: A comparative regional analysis.* ECES Working Paper Series, no. 114. Egypt: the Egyptian Center for Economic Studies.

Philexport Pioneers. 2003. Successful programs for SMEs. *Philippine Employer*, Manila, May.

Refaat, Amal. 2007. *Egypt's global competitiveness: Unlocking the 2006–2007 report.* Policy Viewpoint, no. 20. Egypt: the Egyptian Center for Economic Studies.

———. 2006. Assessing *the impact of the QIZ protocol on Egypt's textile and clothing industry.* ECES Working Paper Series, no. 113. Egypt: the Egyptian Center for Economic Studies.

Sakr, M. Fathi. 2003. Physical capital and challenges of rapid growth … the case of Egypt. Paper presented at the conference "Towards an Egyptian Industrial Policy: The Horizontal Dimension." Center for European Studies, Cairo University and Industrial Modernization Center, unpublished.

World Economic Forum (WEF). 2006. The Global Competitiveness Report 2006–2007.

———. Several issues. *The Global Competitiveness Report.*

World Bank. 2006. Doing Business Report 2007.

———. 2007. *World Development Indicators (WDI).* Online database.

CHAPTER 7

Toward a More Efficient and Equitable Pension System in Egypt

Omneia Helmy

The Egyptian government has recently been engaged in developing a new pension system based on a unified law. The new system aims to provide a decent pension for the elderly; achieve social security for individuals with no pension; and encourage participant employees to target their own pension by changing the methods of defining individual pensions, funding accrued pensions, and managing pension funds.

This new approach has been developed to address the current pension system's inability to achieve fiscal sustainability. The liabilities of the current system are estimated at approximately 141 percent of GDP as opposed to 48 percent in reserves. Moreover, the current system can achieve neither economic efficiency nor equitable income distribution (National Democratic Party 2003 and 2006; Al-Gibaly 2006; Central Auditing Organization 2006; Institute of National Planning 2006; IDSC 2005; Helmy 2004; World Bank 2006a).

However, introducing a new pension system in Egypt has raised concerns about the rights of participants in the current system as well as protection of pensioners and their eligible survivors. Accordingly, this study aims to explore the new pension system and its institutional framework, study and analyze potential impact of its implementation, and offer a set of proposals that would help honor workers' rights. It also aims to protect pensioners and their eligible survivors and achieve the interests of the national economy as a whole in light of relevant international experience.

The study comprises three main sections in addition to the conclusion. Section 1 highlights the different aspects of the current pension system and identifies its deficiencies. Section 2 outlines the main features of the new system and its institutional framework, and analyzes the potential impact of its implementation. Finally, Section 3 proposes a set of measures that would help protect and promote the interests of workers, pensioners and their eligible survivors, as well as the national economy as a whole. Section 4 concludes.

1. The Importance of Shifting to a New Pension System

It is useful to highlight different aspects of the current pension system before pointing out its defects that entail shifting to a new system.

The Current System

The current pension system in Egypt is characterized by wide coverage, being based on four laws (see Table 7.1) that target government employees, public and private business sector workers, private sector employers and the self-employed, casual workers, Sadat Pension eligible recipients, and Egyptians working abroad. In 2004/05, the system covered a large percentage of the employed (93 percent) as compared to merely 30 percent in the Middle East and North Africa countries, and approximately 7.5 million pensioners and their eligible survivors. Additionally, the current system provides protection against several risks that prevent workers from continuing to work, most importantly: old age, disability, and death (World Bank 2006a and b).

Table 7.1. Egypt's Social Insurance Laws: Scope of Coverage and Covered Risks

Law (degree of enforcement)	*Scope of Coverage*	*Covered Risks*
79/1975 (Mandatory)	Government employees and public and private business sector workers	Old age, disability, death, work injury, and maternity
108/1976 (Mandatory)	Private sector employers and the self-employed	Old age, disability, and death
112/1980 (and Sadat Pension) (Mandatory)	Casual workers*	Old age, disability, and death
50/1978 (Optional)	Egyptians working abroad	Old age, disability, and death

Notes: (*) Casual labor includes any worker working for others and does not meet the requirements of becoming subject to the Social Insurance Law 79/1975.
Source: Ministry of Social Insurance and Social Affairs (2003/2004; 2003a; 2000/2001).

Due to Egypt's relatively young population structure, the current pension system's balance of reserves reached 48 percent of GDP in 2004/2005 (National Democratic Party 2006). Next to savings with the banking system, pension funds became the second most important source of long-term funding in the country in 2005. According to the Central Bank of Egypt's 2004/05 annual report, pension funds represented more than 30 percent of total available savings in the Egyptian economy in 2005, compared to savings with the banking system, which amounted to approximately 56 percent of total savings funds.

Shortcomings of the Current System

Despite its several advantages, the current Egyptian pension system is unable to achieve fiscal sustainability. The deficit in collected contributions to cover expenditures on pension benefits rose from LE 2.8 billion to approximately LE 6.6 billion during 2000/01–2004/05 as illustrated by Figure 7.1. Based on available actuarial studies, this deficit is expected to rise to LE 40 billion in 2020, LE 327 billion in 2050, and LE 2 trillion in 2075.[1] Moreover, the current system's liabilities are estimated at approximately 141 percent of GDP as opposed to 48 percent in reserves (National Democratic Party 2006; Institute of National Planning 2006; Al-Gibaly 2006).

Figure 7.1. Inability of Net Collected Contributions to Cover Expenditures on Pension Benefits (2000/01–2004/05) (LE billion)

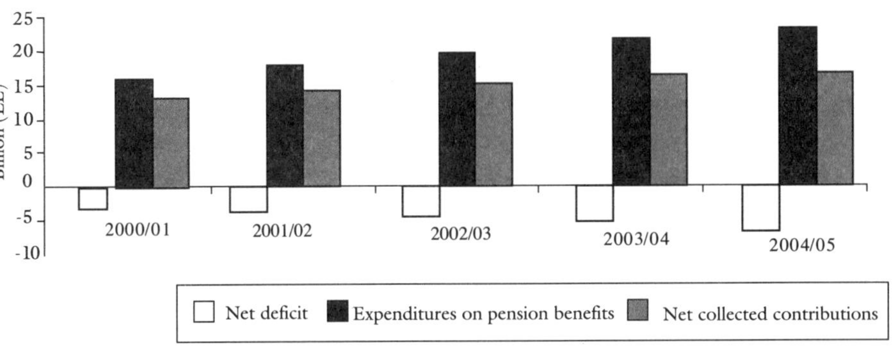

Sources: Ministry of Finance (2006); Al-Gibaly (2006); People's Assembly (2006a, b, and c; 2005a and b; 2004; and 2003a and b).

In addition to its inability to achieve fiscal sustainability, the current system lacks economic efficiency and equity in income distribution. As explained below, there are four main factors responsible for the current system's inadequate performance: high dependency ratios, applied rules, method of funding pension benefits, and the means of managing pension funds.

High Dependency Ratios

Despite Egypt's young population structure, the ratio of pensioners to contributors to the pension system is high (39 percent)[2] compared to ratios prevailing in the Middle East and North Africa (MENA) countries (27 percent), Latin America (25 percent), and Asia (11 percent). The current system's high dependency ratio is attributed to several factors, most importantly: the improvement in life expectancy at retirement, decline in the birth rate,[3] increase in unemployment to 10 percent particularly among the 15–40 age group, and the expansion of the informal business sector. Hence, the number of new entrants to the system is decreasing, and many workers start their careers at a late age thus becoming eligible for pension after merely a few years of service. In other words, contributions are declining while expenditures on an increasing number of pensioners are rising (Ministry of State for Economic Development 2006, Galal 2005, IDSC 2005, International Labor Office 2006, World Bank 2002a, Palacios and Pallares-Miralles 2000, Lindbeck and Persson 2000, Sinn 2000).

Applied Rules

Certain rules of the current system—such as high contribution rate, low ceiling on monthly covered wage, setting individual pension based on the defined benefit technique,[4] and lenient pension eligibility terms for early retirement—weaken its fiscal sustainability and economic efficiency, as well as its ability to achieve equitable income distribution.

High contribution rate

Table 7.2 shows that the contribution rate for government employees, and public and private business sector workers is high; i.e., up to 40 percent and 35 percent of a worker's basic and variable salaries, respectively.

Although this high contribution rate aims to cover accrued pensions, healthcare, and other risks the individual may face—such as work injuries—it is much higher than that prevailing in the MENA countries such as Algeria, Libya, Tunisia, Morocco, and Jordan where it ranges from merely 8 to 14 percent.

A high contribution rate discourages compliance, causing many participants to evade paying their due contributions either for themselves or for their employees or rather contribute at much less than their real incomes (Helmy 2004, Ministry of Social Insurance 2003b, National Democratic Party 2003, Abdel Rahman Mohamed 2002). As a result, outstanding contribution proceeds for the "Social Insurance Fund for Workers at Public and Private Business Sectors" dropped by 17 percent in 2001 compared to the previous year. Additionally, total indebtedness of contributors to this fund rose from LE 2.6 billion in June 2001 to over LE 5 billion in June 2005 (Public and Private Business Sector Employees Fund, annual report and closing accounts, various issues; Central Auditing Organization 2001; Ministry of Social Insurance 2000/01).

Table 7.2. Contribution Shares as a Percentage of Covered Wage

Wage Components	*Government Employees*		*Public Business Sector Workers*		*Private Business Sector Workers*	
	Basic	*Variable*	*Basic*	*Variable*	*Basic*	*Variable*
Employer (E)/ Worker (W)	E/W	E/W	E/W	E/W	E/W	E/W
Old age and disability	15/10	15/10	15/10	15/10	15/10	15/10
Severance compensation	2/3	-	2/3	-	2/3	-
Unemployment insurance	-	-	2/0	2/0	2/0	2/0
Health insurance	3/1	3/1	3/1	3/1	4/1	4/1
Work injuries	1/0	1/0	2/0	2/0	3/0	3/0
Total	21/14	19/11	24/14	22/11	26/14	24/11
Overall total	35	30	38	33	40	35

Sources: National Democratic Party (2006), World Bank (2006a).

The drop in collected contributions negatively affects the system's ability to fulfill its financial commitments towards pensioners and their eligible survivors. Furthermore, contributing at underreported real wages reduces individuals' pensions, and may cause their standard of living to deteriorate (Gillion 2000).[5]

Low ceiling on monthly covered wage

The ceiling on monthly covered wage for a government employee or a public and private business sector worker (Law 79/1975) amounts to LE 1200 (LE 700 and LE 500 for basic and variable salaries respectively), which implies a regressive tax. This means that a low-wage worker pays a contribution reflecting his/her full earnings, while a high-wage worker, whose wage is higher than the ceiling on monthly covered wage, pays a contribution on only a part of his/her income. Thus, the current system imposes higher burdens on low-wage workers, inducing many of these workers to pay contributions on underreported real wages; and fails to collect contributions on a large ratio of higher wages (Helmy 2004, Nagib 2002, James 1997).

Setting individual pension based on the defined-benefit principle

The pension of a government employee or a public or private business worker is determined based on the defined-benefit principle through a formula that takes into account the number of the worker's years of service (maximum 36 years, and minimum 10 years for basic salary and 20 years for variable salary), and a certain accrual ratio (1/45) of the worker's average monthly salary throughout the last two years of his/her service, at a maximum replacement rate of 80 percent (Ministry of Social Insurance 2002, 2000/01; Chemonics International Inc. 1999; Barents Group 1999; International Labor Office 1999).

Linking pension to the individual's average monthly salary during the last two years preceding retirement weakens the link between the individual's contributions throughout his/her entire years of service and the actual pension obtained. It also leads to redistribution in favor of individuals whose salaries increase as their retirement approaches. This may encourage individuals to pay contributions on underreported real wages during most of their years of service, and deliberately exaggerate contributions during the few years preceding retirement in order to get higher pensions that do not match what they actually paid throughout their entire years of service (Helmy 2004).

Lenient early retirement provisions

The current pension system entitles individuals who contribute to the system for 20 years to go on voluntary early retirement (legal retirement age is 60 years), in return for reducing their pension proportionately; i.e., the younger the retiree is, the lower the pension. Furthermore, Table 7.3 shows that under the current system, the "legal" reduction percentages for early retirement are much lower than the "actuarial" reduction rates that should be taken into account to achieve balance between the pension system's revenues and expenses. Lenient provisions for early pension eligibility encourage many individuals to opt for early retirement,[6] increasing the financial burden of funding accrued pension benefits for early retirees while reducing the number of participant workers. The result is a decline in contribution proceeds (Hamdallah Fahim 2002a, Ministry of Social Insurance and Social Affairs 2000/01 and 2000).

Table 7.3. Applied "Legal" Early Retirement Reduction Rates Compared to "Actuarial" Rates

Age at Retirement	*Pension Reduction Rates*	
	Applied "Legal" Retirement Rates	*"Actuarial" Rates*
Less than 45	15	55
45 to less than 50	10	48
50 to less than 55	5	37
55 to less than 59	No reduction	23
59		5

Source: Ministry of Social Insurance and Social Affairs (2000).

Method of Funding Pension Benefits

Although the current pension system was originally based on the fully funded method,[7] it became "partially" funded[8] due to increasing dependence on the government's financial support to pay accrued pension benefits. This is attributed to several reasons, most importantly the lack of an "automatic" mechanism to protect the real value of pension from erosion over time; and the weak link between individual contributions and actual individual pension.

To alleviate the burdens of high cost of living and maintain the real value of pensions, the treasury has been providing funds since 1987 to 2003/04 (article 148 of Law 79/1975),[9] in addition to the government's contribution as an employer (21 percent of basic salaries and 19 percent of variable salaries of government employees). The public treasury's contribution in pension liabilities amounted to approximately LE 13 billion in 2004/05 (8.2 percent of public expenditures). Figure 7.2 indicates that government's contribution as an employer amounted to approximately LE 4.6 billion.

Figure 7.2. Development of Paid Pension Liabilities (2000/01–2004/05) (LE million)

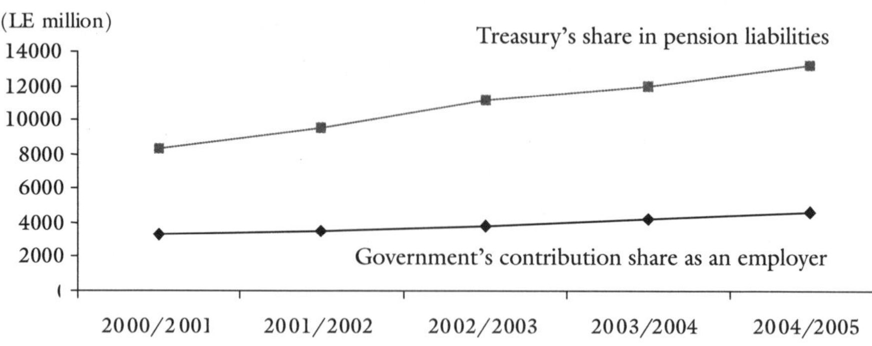

Sources: Ministry of Finance 2006, 2005, and 2003; People's Assembly 2005b.

It is worth noting that over the past ten years, the public treasury was unable to pay in full the financial support to the pension system in order to cover the annual increments granted to face the increasing cost of living. Accordingly, the public treasury's indebtedness to the pension system inflated, amounting to over LE 35 billion in 2004/05 (Central Auditing Organization 2006).[10] Hence, the public treasury has refrained from funding annual increments to pensioners as of 2004/05, and the pension system is now bearing this burden.

Regarding the weak link between individual contributions and actual individual pension, the contribution of a casual worker (casual workers represent approximately 27 percent of total participants in the current system) for instance is LE 1 only per month, but he/she gets LE 80 in monthly pension. Thus, while contributions collected from six million insured individuals amount to only LE 4 million, their actual pension benefits cost the public treasury LE 1 billion annually (Al-Gibaly 2006, Hamdallah Fahim 2002b).

Under this "partially" funded system, saved pension funds (48 percent of GDP in 2004/05) cover merely a ratio of government implicit pension liabilities (141 percent of GDP in the same year). This "hidden" public debt implies intra-generational as well as intergenerational redistribution (Kane and Palacios 1996).

Pension Funds Management

Under the current pension system, the government manages pensions through two funds: the social insurance fund of government employees and the social insurance fund for public and private business sector workers. Articles five and six of Law 119/1980 stipulate that both funds transfer available pension surplus to the National Investment Bank (NIB) and prohibit investment of such surplus without the prior consent of the NIB's board of directors.

This legal obligation restricts efficient investment of pension funds. As shown in Table 7.4, the investment portfolio of pension funds is not sufficiently diversified. The majority of pension funds (92 percent) amounting to LE 239.4 billion in 2004/05 is invested with the NIB (LE 219 billion). Furthermore, a portion of pension funds is used in funding the budget deficit by purchasing government securities (such as Treasury bills, bonds, and debentures).

Table 7.4. Key Forms of Investing Pension Funds in Egypt and their Average Rate of Return, Compared to the Average Rate of Return on Low-Risk Investments (2004/05)

Key Forms of Investing Pension Funds	*Relative Importance (%)*	*Average Rate of Return (%)*
With the National Investment Bank	92	10
Bank deposits	6	8.25–9
Debentures with the public treasury	0.9	5.5
Financial securities	0.9	4–16
Government bonds	0.1	8.75–11
Treasury bills	0.1	9.7–11

Sources: Based on Central Auditing Organization data (2006); Central Bank of Egypt annual reports and economic reviews (various issues).

Calculating the *real* rate of return on pension funds, along with the government's annual increments for pensioners since 1987, shows that this return has become positive and increasing since 1987/1988. It has also exceeded the "real" rate of return on bank deposits (including the annual increments for pensioners) since 1992/93, as shown in Figure 7.3. Additionally, the average investment return on pension funds deposited with the National Investment Bank (10 percent) in 2004/05 became close to the average return on other low-risk investments such as investment certificates and postal savings accounts (10.5 percent) during the same year (Central Auditing Organization 2006; and IDSC 2005).

However, the pension system does not get the actually realized rate of return because the National Investment Bank adds it to the stock of pension funds deposited with it for reinvestment. This may not necessarily be in the interest of pensioners who may prefer to use such return in increasing their pensions. Additionally, these rates of return could substitute for the annual increments funded by the public treasury in order to mitigate the cost of living burdens on pensioners.

Figure 7.3. "Real" Rate of Return on Pensions in Addition to Annual Increment Rates, Compared to that on Bank Deposits (1980/81–2004/05)

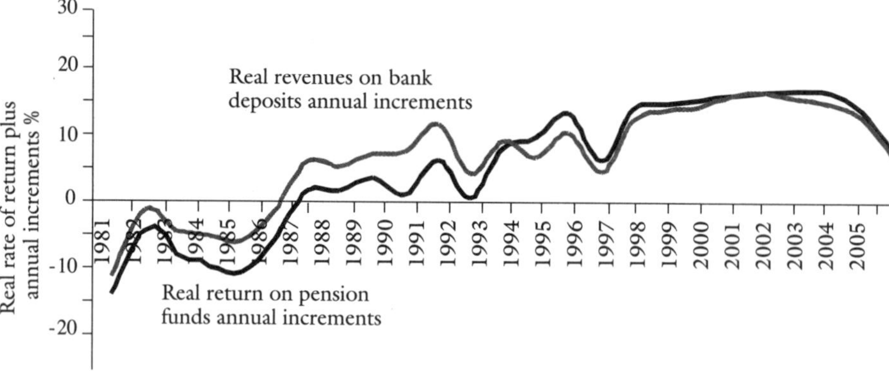

Sources: Author's calculations based on the Central Bank of Egypt, annual reports (various issues); Al-Gibaly (2006); World Bank (2006a).

Pension funds represent approximately 70 percent of financial resources available to the National Investment Bank. The Bank lends the public treasury to fund approximately 86 percent of public investments at a 12 percent annual rate of return (People's Assembly 2006a and b). The public treasury's indebtedness to the National Investment Bank amounted to LE 143.7 billion in 2004/05 (approximately 41 percent of the government's public net domestic debt, which amounted to LE 349.2 billion), and the relevant debt service amounted to LE 21.7 billion (approximately 52 percent of total government public domestic debt service, which amounted to

LE 41.8 billion). Future generations are expected to bear the bigger burden of paying such indebtednesses (Central Bank of Egypt, annual reports (various issues); People's Assembly 2005a and b; Ministry of Finance 2005, 2006).

The above analysis shows that in spite of its advantages, the current pension system is unable to achieve fiscal sustainability, economic efficiency, or equitable income distribution—hence the importance of shifting to a new pension system.

2. The New Pension System and its Potential Impact

Country experience worldwide has shown the futility of reforming partially funded defined-benefit systems, such as the current Egyptian system. Such an approach falls short of achieving fiscal sustainability, efficiency, or equity. Country experience has also stressed the importance of introducing and enforcing a new fully funded pension system based on defined contributions[11] to achieve the above-mentioned goals (World Bank 1997, Loewe 2000, Vittas 1997).

Several countries, including Sweden (1994), Italy (1995), Latvia (1996), Poland (1999), Kyrgyzstan[12] (1997), and Mongolia (2000) realized the difficulty involved in the "direct" enforcement of a new system. This is because current worker contributions would be saved to fund current worker pensions. Thus, the government would bear the high cost of providing the financial resources needed to pay accrued pensions to a large number of current retirees.[13] Therefore, the shift to the new system in these countries occurred gradually.

The strategy of enforcing the system gradually relies on two main pillars. First, maintaining the current system for current pensioners and their eligible survivors, as well as current participants with the exception of individuals below a certain age who "voluntarily" opt to shift to the new system. On its part, the government will issue bonds to guarantee their rights upon shifting (e.g., Poland and Latvia). As for new entrants to the labor market, the new pension system would be "mandatory" (Fox and Palmer 2001, Keller and Heller 2001, Holzmann 2000, Mitchell 1998a and b, Schwarz and Demirguc-Kunt 1999, De Mesa and Bertranou 1997).

Second, combining pay-as-you-go[14] and fully funded financing of pension benefits, and public and private management through two types of accounts: "Notional" accounts based on publicly managed pay-as-you-go defined contributions, and "funded" accounts based on fully-funded defined contributions managed by private companies under rules and regulations established by the government. Table 7.5 shows that at the start of enforcing the new system the majority of contributions goes to the "notional" accounts, while a lesser ratio goes to "funded" accounts. The ratio of contributions allocated to "notional" accounts is reduced gradually; while that transferred to "funded" accounts increases.

Table 7.5. Size of "Notional" and "Funded" Accounts Measured by Contribution Rates in Countries Applying the New System (%)

Country	*Contribution rate*			*"Notional" Account Contribution Rate*	*"Funded" Account Contribution Rate*
	Total	*Employer's Share*	*Employee's Share*		
Sweden	18.5	9.25	9.25	16	2.5
Poland	19.52	NA	NA	12.22	7.3
Italy	32.8	23.91	8.89	32.8	0
Latvia*	33	NA	NA	20	2
Kyrgyzstan	29	24	5	29	0
Mongolia	19	13.5	5.5	19	0

Notes: NA = Not Available. * = In Latvia, although the contribution rate is up to 33 percent, only 22 percent of which is currently credited to "notional" and "funded" accounts. The remaining balance is used to pay pension obligations to current retirees. By 2010, the contribution rate in the "funded" account will rise from 2 percent to 20 percent, and that in the "notional" account will drop from 20 percent to merely 10 percent.
Sources: Williamson (2004), Williamson and Williams (2003), Palme (2003), Palmer (2001 and 1999), Chlon-Dominczak (2002), Rutkowski (2002), Bender and MacArthur (2000), Fox and Palmer (1999), Brugiavini and Fornero (1998).

In light of international experience, the Egyptian government has recently put forth its vision of the new pension system, outlining its main features (National Democratic Party 2006, World Bank 2006a). The discussion below addresses key aspects of the new system and its institutional framework. It also offers an analysis of the system's potential impact.

The New System

Contribution in the new pension system will be mandatory for new entrants to the labor market. The current system will be maintained for current pensioners and their eligible survivors, as well as current participants with the exception of individuals under the age of thirty who wish to shift voluntarily to the new system.

The Structure of the New System

The new system comprises a basic pension and two types of personal accounts for each participant: a "notional" account and a "funded" account, in addition to developing an optional complementary pension system as in Table 7.6.

Table 7.6. Comparing the New Pension System Structure to the Current System Structure

Method Used in:	*Current System*	*New system*			
		Non-Participants	*Participants*		
		"Basic" Pension	*"Notional" Account*	*"Funded" Account*	*"Supplementary" Pension*
Calculating individual pensions	Defined benefits	15 percent of economy-wide average wage	Defined contributions		
Funding pensions	Partially funded	Public revenues	Pay-as-you-go	Fully funded	
Managing pension funds	Government	Government	Government	Private	

Source: The author.

As for the basic pension, to promote social solidarity, the new system provides a minimum pension for every 65-year-old resident citizen in Egypt who does not receive a pension from the state. The basic pension will be funded from public revenues and will require no contribution. It is proposed to be set at 15 percent of economy-wide average wage,[15] and casual labor will be integrated (Law 112/1980).

As for the two personal accounts, both basic and variable salary contributions will be combined into one gross salary that will become a reference contribution in the system. The ceiling on monthly covered wage will be increased from LE 1,200 to LE 2,000, and the contribution rate will be set at 17 percent of the gross salary, 12 percent of which will go to the "notional" account, while 5 percent will go to the "funded" account. It is worth noting that the contribution shares of both employer and employee as well as the nature of risks against which the new system provides protection are not yet clear, although these are significant elements in evaluating the system.

The individual's pension will be based on total individual contributions paid periodically to the "notional" and "funded" accounts throughout the individual's entire years of service in addition to an annual accumulated rate of return set by the government for notional accounts and the market rate of return for the cash stocks invested in diversified financial assets during the years of contribution divided by life expectancy.

In preparation for implementing pay-as-you-go "notional" accounts under the new system, the Ministry of Finance (MOF) announced that the government's debt with the National Investment Bank and the latter's obligations toward the current pension system will be settled and removed from the Bank's budget. A government bond on the public treasury will be issued for all pension system accruals with the National Investment Bank and the MOF. The accrued rate of return will be directly paid to the system. The pension system's accrued interest on the public treasury amounted to LE 15.7 billion in 2004/05. The MOF is to pay such interest in cash to the system in FY2006/07, which will help generate approximately LE 8 billion in cash surplus.[16]

Additionally, the new pension system encourages willing citizens to shift voluntarily to the supplementary pension funds at a contribution rate deemed appropriate by the individual with regards to his/her saving capacity, in order to target the pension he/she would like to get. These funds will be subject to monitoring and supervision by the Egyptian Insurance Supervisory Authority, which is affiliated to the Ministry of Investment.[17] A tax exemption for a specified amount of contributions is expected to encourage individuals to participate in the optional supplementary pension system.

Institutional Framework

Pursuant to presidential decree no. 422/2005, the minister of finance has become responsible for enforcing social insurance legislations. Under this decree, the minister of finance chairs the National Social Insurance Authority, and replaces the minister of social insurance wherever referred to in other laws and legislations. Furthermore, the new pension system's proposed institutional framework includes forming a higher pension committee; renaming the National Social Insurance Authority to the National Pension Management Authority; upgrading the information technology (IT) systems; forming a pension investment board; and establishing a supplementary pensions monitoring and supervision division at the Egyptian Insurance Supervisory Authority.

The *higher pension committee*'s board of directors will comprise the ministers of finance, investment, social solidarity, and labor. It will also include the chairpersons of the Capital Market Authority and the Egyptian Insurance Supervisory Authority. This higher committee will be responsible for formulating legislations and executive directives; and for following up on the performance of monitoring authorities for both the public and supplementary pension systems.

The National Social Insurance Authority (subject to law 207/1994, amending law 79/1975) will be renamed the *National Pensions Management Authority;* and will be responsible for managing the new system and the two accounts thereof as well as supervising the performance of the insurance funds of government employees and public and private business sector employees. Furthermore, a new *center will be established for quality assurance of data processing and supervision of data flow*. Both the current and new systems will be linked.

A *pensions investment board* will be formed and assigned the responsibility of developing policies and frameworks according to which the new "funded" account investment managers will work. Board members will comprise professionals with expertise in investment management. Finally, an independent division called "*supplementary pensions monitoring and supervision division*" will be established at the Ministry of Investment's Egyptian Insurance Supervisory Authority. This division will establish criteria for operating the supplementary pension funds and will monitor compliance with such criteria to protect the interests of participants against any actuarial deficit. Figure 7.4 illustrates the new pension system's institutional framework.

Figure 7.4. The New Pension System's Institutional Framework

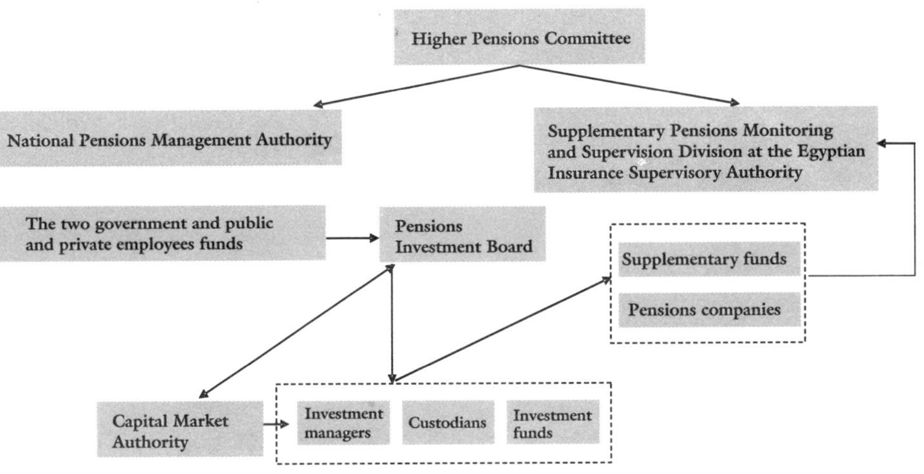

Source: National Democratic Party (2006).

Potential Impact of the New System

The "gradual" enforcement of the new pension system will help reduce the financial burdens incurred by the public treasury in the short run, enhance the system's fiscal sustainability, maintain the role of the state in income redistribution, improve economic efficiency, and develop the capital market. However, it transfers the burden of risk management from the government to individuals, as will be discussed in detail below.

Reduce Financial Burdens on the Public Treasury in the Short-run

Gradual enforcement through directing the higher ratio of contributions (12 percent) to "notional" accounts, and the smaller/lower ratio (5 percent) to "funded" accounts, while making participation in the new system mandatory for new labor market entrants and optional for current system participants below thirty years of age who wish to shift to the new system, is less costly compared to "full and direct" enforcement. The reason is that in case of direct enforcement, current contributions will be saved in current employees' "funded" accounts to finance their pensions. Thus, the government will incur a high cost of paying pension benefits to a large number of current retirees, estimated at approximately 93 percent of GDP, considering the current system's financial liabilities amount up to 141 percent of GDP as opposed to 48 percent in reserves.

Upon enforcement of the new system, current collected contributions recorded in "notional" accounts will be transferred to the public treasury in order to pay pension benefits to current pensioners and other related administrative fees. The public treasury is no longer expected to fund annual pension increments or to bear the cost of borrowing from the National Investment Bank.[18] Thus, the new pension system will help reduce the public treasury's financial burdens by over LE 29.6 billion compared to FY2003/04 as indicated in Table 7.7.

Table 7.7. The New System's Potential Financial Burdens Compared to Those of the Current System (LE million)

Current System's Financial Burdens (2003/04)		*New System's Potential Financial Burdens**	
Government's share as an employer	4,141.2	Net pension contributions (excluding government's share as an employer)	11,271.1
Plus		Minus	
Public treasury's contribution in funding annual increments for "paid" pensions	12,001.9	Paid pensions	6,197.7
Treasury's debt service to the National Investment Bank	18,147.0	Wages and related expenditures	387.3
Total financial burdens	34,290.1	Total financial burdens	4,686.1

Note: * Calculations were made using the most recent available data for 2003/04.
Source: Author's calculations based on People's Assembly data (2006a and b).

Enhance the System's Fiscal Sustainability

Fully "funded" accounts enhance the new system's fiscal sustainability. This is because funding accrued pension benefits based on these accounts will be through employees' saved contributions throughout several years that are invested in diversified assets to achieve a real rate of return to the extent that the present value of saved contributions becomes equal to that of the pension benefits due.

Furthermore, reducing the contribution rate (from 40 percent of basic salary and 35 percent of variable salary to 17 percent of gross salary) helps mitigate the financial burden on new system participants, thus promoting compliance to pay due contributions for real wages, as well as increasing demand for labor in the formal sector. This enhances the system's capacity to honor its financial obligations toward pensioners.

Additionally, defining pension benefits by taking into consideration a coefficient reflecting improvement in life expectancy helps limit expenditures on pensions when a longer life for retirees is expected. As such, there will be no need for legislative amendment to recalculate individual pension benefits.

Maintain the Role of the State in Income Redistribution

The new system explicitly separates income redistribution programs for social solidarity purposes from the contribution-based pensions. The state maintains a leading role in redistribution where it provides a minimum pension guarantee for individuals with no pensions, includes casual labor under the basic pension system, and funds both from public revenues.

It is worth noting that limiting expenditures on the basic pension system requires more accurate targeting of pensioners. For example, it is necessary to exclude certain ineligible categories such as owners of agricultural lands who own less than ten feddans and are classified as casual labor under the current pension system.

Improve Economic Efficiency

Setting pension benefits based on the defined contributions method establishes a closer link between individual's contributions throughout his/her years of service and the individual's pension benefits. Thus, participants will be encouraged to work and save more (Aiyer 1997). When an individual regards his/her contributions as savings to recoup in the future in addition to the market rate of return on funded accounts or that set by the government on "notional" accounts, rather than a tax, he/she will be induced to pay the due contributions based on his/her real salary; continue to work for the longest period possible in order to get a higher pension; and search for the most efficient means of investing such savings (Barents Group 1999; World Bank 1994).

Taking life expectancy into account when calculating individual pensions means that if an individual opts for early retirement, his/her pension will be divided over a larger number of years reflecting increased life expectancy after retirement. Hence, pension benefits will reflect actuarially his years of service and contributions (World Bank 2002b; Gillion 2000; Heller 1998; James 1997).

Develop the Capital Market

Fully "funded" accounts that are based on defined contributions under private management help develop the capital market through providing long-term savings and generating demand for new financial institutions and instruments, which reflects positively on the level of economic development (Barr 2000, 2001, and 2002; Palacios and Pallares-Miralles 2000; Sinn 2000).

Many studies have shown that under regulatory and supervisory rules established by the state, private companies are more capable of investing pension savings in "funded" accounts in more diversified assets, thus maximizing the real rate of return on such savings with the least possible risks. This achieves the interests of participants, pensioners and the overall national economy (Carmichael and Palacios 2003; De Ferranti, Leipziger and Srinivas 2002; Palacios 2002; Iglesias and Palacios 2001).

"Notional" accounts funded on a pay-as-you-go basis are virtual accounts for book-keeping purposes rather than capital assets; therefore, they do not directly contribute to increasing national savings or developing financial markets and institutions. However, "notional" accounts may help increase savings "indirectly" by reducing public expenditures on pensions and reducing the budget deficit.

Transfer the Burden of Risk Management From the Government to Individuals

Pension systems around the world face several risks, most importantly: macroeconomic shocks (such as changes in inflation, unemployment, and productivity), which impact output and prices; demographic risks (such as increased average life expectancy and higher dependency ratios), which impact pension liabilities; investment-related risks (fluctuations in the financial securities market and the correlation between the rate of return and the performance of shares and bonds); administrative risks (fraud and high administrative fees); and the risks of unstable policies (such as the government's decision to alter the methods used in maintaining the real value of pensions).

In spite of its foreseen positive impact, the new pension system transfers the burden of managing the above risks from the government to individuals, although the former is relatively more capable of bearing such burdens. For example, when unemployment rises or wages deteriorate, taxpayers bear the primary burden of funding basic pensions through public revenues. Furthermore, increased average life expectancy "automatically" reduces individual pension benefits. It is difficult to accurately define the burdens to be incurred by individuals because the shares of both employer and employee under the new pension system and the nature of risks that the new system will provide protection against are not yet clear.

As for "funded" accounts, individuals face a major problem of high administrative cost (Zaidi 2006). In many countries, administrative costs (start-up fees, investment cost, bookkeeping and communication costs, and cost of marketing to attract individuals through advertising, for instance) consume a high ratio of returns on invested pension funds in these funded accounts (Stanko 2003; Sunden 2000 and 2004; Weaver 2005).

In Chile, for example, in spite of the high average gross real return on pension funds invested in funded accounts (10.29 percent per annum), administrative cost and commissions consumed approximately 54 percent of this return from 1982 to 1997. Thus, an individual who contributed in 1982 ten percent of his/her income in a "funded" account and retired after 23 years in 2005 found out that the administrative cost consumed over one fifth of his accumulated balance, although his/her contributions were increasing at a real rate of return of 10.29 percent per annum (Keran and Cheng 2002).

3. Proposals for Enforcing the New Pension System in Egypt

Having identified the key potential effects of the new pension system, a set of proposals are offered to ensure employee rights, protect pensioners and their eligible survivors, and uphold the interests of the national economy as a whole in light of relevant international experience and taking into account Egypt's economic conditions.

In order to offer appropriate proposals, it is important to have a clear vision of the various aspects of the new pension system, particularly the shares of both employer and employee in the contribution rate and the nature of risks against which the new system provides protection.

Enhancing Citizens' Trust in Government's Ability to Fulfill Long-Term Commitments

The government's long-term commitments towards the holders of pay-as-you-go "notional" accounts will be explicitly determined, and therefore difficult to reduce in the future. However, relevant information should be made available to enhance citizens' trust in the government's ability to honor such commitments at their retirement and reliance on pension funds in financing budget deficit should be reduced through limiting investment in government bonds. The government should also ensure that the rate of return added to contributors' accounts maintains the real value of pension benefits.

Legislative Amendments

Some of the existing legislations should be reconsidered and combined in a unified law before enforcing the new pension system. For example, to improve the efficiency of using pension funds requires amendment of law 119/1980, which establishes the National Investment Bank, in order to avoid overlapping between the bank and the two insurance funds. It also requires allowing the National Pensions Management Authority and the

Investments Management Board to develop and implement an optimal investment policy for pension funds; and to achieve the highest-possible rate of return, while taking into account the elements of guarantee and liquidity. Furthermore, Article 5 of the Comprehensive Insurance Law (Sadat Pension) should be cancelled as the number of Sadat pension beneficiaries is increasing annually, although the law targets individuals who had no pension before 1980 and their age was 65 at that year; i.e., ineligible categories are benefiting from the said pension.[19]

Prorating the Ceiling on Monthly Covered Wage to the Average Economy-Wide Monthly Wage

Under the new system, the ceiling on monthly covered wage will be increased from LE 1200 to LE 2000 only. Country experience shows that increasing this ceiling four times as much the average economy-wide monthly wage helps increase collected contributions; particularly from employees with relatively high wages (World Bank 2006a and b).

Linking the Rate of Return on Contributions Registered in "Notional" Accounts to the Growth Rate of Wages

The government may set the rate of return on "notional" account contributions according to the nominal growth of GDP (as in Italy); growth in wages (e.g., Sweden, Poland, and Latvia); or interest rate on short-term government bonds (as in China). The aim of linking the rate of return to the growth rate of wages is to provide an appropriate real rate of return for individuals and strengthen the fiscal sustainability of "notional" accounts and (Inter-American Conference on Social Security 2005).

Establishing an "Automatic" Mechanism to Maintain the Real Value of Pensions

Indexing pension benefits to the arithmetic mean of changes in prices and real wages instead of the annual increments granted by the government under specific laws can maintain the real value of pensions and allow pensioners to benefit from the increase in productivity of the national economy (Keran and Cheng 2002; Disney 1998; Hassler and Lindbeck 1998). For example, pension benefits increase annually in Sweden based on the following formula:

Pension increment rate = inflation rate – ("norm" growth rate of real wages[20] – "actual" growth rate of such wages).

In Poland, the inflation rate in addition to a 20 percent increase in real wage rate are taken into account (Chlon-Dominczak 2002). Thus, individual pension depends on the growth rate of wages "*prior*" to retirement, and on the rate of economic growth "*after*" retirement (Fultz and Ruck 2001; Chlon, Gora, and Rutkowski 1999).

Developing Regulatory and Supervisory Rules to Manage Investment Risks

Investing saved pension funds in "funded" accounts requires highly advanced infrastructure in terms of capital markets and related institutions,[21] accurate and continuously updated records for all employees and pensioners and their eligible survivors, intensive IT usage, and individual financial culture.

Moreover, maximizing the rate of return on pension investments with the least-possible risks in favor of employees requires emphasizing the role of the state in establishing a regulatory and legal framework that would ensure efficiency and competitiveness among private firms that will perform this task. It also requires determining the entity responsible for monitoring and supervising these firms in compliance with "prudential" regulations. These regulations aim to ensure avoiding excessive risk-taking, reducing conflict of interest, and limiting concentration of market power. Monitoring and supervision may also be undertaken in accordance with "draconian" regulations regarding the structure of pension funds and their areas of investment as well as performance and profitability criteria. Finally, it requires providing mechanisms for speedy and equitable settlement of potential disputes (Carmichael and Palacios 2003; Palacios 2002; Iglesias and Palacios 2001).

While there is consensus on the need for developing and complying with "prudential" regulations, there are concerns regarding the cost of enforcing "draconian" regulations. This is because requiring the profitability of pension funds to stay within a band such as the industry average may limit competition and reduce the incentive for risk-taking. Furthermore, commitment to confine investment to government securities only achieves low rates of return in most cases and deprives the national economy of a major impetus for capital market development.

Reducing the Administrative Cost of "Funded" Accounts

It is important to reduce the administrative fees so as not to deplete a large portion of the returns on funds invested in "funded" accounts. "Gradually" increasing the ratio of employee contributions allocated to funded accounts can raise the available balances in these accounts, and the administrative fees can be reduced as a result of economies of scale, thus benefiting pensioners (World Bank 2001; Norman and Mitchell 2000). It is worth noting that Chile was able to gradually reduce the administrative fees per unit of assets from 9.4 percent in 1982 to 1.4 percent in 1998 through a set of measures such as contracting to open "funded" accounts with large groups or institutions rather than individual contracting; switching from active investment (such as selecting certain financial stocks and fixed-income assets) to passive investment (such as indexed pension funds) in order to reduce the investment cost; shifting the responsibility for record keeping and communication with individuals from pensions fund managers to the contracted institutions (Soto 2005).

Bolivia opted to confine the management of pensions to only two funds for five years; afterward other funds are allowed to enter the market. Both funds were selected through international bidding, and their investment activities are subject to a set of regulations and supervision by the entity responsible for monitoring the financial sector. Individuals are to participate in one of these two funds for at least two and a half years, after which they may switch to the other fund if they so desire. The two companies managed to keep the administrative fees on assets below 3 percent, compared to Mexico (9.2 percent), and Argentina (7.7 percent).

Achieving More Equitable Income Distribution

In many countries, basic pension represents more than 30 percent of the economy-wide average wage.[22] As for Egypt, the possibility of increasing the basic pension by more than what the new pension system proposes (only 15 percent of the economy-wide average wage) needs to be reconsidered, particularly that salary levels are relatively low.

Individuals forced by certain circumstances to withdraw from the labor market for a certain period (such as unemployment, childcare, or military service) should earn pension rights financed by the state to their "notional" accounts during that period. Table 7.8 identifies contributions that the state incurs on behalf of individuals under certain circumstances and for limited periods in some selected countries.

Table 7.8. Contributions Incurred by the State on Behalf of Individuals under Certain Circumstances and for Limited Periods in Selected Countries

Country	*Unemployment*	*Childcare*	*Disability*	*Others*
Sweden	√	√	√	Pension rights earned during military service and higher education
Poland	√	√	√	X
Kyrgyzstan	X	√	X	X
Latvia	√	√	√	Pension rights earned during military service; and for diplomats' wives
Mongolia	√	X	X	X

Sources: Jorgensen and Van Domelen (1999); Disney (1999); De Mesa and Bertranou (1997).

4. Conclusion

This study argues that despite the current pension system's advantages, it is unable to achieve fiscal sustainability, economic efficiency, or equitable income distribution. This encourages the shift to a new pension system in Egypt. The study attributes the inefficiency of the current system to four main factors: high dependency ratios, applied rules, method of funding accrued pension benefits, and pension management.

The study attempts to identify the new system's basic features, institutional framework, and potential impact, in light of international experience and the Egyptian government's recently outlined vision for the pension system.

Additionally, the study shows that the gradual implementation of the new pension system will help reduce the financial burdens incurred by the public treasury in the short run, enhance the system's fiscal sustainability, maintain the role of the state in income redistribution, improve economic efficiency, and develop the capital market. However, the new system transfers the burden of risk management from the government to individuals. Furthermore, the study offers a set of proposals that would help ensure worker rights, protect pensioners and their eligible survivors, and uphold the interests of the overall national economy in light of relevant international experience and taking into account Egypt's economic conditions.

The study stresses the importance of information availability in order to enhance public trust in the government's ability to honor its long-term commitments at retirement and not to excessively use pension funds in financing the budget deficit. It further emphasizes the necessity that the rate of return added to the savings of individuals maintains the real value of pension benefits to ensure them a decent life.

It proposes legislative amendments to enhance the new system's fiscal sustainability and improve the efficiency of managing pension funds to achieve the highest possible rate of return, taking into consideration guarantee and liquidity factors. Also, the ceiling on monthly covered wage should be prorated to the average economy-wide monthly wage. The rate of return on pension funds invested by the government should be indexed to the growth rate of wages. In addition, an automatic mechanism to maintain the real value of pension benefits needs to be established.

To successfully implement the new system, it is essential to enhance the role of the state in establishing and developing regulations and supervisory rules to improve the efficiency of risk management for the pension funds invested in the financial markets. It also stresses the importance of taking the necessary actions to reduce administrative costs and achieve equitable income distribution.

Notes

1. Under Article 8 of Law 79/1975, when current collected contributions are not sufficient to cover accrued pension benefits, the government bears the financial burden of covering such deficit.
2. This means that approximately every three Egyptian workers support one retiree.
3. The population group over sixty years old represents 9 percent of total population in Egypt. This percentage is expected to rise to 18 percent in 2035. Average life expectancy at birth for the Egyptian citizen rose from 69 years in 2000/01 to 72 years in 2005/06. The growth of birth rates declined from 21.1 (per thousand) in 2000/01 to 19.1 (per thousand) in 2005/06 (Ministry of State for Economic Development 2006).
4. According to the defined benefit formula, an individual's pension represents a certain ratio of his/her average monthly earnings during a certain number of years of service. Pension rises with the increase in the number of years of service (Barents Group 1999; World Bank 1994).
5. It is worth noting that 52 percent of government employees and public and private business sector workers (covered under Law 79/1975) get less than LE 100 in monthly pension (Al-Gibaly 2006).
6. The number of early retirement cases increased from 384,000 at the end of June 2004 to 403,000 at the end of June 2005, representing approximately 40 percent of total retirement cases during the same year (Al-Gibaly 2006).
7. Under the fully funded method, accrued pension benefits are funded using contributions saved in the pension fund by workers who are covered by the system over a period of years and had been invested in diversified assets to achieve a real rate of return. Under this system, the current value of saved contributions equals that of accrued pension benefits, in a way that ensures the system's fiscal sustainability without a need for financial support from the government (Helmy 2004; Barr 2002, 2001, and 2000).

8. A "partially" funded pension system increasingly depends on government financial support to pay accrued pension benefits. Under this system, the current value of accrued pensions is higher than the current value of saved contributions, which leads to implicit liabilities by the government to system participants.
9. Under specific laws, the government has enacted annual increments for pensioners since 1987. Such increments were funded from public revenues as follows: 20 percent in 1987, 15 percent annually 1988–1991, 20 percent in 1992, 10 percent annually 1993–2005, and 7.5 percent in 2006. Since July 2001, the increase has been a maximum of LE 60 and minimum of LE 10.
10. Funds owed to the pension system by the public treasury generate no investment returns as a result of not transferring these funds to the National Investment Bank. Lost returns negatively affect the financial strength of the pension system (Al-Wazeery 2005).
11. Under the defined contributions scheme, an individual pension depends on the contributions he/she actually paid regularly throughout his/her entire years of service. Such contributions plus the compounded annual investment returns thereon would be saved in an account in the individual's name. This scheme ties pension benefits closely to contributions, which stimulates individuals to comply, continue to work for the longest period possible, and exert an effort searching for the most efficient technique for investing the contribution funds saved with the pension system.
12. A country located in Central Asia neighboring China. Its capital is Bishkek. Kyrgyzstan gained independence from the Soviet Union toward the end of 1991.
13. The financial cost of "direct" enforcement of a defined-contributions fully funded system exceeded 90 percent of GDP in Chile, 87 percent in Colombia, and 80 percent in Mexico (Mitchell 1998a and b). These countries financed this high cost by increasing tax rates, reducing pension value, or using a large portion of public companies' privatization proceeds.
14. Under pay-as-you-go financing, the government uses current worker contributions in funding pensions of current retirees; i.e., "notional" accounts are virtual accounts that represent individual rights owed to individuals by the public treasury in the future without having an actual fund to save pensions therein.
15. It is worth noting that the average monthly salary for government employees, public business, and public sector employees is approximately LE 624 (Central Agency for Organization and Administration 2005).
16. According to a statement by the minister of finance to *Al-Ahram* newspaper on May 6, 2006.
17. The number of funds registered with the Egyptian Insurance Supervisory Authority increased from 199 funds in 1980 to 615 funds in 2001. Annual financial resources for these funds rose from LE 30 million to LE 3.6 billion during the same period.
18. The 2006/07 budget does not include any contribution by the public treasury in funding annual pension increments or borrowing from the National Investment Bank. The "interest with the National Investment Bank" item was removed from the balance sheet while a new item "interest on loans to fund public investments" was added.
19. The number of insured individuals under the Social Comprehensive Insurance Law rose from 4.9 million in 1990/91 to approximately 5.2 million in 2004/05.
20. Sweden sets the real wage growth rate "norm" at 1.6 percent.
21. Such as companies for evaluation and classification of financial securities, accounting and law firms, and institutional investors.
22. It is worth mentioning that in Sweden the basic pension for a 65-year-old individual residing in the country for not less than 40 years represents approximately 33 percent of the economy-wide average wage.

References

Abdel Rahman Mohamed, Bareen. 2002. Insurance evasion: Potentials of collaboration with other bodies to avoid this phenomenon (in Arabic). Paper presented at a conference on Social Insurance: Between Hope and Reality, October 13–15. Cairo: Al-Azhar University.

Aiyer, Sri-Ram. 1997. *Pension reform in Latin America: Quick fixes or sustainable reform?* World Bank Policy Research Working Paper, no. 1865. Washington, D.C.: The World Bank.

Al-Gibaly, Abdel Fattah. 2006. *Future of social insurance system in Egypt* (in Arabic). Strategic Papers, volume 16, issue 161. Egypt: Al-Ahram Center for Political and Strategic Studies.

Al-Wazeery, Layla Mohamed. 2005. Unpublished paper on the relation between the social insurance system, Ministry of Planning, Public Treasury and National Investment Bank (in Arabic). Egypt: The National Authority for Insurance and Pensions.

Barents Group, LLC. 1999. Road map to reform: Policy and implementation strategies for Egypt." USAID Reforming Insurance Markets in Egypt Project, Cairo.

Barr, Nicholas. 2000. *Reforming pensions: Myths, truths, and policy choices.* IMF Working Paper, no. 139. Washington, D.C.: International Monetary Fund, August.

———. 2001. The truth about pension reform. *Finance and Development* 38(3): 6–9. Washington, D.C.: International Monetary Fund.

———. 2002. The pension puzzle: Prerequisites and policy choices in pension design. *Economic Issues*, no. 29. Washington, D.C.: International Monetary Fund.

Bender, C, and I.W. MacArthur. 2000. Country profile for Mongolia. (Annex B7). In R. Holzmann, I. W. MacArthur and Y. Sin (eds.), *Pension systems in East Asia and the Pacific: Challenges and opportunities* (Social Protection Discussion Paper, no. 0014. Washington, D.C.: World Bank.

Brugiavini, A. and E. Fornero. 1998. *A pension system in transition: The case of Italy.* Moncalieri: Center for Research on Pensions and Welfare Policies.

Carmichael, Jeffrey, and Robert Palacios. 2003. A framework for public pension fund management. Paper presented at the 2nd Public Pension Fund Management Conference, 5–7 May. Washington, D.C.: The World Bank.

Central Agency for Organization and Administration. 2005. Comparative study on the wages of state workers (government/public/public and private business sectors) (in Arabic). Egypt: Central Agency for Organization and Administration.

Central Auditing Organization. 2001. Annual report on the results of financial monitoring and performance evaluation of the National Social Insurance Authority for the year ending on 30/6/2001 (in Arabic). Cairo: Central Auditing Organization.

———. 2006. Future challenges for investing insurance funds in light of current changes. Central Department for Plan Implementation Follow Up and Economic Sector Performance Evaluation, July (in Arabic). Cairo: Central Auditing Organization.

Central Bank of Egypt (CBE). Various Issues. Annual reports (in Arabic).

Chemonics International Inc. 1999. *Enhancing Egypt's social insurance system. Technical assistance to support the reform activities of the Government of Egypt -(TAPR)-* Cairo, Egypt, September.

Chlon, A., M. Gora, and M. Rutkowski. 1999. *Shaping pension reform in Poland: Security through diversity.* Social Protection Discussion Paper no. 9923. Washington, D.C.: The World Bank, August.

Chlon-Dominczak, A. 2002. The Polish pension reform of 1999. In E. Fultz (ed.), *Pension reform in Central and Eastern Europe Vol. 1: Restructuring with privatization (case studies of Hungary and Poland).* Budapest: International Labor Office.

De Ferranti, David, Danny Leipziger, and P. S. Srinivas. 2002. The future of pension reform in Latin America. *Finance and Development* 39(3): 39–43. Washington, D.C.: International Monetary Fund, September.

De Mesa, Alberto Arenas, and Fabio Bertranou. 1997. Learning from social security reforms: Two different cases, Chile and Argentina. *World Development* 25(3): 329–348

Disney, Richard. 1999. *Notional accounts as a pension reform strategy: An evaluation.* Social Protection Discussion Paper, no. 9928. Washington, D.C.: The World Bank, December.

Fox, Louise and Edward Palmer. 1999. *Latvian pension reform.* Social Protection Discussion Paper, no. 9922. Washington, D.C.: The World Bank.

———. 2001. New approaches to multi-pillar pension systems: What in the world is going on? In Holzmann, Robert, and Joseph E. Stiglitz, eds. *Toward sustainable pension systems in the 21st Century: New ideas about old age security.* Washington, D.C.: The World Bank.

Fultz, E. and M., Ruck. 2001. Pension reform in Central and Eastern Europe: Emerging issues and patterns. *International Labor Review* 140(1): 19–43.

Galal, Ahmed. 2005. The case of formalization of business in Egypt. Policy Viewpoint Series, no. 17 (in Arabic). Egypt: The Egyptian Center for Economic Studies.

Gillion, Colin. 2000. The development and reform of social security pensions: The approach of the International Labor Office," *International Social Security Review* 53(1): 35–63, Jan-Mar.

Government Employees and Public and Private Business Sector Employees Fund. Various Issues. Annual report and closing accounts (in Arabic).

Hamdallah Fahim, Mohamed. 2002a. Early retirement (in Arabic). Paper presented at a conference on Social Insurance: Between Hope and Reality, October 13–15. Egypt: Al-Azhar University.

———. 2002b. Casual workers social insurance: Comprehensive insurance (in Arabic). Paper presented at a conference on Social Insurance: Between Hope and Reality, October 13–15. Egypt: Al-Azhar University.

Hassler, John and Assar Lindbeck. 1998. *Can and should a pay-as-you-go pension system mimic a funded one?* IUI Working Paper, no. 499. Stockholm: Research Institute of Industrial Economics.

Heller, Peter S. 1998. *Rethinking public pension reform initiatives.* IMF Working Paper, no. 61. Washington, D.C.: International Monetary Fund.

Helmy, Omneia. 2004. *Pension system reform in Egypt* (in Arabic). Working Paper Series, no. 94. Egypt: the Egyptian Center for Economic Studies.

Holzmann, Robert. 2000. *The World Bank approach to pension reform.* World Bank Social Protection Discussion Paper, no. 9807. Washington, D.C.: The World Bank, December.

Iglesias, Augusto and Robert J. Palacios. 2001. Managing public pension reserves part I: Evidence from the international experience. In Holzmann, Robert, and Joseph E. Stiglitz, eds. *Toward sustainable pension systems in the 21st century: New ideas about old age security.* Washington, D.C.: The World Bank.

Information and Decision Support Center (IDSC). 2005. Reforming the pension system in Egypt: Options and policies (in Arabic).

Institute of National Planning. 2006. *Pensions and insurance in the ARE (Reality and reform potentials)* (in Arabic). Planning and Development Issues Series, no. 189. Egypt: Institute of National Planning.

Inter-American Conference on Social Security. 2005. *An overview of notional defined pensions plans.* Working paper CISS/WP/05112, November.

International Labor Office (ILO). 1999. Social protection in Egypt. ILO/UNDP/Egypt/R 16, Social Security Department, International Labor Organization, Geneva.

———. 2006. LABORSTA Labor Statistics Database, International Labor Organization, Geneva.

James, Estelle. 1997. Pension reform: Is there an efficiency-equity trade-off? In Nancy Birdsall, Carol Graham, and Richard Sabot, eds. *Beyond trade-offs: Market reforms and equitable growth in Latin America.* Washington, D.C.: Inter-American Development Bank and Brookings Institution.

Jorgensen, Steen Lau, and Julie Van Domelen. 1999. *Helping the poor manage risk better: The role of social funds.* World Bank Social Protection Discussion Paper, no. 9934. Washington, D.C.: The World Bank.

Kane, Cheikh and Robert Palacios. 1996. The implicit pension debt. *Finance and Development* 33(2): 36–438. Washington, D.C.: International Monetary Fund, June.

Keller, Christian, and Peter S. Heller. 2001. Social sector reform in transition countries. *Finance and Development*, 38:(3) 2–5. Washington, D.C.: International Monetary Fund.

Keran, Michael, and Hang-Sheng Cheng. 2002. *International experience and pension reform in China.* The 1990 Institute Issue Paper, no. 16. California: 1990 Institute, April.

Lindbeck, Assar, and Mats Persson. 2000. What are the gains from pension reform? *IUI Working Paper* no. 535. Stockholm: Research Institute for Industrial Economics.

Loewe, Markus. 2000. *Social security in Egypt: An analysis and agenda for policy reform.* ERF Working Paper, no. 2024. Cairo: Economic Research Forum for the Middle East, Iran, and Turkey.

Ministry of Finance. 2003. Financial statement on draft state budget FY2003/04 (in Arabic). Egypt: Ministry of Finance.

———. 2005. Financial statement on draft state budget FY2005/06 (in Arabic). Egypt: Ministry of Finance.

———. 2006. Statistical statement on draft state budget FY2006/07 (in Arabic). Egypt: Ministry of Finance.

Ministry of Social Insurance and Social Affairs. 2000. Study on the impact of early retirement on social insurance systems, unpublished memorandum (in Arabic). Egypt: Ministry of Social Insurance and Social Affairs.

———. 2000/01. Accomplishments and work results report (in Arabic). Egypt: Ministry of Social Insurance and Social Affairs.

———. 2003/04. Accomplishments and work results report (in Arabic). Egypt: Ministry of Social Insurance and Social Affairs.

———. 2003a. Executive stand of ministry assignments stated in government statement dated 29/12/2002 and future prospects (in Arabic). Egypt: Ministry of Social Insurance and Social Affairs.

———. 2003b. Insurance evasion dilemma, unpublished memorandum (in Arabic). Egypt: Ministry of Social Insurance and Social Affairs.

Ministry of State for Economic Development. 2006. Economic performance and development accomplishments, follow-up report of 2005/06 plan and last quarter of the year (April–June), September (in Arabic). Egypt: Ministry of State for Economic Development.

Mitchell, Olivia S. 1998a. Social security reform in Latin America. Review of the Federal Reserve Bank of St. Louis, March/April, 15–18. St. Louis, MO: Federal Reserve Bank of St. Louis.

National Democratic Party, Economic Committee. 2003. Vision for the national social insurance system, unpublished paper, April 9 (in Arabic).

———. 2006. Employment and Investment Policies, fourth annual conference, September.

Norman, Goran and Daniel J. Mitchell. 2000. *Pension reform in Sweden: Lessons for American policymakers.* Backgrounder no. 1381. Washington, D.C.: The Heritage Foundation.

Palacios, Robert J. 2002. *Managing public pension reserves part II: Lessons from Five recent OECD initiatives.* World Bank Social Protection Discussion Paper, no. 0219. Washington, D.C.: The World Bank.

Palacios, R., and Montserrat Pallares-Miralles. 2000. *International patterns of pension provision.* World Bank Social Protection Discussion Paper, no. 0009. Washington, D.C.: The World Bank.

Palme, Joakim. 2003. *The "great" Swedish pension reform.* Stockholm: Swedish Institute.

Palmer, Edward. 1999. *The Swedish pension reform-framework and issues.* World Bank Pension Primer. Washington, D.C.: World Bank.

———. 2001. Swedish pension reform: How did it evolve, and what does it mean for the future? In M. Feldstein and H. Siebert (eds.), *Social security pension reform in Europe.* Chicago: University of Chicago Press.

People's Assembly. 2003a. General report and committee recommendations regarding the final account of the budget for the state, public economic authorities, National Military Production Organization, and the public treasury for FY2000/01 (in Arabic). Egypt: People's Assembly.

———. 2003b. Report of the Plan and Budget Committee on a draft law allocating state's budget FY2003/04, eighth legislative term, third ordinary session, June (in Arabic).

———. 2004. Report of the Plan and Budget Committee on comments and recommendations of the Assembly's specialized committees regarding draft state budget FY2004/05, eighth legislative term, fourth ordinary session, May (in Arabic).

———. 2005a. Report of the Plan and Budget Committee on draft state budget FY2005/06 and draft economic and social development plan for 2005/06, fourth year of the five-year plan (2002/03–2006/07) eighth legislative term, fifth ordinary session, June (in Arabic).

———. 2005b. Report of the Plan and Budget Committee on the closing account of state's budget, public economic authorities, National Military Production Authority, and the public treasury FY2002/03, eighth legislative chapter, fifth ordinary session, February (in Arabic).

———. 2006a. Report of the Plan and Budget Committee on draft state budget FY2006/07 and draft economic and social development plan for 2006/07, fifth year of the five-year plan (2002/03–2006/07) ninth legislative term, first ordinary session, May (in Arabic).

———. 2006b. Report of the Plan and Budget Committee on the closing account of the budget for the state, public economic authorities, National Authority for Military Production, and the public treasury FY2003/04, ninth legislative term, first ordinary session, March (in Arabic).

———. 2006c. Report of the Plan and Budget Committee on committee readings and recommendations regarding draft budget and draft economic and social development plan 2006/07, fifth year of the five-year plan (2002/03–2006/07), ninth legislative term, first ordinary session, May (in Arabic).

Rutkowski, Michal. 2002. *Lessons learned from pension reform in Central and Eastern Europe.* Heritage Lectures no. 729. Washington, D.C.: The Heritage Foundation.

Schwarz, Anita M., and Asli Demirguc-Kunt. 1999. *Taking stock of pension reforms around the world.* Social Protection Discussion Paper, no. 9917. Washington, D.C.: The World Bank.

Sinn, Hans-Werner. 2000. *Why a funded pension system is useful and why it is not useful.* NBER Working Paper, no. 7592. Cambridge, MA: National Bureau of Economic Research.

Soto, Mauricio. 2005. *Chilean pension reform: The good, the bad, and the in between*. An Issue in Brief no. 31. Center for Retirement Research at Boston College, June.

Stanko, D. 2003. *Polish pension funds, does the system work? Cost, efficiency and performance measurement issues*. Discussion Paper PI-0302. London: University of London, Pensions Institute, Birkbeck College.

Sunden, A. 2000. *How will Sweden's new pension system work?* Issue Brief no. 3. Chestnut Hill, MA: Center for Retirement Research at Boston College.

———. 2004. How do individual accounts work in the Swedish pension system? *An Issue in Brief, no. 22*. Center for Retirement Research at Boston College, August.

Vittas, Dimitri. 1997. *The role of non-bank financial intermediaries in Egypt and other MENA countries*. World Bank Country Economic Department Papers no. 1892. Washington, D.C.: The World Bank.

Weaver, Kent. 2005. *Design and implementation issues in Swedish individual pension accounts*. CRR WP 200–05. Center for Retirement Research at Boston College, April.

Williamson, John B. 2004. Assessing the pension reform potential of a notional defined contribution pillar. *International Social Security Review* 57(1): 47–64. International Social Security Association, Massachusetts, United States.

Williamson, John B. and Matthew Williams. 2003. *The notional defined contribution model: An assessment of the strengths and limitations of a new approach to the provision of old age security*. Working Paper 2003–18. Chestnut Hill, MA: Center for Retirement Research at Boston College.

World Bank. 1994. *Averting the old age crisis: Policies to protect the old and promote growth*. A World Bank Policy Research Report. New York: Oxford University Press.

———. 1997. Pension reform, contractual saving, and capital markets. In *World Bank Report no. 1620–EGT., Arab Republic of Egypt Country Economic Memorandum–Working Papers Annex, vol. III*. World Bank Resident Mission in Egypt, March.

———. 2001. *Transition. Paying for a shift from pay-as-you-go financing to funded pensions*. World Bank Pension Reform Primer. Washington, D.C.: The World Bank.

———. 2002a. *Reducing vulnerability and increasing opportunity–Social protection in the Middle East and North Africa*. Orientations in Development Series, Middle East and North Africa Region. Washington, D.C.: The World Bank.

———. 2002b. Notional accounts: Notional defined contribution plans as a pension reform strategy. *World Bank Pension Reform Primer*. Washington, D.C.: The World Bank.

———. 2006a. *Egypt: A framework for an integrated reform of the pension system*. Policy Note, Middle East and North Africa Social and Human Development Group (MNSHD). Washington, D.C.: The World Bank.

———. 2006b. *Pension reform and the development of pension systems: An evaluation of World Bank assistance*. Washington, D.C.: The World Bank.

Zaidi, Asghar. 2006. *Pension policy in EU25 and its possible impact on elderly poverty*. Policy Brief. European Centre for Social Welfare Policy and Research, September. Vienna: European Centre for Social Welfare Policy and Research.

PART III

Sectoral Issues

CHAPTER 8

On Efficient Utilization of Egypt's Energy Resources: Oil and Natural Gas

Tarek H. Selim[1]

Energy is a prime source of livelihood for many nations and is a cause of affluence for others. In Egypt, energy constitutes one fifth of the country's overall economic activity, a little less than half of the country's export revenues, and is a strategic resource for future growth. Yet Egypt's energy reserves are quickly depletable, with a risk of over-consumption, production is aging as far as oil is concerned, and at the same time energy reserves are rather new with respect to natural gas. Hence, there are future tradeoffs between oil and natural gas in the Egyptian economy. Specifically, oil and gas should be considered as demand substitutes in addition to possessing future complementary roles in energy supply.

The strategic importance of the energy sector to the Egyptian economy is evident when examining the country's other sources of comparative advantage: (1) cotton, (2) tourism, and (3) the Suez Canal. Exports of cotton have been declining rapidly in the past couple of decades because of effective world demand for products to substitute for Egyptian long-staple cotton fabrics. In addition, tourism is vulnerable to domestic and external shocks of the Middle East, and the Suez Canal is managed as a fixed income generator of government revenue. Thus, energy is the leading strategic resource on which the Egyptian economy can depend while seeking sustainable development.

Such a positive statement does not come without reservations. Notably, with the continuing decline in Egyptian crude oil production, Egypt's hydrocarbon future lies in natural gas. In particular, the country's gas reserves have increased so substantially over the last decade that it is now feasible to start exporting large volumes of gas as well as catering to growth in domestic demand in the coming decade. Most recent figures estimate Egypt's natural gas reserves, ranked 14th worldwide, at 66 trillion cubic feet (tcf) of proven reserves and up to 140 tcf of probable reserves. However, the recent price hikes in crude oil present an opportunity cost for the economy in terms of hard currency exports. A policy maker is thus faced with the challenge of having to answer the important question of: "What should Egypt do with its energy reserves?" Should the Egyptian economy export a sizable portion of natural gas and leave oil for domestic consumption, even though such consumption is subsidized and creates a strain on the national budget? Or should Egypt predominantly export its scarce oil resources, leaving domestic consumption to abundant natural gas reserves, even though there are switching costs involved? In either situation, there is an opportunity cost. The first situation creates lost opportunities in terms of oil exports at high prices, coupled with domestic over-consumption at subsidized prices. The second situation creates an opportunity cost of natural gas exports and over-depletion of a strategic resource.

This research will tackle the topic of energy policy in Egypt on several fronts. Analysis of the world energy market (Section 1) with reasonable estimates of future prices for oil and natural gas will be conducted, such that the "most likely" scenario from the US Department of Energy's Information Administration database will be utilized (Energy Information Administration 2006). This will be followed by analysis of the energy sector in Egypt including historical production, consumption, and net exports of energy resources (Section 2). In addition, the research will tackle when and to what extent Egypt will turn into a net importer of oil, and analyze the trend of such behavior. Derivation of a time path for natural gas resource depletion, based upon proven reserves, and a forecasted timeline of natural gas consumption until 2025 will be conducted. This will be based upon comparative elasticity analysis (Section 3) between oil and natural gas including the calculation of price elasticity, income elasticity, and energy/GDP elasticity for both resources, and the calculation of the elasticity of substitution between oil and natural gas. The analysis will also include an energy sustainability constraint (application of Hartwick's model) on resource extraction rates, with the objective of guaranteeing future expected energy demand, conditional upon GDP growth rate targets, which guarantee sustainable development (Section 3). Energy sustainability analysis will incorporate alternative energy use including solar and nuclear energy. Policy recommendations will conclude the research (Section 4).

1. The World Energy Market and Future Projections Until 2025

Energy is considered a causal input to economic development, and the performance of the world energy market has a great effect on the quality of life of current and future generations. At the world energy market level, oil and natural gas have very different characteristics. The oil market involves a cartel (OPEC) and has a non-differentiated price element across geographic regions, whereas the natural gas market contains a price advantage within regions, less thermal efficiency, and cleaner emissions than oil. The main future energy challenges are to increase world energy security and to minimize the environmental impact of energy use, especially carbon emissions. Although it is forecast that world energy demand will increase, due to rising demand from key developing countries like China and India, it is also expected that world energy supply will expand and overcome such demand. This scenario has been the main drive for forecasting energy prices by the US Department of Energy, Energy Information Administration in its Energy Modeling System and Forecast Database (World Energy Outlook 2006).

Although price plays a key role in the choice between different sources of energy, oil products are not easily displaced for certain types of use (mainly transportation). Crude oil behaves much like any other commodity with wide price swings in times of shortage or oversupply. Its prices are driven by supply (mainly OPEC) rather than demand. However, natural gas prices are predominantly demand-driven, and the fundamental drivers are weather, season, and inventory levels. The price of natural gas varies widely between regional markets. It tends to settle lower than its oil equivalent, although there are circumstances, such as in East Asian markets, where delivered prices are typically higher than their oil equivalent. Comparing oil with gas reflects the fact that oil deposits tend to be in areas that are not major consumers of oil, but for natural gas the production and consumption regional match is much better. The effect of transportation costs is strongest in the case of natural gas, with crude oil being generally moved via a pipeline because it is the cheapest mode. The thermal efficiency of oil is superior to that of gas as one cubic meter of oil has the same energy content as 1,000 cubic meters of natural gas, yet natural gas produces less carbon emissions than oil, and is therefore more environmentally friendly.

Most experts believe that there will be no shortage of international oil and gas reserves over the next few decades, provided sufficient investment is made into new production, transport, and refinery capacity. Maintaining robust and transparent international markets for energy, including the free movement of capital, is a key policy objective. But many reserves lie in parts of the world ridden with political instability, or where other barriers to investment exist. This, however, is not considered to be a major impediment to energy supply so long as Middle Eastern political tensions are contained and no new wars break out. Moreover, in terms of oil, non-OPEC production is expected to expand rapidly, creating oversupply at future oil prices. For natural gas, reserves are expected to be excessively utilized (or even depleted), especially the abundant natural gas deposits in the former Soviet Union bloc, such as Russia and Ukraine.

Figure 8.1. World Energy Market Forecasted Price Paths for Oil and Gas Until 2025

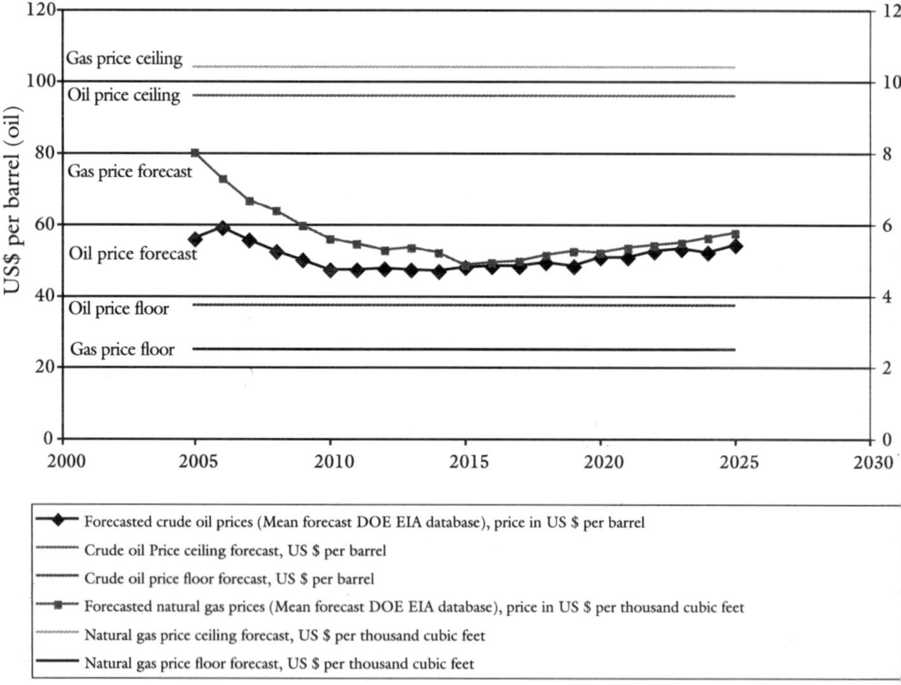

Source: Author's calculations based on World Energy Outlook (2006) and Energy Information Administration (2006).

As seen from Figure 8.1, world energy prices are expected to decrease over time until 2015, due to expanding world supply, expected reserve concessions, and lower growth in China's energy demand. However, analysts predict that oil prices will witness large swings in the future, with an average price of US $52 per barrel, with a price floor of US $37 per barrel and a ceiling as high as US $96 per barrel over the time period of 2005–2025. Thus, oil prices are expected to have a large variance over time, but the average price is expected to be close to the 2004 standards. The assumptions here are that the political turbulence in Iraq will ease with time, the nuclear crisis in Iran will be solved by diplomatic means, and that energy prices will stabilize beyond the Bush administration in the United States. However, if the current problems in the Middle East intensify, particularly the threat of Iran halting its energy exports to the West, oil prices can reach as high as US $96 per barrel. The situation with natural gas is considerably different. Russia and Ukraine, in addition to Qatar and Iran, hold the largest natural gas reserves, with Russian reserves estimated at more than 1,400 tcf at a bare minimum. These world reserves are predominantly underutilized, creating relative resource abundance. The average price for natural gas per thousand cubic feet, for the time period 2005–2025, is US $5.67 for the Middle East region. The lowest estimate stands at US $4.87 and the highest at US $6.66 for the Middle East and North Africa region, although price variations are much higher for other regions (see Figure 8.1 for weighted average world price variations for natural gas).[2] Hence, price variation in the Middle East for natural gas is estimated at 15 percent. This runs counter to future expectations of international oil prices, with upper price variation reaching 80 percent and a lower price variation of 27 percent (see Figure 8.1).

An important element of comparison between oil and natural gas in the international energy market is price. Oil prices behave with wide price swings in times of shortage or oversupply, but those price swings are expected to be short in duration (peak or trough phases) until 2025. Even though oil prices are predominantly supply-driven, natural gas prices, in contrast, are predominantly demand-driven and vary by region due to pipeline transportation costs. In addition, the expected profit margin for oil through 2025 is 70 percent on average, since the cost of oil production is expected to decrease due to process innovation reaching as low as US $3–$7 per barrel (the lower end attributed to Arabian Gulf producers). In contrast, the expected profit margin for natural gas through 2025 is 20 percent, which makes economies of scale in natural gas production more necessary than oil. This runs in line with substantial increases in natural gas production in the future.

Table 8.1. World Energy Market for Oil and Natural Gas: Projections Until 2025

	World Oil Market	*Natural Gas Market*
Pricing	$57 mean price (US $ per barrel). Large price swings until 2025: $37 price floor, $96 price ceiling. High-end price variation at 80 percent, lower-end price variation at 27 percent.	Stable regional prices at $5.7 with $0.8 as standard deviation through 2025 (US $ per thousand cubic feet). Maximum price swings (variation) at 15 percent for Middle East/North Africa region.
Elasticities	Oil is more price inelastic than natural gas, but carries higher income elasticity.	Natural gas has lower income elasticity, but is more price elastic than oil.
Profit margins	There is a uniform world oil price (non-differentiated on a regional level), and profit margin is expected at 70 percent due to cost-reducing process innovations, with least cost estimate at $3 per barrel (Arabian Gulf producers).	Differentiated prices by region, with profit margins expected at 20 percent requiring economies of scale.
Consumption	1.9 percent annual growth rate to 2025. Consumption end use predominantly in transportation with declining power generation demand for oil.	2.2 percent annual growth rate to 2025. Consumption end use in residential, commercial and power generation.
Reserves	1,293 billion barrels (Jan. 2006). Modest expectations of additional reserves.	6,112 trillion cubic feet (Jan 2006). High expectations of probable reserves.
Production	OPEC remaining a key player with declining dominance. Production capacity reaching maturity in 2015 and remaining stable to 2025. Reserves to production ratio of 115 years (Arabian Gulf region)	No OPEC (cartel) equivalent expected. Net production surplus of 16 trillion cubic feet by 2025 in developing countries.
Thermal efficiency	Oil is more thermally efficient than gas. One cubic meter of oil has the same energy content as 1,000 cubic meters of natural gas	Gas is less thermally efficient but is a cleaner fuel.
Kyoto Protocol	Kyoto Protocol carbon emissions reduction standards will affect oil market negatively more than gas.	Kyoto Protocol standards will lead to expansion of natural gas market.
Transportation cost	Alternatives to oil pipeline transportation exist, but pipeline is expected to remain the cheapest mode.	There is no expected alternative to pipeline for natural gas transportation except LNG (Liquefied Natural Gas).

Source: Author's comparison analysis based on data from World Energy Outlook (2006), Energy Information Administration (2006), and Clarkson and Deyes (2002).

2. Egypt's Energy Sector: Historical Trends

During the past several years, production of petroleum products constituted around 8 percent of GDP, and was the largest single industrial activity. The export of crude oil and petroleum products constituted 40 percent of Egypt's export returns and around 20 percent of its GDP.[3] By the start of 2006, Egypt's proven oil reserves have been maintained officially at 3.7 billion barrels with no substantial increase in the past decade. However, export of oil is rapidly declining and Egypt is expected to be a net importer of oil in the short run. Natural gas, on the other hand, is abundant with reserves estimated at 66 trillion cubic feet.

The natural gas sector is one of the fastest-growing sectors in the Egyptian economy and production increased more than two-fold between 1999 and 2003[4] and almost a thousand-fold over the last 20 years by 2005 standards. It is worth mentioning that the substantial increase in the production of natural gas helped to offset some of the negative repercussions of the reduction of crude oil production. The average daily production of natural gas during 2004 was 3.6 billion cubic feet per day (bcf/d).[5] Total gas consumption increased dramatically when thermal power plants were ordered to convert from oil to gas. This was a pivotal and strategic decision made in Egypt's energy policy history. These plants now constitute around 65 percent of total gas consumption.[6] In 2001/2002, Egypt ranked third in worldwide natural gas consumption, with a daily consumption of 2.6 billion cubic feet (bcf).[7] Around 84 percent of Egypt's electric generating capacity is thermal (natural gas), with the remaining 16 percent hydroelectric from the Aswan High Dam. The government has converted all oil-fired plants to run on natural gas as their primary fuel.[8]

Historically, the rate of growth of oil production steadily exceeded that of oil consumption. However, this trend has shifted. With oil production continuously declining and oil consumption increasing due to population growth, oil exports have seen a steep decline. Egypt is thus expected to be a net oil importer in the near future. In addition, Egypt is faced with a trade-off between exporting crude oil and exporting refined oil products. On one hand, if Egypt wants to maintain being a crude oil exporter then it would have to decrease the throughput to refineries and hence decrease its refined oil export revenues. The significance of the petrochemicals industry is further accentuated by the fact that natural gas is one of its primary inputs. On the other hand, Egypt's natural gas reserves provide an excellent potential advantage for the production of petrochemicals. Unfortunately, production of petrochemical products only covers a third of domestic demand. This should encourage the government to develop this sector in a bid to improve its deficit situation. Furthermore, petrochemicals are strategic intermediate inputs to many industries, and strengthening that sector would boost Egypt's industrial base and ensure a sustained raw material supply chain (AmCham 2003, 34). The Egyptian government undertook a long-term investment plan recently to the tune of $10 billion in order to develop the petrochemical industry by 2021. The plan is envisaged to take full advantage of Egypt's gas reserves to maximize value-added benefits. A by-product of this ambitious plan is the import substitution of the current $3 billion bill that Egypt foots to cover its petrochemical imports.[9]

Oil Reserves

Egypt's proven oil reserves were estimated at 3.6 billion barrels on average from 1996 to 1999. In January 2000, the government released a revised estimate of probable crude oil reserves, raising the figure to 8.2 billion barrels, based on new finds and increased recovery ratios. Even though the proven crude oil reserves declined and stood at 2.9 billion barrels from 2000 till 2002 (AmCham 2003, 12), as of 1 January 2006 Egypt's proven crude oil reserves were estimated at the amount of 3.7 billion barrels (APRC 2003, 94).

Oil Production and Consumption

Egyptian oil production in 2003 averaged 618,000 barrels per day (bpd), down sharply from a peak in 1996 of 922,000 bpd (AmCham 2003, 2; Energy Information Administration 2006). In contrast, domestic demand for oil has been climbing from 501,000 bpd in 1996 to 566,000 bpd in 2003. The sharp increase in local oil consumption over the past decade can be attributed to two factors: (1) economic growth in the late 1990s contributed to higher demand for oil, and (2) oil subsidies encouraged over-consumption. The prices of most types of fuel have not moved substantially for the past decade, except due to the recent partial lifting of oil subsidies. This policy, even after partial subsidy removal, has encouraged over-consumption. Increased exploration, particularly in new areas, may lead to new discoveries raising production above the 800,000 bpd level. Figure 8.2 shows the trend of oil production, consumption, and exports in Egypt from 1980 until 2004. By breaking down the country's total production into consumption and exports, it is seen that during the last twenty years (1985–2004) Egypt had squeezed its export revenues by over-consumption.

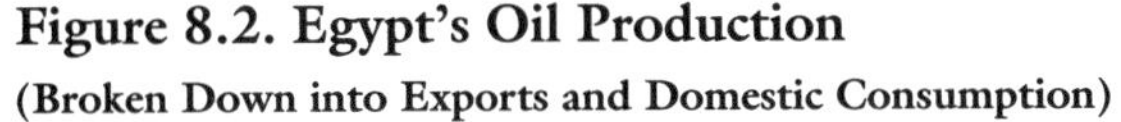

Figure 8.2. Egypt's Oil Production
(Broken Down into Exports and Domestic Consumption)

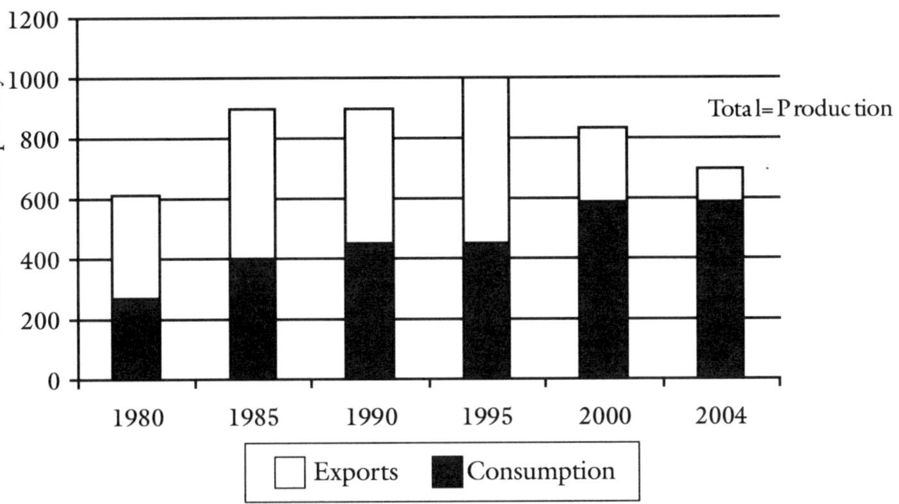

Source: AmCham (2003) and Energy Information Administration (2006).

Moreover, despite the buoyant export activity and the large number of discoveries made each year, which are brought into production as rapidly as possible, there seems little prospect for Egypt to reverse the decline in its crude oil production in the future (see Figure 8.3). Not only is oil production steadily decreasing due to X-inefficiency in production, but proven oil reserves have leveled off, putting a double squeeze on the amount of oil available for export. Some analysts suggest that Egypt could cease to be a net oil exporter sometime between 2007 and 2010 (APRC 2003, 94). As will be analyzed later, the author estimates that net imports of oil will become a fact in the short run for Egypt, as early as 2007/2008.

Figure 8.3. Trend of Egypt's Oil Production, 1992–2004

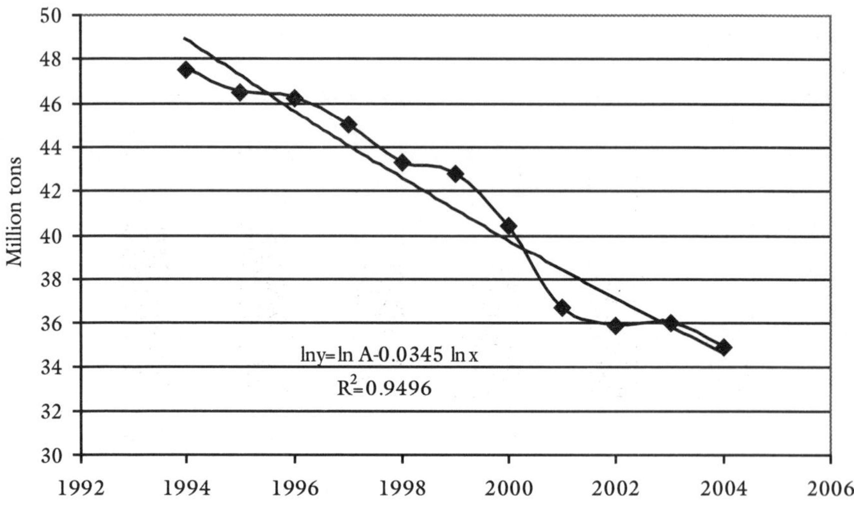

Source: IDSC 2006, Government of Egypt, with declining trend line estimated by the author.

Oil Areas of Production

The Gulf of Suez remains by far the biggest-producing region in Egypt, accounting for about 70 percent of total oil production, although its share is falling. The second biggest oil-producing region is the Western Desert, which accounts for 17 percent. Egypt also draws oil from the Sinai Peninsula (7 percent) and the Eastern Desert (6 percent) (APRC 2003, 94; OFE 2001).

Oil Exports

Egypt has little crude oil left for export, since its domestic refining industry requires nearly 700,000 bpd of feedstock. The Egyptian General Petroleum Corporation (EGPC) is still able to export a small volume of crude, but its exports of refined products are now greater in volume as well as in value. Egypt was a net oil exporter of around 100,000 bpd in 2004 (AmCham 2003, 9; Energy Information Administration 2006). Net exports sharply decreased since 1995 from 560,000 bpd. Recent estimates put Egypt's oil production, consumption, and exports at 700,000 bpd, 590,000 bpd, and 110,000 bpd, respectively. The trend of Egypt's oil exports is seen in Figure 8.4. The author uses a combination of moving averages and non-linear forecast to estimate the expected future trend of oil exports using historical data ($R^2 = 87.89\%$).

The main assumption utilized is constant income elasticity of demand based on historical averages (1980–2005), constant population growth rate, and a targeted increase in average income (GDP per capita) of 6 percent annually. This scenario is seen as the most reasonable with the information currently available.[10] Conditional on those assumptions, the author estimates that Egypt will become a net importer of oil as early as 2007/2008.

Figure 8.4. Historical Trend of Egypt's Oil Exports since 1980

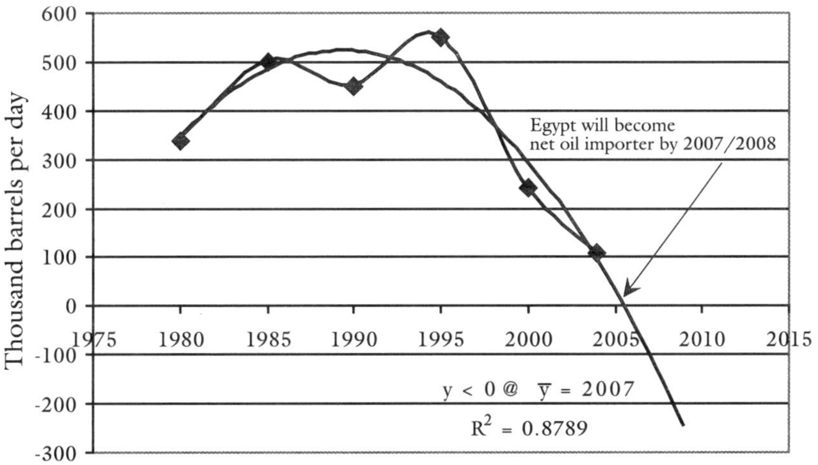

Source: IDSC data with trend estimated by author.

Natural Gas Reserves

Natural gas is destined to become more and more important to the future of Egypt because of recent major discoveries making it an abundant resource. There are vast reserves of natural gas with a strong potential for more discoveries. Beginning in the early 1990s, foreign oil companies began more attractive exploration for natural gas in Egypt, and very quickly found a series of significant natural gas deposits especially in the Western Desert, the Nile Delta, and under the Mediterranean Sea. Proven reserves stand at 66 trillion cubic feet (tcf) in 2006, a little more than the 65 tcf in 2004, up from 55 tcf in 2002, and significantly up from 40 tcf in 2000, with probable reserves estimated at 120–140 tcf as a lower bound range. Major discoveries between 1997 and 2001 in the Nile Delta and the Western Desert doubled Egypt's proven reserves. Figure 8.5 shows the increase in Egypt's natural gas proven reserves over time.

Figure 8.5. Historical Proven Natural Gas Reserves in Egypt

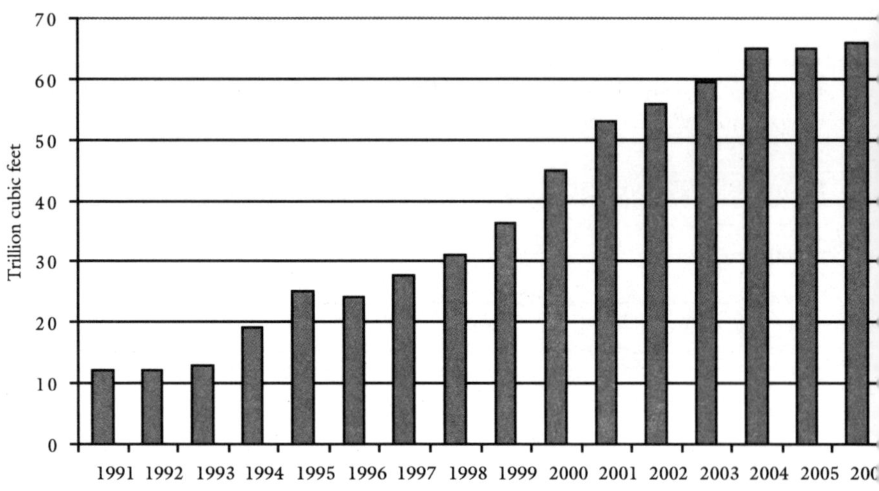

Source: APRC (2003); IDSC (2006); and AmCham (2003).

Natural Gas Production and Consumption

Egypt's natural gas sector has been expanding rapidly, and production has nearly doubled in the last six years. Production in 2005 stood at more than 3 billion cubic feet per day (bcf/d) from 1.6 bcf/d in 1999, and is expected to reach 7 bcf/d in 2006. Output from the Abu Madi and Badreddin fields accounts for more than half of the country's production. In the past, consumption has been almost identical to production—at 98.5 percent of production capacity in the last 15 years. Thermal power plants account for about 65 percent of Egypt's total gas consumption. Large industrial consumers have also been switching to gas, including petrochemical plants, a large new fertilizer plant in Suez, and several major new steel projects in Alexandria, Suez, and south of Aswan. Some 20,000 taxis in Cairo have been modified to run on Compressed Natural Gas (CNG) as part of a pilot program. British Gas heads a group that includes Orascom (an Egyptian construction firm), and Edison International SpA that intends to invest $220 million in a distribution network to serve Upper Egypt down to Assiut, an area with no existing gas service. The network may be expanded as far south as Aswan.

3. Egypt's Energy Sector: Sustainability Analysis and Forecast

Hartwick's energy sustainability model (Hartwick 1977; Hanley, Shogren, and White 1997; and Cairns and Yang 2000) provides an optimal allocation solution to energy resources based on sustainable development constraints. Hartwick's model (usually referred to in the literature as 'Hartwick's Rule') is a dynamic model relating efficient extraction rates to total energy reserves and the forecasted rate of sustainable consumption. Hartwick's Rule, as an application to the model, implies that efficient utilization of energy resources will deliver optimum resources extraction rates, such that current welfare is maximized without compromising the ability of future generations to maximize their own welfare. Consumer welfare, in Hartwick's model, depends entirely on consumption. Production rates are derived from the path of sustainable consumption.

Based on Hartwick's methodology, different economic sensitivity analyses have been conducted on oil and natural gas in this research. Those are based on the assumptions of historical population growth rates, future growth in domestic demand (demand-driven market analysis), and estimated elasticity over time. Dynamic optimization analysis is conducted to reach the rate of resource depletion based on annual resource extraction rates (annual efficient production levels).

For price elasticities, it was found that demand price elasticity for oil is 0.02, while it was found to be 0.26 for natural gas. Hence, oil is almost completely price inelastic, whereas natural gas is generally price inelastic. Thus, for the case of oil, prices are not a key factor in the pattern of domestic consumption over time. Since both oil and natural gas are price inelastic, both are considered necessary goods in consumption. Oil is considered almost completely price inelastic (it is very difficult to be substituted) due to its importance as a necessary input in most of Egyptian industries. Hence, there exists a "resistance to change" on the part of consumers for a significant price increase in oil. In essence, lifting oil subsidies will not generate a sizable reduction in consumption. Even for natural gas, if price increases by a significant 20 percent, domestic consumption will decline by only 5 percent.[11]

With respect to income elasticity, it was found that income elasticity for oil is 0.43 whereas that of natural gas is 1.4. Consequently, relative to income levels and associated budget expenditures of households, oil is a necessary good whereas natural gas is a normal good. A rise in income is associated with more demand increase for natural gas than that of oil. Based on elasticity estimates, it is calculated that social losses (additional economic burdens) per Egyptian household from totally lifting oil subsidies will be LE 110 per month/household (by 2005 standards). This is a substantial portion of a typical citizen's annual average income. Hence, the removal of oil subsidies should be undertaken in phases. In addition, the expected inflationary pressure from lifting oil subsidies is derived. It is estimated that total elimination of oil subsidies will cause an additional 5 to 7 percentage points of inflationary pressure on the Egyptian economy. This is based on multiplier effects of higher commodity prices for most essential goods due to higher input costs and higher transportation costs across the supply chain. Consequently, the political economy and real sector adjustments to this inflationary pressure must be accounted for within a strategy of gradual removal of oil subsidies.

The relationship between oil and natural gas to value of GDP was also estimated. It is found that sensitivity of oil/GDP is 0.3 whereas that of natural gas is 0.9. The weighted average of energy elasticity to GDP is 0.5. Consequently, the decomposition of energy to GDP yields an oil impact share of 67 percent and a natural gas impact share of 33 percent.[12] This has important repercussions on target GDP growth rates. In essence, a target GDP growth rate of 6 percent will necessitate energy demand growth at 1.8 percent annually for oil.

Table 8.2. Comparison and Elasticity Estimates for Oil and Natural Gas in Egypt

	Oil	*Natural Gas*
Reserves	A historical decline in reserves. Total proven reserves at 3.7 billion barrels.	New reserves with strong potential for more discoveries. Total proven reserves at 66 trillion cubic feet.
Production	A decrease in production due to subsidization, technical X-inefficiency reasons and decline in reserves. Historical 3.45 percent annual decline (12–yr horizon).	Production has doubled due to increase in reserves and increase in demand as a substitute for oil as it is environmentally friendly. Historical 12.2 percent annual growth (6–yr horizon).
Consumption	An increase in consumption due to economic growth.	An increase in domestic demand mainly due to thermal power plant conversion.
Price Elasticity	Demand price elasticity is 0.02 (completely inelastic).	Demand price elasticity is 0.26 (inelastic).

(continued)

Cross Elasticity	Cross elasticity between oil and gas > zero, they are substitutes.	
Income Elasticity	Income elasticity is 0.43, which shows that it is a necessary good.	Income elasticity is 1.4 (normal good).
Areas of Production	70 percent from the Gulf of Suez, 16 percent from the Western Desert, 7 percent from the Sinai Peninsula and 6 percent from the Eastern Desert.	The Nile Delta, the Western Desert and under the Mediterranean Sea.
Main Players	EGPC (state-run), Gupco, Petrobel, Badr el-Din Petroleum Company, El Zaafarana Oil Company and Shell.	EGPC (state-run), IEOC, Eni-Agip, BP-Amoco, British Gas, Shell, Edison, International SpA and Repsol-YPF.
Transportation	Suez Canal and Sumed Pipelines.	Pipelines.
Exports	A decline in exports due to increase in local consumption accompanied by a decrease in production.	Beginning of exports in 2004/2005 looking for new opportunities after the increase in reserves.
Elasticity of Substitution	It was found that the elasticity of substitution between oil and gas in production is 3.4; while the elasticity of substitution in consumption is 4.06.	
Energy/GDP elast.	Oil/GDP elasticity is 0.3.	Natural Gas/GDP elasticity is 0.9.

Source: Author's calculations based on historical and forecast results. Assumptions include constant elasticity of substitution between oil and natural gas over time in consumption and production, constant target growth rate of 6 percent for GDP, and data analysis based on proven (not probable) reserves taken as the country's total energy resource endowments. Cross elasticity measure is estimated based on prices, whereas income elasticity measure is estimated based on the economy's per-capita GDP.

A forecasted oil production decline of 3.4 percent annually implies that Egypt's oil imports will average an increase of 5.2 percent annually. Consequently, it is projected that Egypt will become a net importer of oil by 2007/2008, with net oil shortages reaching 100,000 bpd in 2008, 300,000 bpd in 2015, and as high as 600,000 bpd in 2025 (see Figure 8.6).

Figure 8.6. Egypt's Oil Future: Sustainability Analysis and Forecast

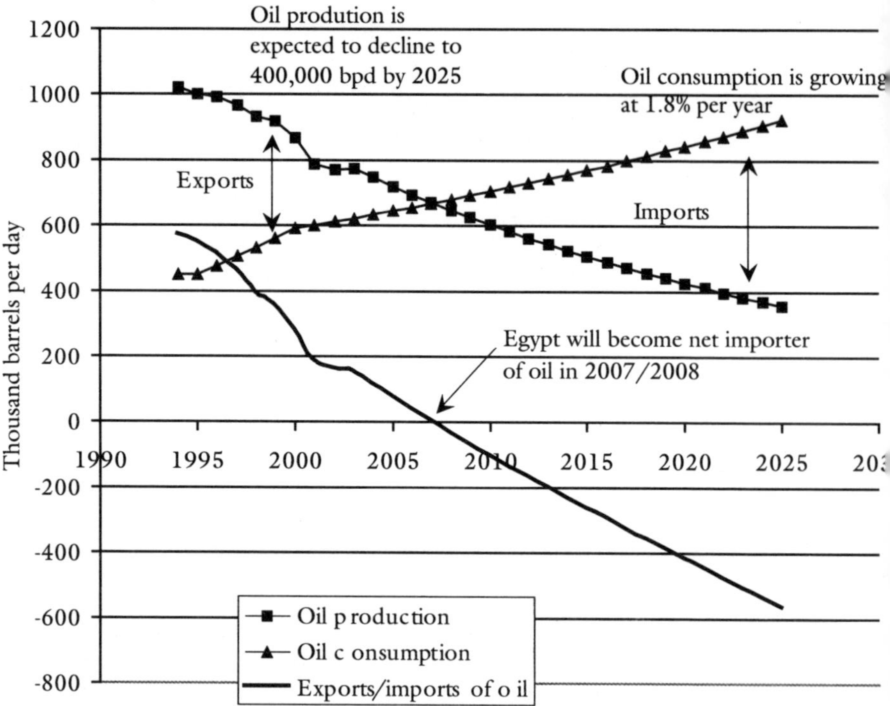

Source: Author's calculations based on model results.

The future of natural gas in Egypt looks brighter (Figure 8.7). Even though consumption of natural gas is expected to rise steeply until 2025, production can overcome such demand and can produce a sizable volume of exports. Consumption is expected to rise by nearly 9.45 percent annually due to the combined effects of population growth, output growth (GDP growth), and the transition from oil to gas in thermal power generation. Production is expected to reach 7 billion cubic feet per day (bcf/d) in 2006, and economic policy should target a production rate of 10 bcf/day by 2010 and 25 bcf/d by 2020. In retrospect, exports are a key opportunity for natural gas in Egypt. Egypt should be able to deliver an export volume of 5 bcf/d by 2010 and 10bcf/d by 2017 (see Figure 8.7).

Figure 8.7. Egypt's Future of Natural Gas: Sustainability Analysis and Forecast

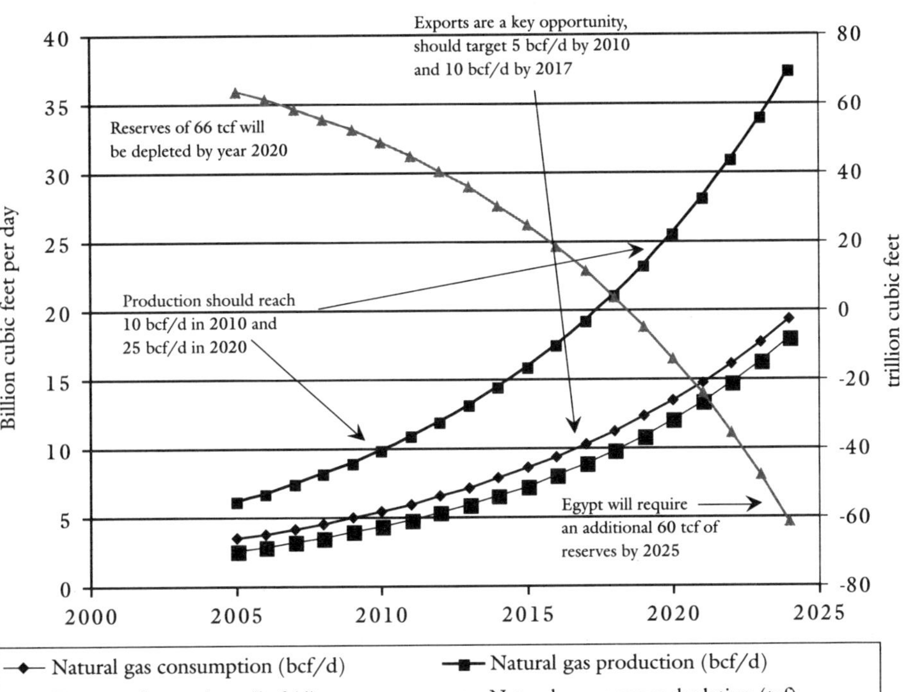

Source: Author's calculations based on model results.

Based on sustainability calculations, the author estimates that Egypt's proven reserves of 66 trillion cubic feet will be depleted by 2020, and that the economy will require an additional 60 tcf of additional reserves of natural gas by 2025. These additional reserves are within the probable gas reserve endowments of the country (120–180 tcf of probable reserves are the current estimate). This, of course, will require complementary investment costs associated with exploration and resource distribution. However, profit margins of 20 percent are expected to persist with time, conditional on economies of scale in production.

4. Egypt's Energy Sector: Future Outlook and Recommendations

In general, the petroleum industry in Egypt should be considered one of the major economic development catalysts in the economy mainly due to investment generation but not particularly because of employment generation. Hence, physical capital requirements are key to the future growth of the industry, especially as those are related to economies of scale and associated reduction in unit production costs (thus creating what has been commonly known as "Stein's competitive advantage"). In retrospect, energy resource endowments are necessary, but not sufficient, conditions to impact long term development. In addition to resource endowments (comparative advantage), a sustainable element of competitive advantage must be present. This can be achieved by process innovations yielding cost-reduction advantages in the energy industry in comparison to other countries. That is not yet achieved in Egypt.

Local investments in the petroleum industry recently amounted to around LE 7.8 million ($1.7 million) while foreign investment was around $2.1 million. However, since the oil and gas industry is a capital-intensive industry, manpower in crude oil was only 33,300 workers in 2004, and in oil products was slightly less at around 30,300 (World Energy Council 2002). It should be noted, however, that since energy is a highly capital intensive industry, it does not hold the key to Egypt's unemployment problem, which ranges between 10 percent (official figures) and 15 percent (unofficial estimates) (World Factbook, CIA, 2006). Future energy sector expansion will rely heavily on the amount of investments rather than the level of employment absorption.

The oil and gas sector fulfils around 95 percent of Egypt's energy requirements, distributed between oil (53 percent) and natural gas (42 percent).[13] Electricity generation is the highest consumer of gas (62.4 percent), followed by manufacturing industries (26.2 percent), petrochemicals (9.4 percent), and residential and commercial users (2 percent). Egypt's energy resources are therefore predominantly demand driven by thermal power generation, and supply driven by the amount of proven reserves. Due to the discoveries of substantial natural gas reserves, Egypt currently has a potential comparative advantage. This should be further developed into a competitive advantage so that export potential is maximized to the fullest extent possible. In particular, Stein's competitive advantage (reduction of unit costs with time through process innovations) can deliver promising future results if Egypt targets a $3 per barrel for the cost of oil extraction. This requires technology transfer with local process innovation, which is not one of the main characteristics of the Egyptian human development path (World Bank 2005). Table 8.3 below summarizes the outlook for Egypt's energy sector until 2025.

Table 8.3. An Outlook for Oil and Natural Gas in Egypt Until 2025

	Oil	*Natural Gas*
Consumption Growth	1.8 percent average annual growth rate until 2025.	9.45 percent average annual growth rate until 2025.
Production Targets	Oil production is expected to decline to 400,000 bpd by 2025, with annual production decline of 3.45 percent.	Production should reach 10 bcf/d in 2010 and 25 bcf/d in 2020.
Exports	An oil shortage is expected by 2007/2008.	Exports are a key opportunity. Gas exports should target 5 bcf/d by 2010 and 10bcf/d by 2017.
Imports	Required imports of oil at 100,000 bpd in 2008, 300,000 bpd in 2015, and 600,000 bpd in 2025.	No required imports of natural gas are expected until 2025.
Pricing	Phased relaxation of oil subsidies is expected. Persistence of consumption characterized as a necessary good.	Longer-term gas subsidy changes are expected. Consumption will remain characterized as a normal good.

Source: Author's calculations based on model results

One of the main critiques of the oil and gas industry in Egypt is its high level of subsidies. Prices are extremely distorted and do not reflect international prices. Furthermore, subsidies carry with them a huge amount of public debt as well as external debt. The government announced in its 2004 budget that it has spent around LE 14 billion to cover petroleum subsidies ($1 is equivalent to LE 5.7 at the time of writing this research).[14] Furthermore, since the oil and gas sector is subsidized both to consumers as well as to intermediate industries, the oil and gas sector actually partially subsidizes all productive activities in the Egyptian economy (Seda 2005). And while Egypt faces falling oil production from its mature oil fields, and hence declining revenues in spite of increasing international oil prices, domestic consumption will force it to become a net oil importer by 2007/2008 as analyzed in this chapter. Unless Egypt reforms its existing pricing mechanism in the oil sector, it would further augment a chronic problem. Moreover, the lifting of oil subsidies should be implemented in phases in order to contain inflation and hedge against increasing poverty. The recent partial lifting of oil subsidies is along those lines. However, as have been estimated in this research, since oil is almost completely price inelastic, a sizable reduction in oil consumption should not be expected even when subsidies are totally lifted.

Overall, the energy sector in Egypt needs major restructuring. As an outcome of this chapter's model results, Table 8.4 below outlines future recommendations for Egypt's energy sector. These recommendations are based on estimated model results for energy resource sustainability.

Table 8.4. Strategies for Egypt's Energy Sector

1. *Optimal Extraction of Energy Sources (Oil and Gas)*
- Re-orient future energy policy toward gas as a new strategic resource in addition to oil.
- Energy growth requirement of 3 percent a year (based on GDP growth rate of 6 percent a year) until 2025.
- Achieve competitive advantage in gas through process innovations based on unit-cost-reducing strategy, while maintaining a target profit margin of 20 percent.
- Gas economies of scale by production expansion from 7 bcf/d in 2005 to 35 bcf/d in 2025.
- Reduce X-inefficiency in oil production through the upgrade of technology by meeting a least cost target of $3 per barrel.

2. *Reduction/Removal of Energy Subsidy*
- Gradual reduction in energy subsidies with a total energy subsidy removal scheme by 2017.
- Oil subsidies should be removed by 2010.
- Reduce household expenditure impacts (additional LE 110 per household per month).
- Enforce minimum wage level as required by Article 23 of the Egyptian Constitution; and determined by UNDP Millennium Development Goals at LE 342 per month.
- Implement 'inflation targeting' to combat an additional 5–7 percent inflationary pressure due to subsidy removal.

3. *Energy Sustainablity (Investment Requirements)*
- Target $120 billion investments in natural gas production at $12 billion per year over the next ten years (2007–2017).
- Target growth in investments for oil production at 5.25 percent per year, such that total oil investments are doubled by the end of the next 15 years.
- Utilize alternative energy sources (solar and nuclear) to cover the energy resource gap starting in 2008 for oil and 2020 for natural gas.

4. *Alternative Energy Sources*
- Alternative energy use must increase to 5 percent by 2010, 10 percent by 2015, and 25 percent by 2025 (currently <1 percent).
- Substitute domestic oil consumption by minimum reduction targets of 7,000 bpd in 2010 and 10,000 bpd in 2025 (lower bound) through solar/alternative energy use.
- Oil import reduction targets of 80,000 bpd in 2015 and 225,000 bpd in 2025 by nuclear energy use as an economic alternative to oil imports.
- Improve environment by a potential gain of $130 per ton of reduced carbon emissions (Kyoto Protocol Standards).

Source: Author's recommendations based on model results. Major assumptions include a 6 percent target GDP growth rate, constant elasticity of substitution between oil and gas, competitive advantage through unit cost reduction (Stein's competitive advantage), X-inefficiency and economies of scale are based on least unit cost of Arabian Gulf producers, household income data based on IDSC data, and nuclear energy feasibility based on announced government policy and opportunity cost analysis to oil imports.

Figure 8.8 Timeline Implementation for Energy Sustainability (Summary of Results)

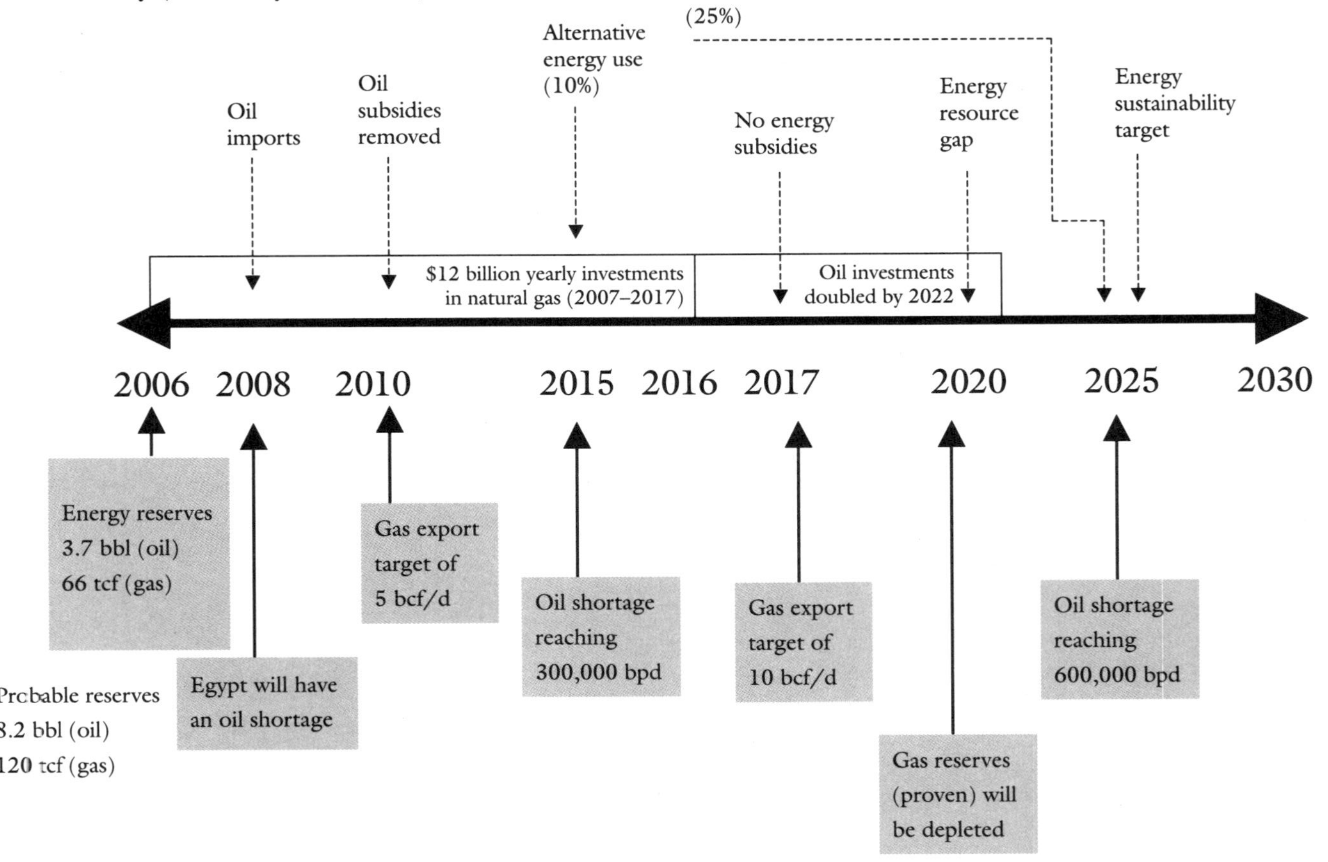

5. Conclusion

The central theme in this research is analysis and forecast of Egypt's oil and natural gas resources, regarding consumption, production, and exports/imports, with proposed strategies for sustainable development. The efficient utilization of energy resources in Egypt requires a major policy shift from oil historically regarded as the country's strategic energy resource, to a future in which natural gas should complement oil as the nation's strategic energy resource for decades to come.

The energy sector in Egypt will remain a high priority sector and a strategic resource for the country's future. Egypt will remain a price taker in world energy markets. Historically, oil has been more price inelastic than natural gas, whereas natural gas has higher income elasticity. Given proven reserves, oil production is declining due to X-inefficiency, and is expected to decline further, reaching as low as 400,000 barrels per day in 2025. Egypt is expected to be a net importer of oil in the very near future and as early as 2007/2008. Oil consumption, on the other hand, is forecast to increase at 1.8 percent per year through 2025, and the removal of oil subsidies, when undertaken, is not expected to guarantee a substantial reduction in oil consumption. On the other hand, natural gas should see a production growth of 10 percent per year, with the proven 66 trillion cubic feet of gas reserves fully depleted by 2020. This depletion, however, includes sizable export proceeds. Comparative advantage alone (i.e., resource endowments) cannot generate sustainable development in the future. Investors can continue to generate comfortable profit margins (70 percent for oil) conditional on economies of scale and the achievement of Stein's competitive advantage (lower comparative unit costs) targeting $3/barrel. Large investment costs are required for natural gas production, accompanied by a 20 percent profit margin. It is estimated that a $12 billion per year investment package over the next ten years (2007–2017) is required for natural gas sustainability, in order to achieve an overall energy growth rate of 3 percent per year, with the economy growing at a 6 percent GDP growth rate.

Subsequently, recommended strategies for Egypt's energy sector have been proposed, summarized as follows: (1) optimal extraction of energy sources, (2) reduction/removal of energy subsidies, (3) energy sustainability (investment requirements), and (4) alternative energy use including solar and nuclear energy. A timeline implementation for such strategies is outlined.

Appendix

Optimal Resource Extraction Model:

The following model (Hartwick's model) was utilized as part of the analysis undertaken in this chapter (based on the works of Hartwick 1977; Hanley, Shogren, and White 1997; and Cairns and Yang 2000):

Let $x(t)$ be the stock (reserves) of resource at time t, the $u(t)$ quantity (production rate) extracted at time t,
$P(t)$ the price path of the resource,
and r is the discount rate.

It is logical to have the following equation of motion for $x(t)$:

$$\frac{dx(t)}{dt} = \dot{x} = -u(t)$$

In other words, the stock (reserves) declines at every time t by the amount of extraction (production).

Assuming extraction costs given by $C(u(t), x(t))$ with $C'(u)>0, C_x \leq 0$, and $C''(u)<0$, such that extraction costs are an increasing function of production flow rate, but such an increase is diminishing with quantity, and including a "stock effect" $C_x \leq 0$ (unit extraction costs are lower for reserves having the potential of economies for scale), the dynamic extraction path will be given by maximizing net benefits over time:

$$Max\{u(t),T\} \in \int_{t=0}^{T} e^{-rt}\left[P(t)u(t) - C(u(t),x(t))\right]dt$$

$$\dot{x}(t) = -u(t) \quad \forall t$$

$$u(t) \geq 0 \quad \forall t$$

$$x(0) = x_0 = \overline{R}$$

$$x(T) \geq 0$$

$$u(t) = D(P(t))$$

Using the current value Hamiltonian (optimal control problem) yields:

$$H_c = P(t)u(t) - C(D(P(t)), x(t)) - m(t)u(t)$$

where $m(t)$ is the current value multiplier,
with $m(t) = e^{rt}\lambda(t)$,
where $\lambda(t)$ is the standard Lagrangian multiplier.

This optimal control problem is then solved by:

$\frac{\partial H_c}{\partial u(t)} = P(\bullet) + P'(\bullet)u(t) - m(t) = 0$	(1)	Sustainability Constraint
$\dot{m} - rm(t) = -\frac{\partial H_c}{\partial x(t)} = 0$	(2)	Equation of Motion
$\dot{x}(t) = \frac{\partial H_c}{\partial m(t)} = -u(t)$	(3)	Resource Depletion
$\lambda(T) = 0$	(4)	Transversality (terminal cycle) Condition

This gives rise to the following solution(s):

(a) When there is no stock effect, $C_x = 0$:

$$\dot{u} = D'(\bullet)\dot{P} = \frac{\dot{m}}{1/D'(P(t)) - C_{uu}}$$

(b) When there is a stock effect, $C_x < 0$:

$$\dot{u} = \frac{\dot{P} - \dot{m} - C_{ux}\dot{x}}{C_{uu}}$$

(c) When there are external costs, $e(t)>0$:

$$\dot{u} = \frac{rP - rC_u}{1/D'(P(t)) - C_{uu}} - \frac{e(t)\left[r - \dot{e}/e(t)\right]}{1/D'(P(t)) - C_{uu}}$$

In solving for the optimal extraction rate, this study assumed no stock effects, and did not account for valuation of externalities (external costs in production were not accounted for). The author recommends extension of his results to incorporate stock effects and externality valuations, but this is beyond the scope of this research.

Elasticity of Substitution between Oil and Natural Gas in Egypt

One of the most common measures of the economy's energy substitution possibilities is the elasticity of substitution (σ). The elasticity of substitution defines the relative change in quantity proportions (in this case, between oil and natural gas) in response to a relative change in their prices. This is done for production (relative change in input proportions in response to relative change in prices) and consumption (relative change in commodity usage in response to relative change in prices). In general, it is possible that the elasticity of substitution will vary; however, it is convenient to assume that elasticity of substitution is constant with time as it is assumed in this study (LeBel 1982, 293; Clarkson and Deyes 2002). The elasticity of substitution between oil and gas in Egypt is calculated for both the production and consumption using the following model:

$$\ln\left(\frac{Q_{OIL}}{Q_{NG}}\right) = \alpha + \sigma \ln\left(\frac{P_{NG}}{P_{OIL}}\right) + \varepsilon$$

where, Q_{OIL}= quantity of oil production or consumption (barrels of oil equivalent).

Q_{NG}= quantity of natural gas production or consumption (barrels of oil equivalent).

P_{OIL}= price of oil (US$ per barrel).

P_{NG}= price of natural gas (US$ per barrel).

σ = elasticity of substitution between oil and gas.

The value of σ is always positive, as the oil-gas ratio moves in the same direction as gas-oil price ratio. If σ is high ($\sigma \rightarrow \infty$), this means that oil and gas can be thought of as perfect substitutes for each other. On the other hand, if σ is very low (σ=0), this case shows that both oil and gas should be used in a fixed ratio regardless of the change in their price ratio. Running the above regression for Egypt for the period 1991–2003 for both production and consumption sides, it was found that the elasticity of substitution between oil and gas in production is 3.4; while the elasticity of substitution between oil and gas in consumption is 4.06.

The period from 1991 to 2003 witnessed economic growth due to implementing the Economic Reform and Structural Adjustment Program (ERSAP) in Egypt from 1991. However, such economic growth has recently slowed down. To forecast the growth of energy demand as a whole or growth of oil and natural gas consumption separately, Energy/GDP elasticity of 0.5 was calculated covering the period 1991–2003. This shows that when Egypt's GDP grows at 1 percent, energy demand would grow at 0.5 percent. Therefore, by applying an anticipated 6 percent rate of economic growth in Egypt, it is expected that energy should grow by 3 percent per year. The Oil/GDP elasticity (sensitivity between oil production and GDP growth rate) was also calculated and found to be 0.3, while the natural gas/GDP elasticity was found to be 0.9. Hence, for 1 percent GDP growth, oil should grow at 0.3 percent and natural gas at 0.9 percent.

Hartwick's Rule and the Sustainability Constraint

Both oil and gas are exhaustible resources that are irreversible. That is, if they are consumed, such consumption cannot be reversed, and if they are not consumed, then there has been an opportunity lost of not consuming or exporting their value. In an influential paper published in 1977, John Hartwick proposed a rule for ensuring sustainability (i.e., non-declining consumption through time), in the case where an economy made use of a non-renewable resource (such as oil or natural gas) in its economic process. Hartwick shows that, so long as the stock of capital does not decline over time, non-declining consumption is also possible. Hartwick stated clearly what has come to be known as Hartwick's rule for this type of economy: "If the accumulation of capital always exactly compensates in value for the resource depletion, then the level of consumption remains constant" (Cairns and Yang 2000, 1; Hanley, Shogren, and White 1997, 426).

Hartwick argued that a sufficient condition to enjoy a constant consumption path is to invest in reproducible capital all the returns from the exhaustible resource use. This incorporates the discount rate (opportunity cost of time), and growth rate of consumption, indexed by uncertainty (relative risk). Using Hartwick's rule to get the social extraction rate to reach a sustainable consumption path for Egypt, we have to use the following formula:

$$r = \rho + \eta g$$

where, r is the social (optimal) extraction rate.

ρ is the social discount rate.

η is the coefficient of relative risk aversion.

g is the growth of consumption of the exhaustible resource (oil or gas).

By applying the above formula to Egypt, and substituting for ρ=15 percent (historical social discount rate in Egypt), η=1 (assuming risk neutrality) and g_o= 1.8 percent (growth rate of consumption of oil in Egypt) and g_{ng}= 9 percent (growth rate of consumption of natural gas in Egypt); the economic extraction rates for oil and natural gas were derived, with the added constraint of GDP growth target rate of 6 percent annually. The study assumes proven oil and gas reserves to begin with as the initial time period (the start of the Transversality cycle), to derive the historical extraction paths, then, calculates for each resource an efficient forecasted extraction path.

Notes

1. The author would like to thank Professor Hanaa Kheir-El-Din and Dr. Omneia Helmy for help and encouragement during the time spent in writing this research. Thanks also go to Professor Robert Mabro and Dr. John Salevurakis. In this study, research assistance was provided by Mr. Amr Al Garhi, MA in Economics, the American University in Cairo. Additional research assistance was provided by Homa Azargoshasb, Abdula Mutualo, and Loubna Olama, MA candidates in Economics, the American University in Cairo. The author would like to thank them all for valuable assistance.
2. The price of natural gas is regional. In the Middle East, the price range is $4.87 to $6.66 per thousand cubic feet. Figure 8.1 shows the weighted average of international natural gas prices including regions outside the Middle East.
3. Energy Information Administration, *Country analysis briefs: Egypt.* US Department of Energy, May 2006: www.eia.gov/emeu/cabs/egypenv.html.
4. Ibid.
5. Ibid.
6. Energy Information Administration (2006).
7. World Energy Council (2002).
8. Ibid.
9. Middle East Economic Digest, *Egypt: Petrochemicals*, January 2003.
10. Income elasticity of demand is calculated to be the prime determinant of effective quantity demanded for oil at a historical GDP/demand elasticity of 0.3, such that future oil exports is the residual of production, after accounting for needed domestic consumption per capita. This is reinforced by a completely inelastic price elasticity of oil demand at 0.02. Hence, the core assumption here is that quantity demanded is a main function of population and future income levels but not predominantly based on future prices.
11. Price elasticities are based on real prices (indexed by consumer prices over time) from 1991.
12. Energy/GDP impact of 0.5 is decomposed into the respective elasticities of oil and natural $0.3\eta^{oil} + 0.9\eta^{gas} = \eta^{energy} = 0.5$
13. AmCham (2003).
14. AmCham (2003).

References

AmCham (American Chamber of Commerce in Egypt). 2003. *The petroleum industry in Egypt: Investment and prospects.* Business Studies and Analysis Center. Cairo, Egypt: The American Chamber of Commerce in Egypt.

APRC (Arab Petroleum Research Center). 2003. *Egypt: Arab oil and gas directory*, 85–120. Paris: Arab Petroleum Research Center.

Cairns, Robert and Zhao Yang. 2000. The converse of Hartwick's rule and uniqueness of the sustainable path. *Natural Resource Modeling* 13(4): 1–10.

Clarkson, Richard and Kathryn Deyes. 2002. *Estimating the social cost of carbon emissions.* UK Government Economic Service Working Paper no. 140.

Colliti, Marcelo and Claudio Simeon. 1996. *Perspectives of oil and gas: The road to interdependence.* London: Kluwer Academic Publishers.

Energy Information Administration (EIA). 2006. *Country analysis: Egypt.* Washington, D.C.: US Department of Energy (US DOE).

Hanley, Nick, Jason F. Shogren, and Ben White. 1997. *Environmental economics: In theory and practice.* Oxford, UK: Oxford University Press.

Hartwick, John M. 1977. Intergeneration equity and the investing of rents from exhaustible resources. *The American Economic Review* 67(5): 972–974.

IDSC (Information and Decision Support Center). Cabinet of Egypt. Available at www.idsc.gov.eg. Accessed on December 20, 2006.

LeBel, Philip G. 1982. *Energy economics and technology.* Baltimore: The Johns Hopkins University Press.

Middle East Economic Digest. 2003. *Egypt: Petrochemicals*, January.

OFE (Office of Fossil Energy). 2001. *An energy overview of the Republic of Egypt.* Energy Overview. Washington, D.C.: Office of Fossil Energy.

Seda, Rodrigo. 2005. *Apache Egypt's contribution to the Egyptian national economy.* Cairo and New York: The American University in Cairo Press.

World Bank. 2005. *Egypt country profile.* Washington, D.C.: World Bank.

World Energy Council. 2002. *Energy in Egypt.* Available at www.worldenergy.org/wec-geis/wec-info/structure-organisation/ea/cairo/stats/eie.asp.

World Energy Outlook. 2006. US Department of Energy (DOE). Available at www.eia.org.

CHAPTER 9

The Impact of Reducing Energy Subsidies on Energy Intensive Industries in Egypt

Abdallah Shehata Khattab

Subsidies are a major item in government expenditures in Egypt. Recent figures indicate that these subsidies exceeded 23 percent of total budget spending in 2005/2006 (more than LE 50 billion), around 74 percent of which was allocated to energy products (excluding electricity).

Due to the rapid increase in oil prices over the past two years,[1] the subsidy bill of energy products has quadrupled. Such increase has posed a critical challenge for the fiscal authority in Egypt. Political and economic considerations have restrained the government from restructuring the existing subsidy system despite its inefficiencies. Starting FY 2005/2006, the fiscal authority has recorded such subsidies *explicitly* in order to reveal the true burden of subsidizing petroleum products and natural gas.

This chapter investigates the potential impact of reducing energy subsidies in Egypt on energy-intensive industries. A partial equilibrium approach is applied to assess such policy. Specifically, it examines the effect of subsidy reduction on energy-driven sectors, under different scenarios of increasing prices of energy products. The effects are assessed through selecting a sample of sectors and industries that depend heavily on energy products, and then measuring the impact on profitability per ton of production in selected industries, holding other factors constant.

The chapter is organized as follows. Following the introduction, Section 1 discusses the concept of subsidy in addition to the rationale behind the energy subsidy system. Section 2 examines the characteristics and challenges of energy subsidies in Egypt. It also assesses the fiscal burden of energy subsidies on government budget. The partial effect of energy subsidy reduction is analyzed in Section 3. Finally, Section 4 sums up the main findings of the study and their policy implications.

1. Subsidy: Conceptual Framework

1.1 What is a Subsidy?

Technically, it is quite difficult to agree on a unique definition of the term "subsidy." As discussed below, it may be understood either in a narrow or broad sense (Schrank 2003). Moreover, the definition differs according to contextual use. The one adopted in free trade zones differs significantly from definitions used by governments, World Trade Organization (WTO), the Organization of Economic Cooperation and Development (OECD), and the United Nations agencies.

In economic literature, subsidy is defined as any action or measure that keeps either consumer prices below market levels, or producer prices higher than market levels (Irrek 2002). The term subsidy is referred to as a *monetary grant* given by government to keep the price of a good lower for consumers, or higher for producers, since this is considered to be in the public interest.[2] This support is given either directly or indirectly, in the sense that it is used to reduce costs for either consumers or producers by giving direct or indirect support to a particular sector/group (Myers and Kent 2001). Furthermore, subsidy is the opposite of a tax, albeit it can also be provided through a reduction of the tax burden.

1.2 Explicit versus Implicit Subsidies

Broadly, subsidies are divided into two categories applying either a narrow or a broad definition of the term subsidy. The narrow definition refers to explicit budgetary subsidies, while the broad one includes implicit support as well. Implicit support (subsidies) encompasses all measures that are not shown in government accounts.

The terms explicit and implicit subsidies are sometimes used as synonyms to the terms *direct* and *indirect* subsidies, respectively (Legeida 2001). However, such usage lacks accuracy as explicit subsidies are sometimes allocated directly or indirectly.[3] Also, some forms of implicit subsidies are allocated directly or indirectly. It is also important to note that explicit subsidies are sometimes accompanied by implicit subsidies. For instance, the government might provide firms with subsidized energy inputs and at the same time encourage them through tax exemption. This makes the distinction between explicit and implicit subsidies not always clear (Valdes 1988).

Fiscal and economic costs[4] differ markedly for explicit and implicit schemes of subsidy (Dodson and Paramo 2001). Moreover, there is a problem measuring the cost of subsidy system as it is a complicated system, given the range of delivering subsidies whether in cash or in kind (Kumar and Alderman 1989). The desirability of using either implicit or explicit subsidies is constrained by different social, economic and political factors. Implicit subsidies seem a desirable option for governments since they do not sometimes imply any marginal fiscal cost to them. Governments may achieve lower prices for goods and services through affecting the incentive system without bearing any explicit budgetary fiscal cost (Valdes 1988).

1.3 Rationale and Effectiveness of Energy Subsidy

1.3.1 Rationale Behind the Subsidy System

Although economic theory has not provided an adequate answer or prescription for the questions of what the state should not do or do and how best to do it, it provides valuable guidance for such questions. As a mechanism of state intervention, the rationale for subsidy is established upon the need for correcting market failures. Thus, the subsidy system (implicit or explicit) is justified based on efficiency and equity considerations.

As argued, the state is often required to subsidize services that the market will not provide, or provides insufficiently. As a rule, the provision of purely public goods—where the marginal cost of an additional unit of consumption is zero—is fully financed by the state. For other goods and services where the market would under-provide them, there is call for some form of government intervention.[5] In this respect, subsidy would be justified on efficiency grounds. However, subsidy is not always justified by efficiency considerations but also because of lack of access to services by poor households and vulnerable groups of society (Saunders and Schneider 2000). Hence, the state should seek to target the provision of these services to such groups on the basis of equity considerations.

For energy activities, it has been argued that free markets do not operate efficiently and effectively, since they do not take into account social, economic, and environmental benefits and costs that might be associated with such activities. Therefore, free energy markets might malfunction in various ways. The problem of over-production and pollution is a typical example of such failure. Also, markets are said to fail when disadvantaged groups of society have limited access to modern energy. In both cases, governments have a responsibility to intervene to protect air quality and provide everyone with access to modern energy (Pershing and Mackenzie 2004).

Although energy subsidies are a widespread practice, they vary significantly in type and magnitude according to product and country. Subsidies on energy products are used widely by governments to achieve a range of policy objectives. For instance, in developed countries governments consider regional employment objectives as a key justification for subsidies on production (Pershing and Mackenzie 2004). For the EU countries, government intervention in the energy sector is justified on the basis of supply security since the oil crisis of the 1970s, environmental improvement, and stimulating particular sectors of the economy or segments of the population (EEA 2004). The rationale for intervention in the energy market is different in developing economies and economies in transition where energy consumption subsidies are often used to guarantee that all members of the population, particularly the poor, have access to a minimum level of energy consumption. This objective justifies subsidized pricing policies of energy products in most developing countries. Furthermore, subsidies are also justified on the basis of encouraging industrial growth through low cost energy (Saunders and Schneider 2000).

1.3.2 Subsidy System Limitations

In economic literature, it has been argued that unless subsidies, as a mechanism of intervention, are introduced to overcome market failure, they might lead to loss of economic efficiency manifested in different forms. Specifically, expansion in production of less efficient industries emerges as a result of subsidies on consumption at the expense of other more efficient industries (Saunders and Schneider 2000). Likewise, subsidies to producers result in less efficient economic operations and investments, as the case of coal production in several OECD countries in which subsidies have hindered efforts to improve productivity (UNEP 2002).

As argued, lower prices of energy due to subsidies expand consumption of energy products beyond its efficient levels (Saunders and Schneider 2000). Furthermore, energy subsidies affect negatively the adoption of certain advanced technologies as they might make certain old-fashioned technologies more economically attractive. Theoretically, lower end-user prices as a result of subsidies lead to higher energy use and reduced incentives to save or use energy more efficiently. Moreover, lower end-user prices of energy products discourage producers to develop and invest in energy projects[6] (UNEP 2002). Price ceilings below market levels may need an administratively costly rationing system. In most cases, rationing systems have not been efficient in reaching target groups.[7]

Direct subsidies in the form of grants or tax exemptions create a challenge for government finances, since they increase the fiscal burden on the budget. For example, according to IMF estimates, the Iranian government's direct spending on energy subsidies amounted to 8 percent of its budget in the late 1990s. Similarly, in Hungary gains of improving energy use jumped from $5–10 million to $80 million per year after consumer price subsidies were removed in 1997 (UNEP 2002). It is also argued that increasing energy use due to subsidies either boosts demand for imports or reduces energy exports. This harms the balance of payments and energy supply security because of increasing the country's dependence on imports. The Indonesian government, for example, estimates that energy subsidies cost the country $16 billion in lost export earnings (UNEP 2002).[8]

Therefore, the literature has outlined the characteristics of an effective/well-functioning subsidy system (UNEP 2004). The key characteristics of such a system are as follows:

- ***A well-targeted system***: it should be directed only to those who are intended and deserve to receive subsidies (target groups).
- ***Efficiency***: it should not undermine incentives for suppliers or consumers to provide or use a service efficiently.
- ***Cost effectiveness***: subsidy programs should be justified based on costs/benefits yardsticks.
- ***Practicality***: resources for subsidies should be affordable and the administrative cost of running subsidy programs should be reasonable.
- ***Transparency***: information on the amount of government funds spent on subsidy and on subsidy recipients should be disclosed.
- ***Transitory***: subsidy programs should be designed in such a way as to avoid consumers and producers becoming overly dependent on such support.

Such conditions or characteristics are the basis in discussing the effectiveness of energy subsidy. The absence of one or more characteristics implies a lack of an efficient and effective subsidy system. Country experience shows that inefficient subsidy programs lacked a timeframe, where they have started as temporary and ended with a permanent, costly system of subsidy. Similarly, a subsidy system is said to be ineffective if it does not reach its target groups.

1.3.3 Magnitude of World Energy Subsidy

Subsidies in most OECD countries are producer subsidies that often take the form of direct payments or support for research and development. For developing countries, most subsidies go to consumers via price controls that keep end-user prices below market level or even below total cost of production (UNEP 2002).

In fact, there is a problem in quantifying subsidies for the world as a whole due to differences in concepts and measurements. This makes most available figures and studies relatively inconsistent and outdated. In 1992, the World Bank estimated world subsidies on fossil-fuel consumption from under-pricing alone at around $230 billion per year. Net global consumption subsidies are also estimated at $235 billion per year. In 1997, the World Bank estimated annual fossil-fuel subsidies at $48 billion in twenty of the largest countries outside the OECD and $10 billion in the OECD (UNEP 2002). Subsidies on the consumption of fossil fuels in developing and transition economies are estimated at US$50 billion in 1995–1996, or 1.3 percent of their GDP (Saunders and Schneider 2000).

Despite increasing reliance on market-based pricing mechanisms, energy subsidies remain significant in developing countries (Legeida 2001). They were estimated at about two-thirds of global energy subsidies. Nonetheless, per capita subsidies in developed countries (OECD) are almost 2.5 times those in developing countries (non-OECD) (see Table 9.1).

Table 9.1. The Cost of Annual Energy Subsidies (1995–1998, $US billion)

	OECD Countries	*Non OECD Countries*	*Total*
Coal	30	23	53
Oil	19	33	52
Gas	8	38	46
All fossil fuels	57	94	151
Electricity	NA	48	48
Nuclear	16	Nil	16
Renewable and end use	9	Nil	9
Non payments and bail out	0	20	20
Total	139	256	395
% of global energy subsidies	35%	65%	100%
Per capita subsidies ($/cap)	88	35	44
Per capita GDP ($/cap)	23,132	3903	7316

Source: Pershing and Mackenzie (2004).

Subsidy rates differ by products as shown in Table 9.2. Clearly, end-user prices are highly subsidized in oil-exporting countries since the estimated rate of subsidy as a percentage of reference price reaches 80 percent in Iran, 57.6 percent in Venezuela, 32 percent in Russia, and 27.5 percent in Indonesia, while it is much lower in non-oil producing countries like South Africa (6.4 percent), China (10.9 percent) and India (14.2 percent).

Table 9.2. Estimated Rate of Subsidy*
(% of Reference Price) in a Sample of Countries**

	Iran	*Indonesia*	*India*	*Russia*	*China*	*Kazakhstan*	*Venezuela*	*South Africa*
Gasoline	59.4	0.0	0.0	9.3	0.0	0.0	26.6	0.0
Auto diesel	93.9	40.2	0.0	0.0	0.0	0.0	35.9	0.0
LPG	89.7	0.0	31.6	0.0	0.0	0.0	26.1	0.0
Kerosene	89.5	55.2	52.6	0.0	0.0	0.0	4.9	2.0
Light fuel oil	82.3	45.5	0.0	1.5	0.0	0.0	19.3	0.0
Heavy fuel oil	88.1	7.8	0.0	0.0	0.0	0.0	39.4	0.0
Electricity	48.1	0.0	24.2	42.0	38.2	56.6	63.0	20.3
Natural gas	77.8	28.4	22.5	46.1	18.7	55.7	85.6	0.0
Steam coal	0.0	0.0	13.1	0.0	8.3	20.7	91.9	8.1
Cooking gas	0.0	0.35	42.3	0.0	73.1	2.7	-	0.0
Total	80.4	27.5	14.2	32.5	10.9	18.2	57.6	6.4

Source: IEA 1999.
* These numbers are weighted by the gross calorific value of all energy used.
** Reference price indicates full production costs including all costs of transport, refining, and distribution.

2. Energy Subsidies in Egypt: Characteristics and Challenges

In Egypt, the government considers the subsidy system as a primary mechanism to reach a reasonable level of equitable income distribution.[9] Therefore, the rationale for the subsidy system in Egypt is justified primarily by equity concerns as in most developing countries. Table 9.3 shows fuel[10] subsidies as a percentage of GDP in 2004 in a sample of developing countries including Egypt. It indicates that Egypt is a leading country in subsidizing fuel products (excluding natural gas) compared to other developing countries. As Table 9.3 shows, the share of subsidy to GDP is to some extent positively correlated with the level of per capita income in the sample.[11] However, per capita consumption of energy products (fuel and electricity) in Egypt is lower compared to many Arab countries and other developing countries (Figure 9.1). Per capita energy use in Egypt is lower than in Algeria, Jordan, Lebanon, Syria, lower and upper middle-income countries, and is even lower than the MENA region. Levels of per capita energy consumption in Egypt are only higher than in Yemen, Sudan, Morocco, and least developed countries (LDCs) (see Figure 9.1).

Table 9.3. Fuel Subsidies as Percentage of GDP

Country	*GDP per Capita (Current US$) 2004*	*Fuel Subsidies (% of GDP) (2004)*
Bolivia	1,073.7	2.2
Ghana	498.4	2.2
Jordan	1,836.4	3.6
Mali	409	2
Sri Lanka	1,133.5	2.1
Egypt	1284.4	4.6
Yemen *	517.2	2.19
Indonesia	1,260.5	3
India **	543.2	0.25
Nigeria **	463.0	3.5

Source: World Bank, *World Development Indicators* (WDI) online database; and Nwafor, Ogujiuba, and Asogwa (2006) *Figures refer to 2002. ** Figures refer to 2003.

Figure 9.1. Per Capita Use of Energy

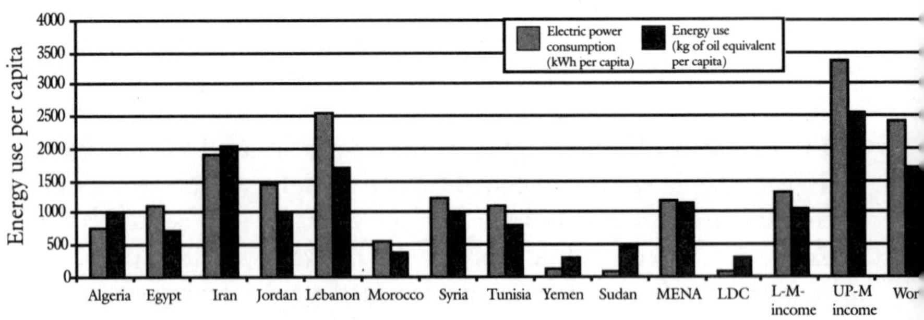

Source: World Bank, WDI online database.

While levels of per capita energy consumption in Egypt are relatively low compared to other developing countries,[12] energy use in production is less efficient. The estimates of oil intensity[13] figures in Egypt are about three times higher than in Indonesia and 1.5 times higher than in Brazil,

Nigeria, India, China, and South Korea (see Table 9.4). Although oil intensity has declined by half over the last 30 years in developed countries and by one-third in developing countries, it is increasing in Egypt (FICCI 2005). Such figures indicate inefficient consumption of energy products by the industrial sector. Highly subsidized prices of energy products have contributed partially to such inefficient use (IDSC 2005a).

Table 9.4. Oil Intensity in a Sample of Developing Countries

Country	*1999*	*2000*	*2001*	*2002*	*2003*
Brazil	0.19	0.16	0.20	0.21	0.19
Egypt	0.27	0.27	0.28	0.31	0.34
Nigeria	0.26	0.24	0.27	0.23	0.22
China	0.22	0.23	0.21	0.21	0.21
India	0.25	0.24	0.23	0.22	0.19
Indonesia	0.11	0.11	0.11	0.11	0.11
South Korea	0.23	0.21	0.22	0.20	0.18
Thailand	0.31	0.30	0.33	0.31	0.29

Sources: FICCI (2005).

In the Egyptian context, subsidies on energy products (excluding electricity) are defined as "subsidies given to the Egyptian General Petroleum Corporation (EGPC) that keep prices of energy products below international prices (prices paid to foreign partners), i.e., the difference between the price paid to the foreign partner and that paid by consumers whether households, businesses or the government sector,[14] in addition to other costs."[15] Specifically, subsidy on energy products includes subsidies allocated to liquefied petroleum gas (LPG), gasoline (80 and 90), kerosene, diesel, fuel oil, and natural gas. The Egyptian government subsidizes energy products through a mix of explicit and implicit subsidies.[16] Until the FY 2004/2005 energy subsidies were not recorded in the state budget and therefore were considered an implicit form of subsidy. Starting FY 2005/2006, subsidies on energy products (excluding electricity)[17] have been recorded in the budget, and are no longer implicit (see Table 9.5).

The fiscal cost of subsidies on energy products (petroleum products and natural gas) was estimated at LE 20.2 billion in FY 2004/2005, and LE 40 billion in 2005/2006 (5.6 percent of GDP) and the same figure was reported in the budget statement for the FY 2006/2007. This significant increase in subsidies can be attributed to the rapid increase in oil prices.

Despite this significant share, figures do not include subsidies on the share of the Egyptian General Petroleum Corporation (EGPC).[18] Adding subsidies to the share of EGPC doubles the volume of such subsidies.

Table 9.5. Allocation of Subsidies in Egypt's State Budget (2002–2007) (LE billion)

Year	*Figures of the State Budget*		*Petroleum Products and Natural Gas Subsidies (2)*	*Total Subsidies*
	Total Subsidies (1)	*Petroleum Products and Natural Gas Subsidies as Recorded*		*(3)= (1+2)[(2002–2005)] (3)=(1) [(2005–2007)]*
2002/2003	6.9*	0	16.1**	23.0
2003/2004	10.3*	0	21.7**	32.0
2004/2005	13.8*	0	20.2**	34.0
2005/2006	52.6	40.0	40.0	52.6
2006/2007	53.7	40.0	40.0	53.7

Source: The People's Assembly, Egypt (2003 and 2004 and various issues).
* Actual figures. ** Figures for energy subsidies that are not recorded in the state budget are obtained from the year-end report of the Budgeting and Planning Committee of the People's Assembly, Egypt.

Subsidy figures for 2005/2006 will change if calculations are based on international prices as shown in Table 9.6, as subsidies[19] exceed LE 58 billion. As indicated in the table below, domestic prices of LPG are highly subsidized where the subsidy ratio[20] is around 93 percent. Similarly, subsidy ratio for products such as natural gas, gas oil and kerosene reaches up to 79 percent.

Table 9.6. Total Subsidies on Energy Products Based on International Prices 2005/2006

Products	*Total consumption (000 Ton)*	*Domestic prices LE/ Ton*	*International prices LE/Ton*	*Differences in prices LE/Ton*	*Amount of subsidies LE million*	*Domestic prices/ international prices (%)*
	(1)	(2)	(3)	(4)= 3–2	(5)=4x1	
LPG	3,380	200.0	2,740	2,540.0	8,585.20	7.3
Gasoline 92	34	1,912.8	3,020	1,107.2	37.64	63.3
Gasoline 90	1,892	1,338.0	2,465	1,127.0	2,132.28	54.3

(continued)

Gasoline 80	765	1,243.8	2,455	1,211.2	926.57	50.7
Kerosene	503	507.0	2,465	1,958.0	984.87	20.6
Gas oil (diesel)	9,362	668.7	2,440	1,771.3	16,582.91	27.4
Fuel oil (mazout)	8,443	293.2	1,160	866.8	7,318.39	25.3
Natural gas	22,470	289.7	1,260	970.3	21,802.64	23.0
Total	46,849				58,370.50	

Sources: Author's calculations based on data from the Ministry of Petroleum (various issues).

The largest share of subsidies in the FY 2005/2006 is allocated to natural gas (40.6 percent), diesel (27.5 percent) and biogas (21 percent) as shown in Table 9.7, whereas the lowest share of subsidies goes to the consumption of kerosene (1 percent), gasoline (4 percent), and mazout (5 percent). However, in 2006/2007 subsidies allocated to diesel, mazout, and gasoline have been significantly increased. Diesel subsidies became a dominant item that accounts for 38 percent of total subsidies while subsidies allocated to natural gas declined to 21.1 percent of total subsidies compared to 40 percent in 2005/2006 budget.[21]

Table 9.7. Percentage of Subsidy to Energy Products Items (2005/2006)

Items	*Amount of Subsidies (in LE billion)*	*%*
Natural gas subsidy	8,963.3	40.6
Biogas subsidy	4,731.4	21.4
Difference of diesel (solar) prices	6,074.9	27.5
Fuel oil (mazout) price difference	1,108.2	5.0
Gasoline price difference	976.5	4.4
Kerosene price difference	223.8	1.0
Total	22,078.10*	100.00

Source: Ministry of Finance (various issues).
* These figures are the projected value of subsidies while the actual figures for the same fiscal year, reported by the budget statement 2006/2007, has reached LE 40 billion.

Over the past two decades, domestic prices of energy products have been relatively stagnant. Prices of energy products have seen changes in different directions, where some items such as gasoline (80 and 90) were increased smoothly until 1992 and then stayed unchanged until July 2006. Changes in the prices of kerosene and gas oil during the period 1982–2006 are similar to those of gasoline prices (see Figure 9.2). LPG has seen two main price movements over the past decades: from LE 0.65 per cylinder in 1977 to LE 1.5 per cylinder in 1990 and finally to LE 2.5 per cylinder in 1991. Although prices of energy products have remained relatively stagnant for a long period of time, the annual growth rate for most energy products has been estimated at 6–14 percent over the period 1982–2004, because of price jumps for most products as shown in Figure 9.2.

Figure 9.2. Changes in Prices of Energy Products (1982–2004)

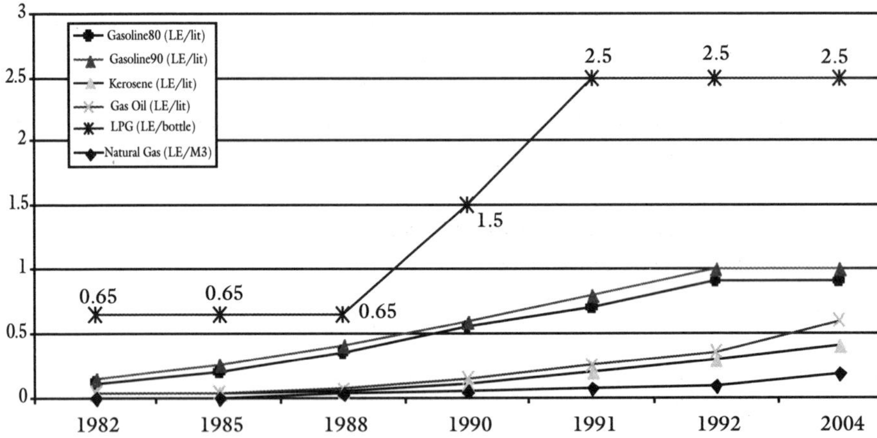

Sources: Ministry of Petroleum (various issues).

Despite this significant burden of energy subsidies in Egypt, the problem with the existing system lies not only in its fiscal cost but also in the extent of distortion resulting from changing market incentives. As argued, the opportunity cost[22] of energy subsidies seems more appropriate than the fiscal cost in evaluating the economic cost of such a system (Gerner and Sinclair 2006). Moreover, reaching poor households or targeting groups of society has also been a challenging task for the effectiveness of such a system. It has been argued that the energy subsidy system is costly both fiscally and economically and even fails to reach and benefit the poor (Helmy

2005). Figures of energy subsidies compared to other fiscal operations in the state budget reveal such inefficient use of resources. As shown in Table 9.8, spending on energy subsidies reaches around 15 percent of total government spending and exceeds 6 percent of GDP. Compared to other fiscal operations in the state budget, allocations for energy subsidies are twice the sum spent on defense, three to four times the spending on health, and exceed that on education (see Table 9.8).

Table 9.8. Energy Subsidies (Excluding Electricity) as a Percentage of Budget Fiscal Operations (2002–2007)

Year	*Energy Subsidies (LE billion)*	*% of Total Expenditures*	*% of GDP*	*% of Social Protection Spending*	*% of Defense Spending*	*% of Education Spending*	*% of Health Spending*
2002/2003	16.1	10.8	4.1	84.7	121.1	78.2	211.84
2003/2004	21.7	13.2	4.8	94.8	148.6	95.6	267.90
2004/2005	20.2	11.2	4.0	71.6	136.5	78.3	276.71
2005/2006	40	16.8	7.2	84.7	256.4	161.9	487.80
2006/2007	40	14.6	6.4	73.7	231.2	146.0	439.56

Sources: Author's calculations based on data from the Ministry of Finance.

Despite the adoption of the economic reform program in the early 1990s, the call for restructuring and reforming the existing subsidy system remained unheeded. This is because reforming the subsidy system has faced social resistance, owing in part to the perception that eliminating subsidies could adversely affect the poor, in addition to the implicit political cost that is taken into consideration. The next section examines the expected effects of subsidy reduction on energy-intensive sectors under different scenarios using a partial equilibrium approach.

3. Impact of Subsidy Reduction on Energy-Intensive Industries

3.1 Assessment of Energy Subsidies Removal (Reduction): Methodological Issues

In economic literature, analyzing the impact of energy subsidy removal (reduction) is conducted basically through two distinct approaches: general equilibrium framework and partial equilibrium models. Both approaches consider the wide use of energy consumption and its impact on producers and consumers. In analyzing the impact of subsidy removal (reduction), general equilibrium models emphasize the extensive use of energy by all sectors of the economy. Such models assume that changes in prices of energy products affect many other sectors, and hence the ultimate effects on any sector depend on the response of others to the changes in the sector in question (Nwafor, Ogujiuba, and Asogwa 2006). General equilibrium models consider that treating energy sector in isolation of the rest of the economy might be misleading. Nonetheless, models that assess the impact of energy subsidy removal (reduction) using a general equilibrium approach are restricted in the sense that they operate with the single household or representative household assumption. Disaggregated models of government spending are scarce and thus disregard the socioeconomic setting of households and sectors (Nwafor, Ogujiuba, and Asogwa 2006). Such abstract framework affects the accuracy of results. On the other hand, partial equilibrium models do not account for variables in some markets since they do not account for inter-sectoral and indirect interactions as a result of price changes. Thus, researchers use the partial equilibrium approach to examine the direct effect of subsidy removal on a specific sector(s) such as energy intensive industries.

The literature[23] identifies three channels through which the impact of subsidy reduction can affect the welfare of individuals: (1) the increase in firms' energy bill, (2) increase in the cost of transportation, and (3) spending re-allocation in government budget.

The reduction of subsidies on energy products increases the energy bill of some sectors, particularly those relying heavily on petroleum products such as cement, fertilizers, electricity, paper, glass, iron, and steel. Such higher prices increase the cost of production. This negatively affects firms' profitability and as a result prices of finished products of such sectors increase,[24] thus negatively affecting individuals' welfare.

The welfare of individuals is also negatively affected by changes in the cost of transportation. The reduction of subsidies increases prices of energy products and hence transportation, leading to an increase in the prices of passenger and goods transportation (Nwafor, Ogujiuba, and Asogwa 2006).

The effect through the third channel of subsidy reduction seems ambiguous (see Figure 9.3). On one hand, the rise in prices due to the reduction of subsidies causes a slowdown in economic growth that brings about a reduction in tax revenue. On the other, increasing resource availability, because of the reduction in the subsidy burden, encourages the government to increase spending on health, education, unemployment benefits, and other social services that are expected to increase the welfare of households.[25] This makes the impact of the change in spending re-allocation of the budget ambiguous since the final outcomes depend on which of these effects will prevail.

3.2 Energy Subsidies Reduction: Country Experience

Country experience and models applied provide valuable guidance regarding the impact of energy subsidy removal (reduction). However, models sometimes have shown different directions of results in assessing such impact (Pershing and Mackenzie 2004). Case studies demonstrate that countries have adopted different approaches in reducing energy subsidies. While some countries adopted a gradual approach in reducing subsidies, others applied severe cuts. Nonetheless, gradual energy subsidy removal (reduction) has proceeded along with compensatory measures to support segments of society that are negatively affected (UNEP 2004).

Figure 9.3. Reduction in Energy Subsidies and Households' Welfare

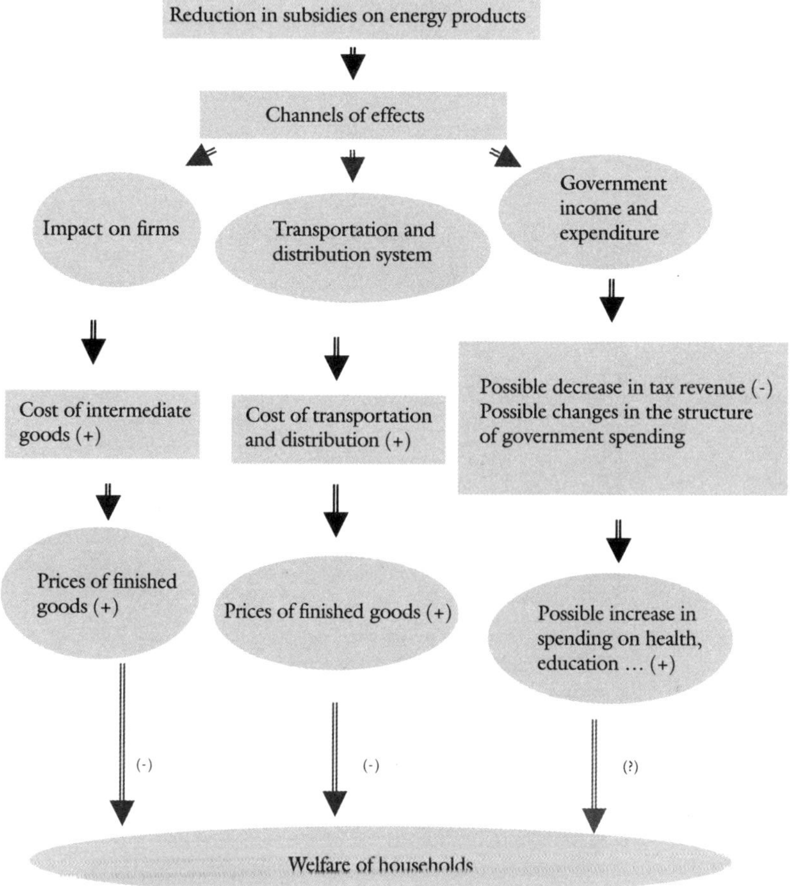

Source: The author based on literature.

Concerning the effects, it has been argued that the economic impact of energy subsidies removal depends mainly on their type, size as well as the structure of the economy (IEA 1999). Examining a number of case studies as shown in Table 9.9 shows that energy pricing reform proved to generate the following positive outcomes: reduction in CO_2 emissions, improving the budget stance, increasing the financial viability of the energy provider and improving the quality of the service provided, encouraging efficient use of energy, and rationalizing domestic energy consumption.

Nonetheless, there is also evidence that structural disturbances caused by the removal (reduction) of energy subsidies might involve economic costs, particularly in the short run as the economy adjusts to higher prices. As argued, output in most energy-intensive industries would normally fall initially unless the government introduces compensatory measures lowering other input costs. Similarly, household spending would also fall unless welfare payments are increased or taxes are cut. Raising energy prices to economic levels also increases the general inflation rate, which in turn may require the government to tighten fiscal and monetary policies, dampening GDP growth, production, and incomes (UNEP 2004).

Table 9.9. The Impact of Energy Subsidy Removal (Reduction) in a Sample of Countries

Country	*Positive Impact*	*Negative Impact*
Czech and Slovak Republics	• Improving energy efficiency • Promoting cleaner energy use	• Adverse effects on poor households • Distorting investment decisions
India*	• Increasing the financial viability of energy providers • Expanding the capacity of networks • Reducing CO_2 emissions • Improving the quality of services	• Raising the cost of living • Raising the producers' cost • Fall in manufacturing sector growth
Indonesia	• Improving national budget balance • Providing a hedge against exchange rate fluctuations • Freeing up resources to support the poor in more effective ways	• Raising the cost of living • Raising the producers' cost
Chile	• Consumption falls slightly • Slightly positive impact on income distribution • Several positive impacts on environmental effects	• Sharp fall in investments • Fall in output in most sectors • Dramatic impact on household budgets
Iran	• Improving budget stance • Spending on social services	• Increasing production cost of goods and services • Increasing cost of living • Increasing inflation
OECD Countries	• Boosting trade • Positive impacts on output • Reducing CO_2 emissions	• Significant negative impact on employment and household spending

Source: UNEP (2004). * FICCI (2005).

In sum, country experience has shown that the effect of energy subsidy removal (reduction) on GDP growth and welfare of households is quite mixed. As argued, subsidy reduction or removal increases economic efficiency as in Iran, Russia, and Venezuela (Table A1 of the Appendix), while in country cases like Chile, the positive impact on output for most sectors is either small or negligible (Table 9.9). Similarly, the effects on households' consumption are also unclear. While energy consumption falls in most subsidizing countries, the size of the consumption decline depends on the magnitude of the price rise and the relevant price elasticity of demand. Because subsidies of different magnitudes are often applied to different fuels in the same economy, there are also shifts in relative fuel prices that lead to inter-fuel substitution within that economy (UNEP 2004).

3.3 Energy Subsidies Elimination in Egypt and its Impact on Energy-Intensive Industries

The Manufacturing Sector and Energy Subsidies

In Egypt, the manufacturing sector, particularly energy-intensive industries, benefit from subsidies on energy products, namely fuel oil, diesel, natural gas, and electricity. Moreover, they benefit indirectly from subsidies given to the transportation sector in the form of lower transportation costs (see Table 9.10). Subsidies granted to the manufacturing sector can be roughly estimated based on the sector's total consumption of different energy products. This includes petroleum products and natural gas, as well as electricity. According to Table 9.10, the *manufacturing* sector consumes around 29.82 percent of total petroleum products consumption in Egypt. This implies that the manufacturing sector receives around 5,514 (LE million) as subsidized diesel, fuel oil (mazout), and others. Subsidies are estimated based on the figures of subsidies allocated to such items in the state budget for FY 2005/2006. Similarly, the manufacturing sector's share of total natural gas subsidies exceeds LE 2.3 billion, as the sector consumes 26.2 percent of total natural gas consumption. In addition, the manufacturing sector's share of subsidies to electricity is estimated at 1406 (LE million). In brief, the *manufacturing* sector in Egypt receives around 5.9 (LE billion) in subsidized energy products that constitute between 20 and 25 percent of total energy subsidies (The Ministry of Finance, various issues).[26]

Table 9.10. Sectoral Consumption of Energy Resources in Egypt (2004)

Sector	*Electricity* (%)*	*Natural Gas (%)*	*Petroleum Products (%)*
Agriculture	4	-	0.54
Electricity	NA	62.4	8.35
Transportation	NA	-	41.68
Manufacturing	38	26.2	29.82
Commercial use	NA	2	15.46
Petroleum	NA	9.4	4.15
Households	37	-	-
Government and public utilities	16	-	-
Total	100	100	100

Source: www.undp.org.eg/workshops. * Figures reported do not add up to 100.

As indicated in Table 9.11, the electricity sector benefits the most from subsidies to natural gas since it is the principal consumer of natural gas (accounting for around 60 percent of natural gas consumption in Egypt). Both the fertilizer and cement sectors are major beneficiaries from natural gas subsidies as their share exceeds that of other industrial sectors. Moreover, fertilizer consumption of natural gas is five times that of households and commercial sectors. In addition, the manufacturing sector also benefits from other subsidies granted to diesel and fuel oil where its share exceeds 45 percent of fuel oil and 15 percent of diesel consumption. Such figures indicate that most energy subsidies are directed to producers.

Assessment Methodology for Energy Subsidy Reduction

The impact of subsidy reduction on production sectors is assessed through two steps. Firstly, a sample of sectors that heavily consume energy (*fuel*[27] *and electricity*) is selected. Secondly, the study considers increasing the cost of energy inputs by 10 percent, 20 percent, 40 percent, 60 percent, and 100 percent.[28]

As a first step, the selection of sectors is based on data provided by the *Annual Industrial Production Statistics* in 2006. Table 9.12 indicates that the cement, fertilizers, steel, and aluminum production sectors depend heavily on fuel and electricity. For instance, fuel and electricity constitute about 30 percent of total production requirements and 21 percent of the

Table 9.11. Sectoral Distribution of Petroleum Products and Natural Gas Consumption (December 2005) (thousand tons)

	Natural Gas		*LPG*		*Gasoline*		*Kerosene*		*Gas Oil (Diesel)*		*Fuel Oil (mazout)*		*Others*	
Sector	Value	%	Value	%	Value	%	Value	%	Value	%	Value	%	Value	%
Electricity	13,698	59.4		-		-		-	100	1.1	4,417	46.7		-
Industry*	2,416	10.5	174	5		-	2	0.4	1,504	15.8	4,334	45.9	110	28.1
Fertilizers	2,024	8.8		-		-		-		-		0		-
Roads and contracts		-		-		-		-	1,023	10.8		0		-
Cement	1,708	7.4		-		-		-		-		0		-
Petroleum	2,480	10.8		-		-		-	425	4.5	161	1.7	24	6.1
HH & Commercial	525	2.3	3,309	95		-	435	92.8		-		0		-
Transport	217	0.9		-	2,847	100		-	2,815	29.6	537	5.7	207	52.8
Agricultural		-		-		-	32	6.8	1,538	16.2		0	51	13
Tourism		-		-		-		-	2,093	22		0		-
Total	23,068	100	3,483	100	2,847	100	469	100	9,498	100	9,449	100	392	100

Source: Author's calculations based on data from the Ministry of Petroleum (various issues).
* The definition of the sector "industry" given by the Egyptian Ministry of Petroleum excludes both fertilizer and cement industries.

value of production at factor cost for the manufacture of cement, lime and plaster.[29] In case the government decides to reduce subsidies on fuel and electricity and hence prices of energy inputs increase, holding other factors constant, changes in the cost of production under different scenarios of energy cost increases are shown in Table 9.13. Adjustments for electricity prices (cost) are made to match the reduction of subsidies on petroleum products and natural gas. This is due to the fact that petroleum products (natural gas, diesel, and mazout) constitute 25 percent in per unit cost of electricity (kw/h) as shown in Table A2 of the Appendix. Thus, adjustments are made assuming that the maximum increase in per unit cost of electricity (kw/h) does not exceed 25 percent, under the scenario of total reduction of subsidies on petroleum products (including natural gas). Thus, scenarios of subsidy elimination reported in Table 9.13 assume that the expected increase in price of electricity matches the increase in prices of petroleum products and natural gas.

These hypothetical increases in the prices of fuel and electricity affect the cost of total production as shown in Table 9.13. Under the scenario of increasing prices of fuel by 100 percent and electricity by 25 percent,[30] as noted, the highest increase in cost appears in the manufacturing of cement (10.92 percent), manufacturing of basic iron (4.52 percent), of casting steel (3.48 percent), fertilizers (4.10 percent), glass and glass products (3.3 percent), aluminum (2.91 percent), and manufacture of paper and paper products (2.2 percent). The lowest effect of increasing fuel and electricity cost appears in the manufacture of concrete, cement, and plaster (0.89 percent), and in chemicals and chemical products (1.53 percent). Moving a step forward, the study has selected some specific industries in order to reach a solid conclusion regarding the effect of subsidy reduction on the cost of production and profitability.

Table 9.12. Percent of Fuel and Electricity in Production Requirements and the Value of Production at Factor Cost* (2006)

	Percent of Total Production Value at Factor Cost			*Percent of Total Production Requirements*		
	Fuel (%)	*Electricity (%)*	*Fuel & Electricity (%)*	*Fuel (%)*	*Electricity (%)*	*Fuel & Electricity (%)*
Manufacture of paper & paper products	1.92	0.95	2.87	2.48	1.24	3.72
Manufacture of chemicals & chemical products	1.27	1.03	2.30	1.92	1.55	3.47
Manufacture of fertilizers & nitrogen compounds	3.45	2.61	6.06	7.56	5.72	13.29
Manufacture of glass & glass products	2.59	2.89	5.48	4.37	4.89	9.26
Manufacture of cement, lime & plaster	7.80	12.47	20.28	10.89	17.41	28.30
Manufacture of articles of concrete, cement & plaster	0.71	0.72	1.43	0.92	0.93	1.85
Manufacture of basic iron & steel	3.89	2.55	6.44	5.84	3.83	9.67
Casting of iron & steel	0.42	12.24	12.66	0.62	18.04	18.66
Manufacture of basic precious & non-ferrous metals (including aluminum)	1.15	7.06	8.21	1.58	9.72	11.30

Source: Author's calculations based on CAPMAS (2006).

* Production at factor cost includes production requirements plus value added.

Table 9.13. Percentage of Increase in Total Production Cost of Main Energy-Intensive Industries due to Reducing Fuel Subsidies and the Resulting Electricity Price Increases*

	10%	*20%*	*30%*	*40%*	*60%*	*100%*
Manufacture of paper & paper products	0.22%	0.43%	0.65%	0.85%	1.28%	2.15%
Manufacture of chemicals & chemical products	0.15%	0.31%	0.46%	0.60%	0.90%	1.53%
Manufacture of fertilizers & nitrogen compounds	0.41%	0.82%	1.23%	1.62%	2.42%	4.10%
Manufacture of glass & glass products	0.33%	0.66%	0.99%	1.30%	1.94%	3.31%
Manufacture of cement, lime & plaster	1.09%	2.18%	3.28%	4.24%	6.37%	10.92%
Manufacture of articles of concrete, cement & plaster	0.09%	0.18%	0.27%	0.35%	0.52%	0.89%
Manufacture of basic iron & steel	0.45%	0.90%	1.36%	1.78%	2.68%	4.52%
Casting of iron & steel	0.35%	0.70%	1.04%	1.27%	1.91%	3.48%
Manufacture of basic precious & non-ferrous metals (including aluminum)	0.29%	0.58%	0.87%	1.09%	1.64%	2.91%

Source: Author's calculations based on CAPMAS (2006).
* It should be noted that electricity prices are adjusted under each scenario to match the increase in prices of petroleum products. For instance, the 10 percent-increase scenario reflects an increase by 10 percent in the cost of petroleum products and a resulting 2.5 percent increase in prices of electricity and so on.

Table 9.14 shows the effects of increasing prices of energy products on cost of production and then the profitability per ton produced for a sample of selected industries. For the *nitrogen fertilizer* industry two companies that produce about 75 percent of total domestic production were selected for measuring the effects of energy subsidy elimination. As noted in Table 9.14, the profit ratio per ton decreases from 22.65 percent to 7.8 percent as prices of energy inputs increase by up to 60 percent and it turns to be negative (-2.2 percent), if prices of petroleum products (including natural gas) and electricity increase by 100 percent. Nevertheless, the profit ratio per ton is higher when those ratios are calculated based on export prices due to the significant gap between domestic and export prices.[31] Under the 100 percent scenario, the profit ratio per ton exceeds 21 percent. Therefore, for companies that export most of their production, increasing energy costs will not profoundly affect their competitiveness and profitability. However, for domestically oriented companies, increasing the cost of energy products causes a significant decrease in their per ton profitability (see Table 9.14). For the cement and aluminum industries the situation is quite different. For the cement industry,[32] with an average price of LE 250 per ton that is below market price in 2005/2006, the profit ratio falls to 15.4 percent as energy prices increase by 60 percent. However, if an average price of LE 300 per ton is applied, the profit ratio exceeds 33 percent and becomes 29.2 percent when prices increase by 100 percent, holding other factors constant (as shown in Table A5 of the Appendix). This indicates that the cement industry compared to other energy-driven industries will not face a critical challenge either domestically or in the international markets, if prices of energy products increase. The same conclusion can be reached for the aluminum industry where profit ratios per ton exceed 27 percent and 26 percent when electricity inputs increase by 60 percent and 100 percent, respectively. Thus, the reduction of subsidy on electricity does not seem to present a critical challenge, since the cost of electricity constitutes about 20 percent of total cost per ton and the reduction of subsidies on petroleum products affects partially the cost of electricity as previously mentioned. However, this is not the case for the steel industry since profit ratios per ton are low as they fall to less than 14 and 13 percent when electricity prices increase under the 60 and 100 percent scenarios, respectively.[33]

Subsidy reduction scenarios shown in Table 9.14 assume that electricity prices match the reduction of subsidies on petroleum products and natural gas given the share of such inputs in the cost of electricity unit. However, the potential benefits of adjusting electricity prices differ according to prices of electricity paid by each company, since prices differ according to the type of electricity consumed. Companies that consume very high voltage electricity power get the lowest prices compared to those imposed on medium and low voltage (see Table A3 in the Appendix). Thus, profit ratios might differ among companies due to the type of electricity consumed.

Table 9.14. Profit Ratio under Energy Subsidy Reduction Scenarios for Selected Energy-Intensive Industries

	Original	*20% inc*	*30% inc*	*40% inc*	*60% inc*	*100% inc*
Fertilizer (nitrogen fertilizer)*						
Profit ratio based on domestic prices	22.65%	19.9%	17.49%	12.7%	7.8%	-2.24%
Profit ratio based on export price***	40.62%	38.5%	36.6%	33%	29.22%	21.5%
Cement industry*						
Profit per ton (LE/ton)	118	114.58	111.51	106.05	100.08	87.71
Profit ratio per ton	39.33%	38.2%	36.2%	35.4%	33.4%	29.23%
Aluminum**						
Profit per ton (LE/ton)	3437	3358.271	3318.907	3295.288	3224.432	3043.355
Profit ratio per ton	29.42%	28.74%	28.41%	28.20%	27.60%	26.05%
Steel industry**						
Profit per ton (LE/ton)	380	372.7	369.05	366.86	360.29	343.5
Profit ratio per ton	14.18%	13.91%	13.77%	13.69%	13.44%	12.82%

Sources: Author's calculations based on information available in the Appendix.
* Calculations are based on 2004 figures. ** Only electricity components of inputs have been increased. *** Figures based on export prices are calculated only for fertilizers since there is a significant gap between domestic and export prices.

Obviously, figures of profitability ratios under various subsidy reduction scenarios indicate that energy-intensive industries shall not be severely affected. This conclusion is supported by another indicator, the after-tax profit ratio. This is to avoid the debate on whether the profitability per unit of production is a good indicator for assessing the impact of subsidy reduction. Table 9.15 shows the after-tax profit ratios for a sample of companies in each industry over the last five years, obtained from the published financial statements for these companies in the Egyptian stock market. Although there is diversity in ratios among companies included in the table, on average profitability ratios—excluding that of the steel industry—are relatively high (ratio exceeds 20 percent) as shown in Figure 9.4.

The highest profit ratios appear in the cement industry where for some companies, profit ratios exceed 40 percent, while the lowest ratios appear in the steel industry. Table 9.15 also reveals the stability in the time path of profitability over the period 2001–2005 for the two leading fertilizer companies (A and B).

This analysis reveals the capacity of cement and fertilizer industries to face a probability of energy subsidy reduction without severely affecting their financial status. The lack of data about profit ratios of other steel companies might lead to a misleading conclusion regarding the ability of the steel industry to adjust to subsidy reduction, particularly because the profit ratios of the two leading companies fluctuate over time (see Table 9.15).

The profit ratios of energy-intensive industries in Egypt are relatively higher than in Europe, North America, and Asia and Pacific. Ratios in Egypt are similar to those in Latin America and the GCC countries. For instance, the average profit ratios (before tax) of the cement industry in the GCC countries is estimated at 22 percent over the last five years (HSBC 2005). This is consistent with the fact that the operating profit margin of two major cement companies, as shown in Table A8 of the Appendix, are higher in the Middle East region (including Egypt) compared to other regions. Similarly, in the fertilizer industry, different reports indicate low profit margin ratios in regions such as Europe and North America compared to those in Egypt. The analysis of 46 fertilizer companies in the UK indicates that the average profit margin does not exceed 2 percent.[34]

Figure 9.4. Average After-Tax Profit Rates in Selected Energy Intensive Industries (2000–2005)

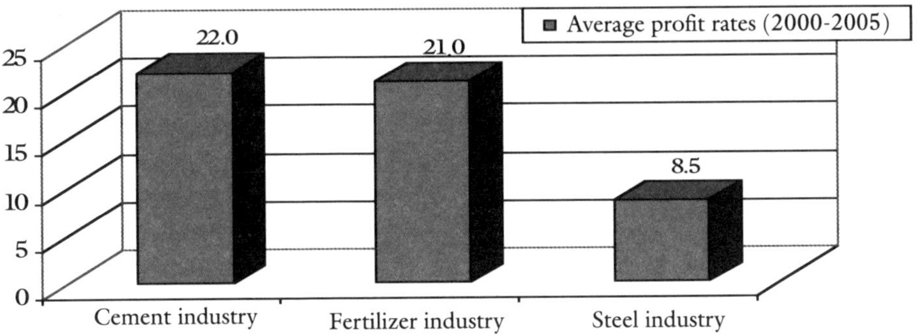

Source: Based on information in Table 9.15.

Table 9.15. Net Profit after Tax and Profit Ratios (% of Sales Revenues) in Selected Companies

Industry/Company	*2000*		*2001*		*2002*		*2003*		*2004*		*2005*	
	Net Profit after Tax (LE mn)	*Profit Ratio (%)*	*Net Profit after Tax (LE mn)*	*Profit Ratio (%)*	*Net Profit after Tax (LE mn)*	*Profit Ratio (%)*	*Net Profit after Tax (LE mn)*	*Profit Ratio (%)*	*Net Profit after Tax (LE mn)*	*Profit ratio (%)*	*Net Profit after Tax (LE mn)*	*Profit Ratio (%)*
*Iron and Steel**												
Company A	16.5	1.6	-40.3	-3.3	-124.9	-10.4	NA	NA	200.4	9.2	450.3	14.7
Company B	-35.3	-2.1	-260.2	-11.8	23.2	0.8	NA	NA	1379.5	18.4	2375.9	30.1
Average Iron and Steel	-9.4	-0.25	-150.25	-7.55	-50.85	-4.8	NA	NA	789.95	13.8	1413.1	22.4
*Fertilizers**												
Company A	261.3	31.7	317.2	33.8	338.4	36.3	345.4	34.6	360.9	28.8	424.5	29.6
Company B	NA	NA	42	21	47.8	21.5	54	18.8	64.3	16.9	90	23.2
Company C	NA	NA	0.7	0.9	0.3	0.4	0.6	1	3	1.9	NA	NA
Average Fertilizers	261.3	31.7	120.0	18.6	128.8	19.4	133.3	18.1	142.7	15.9	257.3	26.4
Cement												
Company A	NA	NA	NA	NA	56.8	60.2	30.5	12.799	80.1	25.309	148.1	35.254
Company B	352.7	27.4	130.1	11.5	59.4	5.2	214	17.463	394.4	26.325	1045.2	44.47
Company C	NA	NA	NA	NA	NA	NA	22.7	11.3	51.5	17.6	132.8	32.7
Company D	7.1	3.9	105.7	58	-100	-52.1	-43.7	-18.5	-43.2	-13.4	86.9	21.9
Company E	NA	NA	78.7	15.7	NA	NA	-91.4	-23.269	27.5	4.763	NA	NA
Company F	NA	NA	26.7	20.3	19.6	9.1	35.6	14.6	80.7	24.6	181.8	43.2
Company G	NA	NA	273.4	33.3	244.1	25.8	306.1	26.6	676.2	42.1	963.1	47.3
Company H	160.4	34	93.9	23.2	49.8	15.303	20.9	5.626	23.6	6.386	48.8	11.622
Average Cement	173.4	21.8	118.1	27.0	55.0	10.6	61.8	5.8	161.4	16.7	372.4	33.8

Source: The Egyptian stock market, published financial statements, different issues.
*Figures of A and B are for the two leading companies in each industry.

These higher profitability ratios indicate that energy-intensive industries are able to adjust to these changes in prices of energy inputs. Therefore, they have somewhat flexible options in the sense that they can choose either not to raise prices or increase them in ways that do not exceed the actual increase in cost. In brief, the results of this analysis are as follows:

- Energy-intensive industries in the Egyptian economy benefit significantly from subsidized energy products either directly or indirectly.
- Higher profit ratios of energy-intensive industries indicate the monopolistic power of such industries. The markets of energy-intensive industries in Egypt are characterized by high market concentration on the supply side. The cement and steel industry present an example of high market concentration. In both industries, few firms are dominating the market. In the cement market, although there are 11 firms in the industry, only three firms account for about 70 percent of total production. The steel industry may be a more striking example since there are about 20 producers in the market, with the market share of two producers amounting to two-thirds of the whole market (Ghoneim and Abdel Latif forthcoming). This phenomenon of supply-side market concentration prevails also in aluminum and fertilizer markets, where Misr Aluminum Company is a clear example of perfect monopoly. Similarly, the market share of three fertilizer companies exceeds 92 percent of the market (IDSC 2004).
- Increasing prices of energy inputs do not constitute a severe challenge for energy-driven industries. Therefore, government intervention through increasing prices of petroleum products and the subsequent rise in electricity prices can be absorbed by energy-intensive companies without raising prices by the same level of increase. The intervention will also be consistent with the enforcement of competition and consumer protection laws, as it might correct for market failure resulting from the monopolistic power of energy intensive industries. Moreover, it enables consumers to stand against exploitation practices of these companies. Protection against exploitation must be extended to include not only the final consumers, as the law states, but also intermediate industries. This is crucial for consumers since the elasticity of demand for such industries is low, which increases the

power of such companies and industries to raise prices in a way that does not exceed the true increase in cost as a result of energy subsidy reduction.

- Since the analysis argues that subsidy reduction will not severely affect the profitability of energy-intensive industries, it strengthens the government's negotiating power with such companies. However, a gradual approach is advisable if the government is to consider a complete elimination of energy subsidies. This will give the energy-intensive sector time to adjust to free-market pricing of energy products.

4. Main Findings and Conclusion

In Egypt, subsidies continue to be a major item of government expenditures. About 74 percent of such subsidies are allocated to energy products (excluding electricity). Specifically, government spending on energy subsidies is around 15 percent of total government spending and exceeds six percent of GDP in 2006. The study argues that energy subsidies are twice those allocated for defense, three to four times those allocated for health, and exceed those spent on education.

Figures of energy subsidies (excluding electricity) have quadrupled due to the rapid increase in oil prices over the past two years. Such increase in the subsidy bill of energy products has presented a critical challenge for the Egyptian fiscal authority. Starting FY 2005/2006, fiscal authority has recorded such subsidies explicitly in order to reveal the true burden of subsidizing petroleum products and natural gas.

The study has investigated the impact of reducing energy subsidies in Egypt on energy-intensive industries applying a partial equilibrium approach. Assessing subsidy reduction on energy intensive sectors, under different scenarios of increasing prices of energy products, has been conducted by selecting a sample of industries that depend heavily on energy products, and then measuring the impact on profitability per ton of production in these industries, holding other factors constant.

The study argues that energy-intensive industries in the Egyptian economy benefit the most from subsidized energy products either directly or indirectly. It shows that increasing prices of petroleum products (including natural gas) and hence electricity prices can be absorbed by such companies without raising prices of their products by the same percentage increase. Higher prices of energy inputs do not constitute a severe challenge for energy-driven industries given their highly profitable activities. Profit ratios of energy-intensive industries in Egypt are higher than those in competitive markets such as Europe and North America. Therefore, energy-intensive industries have flexibility to adjust to subsidy reduction. In other words, they can choose either not to raise prices, due to higher profitability ratios, or increase them in ways that reflect at most the actual increase in cost. The significant reduction in tax rates due to the introduction of the new tax law in 2005 is another aspect to be considered. Reduction of taxes by 50 percent benefits such companies and also lowers the cost of subsidy reduction.

As argued, higher profit ratios of energy-intensive industries in Egypt are partially explained by the monopolistic power they possess. This constitutes an example of market failure that requires corrective measures. Thus, protection for both intermediate and final consumers against the exploitation practices of such companies requires effective government intervention in order to effectively enforce the competition and consumer protection laws.

Finally, it is important to stress that the decision to remove subsidies, either partially or totally, requires compensatory measures to reduce its negative impact, particularly on poor households. These measures should be both targeted and temporary until producers and consumers adjust. They should also be coupled with government intervention to correct for market failure in the energy-intensive market, which in turn will lower the cost of compensatory measures.

Appendix

Table A1. Impact of Subsidy Removal (selected countries)

	Average Subsidization (% of reference price)	*Annual Economic Efficiency Gains (% of GDP)*	*Reduction in Energy Consumption (%)*	*Reduction in CO_2 Emissions*
China	10.89	0.37	9.41	13.44
Russia	32.52	1.54	18.03	17.10
India	14.17	0.34	7.18	14.15
Indonesia	27.51	0.24	7.09	10.97
Iran	80.42	2.22	47.54	49.45
South Africa	6.41	0.10	6.35	8.11
Venezuela	57.57	1.17	24.94	26.07
Kazakhstan	18.23	0.98	19.22	22.76
Total sample	21.12	0.73	12.80	15.96
Percentage of:				
Non-OECD	NA	NA	7.48	10.21
World	NA	NA	3.50	4.59

Source: IEA (1999).

* The percentage reduction in energy consumption was calculated by adding the gross calorific value of the reductions of the different fuels under consideration and expressing the sum as a percentage of TPES. Because the calculations in this study did not take into account the refinery sector (a 5 percent reduction in gasoline use can amount to a reduction of TPES of more than 5 percent), the number thus derived constitutes again a lower bound to the true reductions in energy consumption.

Table A2. Increasing the Cost of Natural Gas and Mazout on Electricity per Unit Cost (Kw/h)

	Per Unit Cost P.T/Kw/h Base-Scenario	*20%*	*30%*	*40%*	*60%*	*100%*
Natural gas	3.6	4.32	4.68	5.04	5.76	7.2
Mazout	0.4	0.48	0.52	0.56	0.64	0.8
Other inputs	6	6	6	6	6	6
Total production cost	10	10.72	11.20	11.6	12.4	14
Transportation cost	2	2	2	2	2	2
Distribution cost	4	4	4	4	4	4
Total production and distribution cost	16	16.8	17.20	17.6	18.4	20
Percentage increase in per unit cost (%)	0	5	7.5	9	13.5	25

Source: Author's calculations based on IDSC (2005a) and Egyptian Electricity Holding Company (2005).

Table A3. Electricity Prices (KW/h) Paid by the Industry Sector

	2004/2005		
	Quantity	*Value*	*Average Price*
Industry			
Very high voltage	11,758	1,044,716	8.9
High voltage	4,604	549,246	11.9
Medium & low voltage	13,922	2,526,378	18.1
Total	30,284	4,120,340	13.6

Source: Egyptian Electricity Holding Company (2005).

Table A4. Effects of Increasing Natural Gas and Electricity on Nitrogen Fertilizer Industry

	*Original**	*10% inc*	*20% inc*	*40% inc*	*60% inc*	*100% inc*
The increase in cost of natural gas prices	0.0	16.400	31.800	62.600	93.400	155
The increase in production cost of electricity	0.0	1.968	3.229	3.986	6.256	12.0575
Total increase in cost (per ton)	0.0	18.368	35.029	66.586	99.656	167.0575
Cost under different scenarios	519.0	537.368	554.029	585.586	618.656	686.0575
Domestic sales prices (per ton)	671.0	671.0	671.0	671.0	671.0	671.0
Export sales price (per ton)	874.0	874.000	874.000	874.000	874.000	874
Profit per ton based on domestic prices	152.0	133.6	117.0	85.4	52.3	-15.1
Profit per ton based on export prices	355.0	336.632	319.971	288.414	255.344	187.9425
Profit ratio based on domestic prices	22.7	19.9	17.4	12.7	7.8	-2.2
Profit ratio based on export prices	40.6	38.5	36.6	33.0	29.2	21.5

Source: Author's calculations based on IDSC (2004).
* Cost structure is an average for both types of nitrogen fertilizers (Yurea + Ammonia), for three leading companies for the year 2004/2005.

Table A5. The Effect of Subsidy Reduction on the Cost (per Ton) of Cement Industry

	Original	*10% inc*	*20% inc*	*40% inc*	*60% inc*	*100% inc*
Increase in cost of producing one ton of cement due to natural gas price inc.	0	1.3992	2.7984	5.5968	8.3952	13.992
Increase in cost of producing one ton of cement due to mazout price inc.	0	1.2	2.4	4.8	7.2	12
Increase in cost of producing one ton of cement due to electricity price inc.	0	0.8602	1.2903	1.54836	2.32254	4.301
Total increase in production cost (LE)	0	3.4594	6.4887	11.94516	17.91774	30.293
Cost per ton	182	185.4594	188.4887	193.9451	199.9177	212.293
Average domestic price (LE/ton)	250	250	250	250	250	250
Profit per ton (LE/ton)	68.8	65.3406	62.3113	56.85484	50.88226	38.507
Profit ratio (%)	27.4	26.1	24.8	22.7	20.3	15.4
Av. domestic price (LE/ton)	300*	300	300	300	300	300
Profit per ton (LE/ton)	118	114.5406	111.5113	106.0548	100.0823	87.707
Profit ratio (%)	39.3	38.2	37.2	35.4	33.4	29.2

Source: Author's calculations based on IDSC (2005b).
* The price chosen is the average price at the end of 2005 and January 2006 price, while market prices reach LE 350 per ton.

Table A6. Cost per Ton of Aluminum and Increasing Prices of Electricity

	Original	*20% inc*	*30% inc*	*40% inc*	*60% inc*	*100% inc*
Quantity of electricity used in producing one ton of aluminum (Kw/h)	14,996	14,996	14,996	14,996	14,996	14,996
Price of electricity (P.T/Kw/h)	10.5	11.025	11.2875	11.445	11.9175	13.125
Cost of electricity used in producing one ton of aluminum (LE)	1574.58	1,653.309	1,692.674	1,716.292	1,787.148	1,968.225
Cost of other inputs	6,672.42	6,672.42	6,672.42	6,672.42	6,672.42	6,672.42
Total cost of producing one ton of aluminum	8,247	8,325.729	8,365.094	8,388.712	8,459.568	8,640.645
Price of aluminum (LE/ton)	11,684	11,684	11684	11,684	11,684	11,684
Profit (LE/ton)	3,437	3,358.271	3,318.907	3,295.288	3,224.432	3,043.355
Profit ratio per ton	29.42%	28.74%	28.41%	28.20%	27.60%	26.05%

Source: Author's calculations based on Ministry of Investment (2005).

Table A7. Cost per Ton of Steel and Increasing Prices of Electricity

	Original	*20% inc*	*30% inc*	*40% inc*	*60% inc*	*100% inc*
Price of electricity (m/Kw/h)	0.105	0.11025	0.112875	0.11445	0.119175	0.13125
Cost of electricity used in producing one ton of steel (LE)	146	153.3	156.95	159.14	165.71	1,82.5
Cost of other inputs (LE)	2154	2,154	2154	2,154	2,154	2,154
Total cost of producing one ton of steel (LE)	2,300	2,307.3	2,310.95	2,313.14	2,319.71	2,336.5
Price of steel (LE/ton)	2,680	2,680	2,680	2,680	2,680	2,680
Profit (LE/ton)	380	372.7	369.05	366.86	360.29	343.5
Profit ratio per ton (%)	14.18%	13.91%	13.77%	13.69%	13.44%	12.82%

Source: Author's calculations based on Egyptian Electricity Holding Company (2005).
* The cost reported is an average figure since the cost of production ranges between LE 2,200 and LE 2,500 per ton. **Prices are also averages and do not include transportation cost.

Table A8. Operating Profit Margin of Two Leading Companies across World Regions in 2004/05 (%)

Region	*CEMEX*	*Holcim*
North America	24.1	8.7
Europe	11.1	14.9
Latin America	18.6	26.2
Africa and Middle East	20.3	22.5
Asia and Pacific	2.6	12.7

Source: Cemex (2005) and Holcim (2005).

Notes

1. The average price of crude oil went up by 16.1 percent in 2003, by 30.4 percent in 2004, and by 37.8 percent in 2005 (BP 2006).
2. The term sometimes extends to include assistance granted by others, such as individuals or non-government institutions. However, the latter form of assistance is more usually described as charity.
3. This case is clear if we look at the Egyptian subsidy system where many explicit subsidies are provided directly and indirectly. For instance, the state budget directly subsidizes the General Authority for Supply Commodities (GASC) and indirectly subsidizes other economic authorities as the state budget continues to finance their deficits.
4. Fiscal costs are those paid by government whether or not they have been shown in government accounts, while economic costs are the benefits foregone from other forms of allocation. Specifically, economic costs are the cost of income transfers that some or a segment of society makes to another segment(s) of society (Valdes 1988).
5. These goods and services—called semi-private or semi-public—may be subject to significant external benefits or costs (positive and negative externalities) such as education and health.
6. For instance, lower prices of energy products discouraged investment in modernizing the electricity sector in India because firms consider the adoption of old-fashioned technology economically attractive. This is a common phenomenon in several developing countries (UNEP 2002).
7. For details, see the case of India where subsidized oil products are rationed (UNEP 2002).
8. In Indonesia all subsidies had almost been phased out by 2003 except for about one percent of GDP in outlays for kerosene.
9. For more details, see the declared objectives of subsidies as revealed in the budget statements.
10. Because the term fuel is a broader concept as it includes petroleum products, natural gas, and wood, the author will specify what items are included when the term comes up in the text.
11. The correlation between percentage of subsidies and GDP per capita is significant with a positive sign and moderate value (0.53) for the existing sample.
12. It is argued that differences in energy consumption among countries are a result of three key factors, namely, the levels of urbanization, economic development and per capita income (Dzioubinski and Chipman 1999).

13. Oil intensity is defined as the number of barrels of oil required to generate $1000 of GDP (FICCI 2005).
14. This definition is based on the state budget statement for the fiscal year 2005/2006 and the People's Assembly Budgeting and Planning Committee reports for 2002/2003 and 2003/2004.
15. There are other forms of cost incurred by EGCP such as transportation and taxes.
16. This definition is based on reports of the Budgeting and Planning Committee, the budget year-end reports of 2002/2003 and 2003/2004.
17. Subsidies allocated to electricity estimated at LE 3.7 billion in 2005, are still implicit (see the budget statement of 2005/2006).
18. The EGPC considers that domestic prices paid by consumers cover the cost for its share. Thus, the concept of subsidies used does not include subsidies on such share. However, this approach is inconsistent with the concept of economic cost since it ignores the opportunity cost of the EGPC share.
19. Value of subsidies = total consumption * (International prices - domestic prices).
20. Subsidy ratio = (1–domestic prices/international prices).
21. For more details see the state budget statement for FY 2006/2007.
22. The calculation of opportunity cost differs for each item of energy products. For instance, the opportunity cost for natural gas is its long run marginal cost, and for oil products is the international price (Gerner and Sinclair 2006).
23. Nwafor, Ogujiuba, and Asogwa (2006) review theoretical and empirical literature that examines the effect of subsidy removal.
24. Country experience shows that the increasing energy bill will raise almost all prices (Nwafor, Ogujiuba, and Asogwa 2006).
25. Such re-allocation of budget spending might also increase the possibility of demand-pull inflation.
26. Such figures represent only the direct benefits of energy subsidies.
27. The term fuel in this context includes natural gas as a source of energy.
28. Increasing prices of petroleum products and natural gas by up to 100 percent does not imply total elimination of subsidies, as doubling prices of such products reduces subsidy rates by up to 60 percent. Similarly, a rise in electricity prices matching the increase in prices of natural gas and petroleum products lowers subsidy rates on electricity by up to 80 percent.
29. Similar results are obtained from the input-output table for the Egyptian economy in the latest Social Accounting Matrix 2005.
30. This is the potential maximum increase in the cost of electricity.
31. Local prices of fertilizers are determined by the government with a profit margin as part of government policies to subsidize farmers. This makes export prices nearly double domestic prices.
32. Calculations are based on the cost structure obtained for three companies with a market share exceeding 45 percent. Those companies are the Egyptian Cement Company (ECC), Suez Cement and National Cement.
33. Scenarios for both aluminum and steel industries assume only an increase in electricity prices. This is due to data availability and to the fact that electricity in both sectors constitutes a major energy component.
34. For more details see www.majorcompanies.co.uk.

References

BP (British Petroleum). 2006. *Statistical review of world energy 2006*. Available at: http://www.bp.com/statisticalreview.

CAPMAS (Central Agency for Public Mobilization and Statistics). 2006. *Annual industrial production statistics*. Cairo, Egypt: CAPMAS.

CEMEX. 2005. Annual report.

Dodson, B.M. and M.G. Paramo. 2001. *The role of the state and consequences of alternative public revenue policies*. Working paper, Spain. The World Bank Institute. Washington, D.C.: World Bank.

Dzioubinski, O. and R. Chipman. 1999. *Trends in consumption and production: household energy consumption*. DESA Discussion Paper No. 6.

EEA (European Environment Agency). 2004. *Energy subsidy in the European Union: A brief overview*. EEA technical report. Copenhagen, Denmark.

Egyptian Electricity Holding Company. 2005. *Annual report 2004/2005*. Cairo: Egypt.

FICCI (Federation of Indian Chambers of Commerce and Industry). 2005. Impact of high oil prices on Indian economy. India, FICCI.

Gerner, F., and S. Sinclair. 2006. *Connecting residential households to natural gas: An economic and financial analysis*. OBA Working paper no.7. The Global Partnership on Output-Based Aid. Washington, D.C.: World Bank.

Ghoneim, A., and Lobna Abdel Latif. Forthcoming. *Competition, competition policy, and economic efficiency: The case of Egypt*. Research project undertaken for IDRC. Cairo, Egypt.

Helmy, Omneia. 2005. *The efficiency and equity of subsidy policy in Egypt*. ECES Working paper no. 105. Cairo, Egypt: Egyptian Center for Economic Studies (ECES).

Holcim. 2005. Annual report. Research and Markets Guinnes Center, Dublin, Ireland.

HSBC. 2005. *Cement industry in GCC countries*. Industry Study. United Arab Emirates.

IDSC (Information Decision and Support Center). 2004. *The economics of price liberalization for the nitrogen fertilizer industry* (in Arabic). Cairo, Egypt: IDSC.

———. 2005a. *Scenarios for reforming subsidies on electricity in Egypt* (in Arabic). Cairo, Egypt: IDSC.

———. 2005b. *The impact of price liberalization of the cement industry inputs on the industry and final consumer* (in Arabic). Cairo, Egypt: IDSC.

IEA (International Energy Agency). 1999. *World energy outlook 1999: Looking at energy subsidies: Getting the prices right*. www.iea.org/textbase/publications

Irrek, W. 2002. *Subsidy reform—moving towards sustainability*. EP Workshop on Energy Subsidy, Energy Institute for Climate, Environment and Energy. www.iea.org/textbase/publications

Kumar, Shubh, and H. Alderman. 1989. *Food consumption and nutritional effects of consumer-oriented food subsidies*. www.ifpri.org

Legeida, N. 2001. *Implicit subsidies in Ukraine: Estimation, developments, and policy implications*. Working Paper no.10. Institute for Economic Research and Policy Consulting. Kyiv, Ukraine.

Ministry of Finance (MOF). Various issues. *The state budget statements*. Cairo, Egypt.

Ministry of Investment. 2005. unpublished data for the Misr Aluminum Company (2005/2006). Cairo, Egypt.

Ministry of Petroleum. Various issues. *Annual Report*. Cairo, Egypt.

Myers, N. and Jennifer Kent. 2001. *Perverse subsidies: How tax dollars can undercut the environment and the economy*. Boulder, WA: Island Press.

Nwafor, M., K. Ogujiuba, and R. Asogwa. 2006. *Does subsidy removal hurt the poor*. Working Paper Series. AIAE (African Institute for Applied Economics). Dakar, Senegal.

Pershing, J. and J. Mackenzie. 2004. *Removing subsidies: Leveling the playing field for renewable energy technology.* Background paper presented at the International Conference for Renewable Energies, Bonn.

Saunders, M., and K. Schneider. 2000. *Removing energy subsidies in developing and transition economies.* Paper presented at the ABARE (Australian Bureau of Agricultural and Resource Economics) Conference.

Schrank, W.E. 2003. *Introducing Fisheries Subsidies.* FAO Fisheries Technical Paper 437. FAO, Rome.

The People's Assembly, Egypt. The Budgeting and Planning Committee Report about the Economic Authorities, 2002/2003. (in Arabic). Cairo, Egypt.

———. (2003). *The End-year Report of Budgeting and Planning Committee 2002/2003.* Cairo, Egypt.

———. (2004). *The End-year Report of Budgeting and Planning Committee 2003/2004.* Cairo, Egypt.

UNEP (United Nations Environment Programme). 2002. *Reforming energy subsidies.* Division of Technology, Industry and Economics. United Nations Publications, USA.

———. 2004. *Energy subsidies: Lessons learned in assessing their impact and designing policy reforms.* Edited by Anja von Moltke, Colin McKee and Trevor Morgan. Geneva: Switzerland.

Valdes, A. 1988. Explicit and implicit food subsidies: Distribution of cost. In A. Andersen (ed). *Food subsidies in developing countries: Costs, benefits, and policy options.* Baltimore: Johns Hopkins University Press.

CHAPTER 10

Public Expenditure on Health in Egypt*

Akiko Maeda and Sameh El Saharty

Over the past decade, Egypt has achieved an overall improvement in health outcomes. There have been significant reductions in infant, child, and maternal mortality rates. Infant mortality decreased from 76 (per 1000 live births) in 1992 to 33 in 2003; and maternal mortality decreased from 170 (per 1000 live births) in 1992 to 39 in 2003. These health improvements are probably attributable to a combination of factors, including improved access to basic health services, hygiene, and safe drinking water, and higher educational attainment of mothers. However, several critical deficiencies remain in the public health system in Egypt, fueling concerns about its sustainability.

First, although overall health outcomes have improved significantly, regional disparities still persist. Disparity in infant mortality rates (ratio of rural/urban rates) reached 1.5 in 2003; and disparity in under-five mortality (ratio of rural/urban rates) reached 1.48 in 2003. Second, Egypt is in the midst of a demographic and epidemiologic transition. Despite the deceleration in population growth rate, the population is expected to continue growing, from 70 million in 2005 to 90 million in 2020. The aging and urbanization of the population will lead to substantial increases in per capita expenditures on healthcare. Third, Egypt has a pluralistic health system, but with a limited level of risk-pooling. Total spending in the health sector is dominated by direct out-of-pocket payments by households, accounting for more than half of all health expenditure in Egypt.[1] Fourth, growth in total health spending outpaced economic growth in the period 1996–2002. Fifth, regional disparities remain in total health spending, as well as inequities in the access to, and use of health services.

Overall, the poor allocation of resources and the lack of a strategic approach to quality improvement are contributing to the loss of patient satisfaction with the public health services. As a result, most Egyptians, including those living in the poorest regions, are more often seeking health services from the private sector.

In July 2005, the government of Egypt embarked on a medium-term strategic framework for reforming the health sector. The strategy aims at the expansion of the social health insurance system, in conjunction with parallel reforms in the tax and budget systems, offering a unique opportunity for creating fiscal space and generating political momentum to extend an effective, affordable, and equitable system of health benefits and financial protection to all citizens.

The remainder of this chapter is organized as follows. In Section 1, the system of health coverage in Egypt is explained. Section 2 tackles the main challenges facing the health system in Egypt, while Section 3 proposes strategies and options for reform. Finally, Section 4 concludes with a brief summary, and a number of short- and medium-term recommendations.

1. Health Coverage in Egypt

On the public side, health coverage for the Egyptian population is provided through a combination of social health insurance and subsidized government health services (Figure 10.1). Social health insurance coverage provided through the Health Insurance Organization (HIO) covers about 48 percent of the population, which includes one-third of the active labor force.[2] The Ministry of Health and Population (MoHP) and other government agencies operate a nationwide network of government healthcare providers, and these function as an "insurer of last resort" by providing free or substantially subsidized health services to the citizens not covered under HIO. Over the past decade, the MoHP has significantly expanded the Program of Treatment at the Expense of State (PTES).

The public sector is divided into government authorities and economic authorities.[3] The healthcare institutions falling under the category of government authorities include the administrative offices and healthcare facilities operated under MoHP, which includes the central headquarters in Cairo, health directorates in the 27 governorates, and the specialized centers for medical care and cancer treatment. Investments in these specialized centers, established in 2001 under the MoHP, comprise a network of about 34 tertiary hospitals, and have contributed to a major increase in the capital and operating expenditures of the MoHP. These services are partly reimbursed through the PTES. In addition, government authorities include hospitals operated by the Public Authority for Teaching Hospitals and Institutes (PATHI), which runs nine specialized research institutes and nine large teaching hospitals, and the university hospitals managed by the Ministry of Higher Education (MoHE), which play a key role in medical education and training and clinical research.

Figure 10.1. Health Benefits Coverage in Egypt

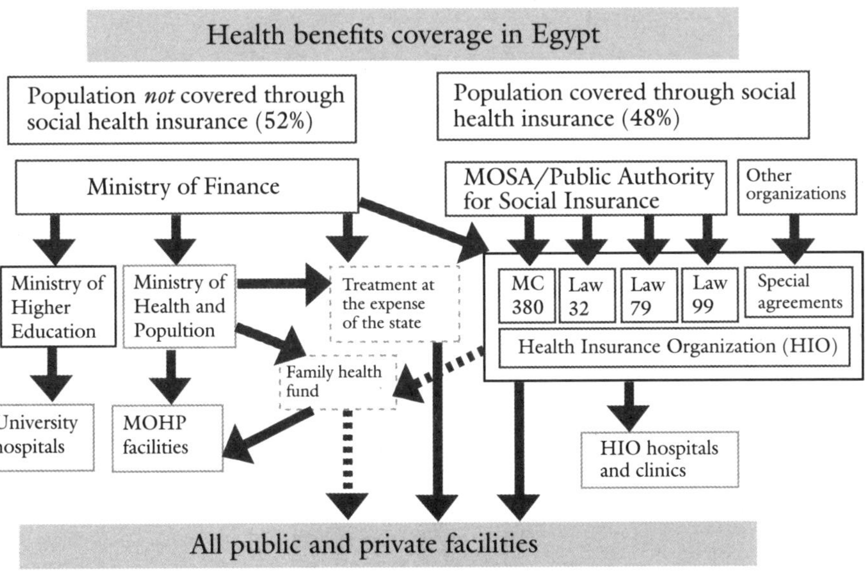

Source: MoHP and World Bank staff.

Healthcare institutions falling under the category of economic authorities include the HIO and the Curative Care Organizations (CCOs). The HIO was established in 1964 after the enactment of Health Insurance Law no. 61, which gave HIO a historic mandate to cover all Egyptians with social health insurance. However, four decades later this objective has not been achieved. At present, HIO manages several separate compulsory social health insurance programs for formal sector workers, pensioners, widows, school children and infants, who are covered on a voluntary basis by a decree. The HIO has 13 regional branches and operates a nationwide network of health facilities for its beneficiaries. It also contracts with public and private providers to extend services for its beneficiaries that it is unable to provide within its own network. More specifically, HIO contracts with individual doctors to work in its facilities (about 25 percent of total staff), as well as with public and private providers and pharmacies to serve the healthcare needs of its beneficiaries. Contracting and outsourcing make up about one-third of total HIO expenditures. Thus, in its present form the HIO functions both as a purchaser and a provider of healthcare services for its beneficiaries.

CCOs were also established in 1964 as autonomous organizations to run nationalized hospitals. The first two were founded in Cairo and Alexandria; four more were founded in the mid-1990s. However, in 2000 three were closed and their hospitals transferred to the MoHP, thereby reducing the overall importance of CCOs in the delivery of health services.

It is worth noting that while the size and scope of healthcare providers operating as government authorities has expanded over the past decade, the number of healthcare providers operating as economic authorities has declined.

Figure 10.2. Trend in Public Expenditures on Health by Budget Chapters, Economic Authorities (constant 1996 LE)

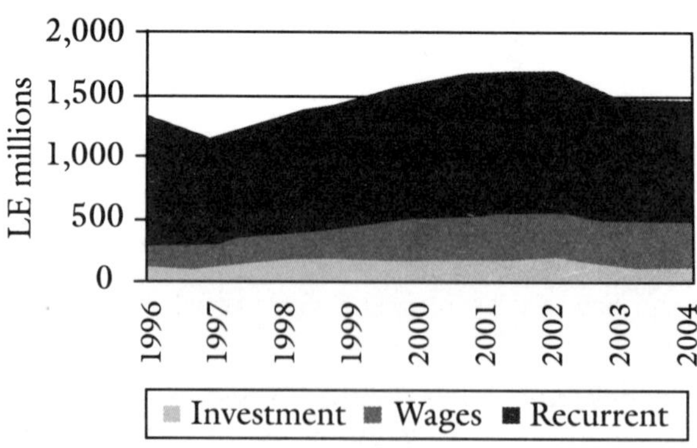

Source: MoHP and World Bank staff.

Figure 10.3. Trend in Public Expenditures on Health by Budget Chapters with PTES Highlighted, Government Authorities (constant 1996 LE)

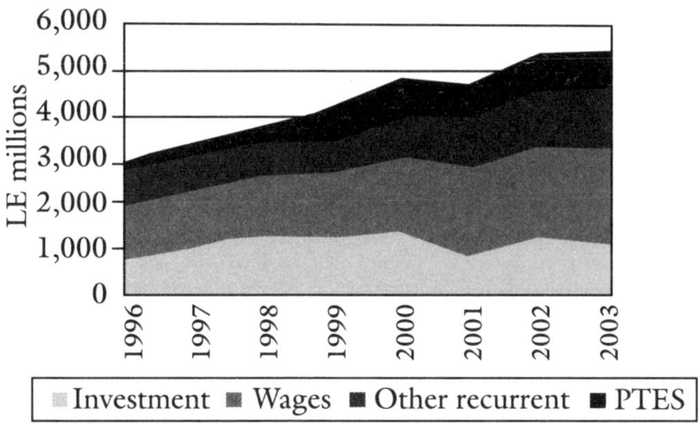

Source: MoHP and World Bank staff.

2. Challenges Facing the Health System in Egypt

2.1 Health Financing

Egypt has a pluralistic health system, consisting of a number of parallel public and private healthcare delivery systems and multiple financing intermediaries. Total spending in the health sector is dominated by direct out-of-pocket payments by households, which account for more than half of all health expenditure in Egypt. About 30 percent is financed through the government budget and another 10 percent through the social insurance contributions. Private health insurance contributes less than one percent of total health spending in the country. From these figures, it is evident that the level of risk pooling and financial protection against an adverse health event available to the Egyptian citizen is limited.

Table 10.1. Distribution of Health Expenditures by Financial Intermediaries, 2004

Financing intermediaries	*LE million*	*Percent*
Government budget[a]	7,927	29.5
of which special treatment at the expense of the state[b]	1,323	4.9
Social insurance[a]	2,020	7.5
Household (direct out of pocket)[c]	16,703	62.2
Private insurance[d]	169	0.6
Others[a]	54	0.2
Total	26,873	100

a. Ministry of Finance (MoF) expenditure data for government and economic authorities for FY 2004.
b. MoHP website: http://www.mohp.gov.eg.
c. EHHUES: 2002 estimated for 2004 based on linear extrapolation from household expenditures in 2002.
d. National Health Accounts (2002) estimated for 2004 based on the assumption of a constant coverage rate.

Growth in total health spending outpaced economic growth between 1996 and 2002. Egypt experienced a rapid escalation in total health spending between 1996 and 2002, averaging 13 percent per year in real terms and outpacing economic growth rate by about 9 percent per year. As a result, the share of GDP spent on health jumped from 3.7 percent in 1996 to 6.0 percent in 2004 (Figures 10.4 and 10.5).

Figure 10.4. Trends in Health Expenditures, 1996–2004 (constant 1996 LE)

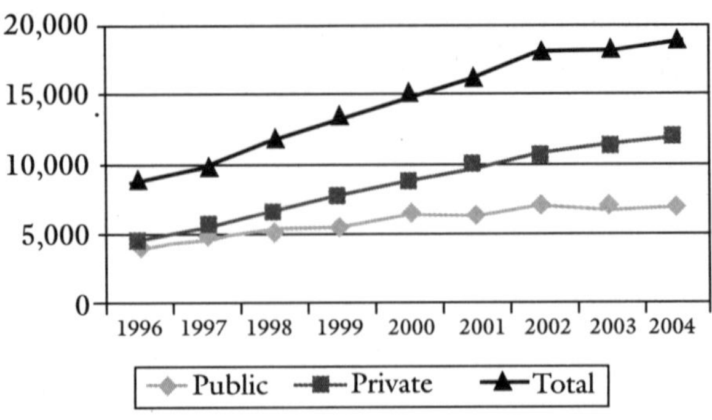

Source: MoHP and World Bank staff.

Figure 10.5. Total Health Expenditures (% of GDP, 1996–2004)

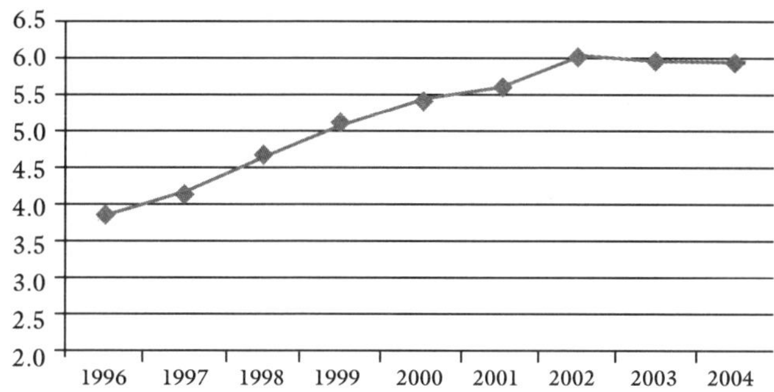

Source: MoHP and World Bank staff.

The increase in spending between 1995 and 2003 brought Egypt's health spending to a level commensurate with countries at comparable income levels (Figure 10.6). Private out-of-pocket spending grew faster than public spending, resulting in a higher share of private spending at the end of the period.

Figure 10.6. Global Trends in Total Health Spending as Percentage of GDP, 2002

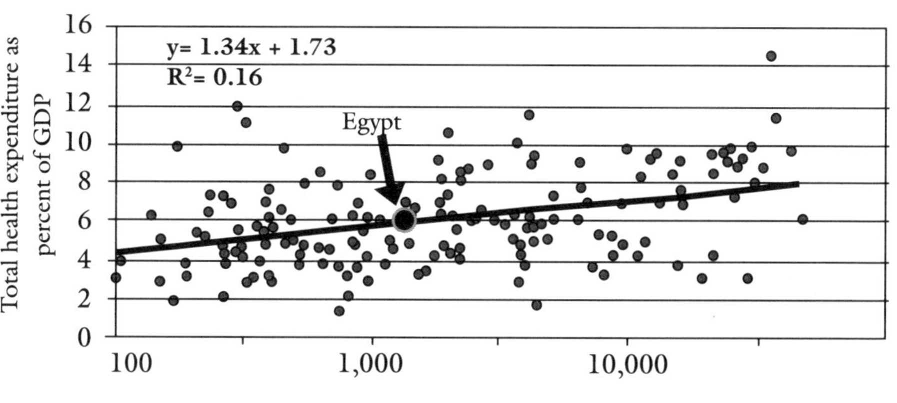

Source: MoHP and World Bank staff.

Table 10.2. Trends in Health Expenditures in Egypt, 1995 and 2002

	1995	*2002*
Per capita total health expenditure, exchange rate US$	38.0	79.4
Total health expenditure, percentage of GDP	3.7	6.0
Public spending on health, percentage of GDP	1.8	2.4
Public spending as a percentage of total health expenditure	49	40

Source: Egypt National Health Accounts, 1995 and 2002.

Although Egypt's public spending on health increased from 1.9 percent to 2.2 percent of GDP between 1996 and 2004, its spending level remains low relative to other countries of comparable income levels. Table 10.3 summarizes the main macroeconomic trends and the growth in health spending from 2001 to 2009.

In 2004, Egypt's public spending on health (including social insurance) accounted for 7.4 percent of total government expenditures, down from 8.0 percent in 2003. By comparison, middle-income countries spent on average 3.5 percent of GDP from public resources, and about 15 percent of total government expenditures, on health.

Table 10.3. Medium-Term Macroeconomic Trends, 2001–09

				Projections		
	2001/02	*2002/03*	*2003/04*	*2004/05*	*2005/06*	*2009/10*
Real annual growth rate of GDP[a]	3.1	3.2	4.1	4.1	5.0	4.5
Real per capita GDP growth rates[a]	1.2	1.4	2.3	2.3	3.2	3.8
Total government revenues (including grants) as percentage of GDP[a]	26.5	27.0	26.7	25.3	26.1	—
Real annual growth rate of total health spending	7.1	11.1	1.5	3.7	—	—
Public expenditures on health (including social insurance) as percentage of GDP[b]	2.2	2.4	2.2	2.2	—	—
Public spending on health as percentage of total government expenditures[b]	7.8	8.0	7.4	7.4	—	—

— = Not applicable

a. IMF 2005.

b. Calculated from government budget data.

The government's proposal to gradually move implicit subsidies onto the budget would help expand fiscal space, increase the transparency of public subsidies, and improve targeting of social programs, including the financing of priority health benefits. Egypt's government revenues are relatively high for its income level, but a significant share of the budget is spent on generalized subsidies rather than on targeted social programs. At about 27 percent of GDP, Egypt's government revenues are above average for middle-income countries. But implicit subsidies on electricity and fuel products are estimated to be significant and crowd out the fiscal space for social programs. The introduction of the new income tax law aims to reduce tax rates, simplify the tax structure, and render it more transparent. While rate reductions may initially lower revenues, other measures in the new legislation to limit loopholes and the expected increase in prices of domestic energy and electricity should offset this shortfall. Overall, these fiscal reform measures should expand the fiscal space for financing priority social programs, including health benefits.

Moreover, the government's new tax reform measures to expand the tax base, including provisions to encourage the informal economy to legalize its status, may benefit the social health insurance system. The social health insurance system currently receives very little contribution from private workers, who face little incentive to participate in the system. Any future expansion of social insurance coverage will depend on improving the incentives for participation in, and contribution to, the social insurance system by non-poor private sector workers.

The rise in public expenditures on health in the 1990s appears due mainly to the expansion of HIO coverage, the expansion of PTES, and the expansion in high-end services provided by government authorities. The HIO showed a rapid increase in spending in the mid 1990s but the rate of spending appears to have slowed over the past four years. By comparison, government authorities have shown an even more pronounced increase in real expenditures over the past decade. Among the main cost drivers in public spending are the wage bill and the introduction of the PTES. The significant investments in the specialized centers under the MoHP in the 1990s contributed to the expansion of the supply of high-end healthcare providers. This development, coupled with the expansion of PTES funding, fueled the rapid increase in health spending among government authorities. The spending increase by the government authorities has been pulled back since 2003. These parallel trends are evident when comparing HIO and PTES expenditures (Figure 10.7).

Figure 10.7. Trend of HIO and PTES Expenditures (constant 1996 LE)

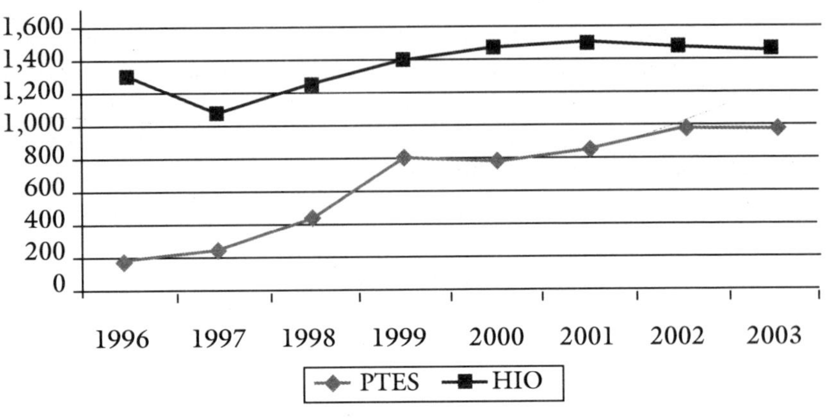

Source: MoHP and World Bank staff.

Deficiencies in HIO, PTES, and Private Spending

The rising deficit of HIO

Since 1996 spending on health services under the HIO has grown faster than revenues, resulting in a persistent and rising operating deficit that more than doubled between 1997 and 2001. An analysis of the HIO's financial flows reveals that workers under Law 32[4] accounted for a significant portion of the net deficit, while workers under Law 79 accounted for little of the deficit, reflecting the substantially higher payroll taxes paid by the latter group. Pensioners and widows represent an even larger share of deficit for the HIO, accounting for some 60 percent of the net deficit in 2001, while they represented only about 6 percent of enrollment. This is not surprising given that the elderly are a higher-risk group: their contribution rates are low while their costs are highest among HIO beneficiaries. School Health Insurance Program enrollees accounted for a modest surplus in all years reported, but the level of surplus has dropped and stabilized at a modest level in 2001. Since the contributions to this program are not indexed to inflation, it is expected that this program will run into deficits in the near future. The expansion of HIO coverage to infants under Decree 380 in 1997 has increased expenditures in this period without providing an additional source of revenues for the HIO. Infants constitute another high-risk group. Cross-subsidization from other sources of revenue is required to ensure the financial sustainability of the program.

HIO has made substantial efforts in recent years to control its expenditures. Measures include restricting the use of non-HIO pharmacies and specialist referrals, reducing HIO staff size through attrition and hiring restrictions, freezing the construction of new HIO health facilities while expanding the contracting of services that could be provided more efficiently by other providers, and engaging in active price negotiations with private providers to obtain better and more competitive prices. These efforts have helped reduce HIO's operating deficits and improve its financial balance. But what is not yet well evaluated is how these cost-containment measures have affected quality of care and access to services for beneficiaries. There is a potential risk that the stringent cost containment by HIO is resulting in cost-shifting of expenses and risks to households and providers.

The cost of PTES

After rapid expansion in the late 1990s, the PTES has also shown signs of moderating expenditures. The average cost of treatment has declined in recent years because of the reduction in spending on overseas treatment. PTES expenditures on treatment abroad decreased from LE 25 million (for 212 patients) in 1997 to LE 1.8 million in 2003 (for 34 patients). This has been made possible by the establishment of the specialized centers that can treat patients. Over the same period, PTES expenditures on the domestic program increased from LE 215 million for 100,000 patients to LE 1.3 billion for almost 1.2 million patients. The PTES is thus playing an increasingly important role as a third-party payer for citizens. It is worth noting that the average cost of LE 1,064 per domestic PTES patient is still high compared with the average cost of the most costly group of HIO beneficiaries. By comparison, the average cost of the "highly specialized services" offered to the pensioners and workers treated outside HIO facilities was LE 482 in 2003.

Increasing private spending

A significant portion of increased private spending could be induced by the increased level of cost-sharing requirements associated with the publicly funded programs such as HIO and PTES. For example, the availability of new health benefits through the PTES may have played a role in inducing demand for treatment that an individual might otherwise have forgone. Since the PTES reimburses only part of the total cost of treatment, a significant amount will have to be paid by the individual. Available data do not distinguish the out-of-pocket spending associated with public programs, such as co-payments for PTES or HIO, and therefore, it was not possible to confirm the extent of private spending induced by the improved insurance coverage. This interaction between private and public spending on healthcare is an important aspect of health expenditures that will require more detailed analysis based on the availability of appropriately disaggregated data.

2.2. Coverage Under Social Insurance: Fragmentation of Risk Pool

Social health insurance coverage is fragmented by beneficiaries. For historical reasons, Egypt's social insurance system has developed into multiple programs with different coverage and benefits package for various segments of the population, resulting in a patchwork of coverage. Social health insurance coverage is extended to only half of the population, including about one-third of the active labor force. In a typical Egyptian family, the father, a public or private sector employee, will be covered by HIO Law No.79; his wife, a government employee, would be covered by Law No.32; his son, a university student, will not be covered; his daughter, a school student, will be covered by HIO Law No. 99; and his infant child would be covered by a decree (Table 10.4). More than half the population, mostly the unemployed, self-employed, and informal sector workers and out-of-school children are not covered under the HIO system.

The different laws in effect under the HIO result in different systems of benefits and co-payments, which complicate the effective administration of the program. Members of the same household have different coverage depending on their status within the household. The "uninsured" population has access to financial protection through the PTES for hospitalization and related high-cost health services. However, the PTES is a passive reimbursement scheme not related to any contribution systems or to a well-defined benefits package. In a limited number of governorates, access to primary care services is financed through the Family Health Fund, but this remains a pilot program without a clear institutional base. The rest of the uninsured population depends on free or subsidized government health services (Figure 10.8).

Table 10.4. Coverage and Eligibility of HIO Beneficiaries, 2005

Governing law	*Law 32 of 1975 (workers)*	*Law 79 of 1975 (workers)*	*Law 79 of 1975 (pensioners)*	*Law 99 of 1992 (schoolchildren)*	*Decree 380 of 1997 (infants)*
Beneficiaries	Government workers	Public and private sector workers	Pensioners and widows	Students up to high school	Infants
Number (millions)	3.74	3.29	1.75	16.89	9.14
Payroll tax or annual premium					
Enrollee share	0.5% of salary	1% of salary	1% pensioners; 2% widows	LE 4 per student	LE 5 (per child)
Employer share or government share	1.5% of salary	3% of salary plus 1% for disability	None	LE 12 (government budget) and cigarette tax	None
Co-payments	General practitioner visit: LE 0.05 Specialist visit: LE 0.10 Tests: < LE 1 Drugs: 50%	None	None	Drugs: 33%	Visit: LE 0.50 Drugs: 33%

Source: HIO, Annual Report for 2002/2003, 2004.

Figure 10.8. Social Insurance Coverage and Access to Government Services

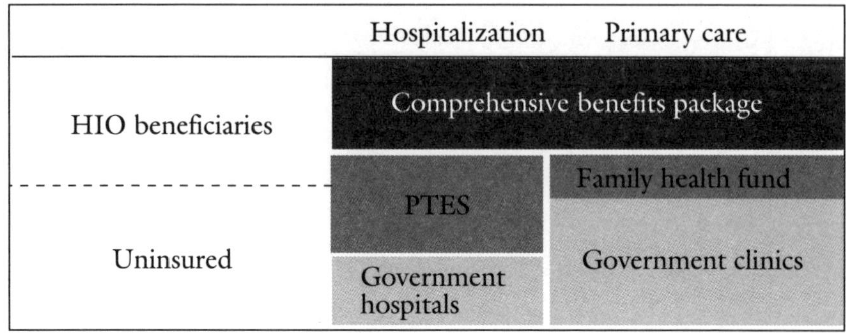

Source: MoHP and World Bank staff.

The level of risk-pooling in Egypt is low. As discussed above, despite the presence of different types of health coverage provided by the MoHP and the HIO, between 1996 and 2002 the share of direct household spending increased from 50 percent of total health spending to 60 percent. This could be due to several causes. *First*, the level of benefits covered under the HIO is limited in scope and requires beneficiaries to make additional payments to obtain services not covered. *Second*, the proportion of the labor force participating in HIO is low (only 30 percent). *Third*, the recent cost containment exercised by HIO could be shifting costs onto households. *Fourth*, the PTES requires a significant level of cost-sharing by patients; therefore, the expansion of PTES would be accompanied by a concomitant increase in household spending to cover the expenses. *Fifth*, the quality of subsidized government health services may be inadequate (shortage of drugs in health facilities, lack of responsiveness), forcing many households to seek private providers.

Table 10.5. Enrollees in HIO by Law and Number of Active Labor Force, 1997–2002 (millions)

	1997	*1998*	*1999*	*2000*	*2001*	*2002*
Law 32 workers	3.1	3.3	3.4	3.5	3.6	3.6
Law 79 workers	2.6	2.6	2.7	2.8	3.0	3.1
Total number of workers covered by HIO	5.7	5.9	6.1	6.3	6.6	6.7
Pensioners and widows	0.8	1.0	1.1	1.3	1.5	1.6
Law 99 (schoolchildren)	15.4	15.8	16.0	16.3	16.6	16.7
Decree 380 (infants)	N/A	1.0	1.6	2.9	4.2	5.5
Total active labor force	16.2	16.8	17.2	17.6	17.9	18.2
Government and public enterprise employees	5.6	5.6	5.9	5.9	—	6.2
Private sector workers	10.6	11.2	11.3	11.7	—	12.0

— = Not available
Source: HIO.

Social insurance coverage of private sector workers is low. In 2002, about 18.2 million Egyptians were in the active labor force, out of an estimated total labor force of 20.2 million. Of these, about 6.2 million were government and public sector employees and 12 million were private sector workers (formal and informal). In the same year, HIO covered about 6.7 million of the working population under both Law 32 and 79 (Table 10.5).

Since all government and public sector employees are covered under HIO by mandate, only about 500,000 private sector workers were covered by HIO—less than 5 percent of the active labor force working in the private sector. There are two explanations for this low coverage rate. *First*, small and medium enterprises are not required to enroll in the social health insurance plan under HIO, although they are required to contribute to the social security administration for pensions. It is likely that this group of employers and employees will not contribute to HIO health insurance, preferring to take advantage of the subsidized MoHP services or the financial coverage offered by PTES. *Second*, larger firms that are required to contribute to HIO would opt out of the scheme, preferring to contribute the mandatory one percent of payroll and enroll in alternative insurance plans.

Participation in well-designed and well-functioning risk-pooling schemes is essential for reducing the likelihood of falling into poverty in the event of a "health shock."

Households in the lower-income groups just above the poverty line are most vulnerable to the impoverishing effects of adverse health events, but even those in the middle-income range are at risk. For example, in Argentina (Maceira 2004) 5 percent of all non-poor households fell below the national poverty line in 1997 as a result of health spending, and in Ecuador (Montenegro 2004) up to 11 percent of non-poor households fell below the poverty line in 2000 because of medical expenses. Even in the industrial economies, medical expenses contribute to economic hardship. For example, in the United States medical expenses accounted for about half of all bankruptcies declared in 2001 (Himmelstein and others 2005). Thus, the availability of risk pooling arrangements plays a vital role in protecting both poor and non-poor households from the impoverishing effects of health shocks.

2.3 Inequities in the Allocation and Use of Health Resources (Inequities in Distribution)

Rural-urban inequities

Total health spending by both public and private sources was 2.5 times higher in urban governorates than in rural governorates and Upper Egypt (Figure 10.9).

Figure 10.9. Annual per Capita Total Expenditures (LE) on Health by Regions, 2002

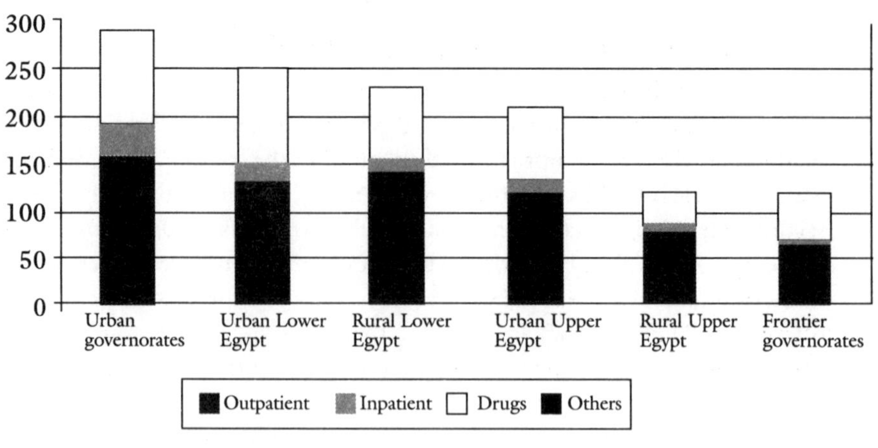

Source: EHHUES, 2002.

Inequities in access and use of health services

There are inequities in the access to and use of health services by region and by income levels. The richest quintile of the population spent 2.3 and 1.6 times as much on hospital and outpatient services as the poorest quintile households.

In principle, the MoHP facilities should be providing free care for the poor. However, a graph of the distributional data reveals a negative correlation between the poverty index and public health spending levels by governorates (Figure 10.10).

Figure 10.10. Correlation between Poverty and Government Expenditures on Health, by Governorate

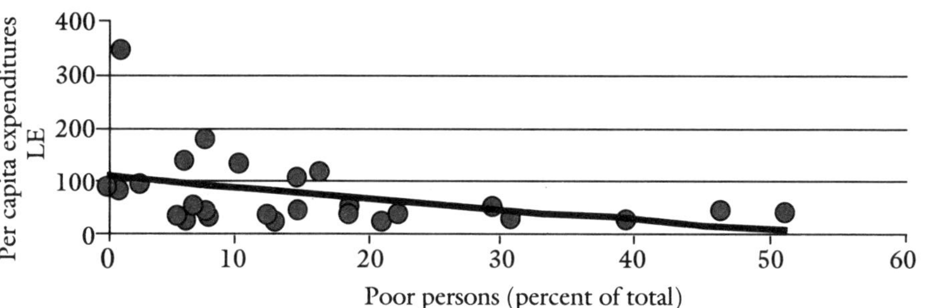

Source: Based on government budget data (2003).

2.4 Inefficiencies in the Health Delivery System

The productivity of the government health delivery system is low. One measure of the low productivity is the very low bed occupancy rate, which indicates that a substantial portion of fixed capital is not well utilized. Although Egypt's bed capacity is comparable to that of other countries at similar income levels, yet it is still far below the average occupancy rate of 80 percent according to the international standard of good practice (Figure 10.6).

Table 10.6. Profile of MoHP Hospitals, 2003

MoHP Hospital Types	*Number of Beds*	*Share of Total MoHP Beds (%)*	*Bed Occupancy Rate (%)*
Specialized centers	5,285	6.6	58.2
General & district hospitals	34,456	42.9	43
Fever hospitals	9,150	11.4	40
Chest hospitals	6,519	8.1	31
Integrated and rural hospitals	8,792	11.0	—
Group health centers	3,219	4.0	—
Other MoHP hospitals	4,818	6.0	—
Total acute care hospitals	72,239	90.0	32.6
Psychiatry	8,021	10.0	50
Total	80,260	100	

Source: MoHP.

Incentives for improving productivity in the government health delivery system are low. Government authorities rely primarily on the state budget, are not held accountable for their financial performance, and have little autonomy and limited ability to generate revenues. Public provider financing is mostly based on historical supply-side financing, with no link between provider revenue and delivery of services to patients. This situation is not conducive to efficient operations in the government sector.

The patient load on HIO service providers has been increasing while budget increases and staffing have been constrained. This could be compromising the quality of care and user satisfaction in the HIO facilities. Another common problem in the HIO program is the delay that beneficiaries face in accessing doctors of reasonable quality in a reasonable time. HIO beneficiaries are required to enroll with an HIO-designated doctor, who subsequently refers patients to specialists. The lack of access to qualified doctors is one of the main bottlenecks in the current system.

3. Strategies and Recommendations

The medium-term strategic framework that the government announced in July 2005 for reforming the health sector is based on six pillars: (a) improving the management capacity and financing sustainability of HIO; (b) expanding the coverage of primary care services under the Family Health Fund; (c) expanding social health insurance coverage to all uninsured Egyptian citizens; (d) expanding primary healthcare services in all governorates; (e) improving the performance of all government-owned hospitals; and (f) merging all these components of the system into a national social health insurance system over the medium term.

The following policy recommendations are proposed as an attempt toward ensuring the adequate financial protection and access to health services, in an affordable and equitable manner. Options and strategies for reform are discussed under four topics: (i) targeting the allocation of government subsidies toward priority programs and beneficiaries, (ii) expanding coverage of social insurance, (iii) consolidating multiple social insurance programs, and (iv) enhancing economic incentives to improve the quality and efficiency of government health services.

3.1 Targeting the Allocation of Government Subsidies toward Priority Programs and Beneficiaries

The use of public resources to subsidize healthcare for the population is justified on at least three grounds. The *first* is to subsidize the cost of healthcare for the poor, who lack the resources to meet the full cost of healthcare. The *second* is to finance public health programs with high externalities and public goods content, such as disease surveillance, immunization, public information, and health education. The *third* is to address market failures in the medical insurance market and offer financial risk protection against adverse health events.

A system of social insurance enables financial risks to be spread over a large number of individuals at different stages in life. It also enables the wealthy to subsidize the poor and the healthy to subsidize the unhealthy.

Figure 10.11. Cost of Health Services and Capacity to Contribute over an Individual's Life Cycle

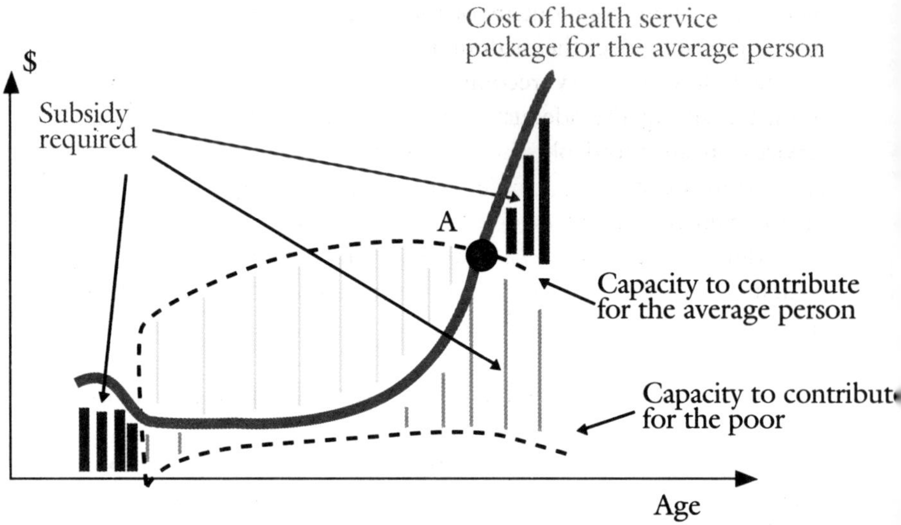

Source: Adapted from Baeza and others (2002).

In Egypt, a significant portion of the government budget is being used to subsidize access to comprehensive healthcare services for a large number of non-poor beneficiaries, while the poor continue to face access problems. There is a need to improve the targeting of government subsidies to priority population groups (the poor and vulnerable) and, by defining the benefits package, to ensure that subsidies are focused on providing effective protection against the impoverishing effects of health shocks.

Promoting Participation in and Contributions for the Social Insurance System by All Non-poor Beneficiaries

Expanding health coverage to new beneficiaries would increase the total liabilities on the social insurance funds. Financial sustainability depends on securing adequate revenues from both the government budget and workers' contributions. Mobilizing contributions directly from the workers and introducing additional cost-sharing schemes would help reduce the dependence on the government budget. But this approach must be balanced with the need to avoid spillover to the labor market, and to avoid creating an excessive contribution-benefits gap. A social insurance system will not function if it lacks credibility and the contribution-benefits gap is perceived to be wide—for example, if appropriate healthcare services are not available or perceived to be of poor quality. This could exacerbate the "informalization" of the workers, who would rather evade than participate in a system perceived to be substandard.

Redirecting Government Resources from Supply-side Subsidies to Active Purchasing through a Third-party Insurer

Establishing a national insurance fund involves a fundamental shift away from supply-side subsidization of government providers, which has been a predominant form of government financing of health services in Egypt, to strategic and performance-based purchasing of services. This transition has often proven difficult in countries that have launched similar reforms. The more successful cases involved a staged approach that built on political consensus and phasing of reforms that maintained the broad consensus. The health system in Egypt does not yet have mechanisms in place to direct resources toward the most cost-effective services and programs, and management of contracts with providers remains rudimentary. Expanding social insurance coverage requires concurrent development of enabling legislations and management capacities. The ultimate objective is to ensure the establishment of a social insurance system with a strong and effective strategic purchasing capacity and a provider market capable of responding efficiently to these incentives.

Defining a Path to Universal Coverage by Introducing a Gradual and Phased Expansion in the Depth and Breadth of the Benefit Package

The breadth of coverage refers to the number of beneficiaries with access to the package, and the depth refers to the richness of the content, including the number and types of interventions included. The fiscal risk and impact of health insurance reform are determined by both the breadth and depth of the benefits package. Countries that have attempted to expand the depth and breadth of coverage simultaneously have tended to face greater political resistance and difficulties in implementation. Countries that have successfully achieved universal coverage have generally opted to take a more gradual approach to expanding the depth of coverage in stages (for example, Chile, Korea, and Taiwan) rather than aim for immediate implementation of a comprehensive benefits package.

3.2 Expanding Social Insurance Coverage

Expanding social insurance toward universal coverage requires different approaches depending on the occupational and social status of beneficiaries. They can be sorted into three distinct groups: (a) those in need of social assistance, including unemployed workers and their families; (b) the non-poor self-employed and informal sector workers; and (c) dependents of the formal sector workers who are currently not covered under the HIO.

Expanding Coverage to the Poor, Unemployed, and Other Vulnerable Groups

It is estimated that one out of every five Egyptians was living in poverty in 2004. This group of beneficiaries should, in principle, be eligible for exemption from premium contributions and co-payments, and have these contributions fully subsidized through the government budget. A major challenge is to target the exemptions effectively to minimize both leakage (extending benefits to the ineligible) and gaps (denying benefits to the eligible).

Subsidization of the poor under the proposed National Health Insurance Fund (NHIF) requires adequate and sustainable fiscal resources. As discussed above, the challenge lies in shifting from supply-side subsidization to subsidization of premium payments for the poor.

Expanding Coverage to Non-poor Self-employed and Informal Sector Workers and Their Families

Non-poor informal sector workers currently do not contribute to or participate in the social insurance system. Their healthcare needs are covered through PTES for catastrophic illness, the Family Health Fund for primary care services in the pilot governorates, or through direct purchase of private health services. To the extent that the recent tax reforms succeed in giving the informal workforce legal status, a segment of these workers will be brought into the formal social insurance system.

For the remaining informal sector workers, participation in the social insurance system would require either enforcing a means-tested contribution system based on an estimation of their income or assets, or establishing a risk-rated contribution system designed to encourage voluntary participation. The first option involves high administrative costs and is extremely difficult to enforce because the income and employment status of informal sector workers are, by definition, volatile and unobservable. The second option also involves the administrative costs of establishing a risk-rating mechanism and also raises the risk of adverse selection if the insurer is unable to evaluate risks effectively. However, this risk could be mitigated if the self-employed and informal sector workers could be organized into groups that would permit community risk rating. For example, some self-employed workers are organized into affinity groups and associations that could form the basis for a collective contribution mechanism. The enrollment of beneficiaries in the Family Health Fund, which involves household contributions to a prepayment scheme within a community setting, also offers a potential entry point for establishing a beneficiary registry and contribution mechanism at the community level for non-poor informal sector workers and their families. Finally, their willingness to contribute will depend on the perceived value of the benefits offered through social insurance. If the benefits are perceived to be inadequate and of poor quality, then the incentive is to avoid contributions.

Expanding Coverage to the Dependents of HIO Workers

Of the three groups, expanding coverage to the dependents of workers covered by HIO would require relatively fewer administrative and institutional reforms, since the head of the household would already be registered and contributing through the HIO contribution system. One option would be to use the existing social insurance system to extend HIO coverage to the dependents of workers. To ensure that the system remains in equilibrium, it would be necessary to revise the contribution rates according to the size of the household and the defined benefits package for the new beneficiaries. Because this option would significantly expand the number of HIO beneficiaries, this step would also require concurrent capacity building and reforms within the HIO to absorb these new beneficiaries.

HIO continues to provide most health services for its beneficiaries through its own facilities. With the expansion in the number of beneficiaries over the years, HIO has turned more frequently to contracting for services from the private sector, but its capacity to manage these contracts effectively remains limited. It has managed to curb cost escalation in recent years by imposing hard budget constraints, but this may be reducing reimbursement rates for the contracted providers. That may produce a negative effect on quality of care as well as potential cost shifting of payments to the beneficiaries.

Restructuring the Co-payment System for Effective Cost-sharing

Expanding social insurance coverage should reduce the share of direct out-of-pocket spending by households on healthcare and increase the share of household budget used for premium contributions to the social insurance scheme. This improves risk-pooling and increases the financial protection of individuals and households against catastrophic health problems. If contribution rates can be linked to beneficiaries' income levels and budget subsidies are well targeted toward the more needy groups, then the system has a progressive contribution structure. However, improved insurance coverage also increases the risk of moral hazard and induced demand problems. To counter these effects it is necessary to introduce a well-designed co-payment system to moderate moral hazard problems on the demand side, as well as active management of providers to moderate moral hazard problems on the supplier side.

Defining the Role of the Private Voluntary Insurance Market in the Framework of the Social Insurance System

The private insurance market could offer three types of plans: for services covered under social insurance (substitution), for services not covered under social insurance (supplementary insurance), and for covering the costs of co-payments and other cost-sharing elements of the social insurance program (complementary insurance). Each type of voluntary insurance plan has advantages and disadvantages to be considered in the framework of a social insurance scheme. In the European context, voluntary health insurance has played an important but relatively limited role within an existing comprehensive statutory insurance system.

The opt-out clause under the health insurance law permits private corporations to opt for a private insurance scheme provided they continue to contribute one percent of their payroll to HIO.[5] This substitution option has two important implications for the expansion of the social insurance system. First, it has the advantage of offering greater choice to corporations and their workers: a private insurance plan may offer better benefits than the HIO. Second, it takes one of the wealthier (and possibly healthier) groups of beneficiaries out of the social insurance scheme, thereby reducing the size of the risk pool and its capacity to redistribute resources across different risk groups. The clause potentially reduces the size of the social security pool, and it simultaneously increases the average household risk and decreases the average household nominal contribution. Thus, it could put at risk the financial sustainability of HIO and that of the NHIF.

3.3 Consolidating Multiple Social Insurance Programs under a National Health Insurance Fund (NHIF)

Harmonizing the Existing Laws and Proposed New Programs Under a Common Legislative Framework

To reorganize the fragmented social insurance programs into a national health insurance system will require regrouping both the beneficiaries and the benefits package into a coherent package of programs organized on principles of fairness, affordability, and administrative efficiency. Based on the assessment of the proposed expansion of social insurance coverage (discussed earlier), a comprehensive framework for the development of the national health insurance system would need to be developed. Such a framework would include definitions of beneficiaries and eligibility criteria, contribution rates, the benefits package including co-payments and other cost-sharing responsibilities, eligible service providers, and administrative bodies responsible for collecting and managing the funds. The agreement on the legislative framework would require an extensive consultative process with the key stakeholders.

A national health insurance system would necessarily involve distinct groups of beneficiaries with different contribution mechanisms and possibly different benefits packages. Consolidation of these distinct social insurance programs under a single NHIF would require stringent management of revenues and expenditures to ensure that any cross-subsidizations across beneficiary groups occur deliberately and transparently, not ad hoc.

Redirecting the Flow of Budget from Government Authorities to the National Health Insurance Fund

One of the major challenges in the transition period would be to redirect the budget going directly to government health services to the NHIF. The Fund, in turn, would contract with providers in its role as a third-party payer.

This step would require close coordination with the proposed reforms of government healthcare providers, which would transform them into autonomous public entities (economic authorities), thereby reducing their reliance on direct budget allocation. In this scenario, HIO would need either to divest itself of direct provision and management of healthcare services to become a third-party purchasing agency, or to transform itself into a provider agency with a network of hospital and clinical facilities. Transferring the existing HIO facilities to an autonomous network of public sector providers would essentially accomplish this transformation. Although this is technically feasible, the political economy of the reform process would require extensive consultation and careful phasing of reforms.

Preparing a Business Model and a Critical Path Analysis for the Establishment of the National Health Insurance Fund

While new legislation will establish the objectives and principles of the NHIF, it will take time to develop essential capacities and functions for the Fund. It will be essential to develop a business model and undertake a critical path analysis for the establishment of the new institution, including an assessment of capacities in HIO, MoHP, and other key institutions that will be closely involved in developing the new structure.

Introducing Economic Incentives by Establishing Effective Contract Management Capacity in the National Health Insurance Fund

Since the expansion of beneficiaries under Law 99, the HIO has been outsourcing and purchasing services from providers outside its network. Expanded purchasing functions of HIO could form the basis of the future NHIF. Contract management is a key function that the NHIF would undertake in its role as the purchaser of healthcare services. Doing so will require developing significant new capacities within the HIO to manage contracts with providers, including private sector providers. It will also require modernizing management information systems at different levels of the health system. A modern health management information system is an essential tool for managing the core functions of the social insurance funds, including managing the beneficiary registry and eligibility checking system, claims processing, payment and billing systems, utilization reviews, and medical audits.

3.4 Enhancing Economic Incentives and Improving the Quality and Efficiency of Government Health Services

Reorganizing Government Providers Under Economic Authorities and Encouraging the Participation of Private Providers in the National Health Insurance Fund

Currently, public sector hospitals and clinics are managed under multiple national organizations, contributing to the fragmentation of services at the governorate level. In line with the government policy toward decentralizing public services, public hospitals belonging to the MoHP, PATHI, HIO, and CCOs could be reorganized into a hospital network under a common management structure at the governorate level. These facilities could be transformed into economic authorities, but doing so would require an in-depth review of performance and rectification of any structural and organizational constraints. This network would be managed as autonomous public entities under a board comprising representatives of the local authority, MoHP, NHIF, medical syndicates, and patient advocates. Budget financing for these networks would be gradually phased out and replaced with the revenues from contracting with the NHIF.

Regulating Investments in New Medical Technologies and Procedures
All public investments in new public hospitals, new technologies, and new procedures should be subject to rigorous review of evidence for need, efficacy, cost-effectiveness, and affordability. The MoHP has introduced the use of a governorate health master plan under the health sector reform program to rationalize investments in primary healthcare services. A similar approach is needed for the hospital sector. With regard to investments in new technologies and procedures, including the registration of new pharmaceuticals, the government should invest in the development of national capacities to undertake a more rigorous assessment of cost-effectiveness and affordability of new technologies.

Introducing a National Quality Improvement and Accreditation Program
The MoHP needs to establish a national program for quality improvement, which would involve public and private sector providers. The proposed Egyptian Council for Accreditation and Quality of Healthcare would play a key role in introducing a process of peer review and enforcement of quality standards at the facility level. The Council will be an autonomous entity under a board of directors representing providers in the public and private sectors. Its primary function would be to establish standards of service, undertake facility inspections to establish accreditation, and provide technical assistance to providers. Accreditation could be one of the key conditions for contract awards by the NHIF.

4. Conclusion

This chapter assessed Egypt's pluralistic health system, and defined the challenges facing it; ranging from financing difficulties, to the low level of risk-pooling, to inequities and inefficiencies of the health delivery system.

The government's proposed expansion of the social health insurance system aims at improving access to health services with focus on equity and access for the poor; extending financial protection against catastrophic health events; setting appropriate incentives for payers/insurers to improve quality and efficiency; and ensuring fiscal and financial sustainability.

The design of an effective social health insurance system in Egypt will depend on careful consideration of five factors: (i) the content of the benefits package; (ii) the availability of fiscal space for sustaining equity subsidies; (iii) the capacity at the HIO for strategic purchasing; (iv) the size of the risk pool and the extent of risk-pool fragmentation; and (v) the regulatory framework for risk-pooling organizations.

In light of the above, options and strategies for reform were proposed under four main topics; (i) better targeting of subsidies, (ii) expanding health insurance, (iii) consolidating multiple social insurance programs, and (iv) enhancing economic incentives to improve the quality and efficiency of government health services.

Based on the World Bank's Policy Note on Health in Egypt, the above options and strategies for reform could be presented in the form of the following concrete short- and medium-term recommendations for the Egyptian government.

Short-term Recommendations

- Launch an initial technical analysis of the definition of the benefit package to be covered by the universal social insurance reform (considering Egypt's health and financial protection priorities).
- Undertake an actuarial estimate and modeling of the revenues and expenditures for the proposed expansion of social insurance to the uninsured.
- Assess the fiscal implications of expanding coverage to the unemployed and other social cases through budget financing; expanding coverage to the self-employed and informal sector workers and their families under a new contribution scheme; and expanding HIO coverage to include dependents.
- Draft framework legislation for the establishment of the NHIF, including the definition of beneficiaries, contribution rates, co-payments and other cost-sharing responsibilities, the benefits package, medical tariffs, eligible service providers, and the administrative arrangements for management of the Fund, and engage in extensive consultation with key stakeholders on the design of the NHIF.
- Evaluate the effectiveness of the Family Health Fund in providing cost-effective and appropriate primary healthcare services; estimate the cost of expanding the system for national coverage; and examine the feasibility of integrating the program into the benefits package to be covered under the NHIF.
- Assess the PTES in terms of the level of financial protection for

the uninsured population, and develop options for redirecting the budget under PTES into the new NHIF framework.

- Develop a medium-term investment plan for rationalizing the network of public healthcare providers, including an expansion of the Governorate Health Master Plan.
- Reorganize the existing government healthcare providers into a network of autonomous providers operating as economic authorities.

Medium-term Recommendations

- Design and implement a social health insurance program for the unemployed and the poor based on the targeting system, and establish clear criteria for budget transfers to subsidize the premiums and co-payments of these social cases.
- Based on actuarial estimates and consultation with key stakeholders, revise the contribution rates for formal sector workers and their dependents, and establish new contribution mechanisms and beneficiary registry systems for the non-poor self-employed and informal sector workers and their dependents.
- Define the roles and functions of private insurance schemes in the context of statutory insurance, including their role in covering services (substitution) for those who opt out of the social insurance system as well as coverage of complementary and supplementary benefits.
- Enhance the capacity of the Egyptian Insurance Supervisory Agency to regulate the private medical insurance market, especially its role in monitoring and assessing new private health insurance products and disseminating information to consumers regarding benefits and restrictions.
- Promulgate a new health insurance law based on the broad consultative process of the draft framework legislation.
- Establish the NHIF based on the analysis of the business model, organizational structure, and staffing requirements, with a phased expansion of social insurance coverage based on feasibility analyses.
- Roll out the reorganization of government providers into economic authorities.
- Introduce a health technology assessment process for evaluating all major public investments in new medical technology or adding new procedures and drugs.
- Establish a national accreditation program and a quality of healthcare agency with an independent board.

Notes

* This chapter was compiled by Sara Al-Nashar and is based on the World Bank's Policy Note No. 9: *Egypt Public Expenditure Review on Health*, prepared by Sameh El Saharty and Akiko Maeda in January 2006; it was presented by Akiko Maeda in the ECES conference entitled the *Egyptian Economy: Current Challenges and Future Prospects* in November 2006.

1. Evidence from several middle-income countries reveals that inadequacies in financial risk protection can cause a significant number of non-poor households to fall below the poverty line. Households in the lower-income groups just above the poverty line are most vulnerable to the impoverishing effects of adverse health events, but even those in the middle-income range are at risk (Maceira 2004).
2. The bulk of the population under HIO coverage (80 percent) is school children and infants.
3. Government authorities are financed directly through the state budget, whereas economic authorities are financed through self-generated revenues.
4. Law 32 covers government sector workers, while Law 79 covers public sector workers (employees of the economic authorities) and private sector workers.
5. An actuarial estimate can determine whether the one percent payroll contribution will sustain the financial viability of the remaining risk group.

References

Baeza, C., P. Crocco, M. Núñez, and M. Shaffer. 2002. Toward decent work: Social protection in health for all workers and their families. *Strategies and tools against social exclusion and poverty (STEP)*, International Labor Organization, Geneva.

Himmelstein, David U., Elizabeth Warren, Deborah Thorne, and Steffie Woolhandler. 2005. Illness and injury as contributors to bankruptcy. *Health Affairs* 24: w63–w73.

Maceira, D. 2004. Mecanismos de protección social en salud e impacto de shocks financieros: El caso de Argentina. (In Spanish) Background paper for the study *Beyond survival: protecting households from the impoverishing effects of health shocks.* Washington, D.C.: World Bank.

Montenegro, F. 2004. Household health expenditures, financial protection and poverty in Ecuador. Background paper for the study *Beyond survival: protecting households from the impoverishing effects of health shocks.* Washington, D.C: World Bank.

IMF (International Monetary Fund). 2005. Arab Republic of Egypt: Article IV Consultation. IMF Country Report 05/177. Washington, D.C.

World Bank. 2005. *World Development Indicators 2005.* Washington, D.C.

Index